THE DESSERT ARCHITECT

Join us on the web at
culinary.delmar.com

ROBERT
WEMISCHNER

THE DESSERT ARCHITECT

Dallas 2011

Betty
Enjoy the sweet journey!

Robert Wemischner

DELMAR
CENGAGE Learning

Australia • Brazil • Japan • Korea • Mexico • Singapore • Spain • United Kingdom • United States

DELMAR
CENGAGE Learning™

The Dessert Architect
Robert Wemischner

Vice President, Career and Professional Editorial:
    Dave Garza
Director of Learning Solutions: Sandy Clark
Acquisitions Editor: Jim Gish
Managing Editor: Larry Main
Product Manager: Nicole Calisi
Editorial Assistant: Sarah Timm
Vice President Marketing, Career and Professional:
    Jennifer McAvey
Executive Marketing Manager: Wendy Mapstone
Marketing Manager: Kristin McNary
Marketing Coordinator: Scott Chrysler
Production Director: Wendy Troeger
Content Project Manager: Glenn Castle
Art Director: Bethany Casey
Technology Project Manager: Chris Catalina
Production Technology Analyst: Tom Stover

Library of Congress Control Number: 2009927869

ISBN-13: 9781428311770
ISBN-10: 1428311777

Delmar
5 Maxwell Drive
Clifton Park, NY 12065-2919
USA

Cengage Learning is a leading provider of customized learning solutions with office locations around the globe, including Singapore, the United Kingdom, Australia, Mexico, Brazil, and Japan. Locate your local office at:
international.cengage.com/region

Cengage Learning products are represented in Canada by Nelson Education, Ltd.

To learn more about Delmar, visit **www.cengage.com/delmar**

Purchase any of our products at your local college store or at our preferred online store **www.ichapters.com**

NOTICE TO THE READER
Publisher does not warrant or guarantee any of the products described herein or perform any independent analysis in connection with any of the product information contained herein. Publisher does not assume, and expressly disclaims, any obligation to obtain and include information other than that provided to it by the manufacturer. The reader is expressly warned to consider and adopt all safety precautions that might be indicated by the activities described herein and to avoid all potential hazards. By following the instructions contained herein, the reader willingly assumes all risks in connection with such instructions. The publisher makes no representations or warranties of any kind, including but not limited to, the warranties of fitness for particular purpose or merchantability, nor are any such representations implied with respect to the material set forth herein, and the publisher takes no responsibility with respect to such material. The publisher shall not be liable for any special, consequential, or exemplary damages resulting, in whole or part, from the readers' use of, or reliance upon, this material.

Printed in the United States of America
1 2 3 4 5 6 7 XXX 12 11 10 09

DEDICATION

This book is dedicated to my wife Leslie, daughter Lauren, and son Chad, whose unfailing patience, support and good humor have made the process of building this book all the sweeter.

CONTENTS

PREFACE

"THERE ARE THREE FINE ARTS: SCULPTURE, PAINTING, AND ORNAMENTAL PASTRY-MAKING, OF WHICH ARCHITECTURE IS A BRANCH."

Pierre Simon Fournier (1712–68), the most famous member of a French family of typographers, was a man of many parts: type cutter, ornament designer, music publishing innovator, inventor of the point system of type measurement—and pastry cook.

How I became a curious, authoritative, experienced, still-enthusiastic-after-all-these years, peripatetic pastry chef and how you can, too

In every creative field, whether architecture, painting, or the pastry arts, one needs to study the past to invent the future. Becoming an artist takes time and a serious commitment whether you use paint and clay or butter, sugar, eggs, and flour. Learning the basics of cookery and baking, studying the styles of those chefs who have come before, and absorbing a broad knowledge of techniques and ingredients from food masters everywhere, all contribute to the formation of the successful pastry chef.

Many different experiences have influenced me in my journey toward becoming a pastry chef and instructor. Growing up in a family who nurtured my interests in food, frequent visits to food stores in the "big city," that is, New York, travel abroad in my college years, studying art and foreign language, and meeting prominent experts in the fields of food journalism, all have played a part in this ever-unfolding journey.

In my youth, I had the good fortune to be raised by two adventurous aunts who encouraged me to try different restaurants with them and early on instilled in me the pleasures of travel as part of a lifestyle. All of this led to apprenticeships in top restaurants and food stores in France in the early 1970s. This experience in turn propelled me further toward a lifelong dream of opening my own specialty food business, bringing back with me the knowledge of and enthusiasm for a whole world of hitherto unknown ingredients and foods. Pioneering in the field of specialty food retailing, I opened and owned French-style *charcuteries* with American flair, preparing foods and pastries to go, and catering to a star-studded clientele on two coasts. Satisfied that I had achieved my long-held goal of gaining national recognition at an early age, I left the retail arena to concentrate on teaching and writing. For the past 20 years, I have been teaching the pastry arts and the art of confidence building to hundreds of students from all over the world, pulling talents and aptitudes from deep inside a highly multiethnic cross section of students from whom I gain in equal measure to what I give. And, as a veteran food writer, I remain emotionally tied to the latest developments in specialty food retailing with visits to stores nationwide, where my pulse quickens upon seeing a particularly inventive and beautiful display of merchandise, and I'm equally thrilled to be able to share these exciting developments with students and readers alike.

Although being based in a highly multicultural metropolis like Los Angeles, I remain thoroughly convinced that no matter where one lives, it is possible to discover people, places, and ideas to whet the appetite, stimulate the creativity, and keep the habit of tasting deeply and widely alive. Developing one's taste for unusual or yet undiscovered ingredients is key in creating innovative pastry art, but the other senses are crucial as well. One's sense of smell, the eye for compelling visual presentation, the aesthetic sense that leads to the use of unusual plates, the ear for and appreciation of the crunch and crackle in a well-made, well-baked pastry, are all critical and can be stimulated by viewing art, listening to music, connecting oneself to the earth from which our food comes and translating this glory to the plate. The German poet Goethe famously observed, "Architecture is frozen music." By extension, I believe that the *Dessert Architect* is composer and conductor, creator and presenter, who orchestrates a symphony of tastes and composes harmonies of ingredients that spell pure pleasure on the plate or in the bowl.

As part of my education, I have been fortunate to meet many passionate individuals involved in growing, producing, selling, processing, or writing about food. Unlike the soul-killing tedium of food shopping in supermarkets, frequent trips to farmers markets are still an intriguing adventure. I suspect it's a holdover from my experience in Europe where shopping for food involves not only getting to know, but also becoming fiercely loyal to, the vendors who sell the highest quality seasonal produce. This experience has enabled me to get to know my local farmers and even visit their farms, where I have been invigorated by the smell of well-tended soil at sunrise, and inspired by the ineffable beauty of pristine produce just pulled from the earth.

The experience of eating in ethnic restaurants provides the twin pleasures of immersion in a foreign culture and experiencing cuisine that is authentic and delicious. This has opened my eyes to the potential of bringing ethnic ingredients in to the pantry of the pastry kitchen, and the recipes in the book reflect that infatuation. I have experienced the collegiality and generosity of chefs all over the world, whose training ranges from the prestigious culinary academy to the School of Mom.

In focused visits to trade shows and manufacturing plants, I have continued to be amazed by the sheer inventiveness of professionals in the field, each willing to put their lives on the line to introduce and promote the next good food idea or ingredient. Yet it is from the artisanal producers of all kinds of foods and beverages that I have learned the most, from cheese makers in rural Washington state to jam makers in northern California, and from coffee micro roasters in LA. In my travels, I've enjoyed tasting first-hand award-winning Calvados produced in France, cardamom and cashews in India, and truly artisanal gelato in Genoa, Italy, and its surrounding towns. I have learned far more than how each artisanal product is made; I have seen the glint in the eye of truly passionate individuals in whom I recognize a kindred spirit and personal pride in the honest quality of the products they produce animating their life's work.

Over the years, I have tasted reflectively and widely. I have been curious and excited to learn the pastry traditions of my ancestors and those from other cultures. I have also learned that what seem like serendipitous discoveries are not happenstance at all. When one is committed to a field, one opens his eyes, ears, heart, and mind to new experiences. One is continuously receptive to what he reads, tastes, and hears— so that the "lovely accidents" that occur are actually no accidents but opportunities a wise eye can identify.

It is my hope that through this book, you will be inspired to be curious and taste widely, to be excited about the many food pleasures you discover, incorporating this lifelong excitement into your career in the pastry arts. I also hope that your pleasure working in the field translates into pure pleasure on the plate for countless diners who are the appreciative recipients of this long-practiced art.

ACKNOWLEDGEMENTS

Writing a cookbook is never solely the achievement of one person. It involves many hands, eyes, palates, and opinions over the long haul. For their immense and unflagging efforts to make this the best book it could be, and for their unerring dexterity and good taste, I wish to thank Sherri Gardiner, Sage Stetson, and Lolita Mendoza, all former students in my professional baking classes at Los Angeles Trade Technical College.

A big shout-out is in order to my longtime friend and writing sage, Diana Rosen, who polished my words to a high sheen, offering friendship and encouragement during the long gestation of this project.

Also, my deepest gratitude to Robert Schueller of Melissa's Produce for the broad range of high quality specialty produce supplied on a moment's notice during the recipe development and testing stages for this book; thanks too to Diane Surfas at Surfas in Culver City, California, for supplying professional culinary tools and specialty ingredients from their broad and deep array; also thanks to all of the other purveyors who widened my horizons and inspired me with their kindness.

Thanks also to Izabel Lam, Fortessa and Steelite for providing me with an array of beautiful table ware which helped to show off the desserts in this book to best advantage.

And many thanks to the accommodating and perceptive team of Elon Schoenholz and Andy Sheen-Turner whose photographs and food styling, respectively, grace the pages of the book.

THE DESSERT ARCHITECT

CHAPTER ONE

The Four Cornerstones

Introduction

Cornerstone n. something that is essential, indispensable, or basic; the chief foundation on which something is constructed or developed

—THE RANDOM HOUSE DICTIONARY OF THE ENGLISH LANGUAGE

In analyzing any successful dessert, from the simplest pie à la mode to the most elaborate multilayered cake or pastry, you will find that what appears simple on the surface may not in fact be so simple.

Building a dessert is not unlike constructing a building. However, instead of using steel, concrete, and glass, the pastry chef's primary building blocks are flour, sugar, dairy products, and flavorings. Each of the elements comprising the whole plays a distinctive and important role in ultimately making the dessert satisfying and successful—successful because it illustrates to at least some degree each of the following Four Cornerstones.

In architecture, when all of the elements of the building work together to create an aesthetically pleasing whole, we consider that building well designed. To the dessert architect, a dessert properly plated and presented, on the right-sized, -shaped, and -colored plate is like a building well suited to its location (appropriate to the tone of the food service venue in which it is served), taking into account the placement and interplay of elements on the plate.

When a building is completed, and aesthetically pleasing, it forms a harmonious whole, making all who enter it feel welcome, comfortable, uplifted, or just secure. Likewise, desserts should comfort, not challenge, offering to the diner a moment when all of the intrusions of the workaday world can be blocked out, a way to escape to a place of pure pleasure and satisfaction, uncomplicated by feelings of guilt or self-doubt.

Chapter Objectives

After reading this chapter, you should be able to:

- **Describe what the Four Cornerstones are and why they are important**

- **Explain the role of ingredients in taste**

- **Describe the importance of different textures in creating a dessert that is satisfying**

- **Understand the interplay and contrasts between elements in a multicomponent dessert**

Building on principles of balance, both visual and physical, knowing fully the weight-bearing capacity of building materials, and applying both principles of good design coupled with functionality, the architect effectively translates a design on paper into three-dimensional reality. So it is, too, with the work of the dessert architect who draws upon a full command of knowledge of ingredients, tools, and techniques to create a well-conceived dessert, informed by what I call the Four Cornerstones: first and foremost, Flavor, and then Texture, Temperature, and Contrast.

All of this work begins with an understanding of the primacy of **Flavor,** the first of Four Cornerstones in the dessert architect's arsenal of knowledge, learning the importance of using high-quality ingredients in correct combinations.

Laying the Cornerstones

In this book, I will systematically present a series of basic preparations and techniques of dessert making that may be combined in countless ways to produce a myriad of extraordinary desserts. All of this flows, however, from an understanding of the primacy of flavor, the first of Four Cornerstones in the dessert architect's arsenal of knowledge, which includes learning the importance of using high-quality ingredients in correct combinations.

How can you learn to create if you haven't yet learned how to taste? All pastry students and practitioners must taste, taste, and then taste again en route to the perfect rendition of a dessert, sharpening their palates to recognize the subtle but important differences in ingredients and how those ingredients shape and influence what ends up on the dessert plate.

The other three nearly inseparable cornerstones of fine dessert making are texture, temperature, and underpinning each of those, contrast. Whether the consumer clearly perceives it or not, the texture of a dessert affects one's perception of its dominant flavors and leads to pleasure on the palate. For example, take note of the texture of a mousse in a dessert. Is it perfectly smooth, one texture throughout, or intentionally enlivened with bits of still-whole fruit? In the context of the other elements on the plate, would one version of mousse be preferable to another?

Temperature also plays an important role and is related to texture. Consider the shatteringly crisp layers of a freshly prepared napoleon pastry compared with one that has been under refrigeration for a day. The former succeeds as a touchstone of the pastry maker's art, while the latter may be perceived as just ordinary, or worse, memorable for the wrong reasons.

Contrast, the last of the Four Cornerstones, represents an essential element in any successful dessert. Thinking about desserts from the perspective of contrast—sweet versus tart, hot versus cold, soft versus frozen, and crunchy versus smooth—is a necessary precursor to crafting desserts that are memorable.

Consider an American favorite, apple pie à la mode. An analysis of its elements—a flaky, buttery crust, soft-crunchy apples, a fortuitous combination of spices, ice-cold ice cream contrasting with warm pie—shows that it includes all of the Four Cornerstones.

The Four Cornerstones

Every recipe in this book was crafted with the Four Cornerstones in mind: flavor, texture, temperature, and contrast. Whether an individual has an intellectual appreciation of these four characteristics or not, the diner's senses nonetheless perceive these multidimensional qualities. The characteristics are described here in enough detail that you will be able to successfully apply them to your pastry creations.

Cornerstone One: Flavor

FLAVOR

n. taste, especially the distinctive taste of something as it is experienced in the mouth

—THE RANDOM HOUSE DICTIONARY OF THE ENGLISH LANGUAGE

It is no accident that flavor is the first cornerstone to any successful dessert. Without it, the pastry chef's work would be pointless. As a pastry chef, keep the following essential question in the back of your mind: Does the dessert have *flavor* or, even though it may be pleasing to the eye, is it bland and does it, therefore, merely represent empty calories?

Regardless of what inspires you, the first point of inspiration must be flavor, whether considering a perfectly ripe peach in season and how it may be treated in a dessert (often minimal manipulation is best) or a well-balanced high-quality chocolate couverture. Even with a mastery of basic techniques, skilled pastry chefs can create desserts only as memorable as the flavors of their prime ingredients. Flavor comes from flavor. What you start with is what you will end up with.

Developing Your Palate

In the quest for a highly flavored dessert, where should you begin?

First, it's essential to taste the main ingredients that you intend to use. How can you create flavorful desserts if you haven't educated your own palate first? As mentioned in the introduction, all students and practitioners of pastry must taste each element of a dessert alone and then in combination to be sure that the end result is satisfying, harmonious, and delicious at least in the eyes of the person producing it. Taste, and taste again. Ask yourself questions such as the following to help ensure that your finished products encompass that first cornerstone, flavor:

- **Does the fruit have a definite flavor? What is its flavor? Is it sweet, tart, floral, or a combination of all of these?**

- **Is the chocolate creamy or coarse? Is its dimension sweet or complex, with what balance of fruity or smoky notes?**

- **Are the nuts fresh tasting or rancid? How do the nuts taste raw? How do they taste when roasted?**

Tasting charts to help clarify your thinking about ingredients may be found below and on pages 24, 27, and 29.

Categorizing Flavor

In order to understand the role of flavor in a dessert, it is best to start by putting flavors into broad categories. Admittedly, this process is often a subjective exercise, so feel free to insert additional ingredients into the following chart, or move ingredients into other categories as your taste impressions dictate. Note that some items with highly complex flavors appear more than once.

When using the chart to analyze the recipes in this book, you will note that the components that make up a single dessert most often will each be drawn from a different category, thereby making the overall flavor profile of the dessert more complex and interesting. When developing desserts of your own, you can also use the chart as a tool to anticipate or plan for the dessert's multiple flavor dimensions.

In analyzing any successful dessert, from the simplest pie à la mode to the most elaborate multilayered cake or pastry, you will find that what appears simple on the surface may not in fact be so simple. The instructions in this book are intended to help you make the final result look effortless to the diner's eyes.

Flavor Inventory Chart

Description of categories of flavor	Ingredients that exhibit these characteristics
Flavors that dominate or are "forward"	Chocolate, banana, berries, cassis (black currant), ripe melons (Galia, cantaloupe, Charentais, pepino), white peach, ginger (fresh, dried, or candied), hazelnut, gianduja (smooth hazelnut chocolate paste), Nutella (sweetened chocolate-hazelnut spread), honey
Flavors that provide a backdrop for other flavors, flavors that recede into the background	Sweet, rich dairy ingredients such as milk and cream, coconut, white chocolate
Flavors that are soft, subtle, mute, faint, otherwise elusive	Cherimoya, egg in pastry doughs or in sauces and custards, cream cheese–based fillings
Flavors that "kick in" after the first few bites	Cardamom, plum, curry
Flavors perceived as sour, tart, acidic, acetic	Apricots, citrus of all kinds (including bergamot orange, lemon, Meyer lemon, kaffir lime, lemongrass, limes, yuzu), tomatoes, persimmons, sour dried plums, pomegranate, quince, rhubarb, tamarind, balsamic vinegar, cranberries, lemon curd, dried hibiscus flowers, star fruit, cassis (black currant), red currant, blackberry
Flavors perceived as salty (even in the arena of sweets-making, undertones of saltiness are present and appropriate, if only as a contrast to the other flavor categories, and to reduce the perceived sweetness of the dessert)	Salted caramel, malted milk powder

Flavor Inventory Chart (continued)

Description of categories of flavor	Ingredients that exhibit these characteristics
Flavors perceived as smoky	Lapsang Souchong tea, Armagnac (brandy from southwest France), Calvados (apple brandy from Normandy, France), Cognac (brandy from the Cognac region of France), Scotch whiskey, certain chocolate couvertures
Flavors perceived as pungent	Ginger (fresh, dried, candied), cardamom
Flavors perceived as sweet, intensely sugary, caramelized (perceived as less sweet)	Lyle's Golden Syrup, sugar cane juice, caramel, dates, dried figs, maple syrup, honey, cajeta (a cooked mixture of goat's or cow's milk caramelized with sugar), condensed milk, soft and hard meringue, angel food cake, butterscotch, milk chocolate, white chocolate
Flavors perceived as bitter, sharp, biting	Astringent aperitifs with herbs and fruits (such as Campari, Cynar, and Punt e Mes), cocoa nibs, dark cocoa, tangerine, lime, key lime, white peppercorns, black peppercorns
Flavors perceived as floral	Lavender honey, violet essence, jasmine flowers and flower-based teas, Darjeeling tea, rose water, orange-blossom water, Asian pears, Muscat grapes, nougat, Forelle pears, lychee, lemongrass, white peaches, Gewurztztraminer and Muscat grape–based wines
Flavors perceived as herbal	Thyme, basil, fennel, tarragon, pandan leaf or extract (a flavoring considered the "vanilla" of Southeast Asian cuisine), Pernod or other anise-flavored liqueur, mint
Flavors perceived as vegetal, vernal, grasslike, "green"	Shiso (Japanese herb, also known as perilla), carrots, beets, fennel, anise, tamarillo, Kabocha squash, pumpkin, green tea, fresh mint
Flavors perceived as earthy	Rice, polenta, couscous, whole wheat flour, prickly pear, chestnut, sweetened chestnut puree, high-percentage couverture chocolate, graham crackers, black teas, beets, carrots
Flavors perceived as spiced, with warm spice notes	Cinnamon, allspice, star anise, cloves, ginger, chai
Flavors perceived as winey, alcoholic, "hot," fermented	Fruits marinated in alcohol, such as brandied cherries; *eau de vie*, white alcohols (such as eau de vie de framboise or eau de vie de poire), port
Flavors perceived as cultured, fermented, tart, or acidic based on dairy products	Crème fraiche, buttermilk, goat cheese, blue cheese, sour cream, yogurt, mascarpone
Flavors perceived as perfumed, exotic	Passion fruit, feijoa (a tropical fruit in the guava family, also known as pineapple guava mango), pineapple, tamarillo, cherimoya, bergamot orange, lychee, mirabelle plum
Flavors perceived as focused, concentrated, memorable, unforgettable, leaving a strong but pleasant aftertaste, with a lingering effect on the palate	Vanilla, praline, coffee made from freshly roasted beans
Flavors containing opposing impressions within one main ingredient—such as sweet and tart, sweet and sour, sweet and pungent	Bittersweet chocolate, coffee, candied citrus rind (orange, lemon, pomelo, grapefruit, sweet lime), kumquats, limequats, raspberries, port wine, peches de vigne (red-fleshed peaches), plums of all kinds, including purple, mirabelle, pluots
Flavors that are perceived as roasted, toasted, burned, intensified by deep roasting	Coffee, nuts, nut pastes (almond, hazelnut, pistachio, walnut), sesame seeds and roasted sesame paste, tahini, halvah, peanut butter, browned butter (beurre noisette), croquantine (commercially made crisp thin flakes of baked pastry), Japanese genmaicha tea (green tea–based flavored with roasted rice), green tea, oven-dried or oven-roasted tomatoes, dried fruit chips (persimmon, pear, apple)

Cornerstone Two: Texture

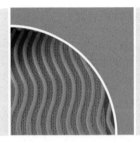

TEXTURE

n. the characteristic physical structure given to a material, an object, etc., by the size, shape, arrangement, and proportions of its parts

—THE RANDOM HOUSE DICTIONARY OF THE ENGLISH LANGUAGE

Key question: What are the textures that can be perceived in a dessert?

Creating Textures

Texture is essential in any successful dessert. Carefully chosen, each element of a dessert lends personality to the whole and keeps the consumer satisfied from first bite to last. A creamy mousse is infinitely more interesting if it is set against a syrup-soaked sponge cake layer which itself has an engaging texture. An ice cream or sorbet may certainly be served as a freestanding dessert, but it, too, becomes much more satisfying when paired with a delicately crunchy, nut-encrusted tuile or other paper-thin cookie. Furthermore, a hot or warm chocolate or fruit sauce poured over a serving of double chocolate or vanilla ice cream adds yet another dimension, both in texture and in temperature. You don't need to go much further than the corner soda fountain of yesteryear to validate the importance of texture in a dessert. That hot fudge sundae is a near-perfect example, delivering a lesson

". . . fruits taste great on their own and they add magic to desserts. . . ."

PICHET ONG

Owner, P*ONG and Batch Bakery, NYC

Pichet Ong needs to look no further than the produce market to gain inspiration for his next dessert. He sums it up this way: "When in peak season and harvested properly, fruits taste great on their own and they add magic to desserts. It is equivalent to what high quality meat or fish is to a savory chef. There is not much you can do with a flavorless steak

or a piece of less than pristine fish. Instead of struggling to make desserts delicious, start off with flavorful fruits." In creating a dessert menu, Ong keeps in mind the flavor palette expressed in the savory side of the menu. "I also think desserts, particularly those served in restaurants, should fit within the context of the menu offerings. I'm a big fan of repeating an ingredient used in one or more of the savory dishes on the menu, but utilizing it in a sweet application. For example, in my restaurant, if I use cherries with foie gras on anise biscotti on a tasting menu, I might use the same fruit again in a warm Black Forest flavored cake, aromatized with kirsch and spiced up with grains of paradise."

in how flavor, texture, temperature, and contrast all work together in a seamless whole. Freezing-cold ice cream paired with scalding hot fudge sauce (temperature and contrast), improved by a crunch of syrup-soaked walnuts (texture), and lightened with a cloud of airy, just slightly sweetened whipped cream (contrast again) show the successful dessert architect (or skilled soda jerk) and the principles of the Four Cornerstones at work on the most elemental level.

What Is Texture?

It's easier to define *texture* by using adjectives that describe the sensation or impressions one gets when tasting the dessert. When considering the overall textural impression of a particular dessert, or the parts of a dessert separately, adjectives can seem imprecise or subjective. But if you asked an individual to describe what texture is being perceived when tasting a dessert, the responses will most likely include such adjectives as shown on the following chart.

Why is it important to identify the textures of your dessert's elements? Any dessert considered complete and satisfying from the point of view of "mouth feel" will include at least two of the characteristics on the following chart. When you design your own desserts, you should first choose flavors of ingredients that work well together, and next consider elements from a textural point of view. All multicomponent desserts should include a combination of textures, with each one perceivable, even if subconsciously, by the person consuming it.

The texture of a dessert affects one's perception of the dominant flavors of the dessert and, when properly executed, leads to pleasure on the palate. Consider the difference between how a fresh-from-the-oven fruit tart with a crisp pastry shell tastes and one in which the juices of the fruits have rendered the pastry soggy and soft. If practical, it is best to bake delicate pastry desserts close to serving time to ensure that the dessert retains the texture you intended.

The following chart lists ingredients and elements of desserts that fall into particular categories of texture. Keeping in mind the importance of including multiple textures in any finished dessert, refer to the chart for inspiration. Deciding which textures your dessert will exemplify and then choosing which ingredients to use to create those textures are both important steps in creating a well-balanced dessert.

Ingredients and Elements of Desserts

Adjective	Elements used to achieve this
Creamy	Dairy products: heavy cream, cheese, sour cream, mascarpone, crème fraiche, softly whipped cream; chocolate ganache using cream at 50% of the weight of chocolate
Crunchy	Nuts (roasted, toasted), coconut, caramelized nuts, caramelized pastry, thin sheets of tempered chocolate; well-baked golden-brown thin sheets of puff pastry, strudel, or filo dough
Silky/Smooth	Bavarian mousses, semifreddo, fruit purees passed through a tamis, caramel deglazed with heavy cream

(continues)

Ingredients and Elements of Desserts (continued)	
Adjective	**Elements used to achieve this**
Thin/Liquidy	Hot caramel sauce, hot chocolate sauce, ganaches where chocolate and heavy cream are in equal proportion
Granular/Sandy	Short pastry dough, biscuit dough, coarse sugar, curded cheese, paneer, ricotta; grains such as semolina, couscous, ground nuts; fresh figs, still-frozen granitas/ices; granulated sugar–coated fried or baked goods
Melt in your mouth	Buttery pastry doughs, caramel sauce with butter in an amount 10% or higher of the weight of the caramel
Flaky	Laminated dough, hand-pulled strudel dough, well-baked filo dough, gently handled chemically leavened biscuit, scone, or shortcake dough, using cold fat when being mixed
Dense	Chocolate, high-fat cakes (pound cake, rustic almond tort), citrus or other fruit-based curds, chocolate ganache using cream at less than 50% of the weight of chocolate
Light	Egg whites, meringues, cocoa butter used to set mousses, poached meringues
Airy, insubstantial, ethereal	Egg whites, Italian meringues, yeasted doughs, foamed dairy products, sponge cakes, chiffon cakes, hot soufflés
Chewy	Invert sugar, molasses, honey, caramel, gelatin; pectin-based fruit gelées, glutinous rice and tapioca
Sticky	Sugar, molasses, honey; glutinous rice and tapioca
Soft	Semifreddo, ice creams, custards
Hard	Toffee bits, crushed peppermint, hard caramel, other hard candies, macadamia nuts
Spongy	Génoise, marshmallows, Italian meringue

Cornerstone Three: Temperature

TEMPERATURE

n. the measure of the warmth or coldness of an object or substance with reference to some standard value

—THE RANDOM HOUSE DICTIONARY OF THE ENGLISH LANGUAGE

Key question: Are all of the elements being served at their optimal temperature?

Temperature, as it applies to the different elements of a dessert—from the filling to the plating to the topping sauce—may be manipulated to stunning effect. Think of a just-baked chocolate chip cookie or how different a hot chocolate sauce tastes on ice cream, compared with a room-temperature or cold sauce. To be sure, each of the sauces has its place in the canon of dessert making.

Exercise in Temperature

Plan to make all of the components of any dessert in this book. When tasting the dessert, serve it with the recommended sauce at different temperatures (well chilled, room temperature, hot) and record your impressions in the following chart.

Rank by order of preference 1, 2, 3, 4	Dessert served with	Describe the flavor of the sauce	Describe the texture of the sauce	Note contrast with other textures in the dessert
	Sauce, almost frozen, 10–15°F	Blunted, dulled not bright	Icy, thick	
	Sauce well chilled, approximately 45°F	Slightly dulled by refrigeration	Thick but flowing	
	Sauce at room temperature, approximate 68–70°F	Pleasant lingering aftertaste	Masking plate consistency	
	Sauce heated to under the boil, approximately 200°F		Flowing uncontrollably on the plate	

Temperature and Contrast

It is impossible to separate temperature from the idea of contrast in a dessert. The consumer perceives as contrasts even subtle shifts in temperature from one component of a dessert to the next, lending interest and excitement to the dessert.

Not every successful dessert features elements served at different temperatures. Sometimes a dessert composed of differently textured components is enough to engage the attention and please the palate of the person consuming it. But when appropriate, for example, serving a hot sauce with a cold mousse, or a pastry-based main element such as a tart or a warm soufflé with a cool, creamy drift of whipped cream, takes that dessert to a transcendent level where the whole is so much more than the sum of its parts. By itself, a warm soufflé is certainly texturally satisfying but becomes even more so when served with its whipped cream accompaniment. Adding one more texture by serving a crisp, thin cookie or a flaky puff pastry baton adds even more textural interest and gives the diner the opportunity to move from element to element, consuming bites of each in succession. With just a little thought and planning on the part of the dessert architect, the overall eating experience is thereby made more complex and more enjoyable.

Serving desserts with elements at different temperatures is, of course, more complex than when elements are all at the same temperature. When composing a mixed-temperature dessert, it is important to consider what is practical and what is not in an operation that serves a considerable number of people at the same time. Think about the following considerations as you develop a strategy for serving multicomponent, multi-temperature desserts:

1. **How is the back of the house staffed?**

2. **Given the physical space allotted to the preparation and serving of desserts, is it practical to maintain a sauce to be served hot, cool, or semi-frozen within easy reach of the other components maintained at other temperatures? How far is the freezer from the refrigerator, and the bain marie from either?**

3. **How much of a dessert might be plated in advance? Is the dessert conducive to being served on a well-chilled plate? Or is a cold plate apt to have a negative, flavor-blunting effect on elements of the desserts that are better served at room temperature (e.g., buttery pastry doughs).**

4. **Will the desserts be delivered to the tables by a waitstaff soon enough to hold up, if one element is hot or warm and another cold or frozen?**

5. **What hot elements of the dessert may be baked to order (if the menu states that this is the case and the waitstaff is diligent about "selling" those desserts that require preordering).**

6. **Does the operation offer tasting menus? If so, and the chef-designed tasting menu includes predetermined desserts (where usually the same dessert or desserts are served to all parties dining at the table), then the timing for last-minute preparation is not an issue, since such a meal progresses on a more predictable schedule. In this case, the pastry kitchen staff may be alerted when to "fire" how many desserts for a particular table with enough advance notice to accomplish serving a fresh-from-the-oven dessert.**

Cornerstone Four: Contrast

CONTRAST

n. a thing or person that is strikingly unlike in comparison; opposition or juxtaposition of different forms, lines, or colors in a work of art to intensify each element's properties and produce a more dynamic expressiveness

—THE RANDOM HOUSE DICTIONARY OF THE ENGLISH LANGUAGE

The fourth cornerstone, contrast, represents the last essential element in any successful work of the pastry maker's art. Contrast can be provided by any opposing dessert elements, such as the following:

Taste and texture contrast

Tart versus sweet—A simple example from the corner diner, lemon meringue pie, combines a thick lemony filling (tart) with an insubstantial whipped egg white–based topping (sweet).

Temperature contrast

Hot versus cold—An example of a hot/cold dessert is the hot chocolate soufflé served with a cold crème anglaise sauce.

Texture contrasts

The following examples of desserts are made from two main elements, each of which exhibits different textures to stunning effect.

Crunchy versus smooth—A flaky puff pastry millefeuille where the crunchy texture of the puff pastry contrasts with the soft velvety-smooth texture of its custard filling.

Dense versus airy—A dense flourless tort topped with a light airy mousse.

Smooth versus crunchy—A smooth panna cotta garnished with a crisp crunchy tuile cookie.

Soft versus frozen—A parfait of soft lemon chiffon mousse topped with a frozen lemon ice cream.

Producing a successful dessert involves not only being able to produce perfect versions of each element of the dessert, but also envisioning how the elements will contrast with each other in a satisfying dialogue that engages the attention, palate, and senses of the person consuming it. A competent pastry chef is able to make a properly textured, light sponge cake, a fine-grained short dough, or a flaky, well-baked, laminated pastry every time. To reach higher than that basic competency, however, pastry chefs must experiment to arrive at new ways to excite the palate. In pursuit of new insights, the successful pastry chef might wish to create a number of different versions of the same dessert, varying the temperature or texture of one element at a time until many permutations have been trialed. An associated required step is taking meticulous notes to record which combinations work together most successfully.

Consider, for example, how a bracingly acidic frozen citrus mousse set onto a warm and mellow honey-sweetened custard sauce would encompass the contrasts of sweet and tart, and warm and frozen. Contrasts in both texture and temperature are represented here, producing a very satisfying and memorable conclusion to a meal.

Key question: How do elements in the dessert contrast with each other, and does that contrast satisfy from first bite to last?

Single-textured desserts do not engage the attention of the diner from first taste to last forkful. Why? The palate becomes bored by the monotony of texture. One cannot fully appreciate a creamy element unless it is paired with a crunchy one. Giving the diner the option to move between creamy and crunchy elements makes for a varied and therefore much more interesting sensory experience.

Likewise, when serving a dessert that has contrasting flavor profiles such as sweet versus tart, or mellow versus acidic, you are providing a welcomed variety of tastes for the diner who can enjoy the back-and-forth sensory experience between sweet and tart elements or mellow dairy notes and bold-flavored caramel.

". . . flavorings . . . with the savory kitchen, are great enhancements to the sweet side of the menu."

SHUNA FISH LYDON

Pastry Chef, San Francisco

Shuna Fish Lydon, with a long and deep résumé including stints at Aziza and Citizen Cake in San Francisco, and Bouchon and the French Laundry in Yountville, California, acknowledges that jobs in culinary arts and pastry demand endless stamina. "This business is brutal but pastry chefs are the most efficient, organized cooks that I know. We are capable of planning our work load and need to manage our time well by considering what can be made in advance and what must be done *á* la minute." Being California-based has influenced her style, leading her to appreciate the melting pot of flavors that the state encompasses. For instance, the use of Asian and Indian spices, flavorings, and other ingredients is only one part of her pantry as a pastry chef. She looks to other fields for inspiration as well. "I hope that school-trained pastry chefs branch out from what they learned in school. It's necessary to stay modern by looking at other art forms and media such as sculpture, painting, photography to get ideas." In her pastry, seasons play a dynamic role. "Looking outside of the standard set of flavorings, fresh herbs normally associated with the savory kitchen, are great enhancements to the sweet side of the menu."

A few words about the recipes

How to read recipes, of course, is far more than being able to sound out the words written in them. As the re-creator of the recipe, you need to truly *absorb* the instructions contained within the recipes, wrapping your mind around the recipe or set of recipes before embarking on the actual process of creating the multicomponent dessert. Be patient and resist the temptation of plunging right in to making the recipe before having fully absorbed its outlines. Instead, read through the entire recipe from beginning to end once, making note of any technique or procedure that might pose a challenge to you or any step that seems unclear. Then read the recipe again with the goal of creating a mental picture of the entire set of procedures involved in accomplishing the dessert. In this way, you are committing to memory the basic outlines of the instructions and the order in which each part of the recipe is to be done. You are coming to "own" the recipe, which makes the actual process of producing the dessert seamless and smooth. This deep reading and comprehension of the recipe will eliminate the risk of any procedure being omitted or executed in the wrong order, leading to needless waste of time, the most precious commodity in the kitchen any chef has, and will ensure that the production of the dessert is accomplished with the greatest economy of movement in the least possible amount of time. At this point you should be able to easily restate in your own words what the recipe entails. When you have grasped the idea of the recipe and learned the techniques involved in making it, then you will be ready to meet any challenges in executing the dessert with confidence. Ideas about the use of ingredients and flavor combinations plus technique equal creativity. Having both an idea and the technique needed to execute that idea, incorporating it into a finished, refined dessert will take you beyond the recipes in the book, unleashing your creative side, leading you to the path on which you can create your own original desserts.

In addition to showing U.S. weight and metric weight and amounts for items that are available in units (such as vanilla beans, fruits or whole spices), where appropriate, the ingredients in many of the components in the recipes are also given in baker's percentage form. Typically applied to yeasted bread doughs, pastry doughs, and cake batters, baker's percentages are an expression of the relationship between the main ingredient and the other ingredients in a recipe. They are an integral part of the baker's or pastry chef's language, and give clues to understanding the architecture of a recipe. Baker's percentages provide a window into the recipe, giving clues to the resulting texture, sweetness and richness of a preparation. Using baker's percentages, the chef can manipulate the formula by easily changing one ingredient in the recipe at a time to achieve different results.

Where flour is the ingredient that there is the most of in a recipe, it is conventional to designate that ingredient as 100%. It is easy then to calculate the percentages for each of the other ingredients in a recipe simply by dividing the weight of each of those ingredients by the weight of flour.

In some of the recipes in the book, flour is combined with another dry ingredient such as cocoa powder or nut flour. In these cases, the combined weight of those ingredients in a recipe is called 100% and the weight of each of the other ingredients in the recipe is compared to that weight leading to a fraction or ratio expressed in percentage form.

In recipes such as pastry creams, custards, sauces and meringues, where either there is no flour or only an insignificant amount of it, then the crucial ingredient that drives the recipe such as milk, other dairy or egg whites is called 100% and each of the other ingredients in the recipe are compared to *that* 100% ingredient. In these formulas, the pivotal ingredients are noted at the top of the baker's percentage column as a guide to how the baker's percentages are calculated.

Finally, baker's percentages are a reliable and precise tool for the baker or pastry chef wishing to change the yields (scaling up or scaling down) of a particular recipe. By simply dividing the desired yield in ounces or grams by the sum total of percentages in the formula, one can calculate the weight of the ingredient that is shown as 100% and then multiply that weight by the percentages of each of the other ingredients in the formula to ascertain the weights of those ingredients used in the new yield.

Deconstructing a Recipe

To become comfortable with the concept of the Four Cornerstones as applied to desserts, deconstruct a few recipes. Examine how each part of the recipe contributes to the whole, and how the elements of the dessert fulfill the Four Cornerstones, working together to lead to a satisfying whole. What follows is a recipe for "A Couple of Doughnuts," a seasonal fruit-based dessert, which combines doughnut-shaped peaches, a deep-fried lightly spiced cake doughnut, and a floral scented panna cotta. Following the recipe, you will find an analysis of the recipe showing how the Four Cornerstones are applied.

A Couple of Doughnuts

YIELD: 12 SERVINGS

A couple of doughnuts—caramel-coated poached white peaches, white dough-nut peach and violet mousse, and a buttermilk spiced doughnut. The placement of elements in this recipe was inspired, in part, by a pop architectural landmark adjacent to one of Los Angeles' busiest freeways where a large cement doughnut is poised above the business known as Randy's Doughnuts. A relatively newly marketed variety of early summer peach, the "doughnut," or Saturn peach, with its flat-tened doughnut shape, helped complete the twinned title of the dessert.

The fresh fruit is first poached in a vanilla-scented syrup and then coated, when served, with a fruity caramel made by reducing that syrup. The fruity floral flavor of the peaches called out for one more element—violet essence, made commercially in France's flower growing and perfume production region, by distilling thou-sands of edible violet petals. The floral notes of violets and this variety of peach seemed to be a marriage made in heaven. Placing the mousse between the doughnut and the doughnut peach creates a tension that works to the advantage of each. Both literally and figuratively, this dish elevates a classic American treat, pairing it with three elegant mainstays from the French classical dessert repertoire: poached fruit, caramel, and mousse.

The order of things:

1. **Make peach mousse**
2. **Make buttermilk spiced doughnut dough** and let rest
3. **Poach the donut peaches**
4. **Make caramel**
5. **Cut and fry the doughnuts**

Equipment list:

Rectangular pan measuring 8 inches by 10 inches, bottom lined with an acetate sheet

Round cookie cutter measuring 2½ inches in diameter by ½ inch thick to cut mousse

Deep fry thermometer

Deep sauté pan or fryer for frying the doughnuts

Peach mousse flavored with violet

YIELD: 12 ROUNDS OF MOUSSE, EACH MEASURING 2½ INCHES IN DIAMETER BY APPROXI-MATELY ½ INCH THICK

Oz	Grams	Each	Name of ingredient
14	420		Commercially prepared frozen **white peach puree,** thawed (this usually contains approximately 10% sugar by weight)
4.3	129		**Powdered cocoa butter** (Mycryo)
17	510		**Heavy cream**
		A few drops	**Violet essence**

→ Heat 5 ounces of the white peach puree to 90°F.

→ Add Mycryo and whisk until melted.

→ Add the remaining peach puree and allow the mixture to cool to room temperature.

→ In the bowl of an electric mixer outfitted with the whisk attachment, whip the cream with the violet essence to soft peaks.

→ Carefully fold the whipped cream into the fruit base and then pour the mousse into an acetate sheet–lined rectangular pan measuring 8 inches by 10 inches.

TIP: Alternatively, you may blanch to remove the peel of fresh ripe, highly fragrant white peaches. Then poach the fruit in a standard simple syrup (equal parts granulated sugar and water by weight) until tender. Remove from the syrup, drain, and then puree. Proceed with recipe as shown below.

→ Spread to an even layer and freeze.

→ When frozen, cut using a 2½ inch diameter round cutter, cutting four rounds along the 10 inch side by three rounds along the 8 inch side, to create 12 rounds of mousse.

→ Keep the mousse frozen until ready to serve the dessert.

Buttermilk spiced cake doughnuts

YIELD: 12 DOUGHNUTS, EACH MEASURING 3 INCHES IN DIAMETER BY ¾ TO 1 INCH THICK, AFTER FRYING

Oz	Grams	Each	Name of ingredient	Baker's percentages
5	150		All purpose flour	31
11	330		Pastry flour	69
.5	15	1 T.	Baking powder	3
		¼ t.	Mace	0.1
		1 t.	Nutmeg	3
		1 t.	Cinnamon	4
		½ t.	Salt	0.3
6.4	192		Granulated sugar	40
7	210		Buttermilk	44
2	60		Unsalted butter, melted	12
1.67	50	1	Whole egg	10
0.5	15	1 T.	Vanilla extract	3
64	1920		Flavorless oil for frying	
As needed to coat the doughnuts after frying			Granulated sugar	

→ Sift flour, baking powder, spices, salt, and sugar together into a medium-sized bowl.

→ Combine buttermilk, melted butter, egg, and vanilla in a separate bowl.

→ Add the liquids to the dry ingredients, mixing gently, only until lightly incorporated.

→ Do not overmix.

→ Turn mixture out onto a lightly floured surface and knead briefly to bring the mixture together into a rough mass.

→ Pat or roll mixture to a rough rectangle measuring 9 inches by 12 inches by approximately ½ inch thick.

→ Using a cookie cutter measuring 3 inches in diameter, cut the doughnuts in rows of three along the 9 inch side, and in rows of 4 along the 12 inch side.

→ Then using a cookie cutter measuring 1 inch in diameter, cut out the center of each doughnut (reserve the doughnut holes for another use, or fry and use as a garnish on the plate).

→ Refrigerate the doughnuts, covered, until ready to fry.

→ Fry just in a heavy deep saucepan half filled with flavorless oil (or electric or gas heated fryer, filled up to recommended level with flavorless oil) heated to 360°F. Fry, carefully turning the doughnuts once halfway through the total of 5 minutes cooking time, or until golden brown and fully puffed.

→ Drain on absorbent paper towels and coat evenly with granulated sugar, just before serving.

Oz	Grams	Each	Name of ingredient
48 to 64 gross weight, 3 to 4 ounces for each fruit, gross weight; 2.5 net weight, after peeling and pit removed	1440 to 1920, approx.; 1200 net weight, approx.	16	**Large doughnut or Saturn white peaches,** ripe but not bruised, peeled by blanching in hot water
16	480		**Simple syrup**
		1	**Vanilla bean,** split
8	240		**Heavy cream**

Poaching more than 12 peaches allows for a few that might appear bruised after poaching, otherwise imperfectly shaped, or asymmetrical.

Poaching the peaches

→ In a large sauté pan, poach the peaches until tender.

→ Using a slotted spoon, carefully remove the peaches from the poaching liquid, *reserving the liquid in the pan for the caramel* as described below.

→ Allow peaches to cool and then remove the pits.

→ Using a small sharp paring knife, free the flesh from the pit. You may need to make a vertical cut on one side of the peach to remove the pit more neatly.

→ Once the pits are removed, refrigerate the peaches, covered, until ready to assemble and serve the dessert.

Making the peach caramel sauce

→ Cook the reserved poaching liquid along with the vanilla bean until the liquid is caramel colored.

→ Remove the vanilla bean and reserve for another use.

→ While the poaching liquid is reducing and cooking to caramel stage (about 318°F), heat the heavy cream in a small saucepan until hot.

→ Remove the caramel from the heat, and carefully add the hot cream to the caramel (it will sputter and steam when first added).

→ Stir until incorporated and set aside.

→ Refrigerate the mixture, when cool, covered, until ready to serve the dessert.

→ It will be necessary to rewarm the caramel over a water bath to re-liquefy it.

Each	Name of ingredient
36, 3 per serving	Candied violets

Assembly and plating

Coat poached peaches lightly and evenly with the caramel sauce. Place a ring of sauce on each plate. Center a peach on top of the sauce. Place a disk of peach violet mousse on top of each peach. Center a doughnut vertically on the disk of mousse. Garnish the plate with candied violets. Serve immediately.

Examined from the point of view of the Four Cornerstones, this recipe illustrates the following elements.

- The cornerstone of *flavor* is well represented here in the ripe floral notes of the seasonal fruit. The peach has intense aroma and lends its floral, fruity flavor to the mousse as well as to the caramel plated sauce.

- The cornerstone of *texture* is illustrated in many places throughout this dessert—

    1. the soft creaminess of the peach mousse flavored with violet,

    2. the pleasantly grainy coating of granulated sugar on the outside of the doughnut,

    3. the silky smoothness of the caramel plating sauce, and

    4. the sugary crunch of the candied violet garnish.

- The cornerstone of *temperature* is embodied here as follows—

    1. the peach is served cold,

    2. the doughnut should be slightly warm, just out of the fryer, and

    3. the accompanying caramel sauce is served warm, contrasting with the cool mousse.

- The cornerstone of *contrast* is found in many places in this dessert—

    1. warm (doughnut) versus cold (the peach, the mousse),

    2. smooth (the mousse) versus granular (the sugared exterior of the doughnut and the coating on the candied violet),

    3. tender and crisp simultaneously (the exterior versus the interior of the doughnut), and

    4. the smooth texture of the caramel versus the crispness of the exterior of the doughnut.

Analyzing the recipes in this way clearly indicates how A Couple of Doughnuts recipe embodies the Four Cornerstones and also shows that these desserts will be enjoyed as multisensory experiences, with their well-planned variety of flavors, textures, and temperatures (underpinned by contrasting elements).

As you work through the recipes in this book, be mindful of how each of the elements of the dessert works in tandem, reinforcing each other, setting up contrasts that are clearly perceivable by the person consuming it. Think about ways that you might alter the recipe, perhaps adding further contrasts in texture or temperature, adding a second sauce to the plate, or designing different garnishes.

Being self-critical and soliciting and acting on constructive criticism from others are important steps in any pastry chef's evolution toward becoming a master in the field. Therefore, evaluating the success of a dessert involves reviewing basics, including the following:

1. Describe the philosophy of this book.

2. Name the Four Cornerstones.

3. Define *flavor* and its importance to desserts.

4. Name three *textures* and possible elements that help achieve these textures.

5. Define *temperature* and its importance to desserts.

6. Define *contrast* and describe why it is considered an underpinning to the other three cornerstones.

Ingredients and Equipment

Introduction

Continuing with the analogy started in Chapter 1, just as when an architect designs a building, starting with decisions about size, form, shape, structure, and decorative facings, the pastry chef constructs the dessert layer by layer, element by element, leading to a harmonious arrangement of elements. Ingredients in the hands of the pastry chef are analogous to the materials an architect uses in planning the design and eventual construction of a building. Just as an architect may make choices among a number of different materials to achieve the desired exterior look of a building, pastry chefs can control the look and overall presentation of a dessert by varying the accompaniments such as sauces and garnishes, but always with the goal of making the most of the flavors inherent in the main ingredients of the dessert.

Flavor

If you examine any ingredient that you use in the pastry kitchen, from spices to nuts to chocolate, coffee, or tea, you will quickly find that no one version of that ingredient defines the category. Often there are significant differences in intensity or pungency of flavor, texture, level of sweetness (or tartness), and many other characteristics in that product, any one of which can affect the outcome of the dessert. The key, therefore, is to taste essential ingredients alone and then in combination with the other main elements in the dessert you are crafting to get an idea of how the final version will taste, taking notes after each tasting for comparison's sake. You

Chapter Objectives
After reading this chapter, you should be able to:

- **Recognize the main ingredients used in the recipes in this book**

- **Gain information about specific ingredients used in a great variety of desserts, which will allow you to create your own original desserts and variations on those offered in the book**

- **Appreciate the importance of developing a true partnership with knowledgeable vendors and suppliers**

- **Recognize the basic and specialized tools and equipment needed to produce visually appealing multicomponent desserts**

may be surprised at how different the outcome can be when using, say, a particular brand of chocolate or vanilla over another. The only way to educate your palate and develop a taste memory is to taste the flavoring ingredients frequently and critically and take careful and thorough notes on your impressions and findings.

Vanilla

The most common flavoring in the bakeshop, vanilla creates the backdrop for all other flavors in a dessert. When you are considering which vanilla to use as an important flavor in the dessert you are building, you must also consider how vanillas of different origin have different flavor profiles. (Tahitian vanilla beans have an *overwhelming* floral character while beans of Mexican origin have an alluring, fruity character.) Obviously, the dessert that features vanilla or uses it as a background note for added flavor in the dessert will taste quite different (and more or less successful with well-married supporting flavors) depending on which vanilla bean (or extract) you choose to use.

The following sample charts are useful tools to assist in choosing the right vanilla for the application.

Vanilla beans

Vanilla Tasting Chart 1

Type of vanilla—country of origin	Flavor profile	Suggested applications	Market forms—whole bean, powdered, paste, extract	Taster's comments
Madagascar-Bourbon				
Tahitian				
Mexican				

Vanilla Tasting Chart 2

Type of vanilla	Flavor profile adjectives	Pairs with spices—if so, which ones	Pairs with custards	Pairs with chocolate	Pairs with fruits
Madagascar					
Tahitian					
Mexican					

Chocolate

There are as many different dark chocolates on the market as there are pastry chefs wishing to use them, each with its own characteristic flavor profile. From sweet to semisweet to bittersweet to practically unsweetened, dark chocolates must be tasted and compared before deciding which to use in a specific recipe. Cost, of course, is always a factor. But if budgets allow, and the clientele is willing to pay a premium for desserts made with high-quality and therefore high-cost ingredients, then considering single varietal chocolates might be indicated.

True single-origin chocolates are made from cacao grown in a single country or growing region within a country. These chocolates each have a specific taste personality, recognizably different from chocolate made in other countries or chocolate made from a blend of beans sourced from a wider swath of cacao-producing countries. From a taste point of view, not all chocolates work equally well for all uses. Fruity,

Bittersweet chocolate

Unsweetened chocolate

Milk chocolate

White chocolate

smoky, woodsy, caramel, or vanilla-scented just begin to describe the range of different flavor notes that are found in high quality couverture dark chocolates. Even within the narrower array of milk chocolates available, there is tremendous variation, from light to darker milk varieties. What is available in white chocolate, too, spans the gamut from sweet and chalky to luxuriously creamy, redolent of vanilla and complex with dairy notes.

The wide range of high-quality chocolate couvertures on the market produced both domestically and internationally make for a somewhat bewildering situation for the pastry chef. Therefore, the only way to arrive at choosing which products to use is to taste widely and frequently. Using the following tasting chart will help you to sort through the many choices available.

Although most manufacturers provide information about the cocoa solids and cocoa butter content of each of their products, these percentages *in and of themselves* are not reliable predictors of the appropriateness of using a specific couverture in a given application. Furthermore, couvertures of different brands with identical percentages will not taste the same due to a myriad of factors, including the terroir (climate, growing conditions, soil) in which the cacao is being grown, manufacturing processes, and length of time for conching (which refines and mellows both taste and texture of the couverture), among others. Additionally, the same couvertures *within* a manufacturer's line of products may not necessarily have the same taste profile from batch to batch, from year to year.

El Rey, Valhrona, Belcolade, Lenotre, Esprit Des Alpes, Felchlin, Michel Cluizel, Guittard, Callebaut, and Cocoa Barry are just some of the more prominent names of brands to be aware of when sourcing chocolate.

Use the following chart in one of two ways:

1. **As a template for tastings of products within a line of one specific brand of chocolate.**

2. **To record comparative information about couvertures from a number of companies (brand name of chocolate) described as containing the same percentage of cocoa solids and cocoa butter.**

Chocolate—Sample Tasting Chart

Brand name of chocolate								
Country of origin								
Name of particular couverture								
Total percentage represented by cocoa solids and cocoa butter								
Manufacturer's guidelines for tempering Temperatures: 1. Melting 2. Crystallization 3. Working, maintaining								
Initial impression of aroma								
Appearance								
Texture in the mouth								
Flavor Profile: (adjectives to describe this chocolate)								
Coarse, smooth, mellow, smoky, bitter, sweet, fruity, others?								
Lingering flavors, if any								
Pairings with other ingredients suggested by the tasting								
Specific ideas for uses								

Coffee

With demand high for most consistently higher-quality coffee, vendors are sourcing beans from carefully tended ecologically sustainable plantations. The result is coffee, available in limited lots, having a refined and complex character. In a dessert where coffee is a prime flavoring, choosing the right one can often make the difference between a result that is ordinary and one that stands out. Simple routes to flavoring desserts with coffee often include the use of pastes or liquid flavorings, but what one gains in convenience and ease of use, one loses in complexity of flavor.

Using properly roasted beans to maximize the inherent flavor profile of the coffee is key when flavoring a cream, ice cream, mousse, or sauce. Over-roasting obliterates flavor, leaving an unpleasant bitterness in the coffee, which translates not only into the cup as a beverage, but also into the dessert as a flavoring component. As with all other ingredients, it's important to taste widely and take good notes whether looking for the right coffee to use in dessert making or to pair with your dessert list.

When making a coffee flavoring from *freshly roasted* whole bean coffee, it is best to use the following proportions: 10 grams of ground coffee to 1¼ ounces of water.

For a more extracted and more intense infusion, reduce the water to ¾ ounce. Once infused, the resulting liquid may be reduced to concentrate flavors by cooking the liquid in a heavy saucepan until reduced to the desired point. It is important to closely monitor the liquid as it reduces, since it burns easily. Once reduced, the liquid may then be reconstituted slightly using hot water or heated simple syrup, as the application requires. The following chart lists the flavors and suggested pairings of different types of coffee.

Types of Coffee

Type of coffee	Characteristics of roasted coffee beans	Flavor characteristics	Suggested pairings
Light roast, also known as the cinnamon roast 	This refers to roasting coffee beans before the bean shows signs of a second crack	Undeveloped, grassy green flavor	Light mousses; fruity desserts; berry desserts; fruit sorbets
Medium roast 	Classic whole bean style; this is roasted to the 2nd crack stage; oil starts to exude from the bean, subtle caramelized notes	Sweeter than light roast; more body exhibiting more balance in acid, aroma, and complexity	Cakes, chocolate tortes, nut tortes; yeast-based desserts, including brioche bread puddings; sponge and chiffon cake–based desserts
Vienna roast 	Medium to medium full roast, decent amount of oil on the surface of the beans	Somewhat spicy; complexity is traded for heavier body/mouth feel, aromas and flavours of roast become clearly evident	Coffee-flavored desserts
Espresso or French roast 	This is pulled from the roaster approximately one minute after the 2nd crack; a lot of oil appears on the beans; dark, almost-carbonized profile; most caramelized	Smoky-sweet; light bodied, but quite intense and mouthfilling	Lemon and other citrus-based desserts; cream-based desserts such as panna cotta, mousses, ice creams

Tea

There are literally thousands of different teas grown worldwide, from India to China to Japan, Southeast Asia, and Africa, each with its own flavor profile. As more good tea is becoming available in the Western world, with the public's increased appreciation of it as a beverage, pastry chefs are discovering its broad and nuanced range of flavors and applying them to the crafting of contemporary desserts. Like coffee, premium whole leaf true tea (as opposed to herbal blends) grown, harvested, and processed according to traditional methods, marries well with other ingredients in a dessert, such as citrus fruit, stone fruit, and chocolate. Tea lends its variously bracing, mellow, smoky, and fruity character to desserts as diverse as ice cream, custard, and crème brulée. It also works well as the base for flavored syrups used as plating sauces, glazes, or gelées.

The taste of tea reflects where it is grown and how it is processed. In general, teas are classified into six main categories: white, yellow, and green, which are not oxidized; oolong, which is oxidized from 2 to 80 percent; and black, which is 100 percent oxidized. The sixth category, puerh, begins as a green tea and is intentionally aged anywhere from several months to decades.

- **Whites:** delicate, lightly sweet, colorless in the cup; made from the leaf bud only.
- **Yellows:** very rare, delicate, lightly sweet, yellow to pale green in the cup.
- **Greens:** vary in taste from delicate to intensely vegetal. Color in the cup and the leaves vary, too, from pale celadon to forest green.
- **Oolongs:** The category of tea with the most variety because of its processing, from delicate to almost hearty; definitely floral in fragrance and taste.
- **Blacks:** Teas that most acutely reflect countries of origin. Chinese have an edge of sweetness and softness; Indian blacks can be intense to delicate (e.g., Assams are hearty and Darjeelings honeyed, or Nilgiris clean and fresh). Ceylon/Sri Lankan teas are brisk, floral, and more delicate than Indian blacks. Hundreds of other varieties exist, making tea a lifelong taste experience.
- **Puerhs** are earthy, a perfect segue for the coffee drinker, and vary from smooth to rough on the palate.

Use the following chart to note your observations and preferences for different types of teas.

Sample Tasting Chart—Tea

Type of tea— white, green, oolong, black	Country of origin	Flavor profile	Brewing time	Desserts suggested to pair with the tea	Suggested uses in making desserts—ice creams, sorbets, mousses, plating sauces

Spices

Strictly speaking, spices are the edible seeds, fruits, and bark of aromatic trees and plants, used to flavor sweet and savory dishes alike. Most are grown in warm tropical climates, and over the centuries have been prized as currency. Today, thanks to controlled cultivation, modern processing, and expedient modes of transportation, chefs take for granted the steady supply and ease of obtaining a wide range of **market forms**, ready for use in pastry kitchens worldwide.

To achieve the most intense flavor in any dessert where spices play a role, using whole spices dry-cooked in a pan or oven, or infused in a liquid is always preferable to using those purchased ground, whose freshness cannot be determined. If stored under less than optimal conditions such as being exposed to strong light or heat, spices lose their potency. In all cases, it's best to buy from reputable vendors who are generous with samples and can provide a wide range of available market forms for all applications.

Cinnamon sticks and ground cinnamon

Cinnamon

Certainly the most prominent and important spice in the baking world, cinnamon is not always cinnamon. It might in fact be cassia, a poor relation to the real thing. True cinnamon (*Cinnamomum zeylanicum*), native to Sri Lanka (Ceylon) first enthralled the Portuguese explorers who came to the island due to the spice's tremendous economic value. Later, also recognizing its value, the Dutch began to cultivate it. Although marketed and processed like true cinnamon, cassia has a less delicate flavor, and is reddish in color, rather than tan like cinnamon. Qualities and flavor profiles of each spice vary widely so it is important to taste the spices both in their whole **quill** or broken shard form, and ground, to choose a spice that works best for any given application.

Fresh and ground gingerroot

Ginger

Available in fresh root form, dried root form, dried ground form, and candied (available chopped, sliced, diced, and pureed), this tropical **rhizome** is a favorite in its fresh form in cuisines throughout Asia and Southeast Asia. In continental Europe, dried ground ginger is a staple in baking and has a long history of use in medieval England, both in savory and then later in sweet dishes. In the northern

European countries from Germany to Scandinavia, ginger is one of many spices commonly used in baking and sweets cookery.

Cardamom

Native to south India and Sri Lanka, in whole seed or ground form, cardamom is the world's third most expensive spice or flavoring (after saffron and vanilla). Warming and slightly pungent, cardamom is used in a geographically broad swath of the world's cooking, from Scandinavia (in baked goods) to the Middle East (as a flavoring for coffee), and from the Indian subcontinent (in sweet and savory dishes) to North Africa (in stews and sauces). Its pungent flavor is well carried in liquids high in fat such as cream (for use in panna cottas, flans, and ice creams) but also strongly infuses sugar-based syrups as a drizzle over crisp pastries as the flavoring for a fat-free sorbet.

Whole and ground allspice berries

Allspice

In the 16th century, when Spanish explorers arrived in the New World searching for the Spice Islands, they landed in what became Jamaica and once there found allspice, the round, dried unripe berry of a myrtle tree. Somewhat resembling pepper, a smaller though unrelated spice, allspice was named pimento (a variant of the word *pimienta*, meaning "peppercorn" in Spanish). Often used in combination with other aromatics such as black pepper, cloves, cinnamon, and nutmeg, allspice is commonly thought to have a flavor personality combining each of those. In its whole form, it is frequently used to infuse liquids of all kinds. It is also often found in sweet or tart pickling syrups and is used to flavor the cooking liquid for meat stews in the Middle East. Usually used in combination with other spices, allspice appears in cakes, puddings and poached fruits.

Nutmeg

Native to islands of Indonesia, nutmeg is common in both sweet and savory uses. Highly fragrant when freshly grated, nutmeg loses its pungency when cooked or baked in a dish. A frequently found flavoring in hot drinks such as eggnog or mulled cider or wine, it lends warm flavor to desserts served warm (rice puddings, custards) and dairy-based beverages served warm such as the wine chaudeau. (See **A Bunch of Grapes**, page 207.)

Whole and ground nutmeg

Whole and ground cloves

Cloves

The unopened bud of an evergreen tree native to Indonesia, convincingly the color and shape of a rusty nail, cloves are a common element in pickling spices, used to aromatize baked hams and brined herring, but it is in the sweet applications that cloves truly shine, as a flavoring for **mulled wine**, in a ground mixture for cookies, pumpkin pies, and syrups made to be drizzled over filo dough–based Middle Eastern pastries of many kinds.

Fruits

Many of the recipes in this book were inspired by the appearance of fresh fruits as they appear on the market, season by season. Making desserts which revolve around **seasonal produce** requires the pastry chef to

"... people eat out to escape and be entertained."

ELIZABETH FALKNER

Owner / Pastry Chef, Citizen Cake and Orson, San Francisco

Elizabeth Falkner believes in using exotic ingredients in innovative ways but always keeps in mind that "people eat out to escape and be entertained." What's on the plate should be both comforting but offer something a bit exotic. Textures of the elements of a dessert should be interesting together or even surprising. Referring to the advantage of starting with produce picked just the night before she uses it, she says, "I don't need to manipulate it to death. I don't have to play too much with it." Here's an example of a seasonal fruit-based dessert that sums up Falkner's philosophy: "I might make a simple sauté of butter and sugar in the base of a sauté pan. Add a bit of wine or fruit juice and reduce it. Add in some high quality freshly

picked peaches, apricots, plums and cherries. Sauté briefly and gently to blend the flavors and release some of the fruits' natural juices into the pan. Then while still warm, the fruits are placed artfully but naturalistically on a plate, without much manipulation. I then top them with a thyme flavored streusel. The plate would then be finished with two more elements: a swath of reduced cream and a fruit puree and then the whole ensemble is crowned with some amaranth microgreens. This spells summer to me."

Where does her inspiration come from? "Sometime a dessert occurs in my head…and I might see it on a plate or not. Then I figure out what plate it should appear on. Sometimes it's just a title that becomes a launching off point for me as in the case of 'A Chocolatework Orange,' a playful twist on the title of a Stanley Kubrick film *A Clockwork Orange.*"

be aware of what's available at any given point within the year and willing to add seasonal items to the menu of offerings. The use of seasonal fruit also represents a marketing opportunity to sell more desserts. With that opportunity, though, comes the need to educate both front and back of the house staff and customers. Consumers who are well educated about what's in season are most apt to be excited by and willing to pay for a dessert based on a fruit that is only fleetingly available. When creating a dessert that places fruit front and center, the pastry chef needs to consider the following:

1. **Seasonality, which affects the quality and ripeness of the fruit (peak of the season fruits not only taste better but they are better priced as well)**

2. **Placing the fruit in a context that is complementary to its inherent flavor and texture where it is only minimally manipulated**

3. **Choosing a treatment that takes full advantage of the fruit's inherent sweetness, fragrance, and personality**

4. **Pairing the fruit with other supporting ingredients that enhance but never mask the delicacy of the fruit's flavor**

5. **Developing good relationships with purveyors, both large and small, artisanal and commercial, farmer-direct and larger distributors**

In addition to fresh fruits, there are other market forms as well, including dried, candied, bottled, canned, and frozen (see next section), all of which have their place in the canon of ingredients that pastry chefs have at their disposal.

Farmers market fruit sellers often are not only a good source for fresh in-season fruits but also highly flavorful artisanal dried versions and fruit-based syrups and juices that offer inspiration for variations on the recipes in the book.

Frozen Fruit Purees

Convenience and true-to-ripe flavor are the best recommendation any product can have. In the dessert making arena, the easy availability of imported frozen fruit purees containing minimal amounts of sugar, made from highly flavored, ripe fruits, processed in season, has led to the universal use of plating sauces, mousses, gelées, ice creams, and sorbets on many upscale dining venues. In fact, using commercially prepared frozen purees made from the fruits currently in season in your growing region, more consistently yields better and more intense flavor than if you were to create your own purees from locally grown fruit in season.

Specialty Fresh Fruits in the Recipes

Baby bananas

Baby pineapples

Blood oranges

Bergamot oranges

Cherimoya, shown ripe

Feijoas

Fig

Muscat grapes

Loquat

Lychee

Indian peach, a variant of the French *Peche de Vigne*

Cactus pear

Persimmon

Pluot

Black cherry pluot

Pomelo

Baby heirloom tomatoes

Key limes

Ojai Pixie tangerines

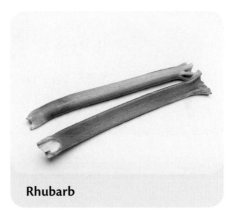

Rhubarb

Tamarillo

Indian mango

Saturn or Donut Peach

Eggs and Dairy Products

If flour and sugar are the tireless workhorses in the pastry kitchen, then dairy products are what makes a dessert delicious, toothsome, luscious, rich, moist, and tender, and above all, satisfying. From eggs to milk to butter to cream, these ingredients are all essential to the success of the dessert. No matter how good the quality of the other ingredients in a dessert, the quality and freshness (or lack thereof) of the dairy products used will be apparent. So it is especially important to source ingredients from this category carefully, taste widely of what's on the market, including artisanal sources where budgets allow, and be vigilant about proper receiving procedures, keeping track of expiration dates and storage temperatures to ensure quality.

Eggs

All of the eggs called for in this book are graded large, weighing anywhere between 1.67 and 1.7 ounces, with the yolks each weighing 0.67 to 0.70 ounces and each white neatly weighing 1 ounce. Fresh eggs are easiest to separate. Older egg whites beat to more stable foams and work well in the flourless French macaroon type cookies and flourless cakes, both of which use finely ground nuts to give stability and flavor to the baked product. Room temperature or even slightly warmed egg whites, when bulked up by sugar and whipped, hold air leading to light airy products such as meringues and soufflés.

Butter

With very rare exceptions, all baked preparations including pastry doughs, cookies, and cakes, icings and butter creams, pastry creams, and browned butter fillings are made with sweet unsalted butter. No other fat provides the mouth feel and flavor that unsalted butter does. Most unsalted butter on the market contains at least 80 percent butterfat (the rest is milk solids and water), although there are higher butterfat-containing butters available that work particularly well in laminated doughs. Vermont Butter and Cheese, for instance, makes an 86 percent butterfat butter that is cultured in the European style with starter cultures that give the butter a rich, deep, and ripened dairy flavor. With the numerous rolling and folding steps involved, higher butterfat butters stay intact, remaining in thin layers, which lead to lighter, flakier pastry with a richer texture.

Clarified butter is another form of this dairy product, which is indispensable to bakers. This involves a slow heating of the butter to separate the fat from the water. When melted without agitating, the melted liquid separates into two layers, the watery layer below and the fat layer above. With continued cooking, the milk solids at the bottom of the cooking vessel turn brown, adding a characteristically nutty flavor to the butter. This browned butter, when combined with sugar, flour, eggs and vanilla, is a perfect filling for tarts and other small pastries. Unbrowned, the clarified butter is often used to brush on layers of thin pastry dough such as filo and strudel, to separate the layers for a flaky result that browns evenly.

Cream

Cream is the ingredient that gives the luxurious mouth feel to dairy-based desserts. The concentrated fat-containing portion of milk, cream is available in different forms, each of which contains a specific percentage of fat, from whipping cream at a minimum of 35 percent, to heavy whipping cream at 36 percent, to manufacturing cream, which is heavier in fat (at 40 to 42 percent) and as the name implies is most commonly used in the manufacture of ice cream. Each of these has a high enough fat content that allows them to be whipped to soft or more solid peaks, depending on the end use.

Cream Cheese

Made from pasteurized whole milk with extra cream added, most commercially made cream cheese is thickened using carrageenan, guar gum, or xanthan. A few more artisanal producers make gum-free versions, which are worth seeking for mousses, flans, cheesecakes, and butter and cream cheese–based pastry doughs.

Farmer Cheese

Farmer cheese is a mildly tangy unripened cheese made by pressing out most of the moisture from cottage cheese. The process involves pasteurizing milk, adding a culture to coagulate the heated milk. The curds form separating from the liquid whey, and then are allowed to drain. Once drained, the resulting mixture is compressed to yield the dry dense cheese, sometimes sold in loaf form, firm enough to slice or crumble.

Mascarpone

Made from the cream of cow's milk, this distant cousin of cream cheese is an uncurded dairy product, high in butterfat, smooth, and rich flavored. Unlike butter, which contains at least 80 percent butterfat and is agitated to make the fat molecules to cohere, mascarpone, which contains 70–75 percent butterfat content, is not churned but instead is thickened with the help of citric acid and then allowed to drain. The best versions taste of sweet cream, are lump free, and work well in mousses, as enrichment in fillings for tarts and strudels, and as a final garnish on fruits, whether fresh, baked into tarts, poached, sautéed, or roasted.

Buttermilk

Traditionally, buttermilk was a by-product of the butter-making process. In modern, commercially prepared versions today, skim milk is fermented with cream cultures after being heated, cooled to stop fermentation, and then slowly stirred to produce a thick, smooth liquid. Its acidic profile works well to produce fine-grained baked and fried goods, and gives just the right amount of dairy richness to delicate sorbets and ice creams.

Sour Cream

This thick and cultured product pairs well with butter as a tenderizing and enriching agent in baked goods. A product made from pasteurized cream with 20 percent milk fat, sour cream gets its characteristic acidic flavor and thick texture from the addition of a pure culture of selected bacteria. Traditionally, fresh cream would be allowed to sour naturally, with unpredictable results and an extremely short shelf life. Today, sour cream is given a second pasteurization to stabilize it, thereby effectively killing all of the live cultures that have given it flavor in the first place. Leaner but firmer than crème fraiche, sour cream is sometimes thickened by the addition of an animal- or vegetable-based rennet to coagulate the proteins in the milk.

Yogurt

A cultured dairy product, yogurt can be made from the milk of cows, goats, sheep, water buffalo, and even camels. Whether commercially made on a large scale or in smaller artisanal dairies, yogurt is fermented using two main species of bacteria. Well drained in a fine sieve lined with dampened cheesecloth, yogurt takes on a soft cheese-like texture and works well in ice creams, sorbets, gelatin-set panna cottas, or sweetened as a filling for thin, flaky pastry such as strudel.

Crème Fraiche

A distinctively tart flavored cream, crème fraiche is made from the cream in cow's milk and thickened by bacterial culture. Aerated, it becomes a more flavorful substitute for whipped cream and with its high fat content (and low enough protein content) it can be directly cooked without curdling.

Goat Cheese

With its fresh, grassy flavor when young and unaged, the coagulated milk of goats may be combined with other dairy products such as mascarpone (see earlier description) for use as a perfect accompaniment to ripe summer fruits such as figs and stone fruit, including peaches and nectarines.

Roquefort and Other Blue Cheeses

Common in Great Britain and much of Western Europe, from France to Italy, blue cheeses are peppered throughout with blue veining, the flavorful result of naturally occurring cultures in the milk or encouraged to grow by the introduction into the cheese of special bacteria. They may be made from cow's, goat's, or sheep's milk (or a combination of milks) and, like other dairy products, may be transformed into mousses, cream accompaniments to fruit desserts, or served as part of a well-balanced cheese course. A special pairing of aged port with Stilton, English blue cheese, is reflected in the recipe **Walnut Torte, Blue Cheese Mousse, Port Sauce, and Puff Pastry Corkscrew with Candied Walnuts** (see page 139).

Sweeteners

Whether the sweetness in a dessert is derived from processed sugar extracted from the boiling of sugar cane or sugar beets, or present in naturally sweet fruits, or from some other form of carbohydrate such as honey, maple syrup, corn syrup, or other by-product of the sugar-making process, when judiciously but not extravagantly used, the result can be memorable. Among the sweeteners available on the market, there are flavor variations to be explored and used to best advantage.

Brown Sugar

Based on their more complex flavor and color, brown specialty sugars are better suited to certain specific applications than others. Originally these specialty sugars were made during the initial stages of processing of the cane juice into unrefined sugar and therefore retained some of the slightly mineralic or burnt edge. However, what is today on the market sold as **Demerara**, **Turbinado**, or **Muscovado** is made in refineries, often far from the source where the plant materials for making sugar are grown. Despite the resulting dilution of flavor in these commercialized versions, thought should be given to which sugars are used for what. Take for instance Demerara, which is golden in color and crunchy in texture, or Muscovado with its sticky quality and very dark brown color.

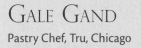

"I think of plating desserts in the same way I approach the canvas when I'm painting."

Gale Gand

Pastry Chef, Tru, Chicago

Chicago-based pastry chef **Gale Gand** takes her inspiration from classical American desserts and French pastries and desserts. I usually use them as a jumping-off point and then riff on them, whether it's by taking them apart and giving them back to the diner in a new way or reinventing a few parts of them. The original dessert is there somewhere in the background if you look closely enough. In this way, something familiar and comforting is there for the customer to latch onto and identify with. On designing the visuals for her desserts, she says, "I think of plating desserts in the same way I approach the canvas when I'm painting. The plate is the canvas. I think about line, shape, shading, negative space, where the eye is led. Then my culinary training kicks in leading me to consider the importance of contrasts in temperature, texture and flavor in the dessert."

The first works well as a crunchy accent to a soft, creamy dessert or as the topping on a thin, crisp cookie. Muscovado, on the other hand, would be appropriate in steamed, well-spiced puddings where its inherently moist character and deep molasses notes contribute to the overall moisture of the finished product.

Light and dark brown sugars

White Granulated Sugar

The crystallized product made from the juice of sugar cane or sugar beets, this common sweetener is available in a wide variety of market forms, from standard to superfine to coarse sanding sugar, and many other gradations in between. Finer-grained sugars dissolve more readily in fat-based creamed mixtures, resulting in lighter textured cakes.

Granulated and superfine sugar

Granulated sugar is the basis for simple syrups, in which sugar is boiled in equal parts by weight with water to create a clear syrup that may be flavored with spices, herbs, fruit purees, and spirits, among many other ingredients. Many of the recipes here make use of simple syrup as an ingredient in sorbets, as a brushing liquid for cakes and other baked goods, and as the basis for plating sauces.

Molasses

In Harold McGee's words, "molasses is generally defined as the syrup left over in cane sugar processing after the readily crystallizable sucrose has been removed from the boiled juice." Long cooked at high temperatures, the resulting liquid has a dark color and a complex flavor profile that includes caramel and licorice notes. Best used in well-spiced cakes, puddings, and cookies, molasses is used here in a number of different applications. (See the smear for the bottom of the molds in **Pineapple Upside Down Cake**, page 227.)

Honey

The product of a complicated process performed by honeybees, honey is a complex flavored sweetener well suited for use in baking. Bees gather nectar from the flowers they visit close to the hives. In a mutually beneficial process, the plants provide food for the bees and the bees carry pollen from one flower to another. Using honey as a sweetener in baked goods has a number of benefits: honey is hygroscopic, which means that it absorbs moisture from the air, resulting in longer shelf life for the baked product, slow staling, and contributes an attractive brown color to the exterior of the baked product. It also plays an important role as the sweetener in meringues for nougat (see **Nougat Glacé**, page 333) and as the basis for plating sauces and syrups that are drizzled over Middle Eastern pastries such as baklava (see **Carrot Halva**, page 369).

Maple syrup

Maple Syrup

The complex flavored processed sap from one principal species of maple tree, the sugar maple, maple syrup is a distinctive and expensive sweetener with many applications in the pastry kitchen. It may be used in cakes, as a flavoring for mousses, puddings, ice creams, and buttercreams and works well in its unmanipulated form as a liquid to pour over baked goods, bread puddings, and other custard-based desserts.

Lyle's Golden Syrup

A syrup made in a refinery from raw sugar, this clear, golden-colored liquid, which is filtered to clarify it, is a specialty of Tate and Lyle, a long-established British sugar manufacturing company. Its mellow sweetness and light caramel notes make it an excellent partner to fragrant citrus desserts. (See **Citrus Walnut Sour Cream Cake,** page 147.)

Nuts
Almonds

The most common nut used in the bakeshop, almonds are available in a wide variety of market forms. Natural with skins on, blanched, raw or roasted, slivered or sliced (these are available in blanched or natural form), and powdered, each has its applications. Almonds are also the basis for marzipan (processed with sugar) and almond paste (two important ingredients in the European pastry kitchen). Careful oven roasting before being used brings out their special sweet flavor.

Walnuts

With a slightly though pleasantly tannic edge, walnuts also benefit from being lightly roasted before using. From the highest quality intact halves to randomly sized pieces, to a flour made from ground nuts, walnuts lend their oily richness in flourless tortes, pairing particularly well with caramel and aromatic spices such as cinnamon. Due to their high oil content, they are best stored in a cool dry and dark place to avoid rancidity. Freezing them, well wrapped, also works, but they are best roasted after being thawed to return the nuts at least partially to their crunchy state.

Almonds

Walnuts

Hazelnuts

With their unique sweet aroma and taste, hazelnuts, sometimes called filberts, are well appreciated in European pastries and gaining in popularity in the United States. Available with skin on and commercially blanched, like most nuts, they gain in flavor and sweetness by being carefully roasted, and pair particularly well with raspberries and chocolate (*gianduja*, a smooth paste of Italian origin combining dark chocolate and hazelnut, is often the basis for confections and pastries). They are also available in an oil-based paste form, which lends itself readily to use as a flavoring in mousses, ice creams, sauces, and buttercreams.

Hazelnuts

Pecans

High in fat and therefore susceptible to staling and becoming rancid, pecans keep well in the freezer, if wrapped airtight, and blend well with deep caramel-flavored sauces. The naturally fruity taste of these nuts seems to be amplified in preparations where vanilla, brown sugar, or molasses is used.

Pistachios

Unique for their bright chartreuse green color, these nuts are actually the seeds of a plant related to the cashew and the mango. Iran, Turkey, and California are the main producers. Pistachios pair particularly well with white chocolate, offering flavor and color contrast.

Pecans

Pistachios

Peanuts

Despite their name, these are actually the seed of a low growing bush, the stems of the flowers of which penetrate the ground, and then swell and mature underground. At harvest time, the whole plant is uprooted, the seedpods are allowed to dry, and then they are shelled, roasted, or processed into meal, paste, or peanut butter. With their high fat content (almost half their weight is fat), they work well in creamy desserts such as mousses, or in their roasted and chopped form as a textural element in cookies, cakes, or boiled sugar confections such as brittle or thin cookies such as florentines and tuiles.

Pine Nuts

As their name implies, these are the seeds from a pinecone, shaken out from the cones after they are sun-dried. Italy, China, Korea, and the United States are the main sources for these tiny nuts. Known as pignoli in Italian, pine nuts become lightly resinous in flavor when toasted. Watch carefully when browning either in the oven or in a dry, heavy skillet as they go from properly toasted to burned in a matter of seconds. With their woodsy aroma and taste, they pair well with herbs such as rosemary and basil and are featured in ice that accompanies the **Tomato Tart** (page 381), and in **Broiled Fresh Figs, Goat Cheese-Mascarpone Crema** (page 235).

Brazil Nuts

Crunchy and gently crescent shaped, the Brazil nut is reminiscent of a mild-flavored coconut and in fact, the nuts are contained in a hard coconut-like hull. Never venturing into the forest in windy weather due to the dangers of being hit by a flying Brazil nut capsule, and given the height of the trees when mature (up to 100 feet), the nuts are harvested solely from the hulls that have fallen to the ground. Second to macadamia nuts in fat content (66 percent by weight), Brazil nuts turn rancid quickly if stored at warm room temperatures. Shaved thinly, the nuts make an attractive addition to cooked sugar brittles.

Macadamia Nuts

With the highest fat content of all tree nuts (74 percent by weight), macadamia nuts have a mild, sweet flavor, crunchy yet finely granular texture. They feel substantial in the mouth and work well in small quantities as a garnish, in combination with caramel, or slivered. Difficult to remove from their hard shells, they are almost always sold shelled, either raw or roasted, or turned into a creamy, rich-flavored nut butter.

Macadamia nuts

Chestnuts

Starchy and mealy in texture, chestnuts are available in many market forms, from fresh, to peeled and jarred, to roasted and vacuum packed, to ground as a flour, candied whole sold in jars or cans (*marrons glacés*), and paste form, both sweetened, often flavored with vanilla and unsweetened. In fresh form, they become rancid quickly so it is best to store them refrigerated if not using within a few days of purchasing. Chocolate, vanilla, and Cognac and other brandies are well matched to the flavor of the chestnut. The **Chocolate Chestnut Cloud**, a flourless torte (page 321), features chestnuts in several forms.

Chestnuts

Coconut

Popular in a wide swath of the tropical world from Southeast Asia to the South Seas, from the Philippines to Mexico, coconut is available in many forms, fresh whole, mature and immature, both sweetened and unsweetened, grated, ground, desiccated (also known as macaroon coconut), flaked, in shards measuring ⅛-inch to ¼-inch wide, and roasted. All of this is in addition to the by-products that include the thin, low-in-fat, but flavorful coconut water from the cavity of the whole coconut and the rich, high-in-fat, creamy coconut milk, extracted from crushing the coconut meat. Its rich sweet taste marries well with a wide range of fruits and other ingredients grown similarly in the tropics, including bananas, pineapple, mango, and papaya. Showing off coconut's versatility and making use of it in numerous market forms are the following recipes: **The Lime in the Coconut Tart** (page 188), **Sticky Rice Cooked in Fresh Coconut Milk** (page 359), **Baby Pineapple with Coconut Rice Pudding** (page 363), **Caramelized Mango Tart with Toasted Coconut Ice Cream** (page 171), and **A South Asian Coupe-Pandan Panna Cotta** (page 183).

Coquitos

Unrelated but similar in taste to coconuts, coquitos are grown on a few varieties of South American palm trees. They approximate the size of macadamia nuts with a white-fleshed interior and a slightly textured brown skin. Their meat is dense and chewy, providing a flavor exactly like coconut meat. Here, they appear in a candied ginger tuile, which complements the **Sticky Rice Cooked in Fresh Coconut Milk** (page 359).

Sesame seeds

Pumpkin seeds

Seeds
Sesame Seeds

Roughly 50 percent oil by weight, sesame seeds are the seeds of a plant native to Africa, and are available in a wide variety of colors, from golden to brown, and violet to black, with white and black by far the most common. Toasted quickly in a low-temperature oven, they develop their characteristic nutty flavor. Asian, Middle Eastern, and Mexican cuisines make frequent use of these seeds. Their nutty overtones make them perfect for flavoring sugar syrups cooked to **hard crack stage** in brittles, and also enhance sugar syrups cooked to caramel stage and then diluted with cream for a plating sauce accompaniment. Complementing other ingredients from the Asian and Middle Eastern/Mediterranean pantries, sesame seeds are found here in a cookie accompaniment to the **Sesame Chiffon Cake with Sesame Halvah Mousse** (page 299) and in the granola base for the cookie under the **Breakfast for Dessert—Yogurt Ice Cream on Granola Cookie with Fresh Fruit** (page 123).

Pumpkin Seeds

As their name indicates, these deep green seeds scooped out from the centers of pumpkins have a nutty flavor when toasted and pair particularly well as an accompaniment to egg-thickened custards made from the fruit of the same winter squash, and like other nuts and seeds, are shown off to good advantage in thin, crisp, sugar-based brittles and other candies. They also pair well with grains such as oats and with nuts as a colorful and flavorful element in cookies and breads.

Recommended Equipment List

As a pastry chef, there are a number of essential tools that it pays to have on hand and in good condition to ensure successful results when embarking on the preparation of any recipe. For this book, the following tools, some very specific, others more generic, were used to produce the full range of recipes. Once having equipped a pastry kitchen, it is essential to monitor the condition of equipment as follows:

1. **Check scales for accuracy frequently.**

2. **Keep knives sharp.**

3. **Keep molds clean and unmarred.**

4. **Keep pastry brushes and vegetable peelers in good shape (replace pastry brushes frequently as they tend to lose their flexibility—and hairbristles—after a while); vegetable peelers' blades tend to dull and therefore the peelers need to be replaced periodically.**

5. **Keep a count of cutters of different shapes and sizes so that the sets are complete.**

6. **Frequently check the condition of sheet pans to be sure that they are unwarped and level (if not, replace).**

The well-equipped pastry kitchen comprises the following list of items, with recommendations for multiples of the equipment and tools depending on the number of people working at any one time, and the volume of production.

- **Digital scale: 5 kg, 11 pounds capacity—US measure and metric, ¼ ounce or 7 gram increments**
- **Digital thermometer with probe**
- **Timer**
- **Calculator**
- **Ruler: US measure and metric**
- **Measuring cups and spoons**
- **Sheet pans: quarter, half, and full size**
- **Speed racks, tabletop cooling racks**
- **Stainless steel bowls: small, medium, large**
- **Cake pans**
- **Loaf pans**
- **Springform pans**
- **Molds: silicone forms—many different shapes and sizes**

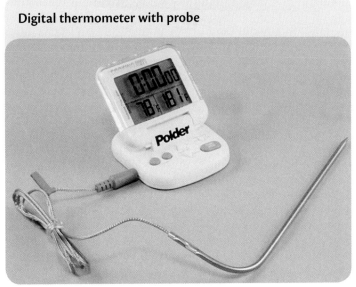

Digital thermometer with probe

Rulers

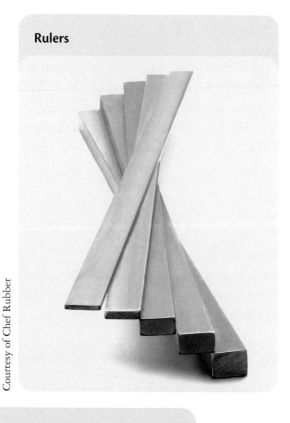

Courtesy of Chef Rubber

Silicone forms

Courtesy of Chef Rubber

Polycarbonate chocolate molds

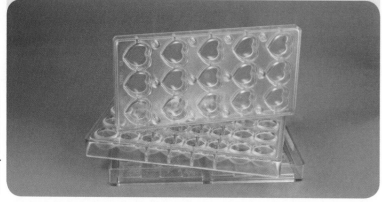

Courtesy of Chef Rubber

- Tart pans with removable bottoms, fluted and straight-sided

- Pie weights: metal, beans, rice

- Entremet rings for mousses, for cutting cakes, mousses, and ice creams

- Bottomless flan rings, with smooth rolled metal edges

- Metal molds: various sizes and shapes, as required in the recipes

- Cutting boards

- Polycarbonate chocolate molds

- Marble slab

- Caramel bars/frames, at least four that work together as a set

- Silpats: quarter-, half-, and full-sheet size

- Acetate sheets, strips

- Thicker-gauge plastic for handmade templates

- Parchment paper

- Cheesecloth

- Various size and capacity paper cups

- Toothpicks/skewers

- Ladles

- Hot pads

- Cutters: sets, rounds, ovals, square, rectangles, triangles, ellipses

- Pastry bags, tips—disposable

- Apple corers

- Melon ballers

- Ice cream scoops: oval, round of several sizes

- Pastry brushes: ½-inch, 1-inch, and 2-inch wide

- Plastic and metal cake combs with various sizes and styles of teeth

- Manual juicer/citrus reamer

- Whisks: stiff wire, flexible wire, straight, and balloon type

- Spatulas: offset and straight

- Plastic bowl scrapers

- Silicone spatulas

- Wooden spoons

- Swivel blade peeler

- Dough cutter

- Knives: small, chef's, serrated

- Mandoline with safety guard with a variety of replacement blades

- X-ACTO knife and replacement blades

- Scissors

- Tuile templates

- Rolling pins

- Wooden dowels

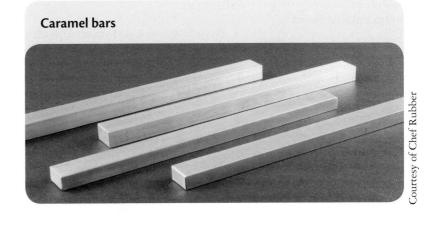

Caramel bars

Courtesy of Chef Rubber

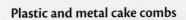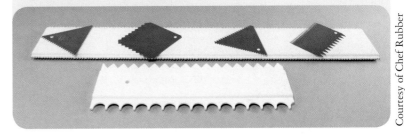

Plastic and metal cake combs

Courtesy of Chef Rubber

Tuile templates

Courtesy of Chef Rubber

Machines:

- Standing 5–6-quart mixer and attachments
- Spice grinders
- Food processor
- Small electric blender
- Immersion blender
- Self-contained (Freon inside) ice cream machine: 1½-quart to 2-quart capacity, preferably with removable bowls, for ease of cleaning
- Electric meat slicer

Smallwares:

- Tamis
- Sifter
- Fine sieves: small, medium, large
- Dredgers
- Heavy saucepans: small, medium, and large
- Heavy sauté pans
- Crepe pans
- Plastic containers with tight-fitting lids
- Squeeze bottles
- Silica gel
- Limestone
- Foaming pitchers
- Espresso machine: for foaming milk, cider, other liquids
- CO_2 cartridge canisters for whipped cream, creating foams
- Nonstick tape to mark plates for decorations
- Styrofoam blocks for allowing caramel dipped items to dry
- Egg crates
- Divided cartons for glasses

Creating a Dessert Menu

Introduction

Designing an effective dessert menu depends on many factors. Given that there is a skilled pastry chef heading the pastry department in the operation, and the kitchen facilities are adequate for in-house production of desserts to begin with, the dessert menu must first reflect the character of the restaurant and be consistent with the style of the rest of the items on the menu. If the menu has international flavors or fuses ingredients from a number of different ethnic cuisines, it stands to reason that the desserts should feature flavors from that palette of ingredients as well. If the menu items are simple, coaxing the best flavor out of a few choice and seasonally fresh, highly flavored ingredients, then the approach to desserts should echo that simplicity. Therefore, when creating or refining the dessert menu, the following questions should be answered:

1. **Is the restaurant casual or formal?**

   Typically an upscale white tablecloth restaurant where high-quality china, flatware, and stemware are used and prices for individual desserts may range from $7.00 to $15.00 per plate, plating of those desserts should make a declaration of style that conforms to the rest of the restaurant's offerings.

2. **Do the menu entries lend themselves to being shared by all the diners at the table?**

   If so, then the desserts might also be served "family style" as a way of inviting diners to share. In this case, multiple plates, flatware, and serving utensils would be brought to the table at the time the desserts are served, with the server

Chapter Objectives

After reading this chapter, you should be able to:

- **Identify what makes a successful dessert menu**

- **Identify desserts from various categories that work well together to create a unified, harmonious, comprehensive but accessible selection of desserts to be offered in an upscale dining venue**

dividing the dessert among those at the table wishing to partake, or leaving that responsibility to the head of the party, if obvious.

3. **Is the plating informal and rustic or highly stylized and architectural?**

   The style of plating of the starters, main dishes, and side dishes should be reflected in the way the desserts are plated and presented. It does not necessarily follow that the desserts need to be in keeping with the plating styles of the savory side of the menu. In fact, desserts might be served in a way that departs significantly from the style of the menu items that have come before, as a way of making a strong statement about the fact that the restaurant serves dessert made in house by a pastry chef (assisted by a team of pastry cooks and others, or not) who sets the style for the sweet side of the menu.

4. **Does the restaurant offer both an à la carte and prix fixe menu?**

   If so, offering different desserts for each kind of menu may be worth considering, according to the price level of each fixed price menu, given that the facility for pastry preparation is suitable for that kind of production.

5. **Is there an area of the kitchen devoted solely to pastry or is the space shared with others on the culinary/savory side?**

   If the preparation area is shared, then dessert preparation is often best scheduled at off hours. This might be in the morning before the restaurant opens to the public (if the restaurant serves only dinner), or, if the restaurant serves both lunch and dinner, then before the lunch preparations begin, or, if practical, at night after the dinner service ends.

6. **How many individuals work in the pastry area?**

   Depending on the size of the restaurant and average number of meals served over the course of a week, it is usually best to schedule production of the bases for the desserts (e.g., cakes, pastry doughs, fillings, creams, ice creams and sorbets, sauces) under the supervision of one individual. This person acts as the principal pastry chef, touching base on a regular basis with all who work under him or her to ensure that all tasks are being done to the standards set by the leader. That individual then can assign tasks to be completed at "off hours" from a master production list, which shows what needs to be accomplished day by day and shift by shift for the most efficient deployment of the staff. During serving times, individuals from the garde manger, or cold-kitchen, side of the operation are often assigned the tasks of finishing the assembly of desserts and plating them as they are ordered.

7. **How many individuals work in the plating area at any given meal-service time?**

   Often restaurants group the tasks in the cold side of the kitchen (assembling and plating appetizers, other cold first courses, and salads) with dessert plating, and even design the workspaces for the garde manger and pastry service area so that they are contiguous or adjacent. In this way, those individuals can easily move back and forth between those two sets of tasks as the orders dictate. The skill set for individuals working in garde manger and in dessert service are similar: the ability to work quickly and accurately, be organized and thorough in setting up the workstations, and have an eye for detail and a good aesthetic judgment. Making a good initial impression with a well-plated appetizer or first course and making a similarly favorable impression on the guest at the end of the meal are equally important and reside in the domain of the individuals working in the garde manger and dessert stations of the kitchen.

8. **Is there adequate storage allocated exclusively for pastry ingredients, desserts in progress, and finished products?**

   As with all other operations in the kitchen, the key to a well-run pastry kitchen is organization. In an efficiently run pastry kitchen, vertical storage—including refrigerated, freezer, and room temperature, preferably in close proximity to each other—allows for the most efficient use of limited space and is essential to the easy retrieval of elements needed to assemble completed desserts to order.

9. **Does the restaurant menu change seasonally or cycle on a regular basis?**

   If so, the dessert menu should change with the seasons, reflecting the produce that is best in each season. Furthermore, warm, comforting desserts should be on the menu in the cooler months while an abundance of cold or frozen desserts should populate the dessert menu during the warmer months.

Once the pastry chef has answered all of the preceding questions and solicited input from all levels of management with whom he or she interacts in the organization, then he or she can sketch out broad categories of desserts that fit into the menu in light of the facilities and available staff resources. Then, going from general to specific, the pastry chef can list actual desserts (or variations of desserts) that are already on the dessert menu or are being considered as possible alternatives. Those desserts can then be listed under each of the following five categories: chocolate, seasonal fruit, nut based, custard based, and frozen desserts. Bear

"I like to use ingredients that are not overused in desserts, such as cucumber and avocado, vanilla-flavored fleur de sel salt, and candied peppercorns."

ADRIAN VASQUEZ

Pastry Chef, Providence, Los Angeles

Adrian Vasquez, pastry chef at Providence Los Angeles (LA) and pastry consultant to the LA Mill Coffee boutiques, insists that his desserts need to be eaten effortlessly. With a background in music and architecture, Vasquez believes that in pastry and dessert making, "form should follow function." In much of his work, layering is key. Verticality appeals to him since all of the flavor components can be appreciated in one bite. Layering flavors, textures, and ingredients characterizes his style.

He is inspired by boredom. "When I get bored repeating the same desserts over and over, I am inspired to create new dishes." I take inspiration from what is happening all over the world. I like to use ingredients that are not overused in desserts, such as cucumber and avocado, vanilla-flavored fleur de sel salt, and candied peppercorns.

Even though he is blessed with the abundance that California produce offers, he says, "Summers are always the easiest; it's in winter that I struggle."

in mind, however, that these examples represent only a small sampling of possible categories and subcategories.

- **Chocolate: Cakes, mousses, ganache-filled tarts**
- **Seasonal fruit: Single-serving pies, tarts, mousses, ice creams, whole poached fruits, compotes**
- **Nut based: Cakes, tortes, tarts, brittles, ice creams**
- **Custard based: Flans, puddings, cheesecakes, fruit tarts with custard bases**
- **Frozen desserts: Ice creams, sorbets, granitas, ices, layered bombes, mousses, and Bavarians**

Once you have determined a sample dessert menu, you will want to arrange for critiquing sessions based on tastings of the dessert with the chef, restaurant (or food and beverage) manager, sommelier or other wine expert on staff, and any other key personnel whose input would be valuable and whose decision-making authority makes them important members of the management team. With the goal of maximizing dessert as the profit center in the restaurant that it can and should be, you should solicit feedback from dining room as well as back-of-the-house staff regarding suggested beverage pairings at this time. The next step is to invite current or prospective coffee and tea vendor(s) to present their product lines as well. Then you can schedule another tasting of the desserts with wine and spirits vendors. Their input will be valuable in setting up a dessert beverage menu (beers, fortified wines, other sweet dessert wines, brandies and other distilled beverages, and clear alcohols) to accompany the dessert menu that you are developing. Be sure to take detailed notes when developing the dessert menu, in particular listing adjectives or other descriptions that arise during these tasting sessions, which can be useful as verbiage on the dessert menu, or used by serving staff when they describe (and sell) desserts to customers.

Making Desserts a Profit Center

Just as the menu for the savory side of the kitchen was designed with profit and efficiency in mind, the dessert menu must take into account both practicality of execution and profitability. Keeping ingredients and labor costs to a minimum without sacrificing the spirit and quality of the dessert offerings is the goal. Once the dessert menu is determined and every time a new item is added to it, a detailed and accurate cost analysis must be generated for each item. Begin by calculating the food costs for the ingredients for a fixed yield (each of the recipes in the book yields twelve portions, so that is a convenient number to use), and next calculate the number of hours spent by the production staff to produce the desserts over a weekly basis.

Because every operation that serves desserts of the kind featured in this book is different, it is difficult to generalize, but the total cost for skilled labor in the dessert-making field should not exceed 45 percent of the revenues produced from sales of desserts. Of course there will be exceptions to this average, with each operation having a production staff of varying skill levels, each demanding different rates of pay. Then add the prevailing percentage for overhead in the operation (this figure is made up of the following: rent or mortgage payment, utilities allocated to the operation, health, property and product liability insurance, fire and other hazard insurances, garbage removal, laundry/linen, repairs and maintenance, credit card expenses, bank fees, accounting/legal services, equipment leases, cleaning and paper/packaging supplies, and any other costs specific to the operation). This total represents the overall costs of the dessert in the operation. Given that some desserts may cost more in ingredients than others and vary seasonally, it is important to allow enough of a markup to make those higher-cost desserts as profitable as the lower-cost items. In fact, it may be that certain items on the dessert list will be more profitable than others, but on average the overall net profit will still be respectable. Since every operation is different, it is difficult to generalize, but industry averages indicate that a food cost for upscale, premium quality ingredient–based desserts should range from 25–30 percent of menu price.

Beyond the revenue produced by desserts, beverages paired and served with those desserts, which have dramatically higher profit margins, can add a considerable boost to the bottom line. (In the case of beverages, the costs beyond the cost of inventory are limited to education of the serving staff and maintaining a good supply of appropriate stemware.) Successful marketing means putting beverages front and center. A list of the liquid offerings should be printed on the page adjacent to the dessert list, with enticing descriptive text designed to help sell the beverages. Alternatively, the beverages can even be bundled with the desserts, showing a price for the dessert and a price for that same dessert with the beverage. (In certain circumstances, granting a discount when the diner chooses both dessert and its suggested beverage pairing is a proven marketing idea.) Maximizing profits means minimizing costs, so efficiency on the production side is essential. As part of that efficiency, the person directing the pastry program in the operation must take the lead in generating well-considered production schedules and insisting that the staff always stick with the schedule, barring any special circumstances involving staff or ingredient shortages, last-minute orders, or other changes in routine. Given that there is adequate freezer storage available to the pastry department of the operation, efficiency increases when production days or parts of days are devoted to producing a week's worth of bases for desserts, such as cake layers in the form of sheets of genoise and pastry doughs (rolled out, stored in molds, ready to bake). This frees the production staff on a daily basis to finish off desserts, making the components that must be served the day they are made, such as ice creams, sorbets, and delicate, perishable garnishes. For efficiency's sake, for instance, plating sauces, more perishable custard-based fillings and tuile batters may be made in bulk every other day, depending, of course, on the volume of desserts served by the operation. In the interest of keeping products fresh, frozen components may be made every other day. This

A well-designed dessert menu should reflect the style of the restaurant (or other food service operation) and also the overall style of the savory side of the menu, from entrees to main dishes.

Here are some suggested dessert menus that reflect a particular sensibility, from rustic to modern, from classic American to classical French, and from European inspired to Asian inflected, among others. In addition to crafting your own dessert menus specific to your own operation, feel free here to follow the suggestions as given or to mix and match from each menu for a more eclectic, less thematically unified but still appealing approach. Most of the following menus include a chocolate-based dessert for those wishing something that tends to be richer or heavier. By contrast, there is at least one fruit-based entry for those desiring something lighter, less indulgent, and less guilt-inducing.

Comforting, American Inspired

MENU 1:
A couple of doughnuts

Carrot beet cake

MENU 2:
A cup of coffee

Root beer ice with Tahitian vanilla ice cream

Broadly European

MENU 1:
Chocolate semolina pudding with spiced coffee syrup

MENU 2:
Caramel poached pear tarte with bourdaloue cream

Hand-pulled strudel with creamy cheese filling

Modern, Contemporary Approach with a Twist

Pineapple upside down cake

Creamsicle in conical mold, orange gelée, vanilla cream semifreddo

A verrine of three mousses

Gateau fondant of candied orange, almond nougatine, and chocolate

Ethnic: Hispanic or Latino Inspired

Citrus walnut cake with cactus pear sorbet

Caramelized mango tart with toasted coconut ice cream, lime sorbet and dried mango tuile

Strawberries and Cream mousse afloat over a mint mojito, lime wafer

Classical French Inspired

MENU 1:

A duo of cream puffs

Topsy turvy Gateau St. Honore

Chocolate cassis roulade

MENU 2:

Blancmange with a nutted almond tuile, roasted apricots

Crepe cake marjolaine

Nougat glacé with roasted peaches

Praline napoleon

Ethnic: Mediterranean-Middle Eastern Inspired

Rustic quince tart, with buttery almond cake, mascarpone cream

Sesame chiffon cake with sesame halvah mousse, orange sections

Broiled fresh figs, goat cheese-mascarpone crema, sweet basil sauce, pine nut tuile

Ethnic: Asian or South Asian Inflected

MENU 1:

A South Asian coupe

Caramelized mango tart with toasted coconut ice cream, lime sorbet

Atualfo mango mousse scented lightly with curry

Carrot halva

Chai chocolate mousse

MENU 2:

Vietnamese coffee ice cream with mango sauce

Chai chocolate mousse

Ros malai, with cardamom milk sauce

Sticky rice cooked in fresh coconut milk, served with mango sorbet

Sample Production Grid

Dessert Name	Made fresh EVERY DAY Ice Cream/ Sorbets	EVERY OTHER DAY Cream/Mousses/Etc.	Made fresh EVERY DAY Sauce/Glaze/Syrup
Chocolate Bombe	Dark chocolate fudgy ice cream		Chocolate sauce
	Bittersweet cocoa sorbet/ice in cone shape		
	White chocolate ice cream base		
Topsy-Turvy Gateau St. Honore		Pistachio pastry cream	Pistachio sauce
		Chocolate pastry cream	Chocolate sauce
		Raspberry pastry cream	Raspberry sauce
			Caramel to stick things together
A Couple of Doughnuts		White peach mousse	
		Violet custard	
Broiled Fresh Figs		Goat cheese–mascarpone crema	Sweet basil sauce/syrup
Walnut Torte		Blue cheese mousse	Port sauce
Yogurt ice cream shaped into yogurt container shape	Yogurt ice cream		Fruit sauces–berry, pineapple, apricot

leaves the staff that works during serving times (lunch, dinner, brunch, depending on the operation) responsible only for the assembly and plating of desserts.

For maximum efficiency, the lead pastry chef in the operation should devise production grids that indicated when and how often components of the desserts need to be made. In particular, this is crucial if the pastry chef takes a more managerial role, ordering ingredients and hiring and training staff, and does not spend all of his or her time on production-related tasks. Staff members who come into work with a clear idea of what is expected of them during their working hours make an efficient use of payroll dollars and also can help lead employees to *owning* their jobs, taking responsibility, and being accountable. Productive use of time (as well as materials and ingredients) is essential for any operation to be profitable.

The production grid on page 61 is just one example of how the work of the dessert preparation station may be organized and therefore delegated to staff, whether the lead pastry chef is on the scene or not. It creates a clear picture of what needs to be done and may also include the names or positions of individuals who are responsible for each part of the day's production. "The order of things" section in every recipe found in Chapter 6 includes production lists for easy production schedule creation.

Sample Production Grid

Garnishes	Tuiles/Cookies	Fruits	Batters/Doughs	Misc
Chocolate filo swath				
Caramel décor	Pâte à choux			
Candied violets			Buttermilk spice doughnuts	
Pine nut tuile				
Puff pastry corkscrew				
Candied walnuts				
	Homemade granola cookie	Fresh pineapple, apricots		

Questions for Review

1. In the broad categories of fruit, chocolate, dairy, and nut-based desserts, should all be represented on a menu?

2. What are some of the factors that determine the scope of the dessert menu?

3. What are the criteria for ensuring timely production, assembly, and service of the choices for your dessert menu?

4. Does seasonal availability of ingredients play a role in your selection of dessert recipes?

Plating

Introduction

Because it is true that people eat with their eyes first, and then appreciate with their palates, the goal of all pastry chefs is—must be—to present desserts that are visually appealing, with an eye for balance, color, interest, and harmony on the plate. Therefore, how the dessert is plated matters. Even the most precise, beautifully executed dessert will suffer if not plated with the care it deserves. Sloppy or imprecise placement of the sauce used to set off the dessert, or the use of a flabby or stale garnish atop the dessert sends the wrong message to the consumer. A restaurant is essentially a place where customers come not only to eat but also to be entertained, to escape their everyday lives. A beautifully plated, well-executed dessert served in a welcoming, comfortable setting is part of that entertainment. The curtain goes up every day anew with a fresh set of customers paying hard-earned dollars, ready to be pleased, served well, and to enjoy the food and the overall dining experience. Therefore, the staff in the back of the house (pastry chefs, pastry cooks, garde manger staff, all who are involved in delivering the sweet side of the menu to the customers) need to care enough to put their best food forward at all times. Otherwise, they run the risk of ruining the customer's dining experience, losing one customer or many who may convey unfavorable impressions about the restaurant to friends and family members alike. No restaurant can afford customers to leave dissatisfied.

As part of offering that overall satisfying experience, the pastry chef must consider himself or herself part of a team serving the public, even if indirectly (depending on whether a small or large staff is in place). Every detail counts in making an

Chapter Objectives
After reading this chapter, you should be able to:

- **Understand the basics of plating a dessert successfully**

- **Have a systematic approach to arrive at the most effective design for the presentation of a dessert**

effort to reach out to customers and please them. Plated desserts that offer pure pleasure are an important part of the many details that the restaurant staff members attend to in the course of a daily operation. (After all, no one *needs* dessert for dietary sustenance; customers simply desire it and they want it to be worth the extra calories and cost.) As a consequence, once the elements to be included in the dessert are decided, carefully considering the color, texture, size, and shape of the plate, bowl, or glass in which the dessert is served, is the first step toward realizing a visually successful dessert. The plate on which it is served should never upstage the dessert. Plates with intricate designs or textures tend to detract from the visual impact of the dessert itself. For example, using white, off-white plates, or slightly tinted or solid-colored bowls or other vessels allows the dessert to be the center of attention.

"...I have been forced to pare down to essentials and the desserts are the better for it."

CLAUDIA FLEMING

Owner/Pastry Chef, North Fork Table and Inn,
Southold, Long Island, New York

Claudia Fleming made her mark by creating seasonally driven, simple but multicomponent desserts at the Gramercy Tavern in NYC, a highly respected restaurant in Manhattan, and then moved on with her husband, Chef Gerry Hayden, to open the North Fork Table and Inn, Southold, Long Island. Here she finds herself completely "hands-on," learning to work on an hour-to-hour basis beside her husband. She says, "I realize that, thankfully, we are grown up and adult enough to recognize that running a restaurant needs to be less ego-driven and more focused on the financials, the nuts and bolts of the business. At Gramercy Tavern, in retrospect, I realize how protected I was from having to worry about the most mundane things. Owning one's own place, however, means that your scope of responsibility is so much broader.

"It's amazing that we get to make our living from something that we are so passionate about. My husband and I try not to take ourselves quite so seriously. We provide a service for people and we don't think of ourselves as artists."

About the process of creation, Fleming says: "As hard as I try to come up with new desserts, I feel like it's always themes and variations. If the basic idea is sound, then I don't need to think of things that are different. I find myself drawing from my bag of basic tricks, dictated by the changing seasons."

On presentation: "Sometimes I feel very behind the times in terms of what I am doing on the plate. I believe that it's not about trends or doing what's the latest and newest thing, or trying to reinvent the wheel. Instead, it's all about trying to make people feel comfortable, and as part of that philosophy, I tend to use a less stylized presentation of my desserts, which fits into the more rustic aesthetic of the operation as a whole.

"Overall, I have found that my desserts have gotten simpler; it was so component-driven before, each one of those components was a dessert. Working on a smaller scale and very hands-on, I have been forced to pare down to essentials and the desserts are the better for it."

Size Does Matter

The size of the dessert and the size of the plate are of equal importance when plating. Although unconventionally shaped plates are becoming more and more common in the dessert serving arena, standard round plates measuring 8 to 10 inches in diameter will never go out of style and reliably provide a suitable canvas upon which the dessert artist can present his or her sweet masterpieces.

Organic, flowing shaped, asymmetrical plates, noncircular bowls, and other flat, almost rimless serving plates are often used in upscale, trendy, and even medium-priced dining establishments wishing to convey a contemporary sensibility. Whether choosing to use the traditional or nontraditional shaped plates, the pastry chef needs to put concerted effort into arriving at a plating style that shows off the dessert to best advantage. Most simply, this process usually involves doing a test run by plating the dessert on different shaped plates before deciding which works best.

Plating Guidelines

Given that aesthetic judgment is rather subjective, there are truly no hard and fast rules that may be applied in all cases. Just as in any artistic field, pastry practitioners ply the pastry arts by relying on their creative impulses, judgment, and aesthetic sense. It is a field that not only encourages but also truly requires a highly individualistic approach. Just as no two pastry chefs using a recipe will produce quite the same dessert, those same two pastry chefs will also each find his or her own way to plate that dessert, rendering the two versions quite different. But there are a few incontrovertible truths about plating desserts that most pastry chefs should follow.

1. **To showcase the dessert, negative space (the empty areas of the plating surface) is as important as positive space (the filled areas of the plate). As a rule of thumb, no more than 50 percent of the plate should be occupied by elements of the dessert.**

2. **Allow the dessert to "breathe" by allowing a border of at least two inches all around to make the most pleasant visual impact. No sauce or garnishes should fall outside of an imaginary line drawn two inches within the outer edge of the plate. This guideline also springs from a practical consideration: leaving the border of the plate empty allows the dessert to be delivered to the customer by the server without marring or smearing the sauce or dislodging any elements of the dessert.**

3. **If the plate is asymmetrical, leaving a 2-inch wide border at the edge of the plate free of sauce or garnish also shows off the dessert to the best advantage.**

How Much Is Just Right?

Whether serving an entrée, main course, or dessert, emphasizing quantity over quality will never win the loyalty of discerning customers. In fact, the opposite is generally true. Individuals who consider themselves sophisticated, perhaps well traveled, and who demand a high quality of food and service, might view dessert as the fitting end for a many-course meal and would consider a dinner incomplete without it. Others might consider dessert an indulgence reserved for special occasions. Whichever the case, diners who eat out frequently tend to be knowledgeable about food and perhaps even consider themselves adventurous when ordering. They are rarely deceived into thinking that they have received good value when served large portions of a dessert of questionable, mediocre, or poor quality. A carefully executed dessert, where each element is part of a seamless whole that also reinforces the other elements, does not need to be overwhelming in size to satisfy the appetite. Although portion size is best determined on a case-by-case basis (depending on the kind of dessert being served, whether creamy, rich, fruity and light, fat-laden, or lower in fat), an appropriate portion of most desserts would weigh between five and six ounces in total, plus the plating sauce, if any, regardless of the number of components being served.

How much sauce is enough? Sauce should be more than a mere design element. It should complement and enhance but not overwhelm the main event on the plate. Calling something a plating sauce is not justified by a few, often-dry decorative droplets of sauce deposited strategically around the main constituent of the dessert. If your vision of the dessert includes an intensely flavored complementary sauce or several sauces, then declare your intentions clearly by using an amount of sauce sufficient to be spooned up with each bite of the dessert.

As part of the plating process, pastry chefs need to consider what shape the main elements of the dessert take and then proceed to position those on the plate to make the most visual impact. Whether rustic or formal, multicomponent desserts derive their character from the interplay of their dissimilar elements. The shape of the main element in a dessert, therefore, is crucial to how the dessert looks on the plate. Round shapes like domes, circles, or ovals, or curved shapes make a different impression from hard-edged squares, diamonds, wedges, or other straight-sided shapes. It is often useful to experiment by making the same dessert multiple times, using different shaped molds (both rectilinear-shaped and curved) or cutting the main elements, such as cakes or firm puddings, into different shapes.

Basic Shapes for Cakes and Mousses

Using two or more of the following well-defined shapes for elements of a plated dessert adds visual tension and excitement to the dessert. The goal is to engage the eye and then engage the palate. Going beyond the tried and true, or the plain and predictable cake-wedge shape, the pastry chef lends interest to the dessert by using other shapes such as the following:

- **Triangles**
- **Squares**
- **Diamonds**
- **Rounds**
- **Ovals**
- **Intersecting double crescents for an oval with pointed rather than rounded ends**

If the budget allows, custom-made metal or silicone molds, of course, allow your desserts to be differentiated from those at another food service venue, making them memorable and making your operation stand out from the crowd. Merely changing the shape of a dessert can often mean the difference between one that sells and one that doesn't. Experiment with a full array of molds and hand-cut shapes (and the plates upon which the desserts will be ultimately served) to arrive at the presentation that pleases you and fits most comfortably within the style of presentation of the rest of the menu at your establishment.

Basic Shapes for Ice Creams, Sorbets, and Other Frozen Mixtures

- **Squares**
- **Batons**
- **Rectangles**
- **Diamonds**
- **Rounds**
- **Triangles**
- **Cones, conical pointed shapes, flat bottom, pointed top or flat topped**
- **Timbale or thimble shapes**

"As you start using seasonal ingredients, you see more and more things that you can do with them."

KATE ZUCKERMAN
Pastry Chef, Chanterelle, NYC

©2009 Laurie Rhodes

Kate Zuckerman, pastry chef at Chanterelle, one of NYC's long-established bastions of haute cuisine, changes her dessert menu every month. "I look at seasonal ingredients as a set of limitations. Limitations make you creative. As you start using seasonal ingredients, you see more and more things that you can do with them." Working in a busy kitchen, she insists on training her staff to respect the importance of serving freshly made product. "The more you have to get ahead, the less fresh the products such as handmade chocolates and cookies will be. If you make a tuile too complicated, then the staff wish to make a lot of them every three days, which leads to a product that is less than pristinely fresh."

Kitchen economy, of course, is essential to running a profitable operation and Zuckerman says that she derives a lot of pleasure in using perfectly good leftovers to serve as inspiration for a new dessert. Success in a high-pressure kitchen depends, she says, on good and frequent communication. "Give people a break when they need it to alleviate the effects of staff burnout. I feel strongly about creating work schedules for my team that are humane and accommodate their needs when possible." Instead of making unrealistic demands on her staff, she says, "I'd rather see the members of my staff take a break by changing jobs, and then return, refreshed. Not asking too much of my staff is the key to keeping them."

She insists on keeping plating simple and often asymmetrical, and tends to incorporate crispy, creamy, cold, hot, salty, and acidic elements into many of her most successful creations.

Saucing It Up

In addition to the shape of the dessert, pastry chefs must consider the shape of any garnishes, including sauces, although *not every dessert requires a plating sauce or is enhanced by serving it with a garnish*. Providing contrast, both visual and textural, is the role of any accompaniments to a dessert. The pastry chef must first consider the complementary quality of the flavors of the sauce, if using, and garnishes as they related to the main element of the dessert. Then, the pastry chef moves on to consider how to position the elements on the plate. Having established that the flavors of the elements of the dessert harmonize well, the pastry chef might consider whether a light-colored sauce would work better to complement a darker-colored main dessert element. Always *first* consider whether one darker-colored sauce would visually set off the dessert to better advantage than one that is pale or light in color.

After a careful trial-and-error process is accomplished by tasting the main element of the dessert with a number of different sauces, choose which sauce works best with the dessert. The sauce selected must be judiciously used. Too much overwhelms the dessert. The dessert should not be "swimming" in the sauce unless the liquid is an integral part of the dessert and is used in what might be considered a greater than normal quantity. For example, in the **Creamsicle in the Round** (page 153), the frozen centerpiece of the dessert is placed into a bowl of blood orange–flavored gelée. Here both the Creamsicle and the gelée are of equal importance in the dessert and, therefore, a greater amount of "sauce," or in this case, gelée, is used than might be otherwise expected.

Too Little Is Just as Bad as Too Much

Likewise, not enough sauce is equally misguided. In most but not all cases, the dessert should be properly served with enough sauce so that the diner can experience each mouthful of the dessert with a bit of sauce. In certain cases, using a sauce to accompany it diminishes the dramatic effect of the dessert. (See the **Fresh Rhubarb Tatin,** page 239, suspended on the cone of ginger ice cream, where five increasingly larger dots of strawberry sauce encircle the base of the ice cream.) Depending on the intensity of flavor and thickness of the sauce, amounts of sauce suggested will usually, but not always, vary from 1 to 2 ounces. Thinner sauces will most likely amount to 1 ounce per serving, while thicker ones, which therefore flow less easily and spread less on the plate, might weigh closer to 2 ounces per serving.

The Shape of Things to Come

The following is a list of basic shapes for sauces, whether smooth, or textured with bits of fruit in the form of a compote. When a sauce is chunky in texture, the shapes tend to be rougher and less precise.

- **Organic and free flowing vs. regular and precise**
- **Swaths**

- Coils

- Pools

- Ribbons

- Series of dots in graduated sizes

- Brush strokes of sauce, applied with a food grade pastry brush (1 to 1½ inches wide)

- Crosshatching, which uses sauces or thin threads of melted chocolate or other semi-liquid sauce, where a set of roughly parallel lines is laid down on the plate and then a second series of parallel lines is laid over perpendicular to the first set—hence *cross* hatching, in which the sets of lines cross each other.

A Few More Ideas for Finishing Plates

Here are three more ideas to create a visually stunning underpinning to the three dimensional elements of the plated dessert. Plates may also be decorated with:

1. Finely pulverized bits of dried citrus peel, confectioners' sugar, cocoa powder, or cocoa powder mixed with finely powdered spices or with confectioners' sugar.

2. Designs made from sprayed cocoa butter (natural or enhanced with cocoa butter-based color) deposited with an airbrush or a paint sprayer.

3. Sifted powders deposited onto plates, using templates with various cutout designs in shapes such as curved swaths, dots, or geometric angular shapes such as squares, diamonds, or triangles.

The Rule of Three

Typically, but not without exception, using odd numbers of elements on a plate is most visually pleasing. As a general rule, that odd number is usually three. Groups of three provide just the right degree of complexity without losing clarity of composition. Even numbers are predictable, static, and feel contrived. Using only two items makes for an ordinary and even uninteresting presentation. On the other hand, if the dessert comprises five or more separate elements, then chaos results. The eye is confused and the senses are on overload, with the diner not knowing which element to taste first, second, and so on.

How the elements are placed on the plate, of course, matters, as does plate or serving vessel size and shape. In the case of flat or plates or ones with a slightly upturned edge, the elements of the dessert should be positioned within an imaginary border, measuring at least 2 inches from the edge, all around the perimeter of the plate. The elements on the plate should be close enough to each other so that the diner may go from one to the other easily. Visually speaking, each element should be just close enough together that they seem cohesive, all parts of one dessert, but far enough apart so that there is some blank space visible. As in any work of art, the negative, or blank, space is as important as the areas that are painted or otherwise filled in. This is also true in plated desserts where each element is shown off to best advantage when framed by some white (or whatever pale, solid color the plate or serving vessel may be).

Consider also symmetrical versus asymmetrical placements of elements on the plate, or in a glass or bowl.

Draw Before You Plate

Without actually plating the components on a plate, it is difficult to tell how the elements will interrelate or whether or not there will be a visually appealing dialogue between them. Since perishable or meltable items such as ice creams and mousses do not allow for a leisurely experimental placement on a plate, the next best thing is to draw out the elements in their actual portion size and place them on a paper template of the size and shape plate that you intend to use, with plating sauce, if any, drawn out and colored to give you a more accurate representation of what the finished dessert will look like. A good place to start is with a sketchpad and some colored pencils or markers. If possible, even better yet, would be to use three-dimensional objects—cookie cutters covered in colored construction paper or shiny wrapping paper work for this purpose—as rough representations of the elements in the dessert to stand in for the actual components of the dessert. Or you could use a scoop or oval shape for ice cream or sorbet, geometric shapes (such as wedges, rectangles, squares, or circles) for cake or pastry elements, set on the desired plate or a paper template of the plate with a paper or plastic cutout representing the sauce, colored and shaped as it would be if using the actual sauce. You can easily move these stand-ins around to arrive at the best positioning before committing to the plating design of the dessert.

Commonsense Plating Ideas

The importance of contrast in color, height, and proper positioning of elements for maximum effect cannot be underestimated. It helps to examine each of the components of the dessert for shape, size, and color to discover the most dynamic arrangement for the final plating of the dessert.

Questions to consider:

- **Is the main element angular, round, flat, tall, or asymmetrical?**
- **Is there an obvious center point around which the other elements of the dessert might be best arranged?**
- **On which element of the dessert do you want the diner to focus?**

- Would an off-center placement of that element or others bring drama to the overall impression of the dessert?

- Is the main element proportionate in size to its supporting elements?

In higher-volume operations such as caterers that execute large-scale events, it is important to consider the choice of dessert to be served from the practical point of view of logistics, volume, and timing. Choose carefully when recommending a particular dessert for a large group, to be sure your facility has enough horizontal surfaces to plate a large number of desserts at any one time (or vertical racks to accommodate the height of the finished dessert). Plan for enough staff to accomplish the plating of elements just before service time. Consider using elements that are *cool* room-temperature–stable and plate those first, adding the perishable elements just before serving the dessert. The closer to service time that the desserts are plated, the fresher and more impressive they will be, adding one more positive element to the customer's overall impression of the event. Attention to detail, precision, and freshness are necessary attributes to any successful dessert, and have the added advantage of positive word of mouth that all pastry chefs need to build referral business. As a pastry chef, you are in the critical position of orchestrating the customer's last impression about a meal. All of the hard work that goes into the making of the elements of the dessert must be presented at serving time in peak condition, both visually and gustatorily.

Questions for Review

1. Is it important to take into account the shape of a dessert when deciding how to position the sauce on the plate?

2. What is the rule of three?

3. What visual tools can you use when designing a dessert?

Dessert & Beverage Pairings

Introduction

Desserts may be enhanced by serving them with the appropriate beverages, making dessert an even stronger profit center for the food service operation. An enhancement might be as simple as serving a properly brewed cup of tea made from premium, whole leaf tea leaves, or coffee made from freshly roasted coffee beans. At other times, adding a layer of excitement to the dessert experience may be accomplished by serving a dessert wine such as port, Madeira, sweet Banyuls, or Sauternes. Still others are well suited to being paired with flavor-infused beers, such as Belgian lambic, which work particularly well when paired with desserts based on intense chocolate and highly aromatic height-of-the-season berries, for example.

Some desserts require no liquid accompaniments and are in fact best served on their own, with the end-of-the-meal cup of coffee or tea served after the dessert has already been consumed. But first, it is essential to consider the flavor profile of the dessert for which you are seeking beverage partners, since with all food and beverage pairings the goal is to create a harmonious dialogue between the food and the beverage. The beverage should not compete with the dessert. In a successful pairing, a bite of the dessert should lead seamlessly into a sip of the beverage, which in turn should lead the diner back to the next bite of the dessert, and so forth, until both dessert and beverage have been fully consumed. Enjoying the dessert and the beverage side by side should lead to a greater enjoyment of each than if they were being consumed separately. The pairing should allow the diner to appreciate the complexities of flavor in both the dessert and the beverage as each transforms the other.

Chapter Objectives

After reading this chapter, you should be able to:

- **Describe the basics of pairing beverages with desserts**

- **Be inspired to create your own dessert/beverage pairings from a sample menu**

- **Describe the marketing potential of suggesting dessert/beverage pairings to the diner**

"... there will always be new things to learn, and for every path taken or decision made, there are perhaps a dozen more alternative ideas left to explore!"

Michael Laiskonis

Pastry Chef, Le Bernardin, NYC

"My 'style' or 'philosophy' involves the subtle (or not so subtle) modernizing of classic ideas, techniques, and flavor combinations," says **Chef Laiskonis**. Although he believes that there is nothing new under the sun, he recognizes further that "We all have our own experiences and perspectives; the possibilities of such individual interpretations are then indeed infinite. That's why this job is so rewarding and satisfying; there will always be new things to learn, and for every path taken or decision made, there are perhaps a dozen more alternative ideas left to explore!"

When asked where his inspiration comes from, he points to fields outside of the culinary realm such as architecture and design, art and photography, even nature. He acknowledges that it isn't always easy to trace a direct line from the source of inspiration to the dessert which drew inspiration from that source. Similarly, ingredients from the exotic to the everyday that excite him one week might find a place in a dessert almost immediately. The next week might bring new ingredients to taste and work with, but he always sees a need to experiment until the dessert is the best it can be, with all ingredients in harmony before it makes it onto the dessert menu.

Appearances and plating presentation count—he subscribes to an aesthetic that is fairly sparse, often asymmetric, and with clean lines. "I especially like mixing hard geometrical shapes with natural organic ones," but in his mind, flavor rules. "We must never lose sight of the fact that what we prepare has to be delicious first and foremost. Whether it's a hot apple gelée concocted from the trendiest hydrocolloid, for example, or the most basic and rustic apple tart, flavor is paramount."

Laiskonis's advice for the budding pastry chef: Travel when possible to experience other people's work, read when travel is not possible, and taste widely. Never be satisfied with mediocrity, work hard and smart but don't burn yourself out. And since working in the world of pastry is a collaborative art, he urges all pastry chefs to "learn management and team-building skills. Your co-workers or assistants are ultimately your greatest tools in the kitchen, and they will more than likely follow your example, not only when it comes to technical skill, but also how you well you treat other people."

Conscious that the dessert menu should flow seamlessly from the restaurant's first courses and main dishes, Laiskonis asserts: "One's individual ego should never clash with the overall vision of the restaurant's chef. I've always had great relationships and open lines of communication with the chefs I've worked for, and when you have that collaborative spirit, the food, both sweet and savory, will be that much better."

Pairing Chart

The following chart shows beverages and the broad dessert categories and specific flavoring ingredients used that complement them.

White wines: fragrant, floral grapes Sauternes whose sweetness is caused by the *noble rot*, which consumes most of the grape's acidity and the water content in the grape, leaving an intensely sweet fruit Muscat, muscatel, moscato—wines made from grapes with a distinctively musky aroma and fruity flavor Tokay, tokaji—Hungarian wine produced with grapes affected by the noble rot (see Sauterne above for information) Banyuls—called *vin doux naturel*, made from very ripe grapes and fortified with pure grape spirit, available in red, white, rose or tawny colored	Fruit-based desserts such as mousses, ice creams, Bavarian creams, semifreddo, fruit tarts, roasted and caramelized fruit-containing desserts
Champagne and sparkling wines: rosé and even red sparkling wines from France and Italy are considered here Brut—dry Sec—medium to medium sweet Demi sec—sweet, the sweetest of all, and most commonly paired with desserts	The demi sec is the easiest to pair with all desserts, although in the case of desserts based on exotic and tropical fruit (such as lychee, cherimoya, pineapple, feijoa, passion fruit, mango, pandan, and those lightened with cream and Italian meringue), other drier champagnes can sometimes work well. Intensely dark chocolate–based desserts for the sweeter champagnes
Eiswein: Made in Germany and Canada, also known as *vin de glace*—made from grapes allowed to freeze and then immediately pressed into richly concentrated grape juice and allowed to ferment	Grape and raisin–based desserts, desserts featuring fall–winter tree fruit such as apples, pears, quince, pomegranate, persimmon, and Asian pear; spiced desserts flavored with cinnamon, star anise, ginger, allspice, cloves, nutmeg
Fortified wines: Port, Madeira	Chocolate desserts of all kinds, poached fruit desserts
Eau de vie: White alcohols Framboise (raspberry), myrtille (blueberry), mures (blackberry), fraise des bois (wild strawberry), poire (pear), pruneaux (plum)	Fruit-based desserts, including cassis, plum, pear, dried or confited fruit, almond-based desserts, desserts with toasted nuts, praline
Brandies: Cognac, Armagnac, Calvados	Tea-based desserts, caramel containing desserts, fruit desserts based on apple, pear, cider, peach, pumpkin, maple syrup or maple sugar sweetened, custard-based such as bread puddings, flans, crème brulée
Beers	Berry-based desserts, desserts with a strong vanilla flavor (especially with flavored beers) Stout and other dark beers pair particularly well with chocolate-based desserts
Spirits: Scotch, Bourbon	Vanilla-based desserts
Coffees Kinds of coffee: Central American, South American, Mexican, Ethiopian, Yemeni, Africa, Indonesia, South Asia	Coffee-based desserts, all chocolate desserts, caramel-based desserts
Teas Green tea served with green tea–based desserts (matcha, Sencha, Chinese Dragonwell, Gunpowder, Lung Ching, Pi lo chun) Black teas including Chinese Keemun, Yunnan, Lapsang Souchong (smoky), Indian Assam (rich red-colored liquor, strong and malty flavor at its best) and Darjeeling (delicate, peachy, "the champagne of teas") Semi-oxidized Oolong tea served with oolong tea–based desserts (Ti Kuan Yin, Pouchong—floral, orchid like, sweet)	Tea-based desserts, citrus-based desserts, mellow fruit–based desserts such as pear and apple; chocolate-based desserts work well here paired with black teas Serve with fragrant fruit desserts featuring Asian pears, stone fruits such as peaches, plums, and apricots

Flavor Categories of Desserts

Let's now examine each of the flavor categories of desserts that follow in the next chapter to uncover some of the many possible beverage pairings. Bear in mind that the flavor profiles of the desserts may vary somewhat depending on the ripeness of fruits used, the sweetness level of fruit purees, the intensity of chocolate flavor, the freshness and pungency of spices used, and many other variables in ingredients that cannot be fully predicted. Let your taste buds be your guide as you arrive at what you consider the best dessert and beverage pairings, given the desserts that you have produced from the recipes in the book.

Furthermore, taste is subjective, and therefore what you consider an ideal pairing may not register the same on others' palates. In a well-run restaurant, with the over-riding goal of making the dining experience entirely pleasurable, waitstaff should always be prepared to offer alternate suggestions for pairings, even replacing the beverage initially chosen if the customer does not like the pairing. Here satisfying the customer costs far less than the loss of revenue that unfavorable word of mouth can cause as a result of the diner's negative last impression.

Sample Dessert Menu

Dessert Menu with Beverage Pairings

Desserts

White chocolage mousse with pistachios	$9
Paired with Brut champagne	$20
Hand pulled cheese strudel with dried pears	$8
Paired with icy thimble of eau de vie de poire	$18
Chocolate framboise	$12
Paired with Belgian raspberry flavored beer	$18

Beverages to Enhance the Dessert Experience

Dessert wines

Sparkling wines—champagne, vin mousseux, vin petillant

Fortified wines—sherries, ports, madeiras

Distilled spirits—bourbon, scotch, cognac, calvadoes, armagnac, Eaux de Vie

Beers

Coffees

Teas

Questions for Review

1. Select five desserts and choose appropriate beverages to pair with them.

2. Why should you choose one beverage over another for a particular dessert?

3. What other criteria are important to making satisfying dessert/beverage pairings?

Desserts

Introduction

All of the recipes are designed to yield 12 servings, given in both US and metric measurement. Where appropriate, baker's percentages are offered for each master recipe formula—cakes, pastry doughs, custards, and sauce bases.

After completing each recipe, take a moment and answer the following questions:

1. **What alternate equipment or tools could be used in the recipe to achieve the same or similar results?**

2. **Using this recipe as a launching pad, how would you do something similar using *x* ingredient?**

3. **How would you plate this dessert differently than shown in the photograph? Using a plate template (a sample is included in the book, to be copied by reader for such exercises), draw out other possible presentations.**

Record your answers and experiment the next time you make the dessert again.

RECIPES

Non Seasonal Recipes

Nut Recipes

Rice and Grain Recipes

Vegetable Recipes

Chocolate Bombe

YIELD: 12 SERVINGS

Chocolate bombe with intensely dark chocolate ice cream and white chocolate ice, paired with bittersweet chocolate ice, ganache plating sauce, dark cocoa shortbread confetti cookies, and white and dark chocolate décor. Here's a dessert that epitomizes the "wow" factor and though not difficult to achieve, requires patience and accuracy. However, visual impact does not alone make a dessert that is satisfying. Good looks and taste have to go hand in hand and they certainly do here. Premium-quality dark and white chocolate couverture star in two different ice creams that are molded together into a striking pattern. Several different chocolates work together on the plate to indulge the most diehard chocolate fan. Silky, dense ice cream in the bombe contrasts with a granita-textured bittersweet chocolate ice. Crunch appears in the form of the miniature dark cocoa shortbread cookies, ready to be dipped into the pool of ganache on the plate. A thin square of striped chocolate garnishing the bombe is the final bravura touch, lending textural as well as visual snap to the elegant ensemble.

The order of things:

1. **Make the dark chocolate ice cream and the white chocolate ice cream**

2. **Mold the dark chocolate ice cream** into conical cups and support them so that they freeze upright

3. **Freeze water in six conical cups** and support them so that they stand upright in the freezer

4. **Make white chocolate ice cream** and when semi-firm, line the six thimble or flower pot–shaped molds, each measuring 4 inches in diameter at the top by 2 inches in diameter at the bottom, by 1¾ inches tall, with the mixture

5. **Place the conical waxed paper cups of ice, from above, into the molds** lined with white chocolate ice cream to act as place savers for the dark chocolate ice cream that will be placed into them after the white chocolate ice cream is fully frozen

6. **Make the bittersweet chocolate ice** and freeze

7. **Remove the place savers of frozen water and fill** the now empty space with the conical shaped dark chocolate ice cream

8. **Scrape the bittersweet chocolate ice** occasionally during freezing and when frozen fill six cup-shaped molds and freeze

9. **Make the dark and white chocolate striped decorations**

10. **Make shortbread dough** and chill

11. **Cut and bake shortbread cookies,** cool and set aside at room temperature

12. **Make ganache** as plating sauce

Equipment list:

Six **thimble or flower pot–shaped molds,** each measuring 4 inches in diameter at the top by 2 inches in diameter at the bottom, by 1¾ inches tall

Twelve conical **waxed paper cups,** cut to measure 2 inches in diameter at the top (which will become the bottom when the bombe is served) by 1¾ inches tall, six for the dark chocolate ice cream and six for the frozen water place savers

Clean and empty **cardboard egg crates** to keep the conical waxed paper cups upright and perfectly level while the ice cream and the water for the place savers is freezing

Six **cup-shaped molds** for the bittersweet chocolate ice, each measuring 2½ inches in diameter by 1½ inches tall

Small **truffle cutters** used to cut the dark cocoa shortbread confetti cookies into a variety of shapes (squares, rounds, diamonds, triangles)

Rectangular sheet of **food-grade acetate,** measuring 10 inches by 14 inches

X-ACTO knife

Propane torch

Heavy chef's knife, used to cut the chocolate bombe vertically into two equal parts

Squeeze bottle for the plating sauce

Intensely dark chocolate ice cream

YIELD: 12 SERVINGS

Oz	Grams	Each	Name of ingredient
16	480		**Chocolate couverture**, chopped
6	180		**Whole milk**
4	120		**Granulated sugar**
8	240		**Heavy cream**
		1 Pinch	**Salt**

- → In a medium saucepan, heat the milk.
- → Add the sugar and cook to dissolve.
- → Remove from the heat, add the chocolate, and stir to melt completely.
- → Pass the mixture through a fine sieve into a stainless steel bowl set over an ice water bath.
- → Add the salt and stir to dissolve.
- → Allow the mixture to cool and then stir in the heavy cream.
- → Transfer to the bowl of an electric ice cream machine and freeze until semi-firm.
- → Spoon and compress the mixture into six conical waxed paper cups, cut to measure 2 inches in diameter at the top (which will become the bottom when the bombe is served) by 1¾ inches tall. Freeze until firm.
- → When firm, peel off the paper and place the cones of ice cream flat side down onto a parchment-lined sheet pan.
- → Cover and return to the freezer until ready to assemble the bombes.

White chocolate ice cream

YIELD: APPROXIMATELY 2 POUNDS, 4 OUNCES

Oz	Grams	Each	Name of ingredient
3.3	100		**Egg yolks**
2	60		**Granulated sugar**
12	360		**Whole milk**
		1	**Vanilla bean**, split
12	360		**Premium-quality white chocolate**, chopped
	1	Pinch	**Salt**
8	240		**Heavy cream**

Prepare the molds as follows

- → Fill six conical waxed paper cups with water, each measuring 2 inches in diameter at the top by 1¾ inches tall.
- → Place the cups into a stand or arrange them in an empty, clean cardboard egg crate to keep them upright and perfectly level while they are freezing.
- → Place carefully into a level shelf in the freezer.

Make the white chocolate ice cream as follows

- → In the bowl of an electric mixer outfitted with the whisk attachment, beat the egg yolks and sugar until thick and light.
- → When the whisk is lifted, the mixture should flow slowly from it in a thick ribbon.
- → In a heavy saucepan, heat the milk with the vanilla bean to infuse, cooking for 5 minutes.
- → Remove from the heat, cover, and allow the mixture to infuse for 15 minutes. The flavor of vanilla should come through clearly.
- → Remove the vanilla bean, rinse, dry, and set aside for another use, and then reheat the infused liquid.

- → Stirring without aerating, add it gradually to the egg and sugar mixture to temper.
- → Transfer the mixture to a stainless steel bowl and cook over a pan of simmering water (the water should not touch the bottom of the bowl), stirring with a wooden spoon, without aerating, until the mixture reaches 180°F.
- → Remove from the heat and add the chocolate and stir to melt.
- → Add the salt and stir to dissolve.
- → Transfer the mixture to a clean stainless steel bowl, set over an ice water bath.
- → Stir, without aerating, to cool evenly.
- → When cool, add the cream and then pour the mixture into an electric ice cream machine and freeze until semi-firm.
- → Spoon equal amounts of the semi-firm ice cream into six thimble or flower pot–shaped molds, each measuring 4 inches in diameter at the top by 2 inches in diameter at the bottom, by 1¾ inches tall.
- → Use a metal spatula to press the ice cream firmly against the walls of the molds, thereby creating a shell of white ice cream in the mold.
- → Place the conical waxed paper cups of ice, from above, into the molds to act as place savers for the dark chocolate ice cream that will be placed into them after the white chocolate ice cream is fully frozen.
- → Place the molds into the freezer.
- → Note that there will be some leftover ice cream.
- → Reserve, frozen, for another use.
- → When the white chocolate ice cream is fully frozen, remove the molds from the freezer.
- → Remove the paper cups of ice from each mold and discard, replacing them with the cone-shaped portions of the dark chocolate ice cream, from above. Be sure to press the chocolate cone firmly into the white chocolate shell.
- → Return the molds to the freezer and make the bittersweet chocolate ice.

Oz	Grams	Each	Name of ingredient
16	480		Water
8	240		Granulated sugar
0.75	23		Glucose
0.75	23		Cocoa powder
3	90		72% **Dark chocolate,** chopped into small pieces
	1	Pinch	Salt

Bittersweet chocolate ice

YIELD: APPROXIMATELY 28½ OUNCES, ENOUGH FOR SIX ROUNDS, EACH WEIGHING ABOUT 2⅓ OUNCES, MEASURING 2 INCHES IN DIAMETER BY 1 INCH TALL; WHEN PLATING THE DESSERT, THESE ARE EACH CUT IN HALF TO YIELD 12 SERVINGS

- → In a medium-sized heavy saucepan, bring the water, sugar, and glucose to the boil.
- → Add cocoa powder, whisking to smooth.
- → Add the chocolate and whisk again until melted and smooth.
- → Add the salt and transfer the mixture to a stainless steel bowl, set over an ice bath.
- → Stir to cool evenly, and when cold, transfer the mixture to an electric ice cream machine.
- → Freeze until semi-firm and remove the mixture to a container with a tight-fitting lid. Freeze.
- → When frozen, remove from the freezer and scrape the mixture into six cup-shaped molds using a fork to create a granular, cratered texture, each measuring 2½ inches in diameter by 1½ inches tall.
- → Freeze in the molds.
- → Unmold and cut each round into two halves vertically, yielding 12 halves, one for each dessert.
- → Place onto a parchment-lined sheet pan and freeze, covered, until ready to plate the dessert.

Dark and white striped chocolate decorations

YIELD: TWELVE 3 INCH SQUARE DECORATIONS, ALLOWING FOR EXTRAS IN CASE OF BREAKAGE

Oz	Grams	Name of ingredient
6	180	**White chocolate couverture,** tempered or non-tempering white chocolate coating
6	180	**Chocolate couverture,** tempered or non-tempering chocolate coating

TIP: *Precision here is what makes this decoration "pop." The layers of dark and white chocolate must be the same thickness. Practice makes perfect. Once dried, the chocolate can be scraped up, laid down again numerous times, and reused for other preparations. Practice using either white or dark chocolate so you can use it over and over again before superimposing one over the other. The way to gain mastery over this process is through repetition.*

If using couvertures, temper as follows

→ If tempering the chocolate, heat two thirds of it in a stainless steel bowl over simmering water.

→ Melt it, stirring occasionally, until it reaches 122°F.

→ When it reaches this temperature, remove from the heat and add the remaining one third of the chocolate to lower the temperature of the chocolate to 81°F.

→ Stir constantly during this process to encourage the production of many small cocoa butter crystals that will lead to a good temper for the chocolate.

→ Then carefully rewarm the dark couverture to 90°F and the white couverture to 86°F.

→ Maintain each at these prescribed temperatures.

→ To test to see if the chocolates are in temper, dip the corner of a small piece of parchment paper in each chocolate and then place the parchment pieces on a work surface. If the chocolates are in temper, they should dry within minutes and break cleanly when the paper is folded. They also should not melt readily when touched.

If using non-tempering chocolate

→ Chop the coatings and place each one into a stainless steel bowl, set over a water bath of simmering water.

→ Stir to melt and keep warm so that the coatings flow easily.

Completing the chocolate decorations

→ Onto a rectangular sheet of food-grade acetate, measuring 10 inches by 14 inches, using a long metal spatula, wide palette knife, or plastic scraper, spread a thin but not translucent layer of the white chocolate couverture or non-tempering white coating.

→ Using a fine-toothed cake comb, beginning at the short end, scrape firmly and with even pressure along the length of the rectangle to create thin stripes.

→ Allow the white chocolate to dry and then spread a thin but not translucent layer of the dark chocolate couverture or non-tempering dark chocolate coating to cover the white chocolate stripes.

→ Allow to dry and then using an X-ACTO knife or small sharp knife, using a ruler as a guide, score the chocolate sheet into twelve 3 inch squares, in rows of three along the 10 inch side, and in rows of four along the 14 inch side, totaling twelve squares.

→ Carefully remove the decorations from the acetate sheets and set aside in a cool place until ready to garnish the dessert.

→ Make shortbread dough.

Chocolate shortbread confetti cookies as garnish

YIELD: 8 OUNCES OF DOUGH, YIELDING 60 TINY VARIOUS-SHAPED COOKIES

Oz	Grams	Each	Name of ingredient	Baker's percentages
3	90		**All purpose flour**	80
0.75	23		**Unsweetened dark cocoa powder**	20
	1	Pinch	**Salt**	0.8
2.5	75		**Unsalted butter,** room temperature	66
1.25	38		**Granulated sugar**	33
1.67	50	1	**Whole egg**	44
0.16	4.8	1 t.	**Vanilla extract**	4

Oz	Grams	Each	Name of ingredient
0.67	20	From 1 large egg	**Egg yolk,** from a large egg
0.5 to 0.75 ounce, approximately, or enough to make a paintable glaze	15 to 23		**Water**

Oz	Grams	Name of ingredient
1	30	**Pearl sugar**

→ Sift the flour, cocoa powder, and salt together onto a sheet of parchment paper and set aside.

→ In the bowl of an electric mixer, cream the butter with the sugar until light.

→ Add the egg and the vanilla and mix to incorporate, scraping the bottom and sides of the bowl to ensure that the mixture is well blended.

→ Add the sifted dry ingredients and mix just until they disappear into the mixture.

→ Remove the dough from the bowl and knead briefly on a lightly floured surface.

→ Wrap and chill until firm.

→ Roll the chilled dough on a lightly cocoa-dusted surface to ⅛ inch thickness.

→ With small truffle cutters, cut the dough into 12 each of a variety of shapes (squares, rounds, diamonds, triangles).

→ Place the cookies on Silpats or parchment-lined baking sheets.

→ Chill again until firm.

→ Brush lightly with eggwash and sprinkle the pearl sugar lightly and evenly on the cookies, as desired.

→ Bake in a preheated 350°F oven for approximately 8–10 minutes.

→ Remove from the oven and allow to cool on a cooling rack.

→ Set aside at room temperature until ready to plate the dessert.

Oz	Grams	Name of ingredient
6	180	**58% Premium-quality dark chocolate,** chopped
6	180	**Heavy cream**

→ Place the chocolate into a heat-proof stainless steel bowl.

→ In a small, heavy saucepan, bring the cream to the boil.

→ Remove from the heat and pour over the chocolate.

→ Stir, without aerating, to melt evenly.

→ Set aside to cool and then transfer to a squeeze bottle, covered, until ready to plate the dessert.

→ Refrigerate, covered, if not using within an hour.

→ When ready to use, remove from the refrigerator and place the bottle into a hot water bath to re-liquefy.

Assembly and plating

As needed, remove an ice cream bombe from the freezer. Using a heavy chef's knife dipped in hot water and then dried, or heated lightly with a torch, cut the bombe in half vertically to expose the two-toned pattern. Place one half on the serving plate. Position one semi-circle of bittersweet chocolate ice to the left, and in front of, the bombe. Place a group of assorted shapes of the chocolate shortbread cookies to the right of the bombe. Center a generous dot of the chocolate ganache in front of the bombe. Place a striped square into the top of the bombe, shiny side facing the front of the plate. Serve immediately.

Chocolate Cassis Roulade

YIELD: 12 SERVINGS

Chocolate cassis roulade, layered with cassis sorbet and served with kir royale sauce–champagne cassis-flavored sabayon, chocolate décor. Intense meets intense in this cantilevered dessert. The deep purple, tart black currant, cultivated since the 16th century in northern Europe, and only recently available fresh commercially in the United States, appears here in five different components, as a sorbet, as a syrup to soak the cake, in a champagne-based custard sauce for plating, as a jam or compote, and in preserved berry form as a final garnish. Made from the black currant, *crème de cassis*, a specialty of Dijon, in the Burgundy region of France, is best known as the flavoring in *kir*, the delightful aperitif, in which a dollop of the alcoholic black currant syrup gives a sweet/tart savor to a glass of white or, less commonly, red wine. The plating sauce here is inspired by *kir royale*, the champagne-based version of this drink. In fact, instead of coffee or tea, a glass of a fruity champagne would be the perfect accompaniment to the very dessert offered below.

Note that the tartness of cassis purees varies, so the amount of simple syrup used in making the sorbet may vary.

The order of things:

1. **Make cake and bake it,** then cool slightly and roll
2. **Temper chocolate,** if using, and then make chocolate décor from it
3. **Make Italian meringue** for chocolate mousse
4. **Complete chocolate mousse**
5. **Unroll cake and fill with mousse**
6. **Make cassis sorbet**
7. **Make kir royale sabayon** and refrigerate, or freeze it to use as a scoopable accompaniment to the dessert, if desired

Equipment list:

Round metal cookie cutter, measuring 2½ inches in diameter to cut the sorbet

Drum sieve or other fine sieve to sift confectioners' sugar used to dust the roulade when unmolding and rolling it

Heavy aluminum foil used to give shape to the roulade after rolling it up

Sharp, serrated knife to cut roulade when serving

Rectangular pan measuring approximately 7½ inches by 10 inches for sorbet

Paper parchment cone to pipe out chocolate décor

Chocolate sponge roulade

YIELD: APPROXIMATELY
32 OUNCES, ONE ROULADE,
APPROXIMATELY 18 INCHES
LONG BY 3 INCHES IN
DIAMETER

Oz	Grams	Each	Name of ingredient	Baker's percentages—Cake flour, cocoa powder, and cornstarch total 100%
2	60		Cake flour	34
1.75	53		Cocoa powder	32
2	60		Cornstarch	34
		½ t.	Baking soda	2
7	210		Egg yolks	121
8.8	264		Granulated sugar	152
0.16	4.8	1 t.	Vanilla extract	3
10.6	318	10–11	Egg whites	183
		As needed to sift onto parchment paper before unmolding cake onto it, and rolling it up	Confectioners' sugar	

TIP: *Do not overbeat the egg whites here. They should be shiny but still have a creamy, moist quality to them. If they are beaten until stiff, they will not incorporate easily into the egg yolk base. Folding the whites into the base should be done gently so that the cake batter retains maximum lightness before being baked, yielding a light, airy cake.*

→ Sift together onto a sheet of parchment paper the cake flour, cocoa powder, cornstarch, and baking soda.

→ Beat egg yolks and sugar over a double boiler until warm.

→ Place on electric mixer and using whisk attachment, beat until light in color and texture.

→ Add vanilla extract.

→ Set aside.

→ Using whisk attachment, whip egg whites in a separate mixing bowl until soft peaks form.

→ Alternately, fold dry ingredients and beaten egg whites into the egg yolks and sugar mixture.

→ Immediately pour into parchment-lined and greased half-sheet pan.

→ In preheated 350°F oven, bake for about 13–15 minutes.

→ Remove the cake to a clean sheet of parchment that has been lightly dusted with sifted confectioners' sugar.

→ Roll the cake tightly using the parchment paper to help form the cake into a tight roll.

→ Allow the rolled cake to cool and then unroll when ready to fill with the following filling.

Chocolate mousse

YIELD: APPROXIMATELY
40 OUNCES

Lbs	Oz	Grams	Each	Name of ingredient
1		480		High-quality 70% chocolate couverture, melted
	4	120		Unsalted butter
	6	180	6	Egg whites, from large eggs, room temperature
	4	120		Granulated sugar
	4	120		Water
	12	360		Heavy cream

→ Set a stainless steel bowl over a saucepan of simmering water and melt the chocolate and butter together, stirring until fully melted and smooth.

→ Remove from the heat and set aside.

Make an Italian meringue as follows to use in the mousse

→ In a small, heavy saucepan, bring the sugar and water to the boil and then cook to 240°F.

→ In the bowl of an electric mixer outfitted with the whisk attachment, place the egg whites.

→ Whip to a froth, and with the machine running, add the hot syrup in a thin stream, whisking until the mixture is thick and shiny.

→ In the bowl of an electric mixer outfitted with the whisk attachment, beat the heavy cream until soft peaks form.

→ Fold the chocolate-butter mixture into the Italian meringue and then fold in the whipped cream.

→ Set mousse aside.

Cassis syrup

YIELD: APPROXIMATELY 8 OUNCES

Oz	Grams	Name of ingredient
4	120	Cassis puree
4, *approximately*	120	Simple syrup

The syrup should be sweet-tart; adjust the amount of simple syrup used, accordingly.

→ Bring the puree to the boil with the simple syrup.

→ Allow to cool and then unroll the cake, above, brush the top side of the cake lightly with the cooled cassis syrup, allow the syrup to soak in, and then brush again.

→ Fill with the chocolate mousse, using a long metal spatula to spread an even layer to within 1 inch of each edge of the cake.

→ Roll the cake tightly using the parchment to help the process.

→ Place the parchment-wrapped cake onto a large sheet of heavy aluminum foil and enclose the cake tightly to shape it into a firm roll.

→ Refrigerate until ready to serve the dessert.

Cassis sorbet

YIELD: APPROXIMATELY 30 OUNCES, 12 SERVINGS, EACH WEIGHING LESS THAN 2½ OUNCES

Oz	Grams	Name of ingredient
16, approximately	480	**Cassis puree,** from fresh black currants or commercially prepared frozen puree, thawed
12, approximately	360	**Simple syrup**
2, approximately	60	**Fresh lemon juice,** sieved

Commercially prepared purees commonly contain 10% sugar by weight, so adjust the amount of simple syrup accordingly.

→ Combine the ingredients, taste for sweetness (adding more simple syrup or cassis puree as needed to achieve a good balance between sweet and tart) and then pour into the bowl of an electric ice cream machine.

→ Freeze until semi-firm.

→ Remove the sorbet from the machine, spread the mixture in an even layer, approximately ½ inch thick, into a rectangular pan measuring approximately 7½ inches by 10 inches, and place the pan into the freezer, well wrapped, until fully frozen.

→ When frozen, use a round cookie cutter, measuring 2½ inches in diameter to cut the sorbet into circles.

→ With the long side of the rectangular pan of sorbet facing you, begin at the top left corner and moving to the right along the top 10 inch long side, cut four circles of sorbet.

→ Moving down along the left 7½ inch side of the rectangle, cut four more circles, from left to right, and then finally move down to the bottom left corner of the short side and starting there, cut the last four circles, moving from left to right.

→ You should now have cut 12 circles of the sorbet.

→ Return the sorbet circles to the freezer and remove them from the freezer as needed to assemble the dessert just before serving.

Note: There will be some sorbet left from the areas between the circles that you have cut out. Save for another use.

Kir royale sabayon

Oz	Grams	Each	Name of ingredient
3	90		**Crème de cassis** (black currant liqueur)
8	240		**Dry champagne**
6	180	From 9 large eggs	**Egg yolks**

TIP: *Instead of using the sabayon as a plating sauce, this mixture may be frozen in a small, shallow, rectangular pan and served as a scooped or spooned accompaniment to the roulade.*

→ Combine all ingredients in a large stainless steel bowl.

→ Place the bowl over a saucepan half filled with simmering water (the bottom of the bowl should not touch the simmering water) and stir, without aerating, until the mixture reaches 180°F and thickens lightly and is foamy.

→ Place the mixture, once cooled, into a squeeze bottle and then store in the refrigerator until ready to serve the dessert.

Cassis (black currant) berries garnish

Oz	Grams	Name of ingredient
8	240	**Cassis jam with whole cassis berries**

→ Strain the berries out of the jam by placing the jam in a wide-meshed sieve.

→ Reserve the jam and cassis berries in two separate containers.

→ Reserve 3 berries per serving and mix the rest of the berries back into the jam.

If the cassis jam is unavailable, you can instead use wild blueberry or huckleberry jam.

Chocolate garnishes

Oz	Grams	Name of ingredient
12	360	**Tempered chocolate, or non-tempering chocolate, melted and held at 90°F**

→ If tempering the chocolate, heat two thirds of it in a stainless steel bowl over simmering water.

→ Melt it, stirring occasionally, until it reaches 122°F.

→ When it reaches this temperature, remove from the heat and add the remaining one third of the chocolate, stirring to melt and thereby lowering the temperature of the chocolate to 81°F.

→ Stir constantly during this process to encourage the production of many small cocoa butter crystals that will lead to a good temper for the chocolate.

→ Then carefully rewarm the chocolate to 90°F, which is the temperature at which it should be held for creating the chocolate décor.

→ To test to see if the chocolate is in temper, dip the corner of a small piece of parchment paper in the chocolate and then place the parchment on a work surface.

- → If the chocolate is in temper, it should dry within minutes and break cleanly when the paper is folded. It also should not melt readily when touched.
- → Maintain the chocolate in temper at 90°F in a stainless steel bowl set over a pan of simmering water. Do not allow the chocolate to exceed 90°F or it will go out of temper and need to be retempered before using.
- → Fill a paper parchment cone with the tempered chocolate or non-tempering chocolate coating and pipe out 12 designs of your choice onto a parchment-lined half-sheet baking pan.
- → Allow to dry and store at cool room temperature until ready to plate the dessert.

You may have more tempered chocolate than needed for 12 chocolate garnishes. Reserve any leftover for another use.

Consult the chocolate manufacturer's recommendations for precise holding temperature, as temperatures vary from chocolate to chocolate.

Assembly and plating

Holding a serrated knife at a 45 degree angle, cut the roulade into twenty-four ¾ inch thick diagonal rounds. You will use two rounds per serving. Place one round of the cake on each serving plate. Then place a round of cassis sorbet onto the cake, protruding over the right edge of the cake. Top the sorbet with another slice of cake, lined up with the cake below. Spoon some cassis jam to the side of the cake and then squeeze a swath of the kir royale sabayon beside the cake. Garnish the kir royale sabayon with a few cassis berries, which had been set aside. Garnish the top of the dessert with the chocolate décor.

Gateau Fondant of Candied Orange, Almond Nougatine, and Chocolate

YIELD: 12 SERVINGS, EACH WEIGHING APPROXIMATELY 3 OUNCES

Chocolate gateau fondant with almond praline and orange confit, served with citrus shake. Although candying fruit was known to the ancient Romans, today it is a dying art, the province of a shrinking number of French, Italian, Spanish, and Portuguese (and by extension, Mexican, Latin American, and Philippine) confectioners whose cultures still appreciate the beauty of a perfectly intact, uniformly translucent whole fig, orange, prickly pear, baby pineapple, or small melon. This painstaking and time-consuming process involves replacing the water content of the fruit with sugar syrup in which traditionally the concentration of sugar in the cooking syrup is gradually increased, day by day. Small fruits may be candied over a few days-long process while larger whole fruits may take up to 10 days or more. Here, in the interest of practicality, the process has been telescoped to produce what properly would be called *confited* (meaning preserved) oranges rather than candied. Despite the albeit abbreviated process, allow at least 2 hours from start to finish to make the confited oranges. Therefore, tackle this part of the recipe first, before moving onto the other elements. Here the preserved fruit is used in two elements of the dessert. First, it flavors the gateau fondant, a tender flourless chocolate cake (*fondant* means melting, which refers to the desired texture of the cake) and it then is used in an accompanying vanilla ice cream–based shake, a soda fountain treat gone upscale.

Chocolate, caramelized almonds, and the confited orange come together here in a three-part harmony of flavors. If **briefly** microwaved to warm (approximately 10–15 seconds on high power), the cake is then in sharper contrast to the icy chill of the shake. The yielding softness of the slightly heated cake is balanced by the shattering crispness of the almond praline shard positioned at its center.

The order of things:

1. **Place freezer-safe tall glasses for the citrus shake into the freezer** to give them a frosty appearance, and remove as needed when assembling the dessert
2. **Make confited oranges; Note: this process requires at least 2 hours,** including the multiple blanchings of the fruit in water and then slow simmering in sugar syrup so plan accordingly
3. **Make vanilla ice cream**
4. **Make almond praline**
5. **Make chocolate gateau fondant**
6. **Make chocolate ganache**
7. **Make citrus shake** just before serving the dessert
8. **Whip the cream to soft peaks** to use as an accompaniment to the cake

Equipment list:

Freezer-safe tall glasses for the citrus shakes, approximately 8 ounces capacity

Mandoline to thinly slice the oranges

Heavy saucepans used for making the almond praline and for the candying of the oranges

Fine-meshed cooling rack used when draining the blanched orange slices, and again to drain the confited orange slices

Silform plaque with 12 oval, round, or hexagonal-shaped indentations, as desired, each holding 3 ounces of batter

Covered canister-style electric blender *or* **immersion blender and tall stainless steel cup** in which to make the citrus shake

Vanilla ice cream for citrus shake

YIELD: APPROXIMATELY 25 OUNCES

Oz	Grams	Each	Name of ingredient
12	360		**Whole milk**
		1.5	**Vanilla beans**, split
4	120	From 6 large eggs	**Egg yolks**
3	90		**Granulated sugar**
6	180		**Heavy cream**
	3	Generous pinch	**Salt**

→ In a medium-sized heavy saucepan, bring the milk and vanilla beans to a simmer.

→ Cover the pan and allow to infuse for 30 minutes.

→ Remove vanilla beans, rinse and dry, and reserve for another use.

→ In the bowl of an electric mixer outfitted with the whisk attachment, beat egg yolks and sugar to thick ribbon stage.

→ Reheat milk and temper half of it into the egg and sugar mixture.

→ Add remaining milk and then cook the mixture over medium heat, stirring with a wooden spoon constantly, without aerating, until the mixture reaches 185°F.

→ Stir in salt and mix to dissolve.

→ When the mixture reaches temperature, immediately remove from the heat and pass through a fine sieve into a stainless steel bowl set over an ice bath.

→ Cool quickly, stirring occasionally, and when cold, freeze the mixture in the bowl of an electric ice cream machine.

→ Once frozen, remove to a container, covered, and freeze until ready to make the citrus shakes below.

Confited orange

Oz	Grams	Each	Name of ingredient	Notes
12 to 16, approximately, depending on the size of the oranges	360 to 480	From 4 large oranges, with bright orange colored skin	Orange slices	
96 for **each** of three blanchings of the oranges	2880 (2.8 kg)		Water	Used to boil and tenderize the orange slices before cooking them in sugar syrup
16	480		Granulated sugar	
6	180		Corn syrup	
16	480		Water	

→ Wash and dry the oranges.

→ Using a mandoline or sharp knife, slice the oranges into ¼ inch thick slides.

→ Place 3 quarts of water into a large saucepan and then add the orange slices.

→ Bring to the boil and then drain.

→ Repeat this process two more times to remove the bitterness from the skins using enough water each time to allow the orange slices to float freely.

→ After the third boil, remove the slices from the water, discard the water and set the now-tender orange slices on a cooling rack in a single layer while you make the syrup.

→ In a medium-sized heavy saucepan, bring the sugar, corn syrup, and water to the boil.

→ Add the cooked tender orange slices to the syrup, reduce the heat and cook, at the barest simmer, for approximately 60 to 90 minutes, or until the slices are tender, but not disintegrating.

- The key here is to cook the fruit slowly enough so that it remains relatively intact while absorbing the sugar syrup evenly and thoroughly.
- Taste to check that the fruit has absorbed the sweetness of the syrup.
- At this point, the tanginess of the peel should be muted.
- Then, using a large perforated spoon, carefully remove the confited orange slices from the syrup and place them in a single layer on a fine-meshed cooling rack set on a half-sheet pan, and allow to drain at room temperature.
- Refrigerate the extra slices, covered, in a single layer. They will keep well refrigerated for at least a few weeks.
- Reserve the syrup for the citrus shakes, and for any other desserts where an orange-flavored syrup may be used, such as as a moistener on a cake or as a flavoring for ice creams, sorbets, pastry cream, buttercream, or other preparations. The syrup keeps well, refrigerated, in a container with a tight-fitting lid.
- Now make the almond praline as follows.

Note that this recipe yields more candied orange slices than are called for in the dessert.

Almond praline
YIELD: APPROXIMATELY 18 OUNCES

Oz	Grams	Each	Name of Ingredient
7	210		Granulated sugar
4	120	½ c.	Corn syrup
8	240	1 c.	Water
4.5	135		Slivered almonds

- In a heavy saucepan, bring sugar, corn syrup, and water to a boil.
- Cook, without stirring, to 230°F.
- Quickly stir in almonds and pour mixture onto a heated Silpat-lined sheet pan.
- Heating the pan before pouring the mixture onto it allows the nut mixture to spread more evenly and thinly for a more even bake.
- Bake in a preheated 350°F oven for approximately 10–15 minutes, or until evenly golden brown, rotating the pan to ensure uniform browning of the praline.
- Remove immediately from the oven and allow to cool before using.

TIP: *You may find that some of the praline mixture has flowed over the edges of the Silpat and baked under the Silpat. If you use a full-sheet pan–sized Silpat, this may be avoided.*

Mix hot syrup with nuts in a heated bowl. Carefully pour the mixture onto Silpat placed onto a heated sheet pan and allow it spread out as thinly as possible.

Carefully remove the finished nut brittle, when cool, from the Silpat.

Break the brittle into shard-like garnishes.

Gateau fondant

YIELD: APPROXIMATELY
39 OUNCES, 12 SERVINGS,
EACH APPROXIMATELY
3¼ OUNCES

Oz	Grams	Each	Name of ingredient	Baker's percentages— Chocolate at 100%	Baker's percentages— Chocolate
12	360		High-quality 70% bittersweet chocolate couverture, chopped	100	25
6	180		Unsalted butter	50	25
6	180	From 9 large eggs	Egg yolks	50	16 to 25
9	270	From 9 large eggs	Egg whites, at room temperature	75	100
3	90		Confited orange (from above)	25	50
3	90		Almond praline (from above)	25	50
2 to 3	60 to 90		Unsalted butter, melted, to grease the cake molds	16 to 25	75

→ In a stainless steel bowl, set over simmering water, melt chocolate with butter, stirring until melted and smooth.

→ Remove from the heat, allow to cool briefly, and then add egg yolks, stirring them in one by one.

→ In a food processor, process the confited orange slices into a smooth paste.

→ In a food processor, process the almond praline (from below) to a fine powder.

→ Fold each of the mixtures into the chocolate mixture and set aside.

→ In the bowl of an electric mixer, outfitted with the whisk attachment, whip the egg whites to soft peaks.

→ Fold beaten whites gently into the chocolate mixture.

→ With melted butter brush 12 Silform molds, either oval, round, or hexagonal-shaped, as desired, each holding 3 ounces of batter.

→ Bake in a preheated 350°F oven for about 10–15 minutes, or until just barely cooked inside.

→ The cakes should remain somewhat moist and fudgy inside.

→ Remove the cakes from the oven and place on a cooling rack. These cakes, which are flourless, will deflate some as they cool.

Chocolate ganache

YIELD: APPROXIMATELY
12 OUNCES, 1 OUNCE PER
SERVING

Oz	Grams	Name of ingredient
6	180	58% dark chocolate couverture
6	180	Heavy cream

→ In a small heavy saucepan, heat the cream to boiling.

→ Pour the hot cream over the chocolate and stir until melted and smooth.

→ Use immediately or store in a covered container, refrigerated, and rewarm over a hot water bath to liquefy, as needed, just before serving the dessert.

Oz	Grams	Name of ingredient
8	240	Heavy cream

→ In the bowl of an electric mixer, outfitted with the whisk attachment, whip the cream to soft flowing peaks. Do not overbeat.

→ Use immediately or store in a container, covered, refrigerated, until ready to serve the dessert.

→ You may need to rewhip the cream briefly to stiffen it a bit, if it has become deflated and liquidy.

Oz	Grams	Each	Name of ingredient
24	720		**Vanilla ice cream** from above
48	1440		**Whole milk**
6	180		**Confited orange** from above
6	180		**Orange syrup** from the confited orange above
1	30	2 T.	**Vanilla extract**

These shakes are to be made just before serving the dessert. They should be thick and foamy, flecked lightly with bits of confited orange.

Assembly and plating

Break the almond praline into 12 roughly triangular shards, using one per serving in the dessert. Place a pool of liquid ganache on each plate. Using a sharp serrated knife, slice the cakes horizontally in half at a sharp angle. Just before serving, if desired, warm the cake briefly in the microwave on low to medium power for a few seconds and then proceed with the next step. Place the bottom half of the cake on the plate. Place the almond praline shard on top of the bottom cake and then place the top half of the cake on top of the praline. Place the cake on top of, and halfway back, onto the pool of ganache. Spoon some softly whipped cream to the side of the cake, and a confited orange slice to the front left of the cake.

Just before serving, make the citrus shake as follows. In a blender, combine all the ingredients (or a proportionately scaled down amount of each ingredient per serving) until smooth. Pour into a freezer-safe glass that has been stored in the freezer to give it a frosty appearance, and serve as an accompaniment to the chocolate fondant.

Serve the citrus shake in a glass on a separate plate, behind the dessert plate. Serve immediately.

TIP: *Alternatively, you may use an immersion blender set into a deep stainless steel cup to puree and aerate the mixture.*

A Cup of Coffee

YIELD: 12 SERVINGS

A cup of coffee—espresso soaked genoise, coffee custard filling, topped with cappuccino foam, layered in a latte cup. The fun of this dessert lies in the presentation, which juxtaposes elegant components within the setting of a coffee cup that would fit comfortably into any retro corner diner in Smalltown, USA. A layer of light sponge cake heavily drenched in a sweetened lemony espresso syrup almost dissolves into the intensely coffee flavored custard. All of this creamy softness is set off nicely by a coffee-bean studded biscotti, which is fine grained, moist, and crunchy all at the same time.

The order of things:

1. **Make genoise** and allow to cool
2. **Make coffee custard**
3. **Make biscotti**
4. **Make espresso sauce**
5. **Make whipped cream**
6. **Make cappuccino foam** as the dessert is ordered

Equipment list:

Cheesecloth for sieving coffee grounds from steeped espresso liquid

Pastry bag, outfitted with a plain round tip, measuring ½ inch in diameter

Twelve **clear glass mugs** to serve the layered dessert, 8 to 10 ounce capacity

Steamer from an espresso machine to foam the milk to top the dessert

Genoise sponge layer in coffee cup

YIELD: ONE HALF SHEET CUT INTO 12 ROUNDS, APPROXIMATELY 3 INCHES IN DIAMETER, OR JUST SLIGHTLY SMALLER THAN THE INTERIOR DIAMETER OF THE CLEAR GLASS COFFEE MUGS IN WHICH THE DESSERT IS SERVED

Oz	Grams	Each	Name of ingredient	Baker's percentages
6	180		Cake flour	100
	1.5		Salt	0.8
12	360	7	Large eggs	200
6	180		Granulated sugar	100
.25	7.5	1½ t.	Vanilla extract	4
3	90		Butter, melted and warm, not hot	50

TIP: *To best incorporate the butter into the whipped egg and sugar mixture without deflating the mixture, make sure that the butter is lukewarm, not hot, as hot butter will sink to the bottom of the bowl, requiring more mixing than is advisable and thereby dissipate the air that has been beaten into the mixture instead of allowing it to be airy and light.*

→ Sift flour and salt three times, depositing the mixture onto a sheet of parchment paper and set aside.

→ Place the eggs and sugar into a stainless steel bowl set over a pan of simmering water (the water should not touch the bottom of the bowl).

→ Heat the mixture, whisking constantly, until it reaches 110°F.

→ Transfer the mixture to the bowl of an electric mixer, outfitted with the whisk attachment.

→ Whip until light in color and tripled in volume.

→ Fold the sifted dry ingredients gently into the egg base, adding the vanilla and melted butter as you fold.

→ Handle carefully to avoid deflating.

→ Pour the batter immediately into a parchment-lined and greased half-sheet pan, and bake in a preheated 375°F oven for approximately 15 minutes.

→ Remove from the oven to a cooling rack and store, at room temperature, if using the same day, covered, until ready to assemble the dessert. If not using the same day, refrigerate, covered, and use within two days.

→ First, trim off an inch-wide strip from the four sides of the sheet cake. (This kind of cake often has edges that are too brown or too crisp to use and therefore those edges should be removed before cutting the squares of cake for use as the mousse base.)

→ Now using a cookie cutter just slightly smaller than the interior diameter dimension of the clear glass coffee cup in which the dessert is served, cut the cake into 12 rounds, 3 inches in diameter, in rows of four along the long side and in rows of three along the shorter side, totaling 12 rounds.

→ Set aside, covered, until ready to assemble the dessert.

Coffee custard

YIELD: APPROXIMATELY 23 OUNCES

Oz	Grams	Each	Name of ingredient	Baker's percentages—Milk at 100%
8	240		Whole milk	100
7	210		Sugar	33
4	120	2	Large eggs	50
1	30		Cornstarch	6
1.25	37.5		Coffee beans, coarsely ground	16
		1	Vanilla bean, split	1
2	60		Unsalted butter	25

- In a medium-sized heavy saucepan, bring the milk to a boil with vanilla bean and coffee beans.
- Pass through a fine sieve lined with cheesecloth dipped in water and wrung out, reserving the liquid and discarding the solids.
- In a medium-sized bowl, using a whisk, beat the sugar, eggs, and cornstarch until smooth.
- Temper the egg mixture with the hot milk, pass through a fine sieve again, and pour the liquid into a heavy saucepan.
- Cook over medium heat, whisking constantly, until the mixture thickens and is smooth.
- Remove from the heat and whisk in the butter.
- Transfer to a stainless steel bowl, set over an ice water bath, and cool quickly.
- When cool, transfer to a container, cover, and refrigerate until ready to assemble the dessert.

Oz	Grams	Each	Name of ingredient	Baker's percentages
4	120		Unsalted butter, room temperature	50
4	120		Granulated sugar	50
3.2, approximately	96	2	Large eggs	40
.16	4.8	1 t.	Vanilla extract	2
8	240		All purpose flour	100
.17	5	1 t.	Baking powder	2
.05	1.5	¼ t.	Salt	1
	4		Coffee beans, weighed and then coarsely ground	2
1	30		Dark chocolate couverture, 66%, finely ground	12

Coffee bean biscotti

YIELD: 30 BISCOTTI, EACH MEASURING APPROXIMATELY 5½ INCHES LONG BY 5/16 INCH THICK, EACH WEIGHING APPROXIMATELY ½ OUNCE

- In the bowl of an electric mixer, outfitted with the paddle attachment, cream the butter and sugar until smooth and light.
- Add the eggs and vanilla and mix to blend.
- Sift the dry ingredients onto a sheet of parchment paper and then add to the mixer bowl.
- Fold in the coffee and chocolate and spread the mixture into a rectangle, measuring 5 inches wide by 13 inches long by ½ inch thick (before baking).
- Bake in a preheated 350°F oven for 25 minutes, or until golden.
- Remove from oven, allow to cool 10 minutes.
- Then cut the baked rectangle at a slight diagonal into baton shapes, 5½ inches long by 5/16 inches wide.
- Place the cut pieces onto a cooling rack set on a sheet pan.
- Return the biscotti to the oven for 15 more minutes, or until lightly golden and somewhat dry.
- Cool.

Espresso sauce

YIELD: 8 TO 9 OUNCES, AFTER SIEVING

Oz	Grams	Name of Ingredient
12	360	**Simple syrup**
2	60	**Espresso beans,** coarsely ground
1	30	**Fresh lemon juice,** sieved

→ In a medium-sized heavy saucepan, heat the syrup and the coffee beans.

→ Bring to the boil, reduce to a simmer and cook for 5 minutes.

→ Remove from the heat, cover the saucepan, and allow the liquid to infuse for approximately 15 minutes.

→ Pass through a fine sieve, lined with a double layer of cheesecloth that has first been moistened with water and squeezed out.

→ Discard the solids, reserving the liquid.

→ Stir in the lemon juice and place into a squeeze bottle.

→ Place the sauce, covered, in the refrigerator until ready to assemble the dessert

Sweetened whipped cream

YIELD: ENOUGH FOR 12 SERVINGS, USING ONE ½ INCH THICK LAYER IN EACH CUP

Oz	Grams	Name of ingredient
10	300	**Heavy cream**
2	60	**Granulated sugar**
.5	15	**Vanilla extract**

→ In the bowl of an electric mixer, outfitted with the whisk attachment, whip the cream with the sugar and vanilla extract, to soft peaks.

→ Transfer to a pastry bag, outfitted with a plain round tip, measuring ½ inch in diameter and seal the bag.

→ Refrigerate until ready to assemble the dessert.

Cappuccino foam

Oz	Grams	Name of ingredient
1 oz per serving	30 per serving	Cold **low-fat milk**

→ Using the steamer from an espresso machine, foam the cold milk to a fine textured creamy white foam.

→ Alternately, you may heat the milk in a small saucepan, whisking constantly, until you have achieved a stiff frothy mixture.

→ Spoon carefully into the coffee cup, mounding the foam slightly.

→ Serve immediately.

Assembly and plating

Squeeze in a layer of espresso sauce in the bottom of the cup. Top with a round of genoise, which has first been soaked on both sides with the espresso sauce. Then using a pastry bag, next pipe in a layer of coffee custard, about ½ inch thick. Then pipe in a layer of whipped cream, about ½ inch thick, and cover the whipped cream evenly with a layer of the espresso sauce. Make the cappuccino foam and then immediately spoon a generous portion of it on top of the espresso sauce, allowing it to dome over the rim of the cup. Serve immediately with two biscotti on the underplate.

Chai Affogato

YIELD: 12 SERVINGS

Chai affogato—hot spiced milk tea poured over ginger ice cream, served with a pan-seared Forelle pear and chocolate ginger snap cookies. *Affogato*, meaning "drowned" in Italian, is a beloved, simply executed dessert from the Italian repertoire, which involves pouring a freshly made strong, hot espresso over a scoop of good-quality vanilla gelato. Here boldly spiced black tea takes the place of the coffee and instead of vanilla, the ice cream is flavored with fresh and candied ginger which echoes the richly fragrant personality of the chai, the spiced tea of India. Descended from trees in central Asia where the pear was first seen in antiquity, the ripe fragrant miniature variety pear used here with its slightly caramelized edge adds one more creamy and decidedly fruity note to the ensemble. For further textural contrast, the crisp cookie, with its spicy notes and dark cocoa richness, completes the experience.

Ginger ice cream

YIELD: APPROXIMATELY 21 OUNCES, 12 SERVINGS 1¾ OUNCES EACH

Oz	Grams	Each	Name of ingredient
8	240		**Whole milk**
1	30		**Fresh peeled gingerroot,** roughly chopped
4	120		**Egg yolks**
2.5	75		**Granulated sugar**
	1		**Salt**
0.08	2.4	½ t.	**Vanilla extract**
6	180		**Heavy cream**

TIP: *Use fresh gingerroot whose unblemished skin is tautly stretched over the root, with no visible signs of deterioration. If the root has soft spots or is shrunken, it will have an off flavor and should not be used. As the flavor can vary from season to season and root to root, taste what you plan to use to determine how much to use and how long to infuse it in the milk for the ice cream base.*

Finishing the ice cream

Oz	Grams	Name of ingredient
1	30	**Candied ginger,** cut into ¼ inch dice

→ In a medium-sized heavy saucepan, bring the milk and fresh gingerroot to a simmer.

→ Remove from the heat, cover the pan, and allow to infuse for about 15 minutes. The fresh ginger flavor should come through clearly. Taste to confirm. If necessary, infuse for a few minutes.

→ Then pour through a fine sieve into a stainless steel bowl.

TIP: For ease of service, it is advisable to portion the ice cream into ¾ ounce scoops, using an ice cream scoop measuring 1½ inches in diameter, placing the scoops on a parchment-lined sheet pan, covered, and set back into the freezer. Remove two scoops per serving as needed just before assembling and serving the dessert.

- → In the bowl of an electric mixer, outfitted with the whisk attachment, beat the egg yolks and sugar to ribbon stage.
- → Reheat the ginger-infused milk and temper the hot liquid into the egg yolks–sugar mixture, stirring but not aerating.
- → Transfer this liquid to a small heavy saucepan and cook, stirring with a wooden spoon, without aerating, until the mixture reaches 185°F. The mixture should coat the back of the spoon.
- → Remove from the saucepan and immediately transfer the mixture to a stainless steel bowl set over an ice water bath.
- → Stir in the salt and mix to dissolve.
- → Then add the heavy cream and vanilla extract.
- → Allow the mixture to chill over the ice water bath, and when cold, transfer to the bowl of an electric ice cream machine and freeze until semi-firm, adding the chopped candied ginger at the last minute, just to incorporate.
- → Remove to an airtight covered container and store in the freezer until serving time.

Pan-seared Forelle pears

YIELD: 12 SERVINGS, EACH OF WHICH IS ONE HALF PEAR

Oz	Grams	Each	Name of ingredient
12 to 15	360 to 450	6	**Whole ripe Forelle, Seckel, or other small variety pears,** each weighing 2 to 3 ounces
8	240		**Acidulated water** containing the juice of 1 large lemon
2	60		**Butter,** clarified
1			**Granulated sugar**

- → Cut each pear into two halves, removing any obvious seeds.
- → Store in acidulated water for up to 15 minutes, to prevent oxidation.
- → Just before sautéing, remove from the water, drain and dry on absorbent paper towels, and set aside.
- → Heat clarified butter in a heavy sauté pan.
- → Carefully place the pear halves, a few at a time, into the pan to sear.
- → Sprinkle with sugar and cook just to brown the edges of the cut sides of the fruit.
- → Remove the pears to a baking sheet and bake in a preheated 350°F oven for approximately 10 minutes until tender but not mushy (oven time is dependent on the degree of the fruits' ripeness).
- → Set aside at room temperature for up to 1 hour before serving the dessert.
- → For longer storage, store, covered, in the refrigerator and rewarm just before serving.

TIP: Clarified butter is used here because it has a higher smoke point than whole butter, yielding pears that have a caramelized but not burnt taste. Clarified butter is made by melting butter slowly in a heavy saucepan and continuing to cook it without stirring until the milk solids sink to the bottom of the pan, are separated from the butterfat, and most of the water in the butter has been cooked away. Using a wide spoon, skim any residue that floats to the top of the liquefied butter and carefully pour off the clear yellow layer, leaving the white milky solids in the bottom of the pan, which are discarded.

TIP: Alternatively, instead of sautéing them, the pears may be dipped in clarified butter and then coated lightly with granulated sugar and then placed under a broiler or salamander to brown slightly and then placed into the oven, as noted above, to continue cooking until tender but not mushy.

Oz	Grams	Each	Name of ingredient	Baker's percentages—Flour and cocoa powder total 100%
4	120		Butter	80
3	90		Sugar	60
4	120		All purpose flour	80
1	30		Unsweetened cocoa powder	20
.06	2		Ground cinnamon, allspice, and ginger	1
.03	1		Ground cloves	.6
0.5	15		Molasses	10
1.67	50	1	Large egg	33
As needed for rolling out the dough			Unsweetened cocoa powder, sifted onto the surface where the dough is being rolled	

YIELD: APPROXIMATELY 13 OUNCES, ENOUGH FOR 12 COOKIES, EACH MEASURING 4 INCHES LONG BY 1 INCH WIDE.

→ In the bowl of an electric mixer, outfitted with the paddle attachment, cream the butter and sugar until light. Sift the dry ingredients together into a bowl and set aside.

→ Add the molasses and the egg to the creamed butter mixture and mix to combine, scraping the bottom and the sides of the bowl to ensure a well-blended mixture.

→ Add the dry ingredients and mix on low speed until they disappear.

→ Remove the dough from the mixing bowl and wrap in plastic wrap.

→ Chill the dough for approximately 1 hour or until firm enough to handle. If the dough is kept well chilled, when rolling out, it will not stick to your work surface.

→ On a surface lightly dusted with sifted unsweetened cocoa powder, roll the dough to about ¼ inch thickness, being careful not to incorporate any more of the powder than necessary.

→ Using a rolling toothed pie jagger, cut the dough into strips 1 inch wide by 4 inches long.

→ Place the strips on a parchment-lined baking sheet, chill until firm, about 15 minutes, and then bake in a preheated 375°F oven for 10 minutes or until dry to the touch but not overly browned.

Chai

Oz	Grams	Name of ingredient	Notes
	10	**Mulling spices** (A mix of whole cloves and allspice, pieces of cinnamon bark, and dried orange peel, in equal parts)	
	15	**Black tea**	Indian premium, whole leaf Assam or Nilgiri teas are suggested for use here.
16	480	**Whole milk**	
1	30	**Mild-flavored honey** such as clover honey	

The hot chai should be prepared **just before serving** the dessert. However, for ease and efficiency of preparation, measure out mulling spices and tea in the amounts shown above, which are enough for **two** servings. Make six times these amounts for 12 servings. If making one serving at a time, divide the two serving amounts into two equal parts and proceed.

→ In a medium-sized saucepan, bring the milk to the boil.

→ Reduce the heat and add the mulling spices and simmer for approximately 5 minutes, or until the spice flavors come through clearly. Taste to confirm. If necessary, continue to simmer for a few minutes more.

→ Add the tea and simmer again for 5 minutes. The tea should color the liquid and the flavor of the tea should come through clearly. If not, continue to simmer the mixture again briefly until the liquid has a pleasant tea flavor.

→ Pass the mixture through a fine sieve set over a bowl, discarding the solids, sweeten it with honey, stir, and transfer to a heat-proof pitcher.

→ Just before serving, pour the liquid over the ginger ice cream in a tall iced glass, which will foam up and float up to the top of the glass as it begins to melt.

Assembly and plating

Prepare the chai just before serving the dessert, as noted above. Place two previously portioned scoops of ginger ice cream, each measuring about 1½ inches in diameter, into a tall, heat-proof glass. Pour the hot chai over the ice cream. Place a sautéed pear to the side and slightly behind the glass; garnish the plate with a Chocolate Spice Snap cookie and serve immediately with a long spoon, knife, and a fork.

Chocolate Melting Moments Torte Flavored with Assam Tea

YIELD: 12 SERVINGS

Chocolate melting moments torte—flavored with Assam tea, served with malted milk chocolate ice cream, tea-infused sauce, and Isomalt and tea décor. The teas grown in the Assam region of northeast India often have an almost roasted edge that pairs particularly well with dark chocolate. Their rich aroma and full body in the cup allow them to stand up to the addition of milk or cream and shine through in a buttery cake redolent of chocolate and cocoa. Accentuating the inherently malty character of the tea, malted milk powder made from barley grain, appears in the cake as well as in the milk chocolate ice cream, with its own caramelized dairy personality. Tea appears in three different places in the recipe; first as a liquid flavoring for the cake; next in the cream-based plating sauce (which illustrates that fat is the carrier of flavor to the palate), and finally in the delicate tracery on the clear, thin, glassy Isomalt garnish. What beverage should accompany the moments of chocolate intensity? A well-brewed cup of malty Assam tea.

The order of things:

1. **Make chocolate Assam tea torte**
2. **Make the ice cream** and freeze until firm
3. **Make the tea-infused sauce**
4. **Scoop the ice cream,** if desired, and place on a parchment-lined sheet pan, covered, and return to the freezer until ready to assemble the desserts to order
5. **Make the Isomalt and tea décor** and set aside at cool room temperature

Equipment list:

Rectangular baking pan measuring approximately 8 inches by 10 inches by 2 inches deep, in which to bake the tort

12 eight-sided cutters (or other similar-sized shape of your choice), measuring 2¼ inches across by 1½ inches high, as molds for the torts

Ice cream scoop, measuring approximately 1¾ to 2 inches in diameter, to scoop the malted milk chocolate ice cream

Chocolate Assam tea torte

YIELD: APPROXIMATELY 58 OUNCES, 12 SERVINGS, EACH APPROXIMATELY 4 OUNCES

Lbs	Oz	Grams	Each	Name of ingredient	Baker's percentages
1		480		58% bittersweet chocolate couverture	228
	8	240		Unsalted butter	114
	2	60		Premium whole leaf Indian tea such as Assam	29
	8	240		Water	114
	2	60		Unsweetened, good-quality cocoa powder	29
	17	510	10	Large eggs, separated	242
	6	180		Granulated sugar	86
	0.33	10	2 t.	Vanilla extract	5
	7	210		All purpose flour	100
	2	60		Malted milk powder	29

- → Prepare a rectangular baking pan measuring approximately 8 inches by 10 inches by 2 inches deep.
- → Spray with pan release spray, line with parchment, and then spray again.
- → Set aside. Preheat the oven to 350°F.
- → In a stainless steel bowl set over simmering water, melt the chocolate and butter, stirring until fully melted and smooth.
- → Remove from the water bath and set aside.
- → Brew the tea in the water, steeping for just 3 minutes.
- → Pass through a fine sieve, discarding the tea leaves and reserving the liquid. Place the cocoa powder into a medium-sized bowl.
- → Using a whisk, add the brewed tea slowly to the cocoa powder.
- → Then blend the cocoa-tea mixture into the melted chocolate.
- → Separate the eggs, placing the egg whites into the bowl of an electric mixer.
- → Add the yolks to the chocolate mixture.
- → Whip the egg whites, using the whisk attachment, until foamy.
- → With the machine running, add the sugar gradually, beating until stiff but not dry.
- → Sift the flour and malted milk powder into a medium-sized bowl.
- → Gently fold the beaten egg whites and the dry ingredients into the chocolate mixture. Do not deflate the batter.
- → The batter should remain light and airy.
- → Pour the batter into the pan and bake for approximately 30–40 minutes. The cake should remain somewhat soft and fudgy in the middle. Do not overbake.
- → Remove from oven and cool on the rack.
- → Using an eight-sided cutter (or other similar-sized shape of your choice), measuring 2¼ inches across by 1½ inches high, cut the cooled cake into 12 individual portions, cutting in rows of four along the 10 inch side of the rectangle and in rows of three along the 7 inch side.
- → Cover the cut cakes to keep moist and set aside at room temperature.
- → Make malted milk chocolate ice cream as follows.

Malted milk chocolate ice cream

YIELD: APPROXIMATELY 46 OUNCES, 12 SERVINGS, EACH WEIGHING SLIGHTLY MORE THAN 3¾ OUNCES

Oz	Grams	Name of ingredient
16	480	Whole milk
16	480	Heavy cream
12	360	Premium-quality 41% milk chocolate, chopped
2	60	Malted milk powder
1	30	Trimoline, glucose or corn syrup
	1	Salt

- → Bring milk and cream to the boil.
- → Remove from the heat, add the chocolate, and stir until smooth.
- → Remove about 1 cup of the liquid and whisk it gradually into the malted milk powder to yield a smooth paste.
- → Gradually add more of the liquid, stirring constantly, to keep the mixture smooth.

- When all of the liquid has been added, stir in the Trimoline (glucose or corn syrup) and the salt, stirring to dissolve thoroughly.
- Chill the mixture in the refrigerator, covered, and when cold, pour it into the bowl of an electric ice cream machine.
- Process until semi-firm. Remove the mixture to a container, covered, and freeze until firm.
- Return to the freezer, cover the pan well with plastic wrap, and remove from the freezer, as needed, to complete the desserts to order.

TIP: *To save time when the desserts are being served, once the ice cream is frozen, using an ice cream scoop measuring 1¾ to 2 inches in diameter, scoop it into well-shaped round balls and place the ice cream balls onto a parchment-lined baking sheet.*

Tea-infused plating sauce

YIELD: APPROXIMATELY 5 OUNCES, 12 SERVINGS, EACH LESS THAN ½ OUNCE

Oz	Grams	Name of ingredient
6, plus additional as needed to mellow the sauce, to taste	180, plus additional as needed to mellow the sauce, to taste	Heavy cream
	20	Assam tea leaves—decaffeinated works very well here
2	60	Granulated sugar

- In a medium-sized heavy saucepan, heat the cream to the boil.
- Add the tea leaves and sugar, stirring to dissolve the sugar.
- Remove from the heat and allow the mixture to infuse, covered, for approximately 2 minutes and sieve, pressing hard on the solids. The liquid should be a slightly golden brown color.
- Taste and add more cream to dilute to arrive at a well-balanced mellow tea and dairy flavor.

TIP: *Taste the mixture every few seconds to monitor the progress of the infusion. The tea should come through clearly here but should not be aggressively tannic or bitter.*

Isomalt and tea décor

YIELD: 12 GARNISHES

Oz	Grams	Name of ingredient
4	120	Isomalt
1, approximately	30	Water
	5	Assam whole leaf tea leaves

- In a small heavy saucepan, melt the Isomalt with enough water to moisten.
- Cook without stirring until liquefied.
- Pour the hot and flowing Isomalt onto a Silpat in a thin layer.
- Sprinkle tea leaves sparingly over the Isomalt, allow to cool, and then break into irregular-shaped shards to use as a garnish.

Assembly and plating

Place one cake on the left side of each rectangular-shaped plate. Spoon the tea sauce onto the plate, beginning behind the cake and moving to the right, toward the front of the plate, in a long, curved, snake-like shape. Using an ice cream scoop, measuring approximately 1¾ to 2 inches in diameter, scoop the ice cream and place the scoop on top of the cake. Then set the Isomalt and tea décor on top of the ice cream. Serve immediately.

Vietnamese Coffee Ice Cream with Mango

YIELD: 12 SERVINGS

Mekong Magic: Vietnamese coffee ice cream with mango balls and mango sorbet in a tuile boat, accompanied by plating sauces of condensed milk and espresso coffee syrup and mango sauce. With a presentation inspired by the meandering rivers and the graceful flat-bottom boats of the Mekong River delta, this dessert combines three important elements of the Southeast Asian dessert tradition: mango, coffee, and condensed milk. And the cinnamon accents in the ice cream revere another high-quality local ingredient, Saigon cinnamon, grown not in southern Vietnam around Saigon but rather in the central highlands of the country. Although misnamed, since it is strictly speaking made from the bark of the cassia tree, botanically in the same genus as true cinnamon, this spice figures prominently in the soups, broths, and sausages of Southeast Asian cookery and lends its haunting presence here as a backdrop for the coffee, which is the star player.

Here, the heady combination of high-octane Vietnamese coffee and creamy sweetened condensed milk borrows the best from the East and the West. The strong coffee, a holdover from the time of French colonial rule in Vietnam, enriched by sweetened condensed milk, is served as *cà phê sũa đá* in cafes throughout Vietnam.

The tradition involves the use of an ingenious but simple version of the French press pot. Finely ground dark-roasted coffee is placed in the bottom of a round perforated metal one-serving drip filter outfitted with a screw in the center of its bottom. Then boiling water is poured over the grounds. A perforated metal disc fits onto the screw and is tightened just enough to allow the water to flow through the coffee grounds slowly for maximum flavor. The whole apparatus is placed on a glass containing a generous layer of condensed milk. When the coffee has finished dripping into the glass, the lucky imbiber uses a long spoon to combine it thoroughly with the condensed milk and then pours the resulting liquid into a tall glass filled with ice cubes. The result? Pure liquid nirvana and caffeine contentment in a glass. Here all of these elements come together on the plate in a dessert that satisfies both the eyes and the palate.

The order of things:

1. **Infuse cream** for Vietnamese coffee ice cream
2. **Make ice cream base**
3. **Complete ice cream** and freeze
4. **Make mango sorbet** and freeze
5. **Mold the mango with apricot glaze** and chill
6. **Make tuile batter** and let rest
7. **Make condensed milk sauce**
8. **Make espresso coffee syrup**
9. **Make mango plating sauce**
10. **Deposit tuile batter through templates** for boats and oars and bake
11. **Scoop ice cream and sorbet** and place scoops on sheet pans, covered, in the freezer

Equipment list:

X-ACTO knife to make cutout in a heavy acetate sheet for tuile "boat" and "oar"

Tuile template made of heavy acetate, with a canoe-shaped cutout, measuring 10½ inches long by 3 inches wide, measured at the widest point, tapering to a point at each end

Tuile template made of heavy acetate for the "oar" cutout, measuring 11 inches long by ¾ inches wide

Silicone plaque with twelve demispherical indentations, each measuring 3 inches in diameter by 2 inches deep

Round ice cream scoop, measuring 1 inch in diameter

Two squeeze bottles for depositing the plating sauces onto the plates

Vietnamese coffee ice cream

YIELD: 12 APPROXIMATELY
1½ OUNCE SCOOPS, ONE PER
SERVING FOR EACH DESSERT

Oz	Grams	Each	Name of ingredient
7	210		Heavy cream
1.75	53		Finely ground espresso coffee
		1	Whole cinnamon stick
7	210		Sweetened condensed milk
1.3	39	2	Egg yolks from large eggs
3.4	102		Whole milk
		1	Pinch salt

→ In a small heavy saucepan, heat the cream with the ground coffee and the cinnamon stick.

→ Bring to the boil and simmer for 5 minutes.

→ Remove from the heat, cover the saucepan, and allow the mixture to infuse for approximately 15 minutes. The coffee and cinnamon flavors should come through clearly. If not, infuse for a few more minutes.

→ Taste again to confirm the intensity of the flavor and then proceed.

→ Remove the cinnamon stick and then pass the mixture thorough a cheesecloth-lined sieve, pressing hard on the coffee to extract as much liquid as possible.

→ Discard the coffee grounds and reserve the coffee-infused cream, placing it into a medium-sized stainless steel bowl, set over a pot of simmering water (the water should not reach the bottom of the bowl).

→ Add the condensed milk, egg yolks, and whole milk to the coffee-infused cream mixture and cook over medium heat, stirring constantly without aerating, until the mixture thickens slightly and the egg yolks are cooked.

→ The mixture should reach 180°F.

→ Remove from the water bath and stir in salt to dissolve. Place the bowl over an ice water bath to chill the mixture until cold and then freeze in an ice cream machine until firm.

→ Remove to a covered container, place in the freezer until firm.

→ Using a round ice cream scoop, measuring 2 inches in diameter, scoop 12 portions of the ice cream, placing them on a parchment-lined sheet pan. Cover and return to the freezer until ready to assemble the desserts to order. Remove as needed from the freezer.

Cubed mango

YIELD: APPROXIMATELY
16 OUNCES, ENOUGH FOR
12 BALLS OF CUBED MANGO,
EACH WEIGHING APPROXI-
MATELY 1⅓ OUNCES

Oz	Grams	Each	Name of ingredient
4	120		Apricot or clear glaze
2	60		Water
12	360	From 2 to 3 medium-sized fruits	Fresh mango, peeled and cubed into ½ inch cubes

TIP: *Alternatively, you may use a demispherical ice cream scoop, measuring 2 inches in diameter, to form the balls, then torch briefly or dip the rounded side of the scoop into boiling water briefly to release the mango from the scoop, placing the balls on a parchment-lined baking sheet as they are released from the scoop. Then chill until ready to assemble and serve the dessert.*

→ In a small heavy saucepan, heat the glaze with water, stirring with a spoon until liquefied and lump free.

→ Place mango cubes into a stainless steel bowl.

→ Gently combine hot glaze with mango cubes, making sure that all of the mango cubes are coated lightly and evenly with the glaze.

→ Then divide the mixture evenly and quickly pour the mixture into a Silicone plaque with 12 demispherical indentations, each measuring 3 inches in diameter by 2 inches deep, set on a baking sheet.

→ Chill in the refrigerator until firm.

→ Once the mixture is set, remove from the refrigerator and dip the plaque of molds into hot water briefly and invert onto a parchment-lined baking sheet to unmold.

→ Keep chilled until ready to assemble and serve the dessert.

Oz	Grams	Name of ingredient
6	180	**Mango puree,** fresh or frozen, thawed
1.25	38	**Simple syrup**
0.5	15	**Fresh lime juice,** sieved

→ In a bowl, combine all of the ingredients and then chill until cold.

→ When cold, process in an electric ice cream machine until firm.

→ Remove to a well-covered container, freeze, and then scoop into twelve ⅗ or slightly more than a half of an ounce balls, using a round ice cream scoop, measuring 1 inch in diameter.

→ Freeze the scoops, covered, until ready to assemble and serve the dessert.

Oz	Grams	Name of ingredient
10	300	**Strong, brewed liquid espresso coffee**
3	90	**Granulated sugar**
1	30	**Cornstarch**
3	90	**Water**

→ In a small heavy saucepan, heat the brewed espresso with sugar and cook just until sugar is dissolved.

→ In a separate small bowl, combine the cornstarch and water.

→ Add the cornstarch mixture and cook over low heat, whisking constantly, just until the mixture thickens and the raw taste of cornstarch disappears.

→ Cool to room temperature. If using immediately, store at room temperature. If you are serving the dessert later in the day or the next day, store the sauce in a container, covered, in the refrigerator.

→ After refrigerating it, the sauce will congeal some.

→ Set over a hot water bath to re-liquefy, stir briefly, and then hold at room temperature during the serving of the dessert.

Oz	Grams	Name of ingredient
14	420	**Condensed milk**
2, or as needed, depending on the thickness of the condensed milk	60, or as needed	**Heavy cream**

→ In a small bowl, combine the condensed milk with heavy cream as needed, without aerating excessively, to thin slightly.

→ Refrigerate until ready to serve the dessert.

Tuile batter

YIELD: GENEROUS
12 OUNCES, ENOUGH FOR
12 "BOATS" AND 12 "OARS,"
ALLOWING FOR EXTRA IN
CASE OF BREAKAGE, OR
IMPROPERLY SHAPED OR
BAKED COOKIES

Oz	Grams	Each	Name of ingredient	Baker's percentages
4	120		**Unsalted butter,** room temperature	100
4	120		**Confectioners' sugar**	100
4	120	4, from large eggs	**Egg whites** from large eggs	100
.16	4.8		**Vanilla extract**	4
4	120		**All purpose flour**	100

→ Using two sheets of heavy acetate, with an X-ACTO knife or box cutter, cut an elliptical "boat"-shaped template into one, and then cut an "oar"-shaped template in the other. (Transparent report covers work well here.) The opening for the "boat" should be 10½ inches long by 3 inches wide, measured at the widest point, tapering to a point at each end. The opening for the oar should measure 11 inches long by ¾ inches wide.

→ In the bowl of an electric mixer outfitted with the paddle attachment, cream the butter until light and smooth.

→ Add confectioners' sugar and mix to blend, scraping the bottom and sides of the bowl to ensure that the mixture is well blended.

→ Add egg whites and vanilla and mix to incorporate.

→ Add the flour and mix just until flour disappears.

→ If time allows, set batter to rest in the refrigerator for approximately one hour.

→ Then using a small metal spatula or plastic bowl scraper, spread the mixture in a thin but not translucent layer onto the boat-shaped template placed on a Silpat set onto the back of a baking sheet.

→ It is best to make only a few of these at a time, as they need to be shaped quickly upon removal from the oven.

→ Bake in a preheated 350°F oven for about 10 minutes or until lightly golden, rotating the sheet pan as necessary to achieve even color.

→ Remove the tuiles from the oven and shape immediately over a shallow, flat-bottomed bowl, measuring approximately 9 inches in diameter, to create a gently curved boat shape, with the ends upturned and the middle left flat (when serving the dessert, the cubed mango ball, espresso ice cream, and mango sorbet will be placed in the flat area).

→ Repeat the process until you have 12 "boats."

→ With the remaining batter, make 12 "oars."

→ Using a small metal spatula or plastic bowl scraper, spread the mixture in a thin but not translucent layer onto the oar-shaped template placed on a Silpat set onto the back of a baking sheet. It is best to make only a few of these at a time, since they need to be shaped quickly upon removal from the oven.

→ Bake in a preheated 350°F oven for about 10 minutes or until lightly golden, rotating the sheet pan as necessary to achieve even color.

→ Spread through the long, thin template shape.

→ Bake as above, remove from the oven, and using both hands, hold the ends of the strip, with one end in each hand, twist gently and then set the "oar" onto the Silpat as you continue to shape the others.

→ Store the "boats" and "oars" at room temperature in a single layer in a container with a tight-fitting lid, outfitted with a piece of limestone or a packet of silica gel, to help retain crispness.

Oz	Grams	Name of ingredient
12	360	**Mango puree,** either fresh or commercially prepared frozen puree (this kind typically has 10% sugar by weight)
As needed, if needed		**Simple syrup**
2	60	**Fresh lime juice,** sieved

Depending on the sweetness of the fruit, the simple syrup will vary, or perhaps not be needed at all. Taste the sweetness of the fruit first, before adding any simple syrup.

→ In a small bowl, combine the puree with the syrup, if using, and then add the lime juice.

→ Taste to achieve a balanced sweet-tart flavor, adding more simple syrup if needed.

→ If you are using the commercially prepared mango puree, you may not need to use any simple syrup.

Assembly and plating

Fill one plastic squeeze bottle each with the condensed milk sauce and the espresso plating sauce. Onto each plate, squeeze out a long rectangular strip of the condensed milk sauce. Then squeeze out two lines of the espresso plating sauce, one on each side of the condensed milk sauce. Place the tuile "boat" at an angle on top of the sauces. From left to right, place the cubed mango ball, the coffee ice cream, and then the mango sorbet on top of the flat center area of the tuile boat. Garnish with a tuile twist and a pitcher of mango sauce and serve immediately.

Breakfast for Dessert— Yogurt Ice Cream on Granola Cookie with Fresh Fruit

YIELD: 12 SERVINGS

Breakfast for dessert: Yogurt ice cream shaped into yogurt container shape, set on granola cookie, fresh fruits, fruit purees, pineapple fruit leather garnish. You might say yogurt ice cream is a contradiction in terms. Not here. In this play on serving breakfast for dessert, yogurt, normally at home early in the day, plays the flavoring role, but freezing it with a bit of sugar and flavorings and enriching it with cream make it shine after dinner. Thick, well-drained, Greek-style yogurt is used here, in an ice cream accented with notes of vanilla and highly fragrant low-acid Meyer lemon peel. If drained yogurt is not available, simply use whole milk yogurt and allow it to drain, refrigerated, overnight, in a fine sieve, set over a bowl. You may discard the whey, the liquid left in the bowl, or use it as a protein-rich addition to bread dough or in a smoothie, using the now-thick yogurt in the ice cream. (If Meyer lemons are unavailable, feel free to substitute the everyday variety but be aware that the result, while still delicious, will be less complex in flavor, with less of that *je ne sais quoi*, that undefinable something, that makes the ice cream so addictive and memorable.) The yogurt ice cream is shaped to resemble a yogurt cup, set on a cookie base made from a homemade oat granola, studded with dried fruits, nuts, and sesame seeds. The cookie provides a wholesome crunch, the fruit provides color and some tart and sweet contrasts, and the minimally sweetened fruit leather introduces a refreshingly chewy note.

The order of things:

1. **Infuse the cream with the lemon peel**
2. **Complete making the yogurt ice cream** and place into paper cups, topping each with a second waxed paper cup to create an indentation in the top of the ice cream; freeze
3. **Make the granola**
4. **Make the granola cookie mixture**
5. **Bake the cookie mixture** and allow to cool to lukewarm, then cut
6. **Make the pineapple fruit leather garnish**
7. **Prepare the fruit garnish**
8. **Prepare the fruit purees** to be used as plating sauces
9. **Remove the ice cream from the paper cups** and return it to the freezer, covered, until ready to assemble the dessert

Equipment list:

Twenty-four **waxed paper cups,** measuring 3¾ inches high by 3 inches at the top and 2 inches at the base, 12 to use as the container in which the yogurt ice cream is formed, and 12 to act as place savers, creating an indentation at the top of the ice cream to create a thin lip at the top of the ice cream in which the fruits are placed when the dessert is served

Round metal cookie cutter measuring 2 inches in diameter to cut the granola cookies after baking

Squeeze bottles for fruit purees used as plating sauces

Yogurt ice cream

YIELD: APPROXIMATELY
30 OUNCES, 12 SERVINGS,
2½ OUNCES EACH

Oz	Grams	Each	Name of ingredient
8	240		**Whole milk**
From 1 large Meyer lemon			**Meyer lemon** peel from 1 large fruit, cut into strips, without pith
			Note: Regular lemon may be used instead, if Meyer lemons are unavailable.
		1	**Vanilla bean,** split
8	240		**Granulated sugar**
17.6	528		**Whole milk Greek-style drained yogurt**
8	240		**Heavy cream**
		1	**Salt**

→ In a medium-sized heavy saucepan, heat milk with Meyer lemon peel and vanilla bean.

→ Bring to a boil and then simmer for 5 minutes.

→ Remove from heat, and allow mixture to infuse, covered, for 15 minutes.

→ Pass through a sieve, discarding peel and reserving vanilla bean for another use.

→ Return infused milk to a medium-sized heavy saucepan, add sugar and heat until sugar is dissolved.

→ Allow to cool to lukewarm and add to the yogurt, stirring just to blend, without aerating.

→ Add heavy cream and salt, mix to blend and freeze in an electric ice cream machine.

→ When firm, remove mixture from the machine and fill waxed paper cups, measuring 3¾ inches high by 3 inches at the top and 2 inches at the base.

→ Place another cup of the same size on top of each cup to make an indentation which should leave a raised rim of yogurt ice cream measuring approximately ½ inch wide all around.

→ This creates a well into which the fresh fruit garnish will be placed when the dessert is served.

TIP: *If you wish to create more of a yogurt parfait look, you can half fill the cups, double the following recipe for the granola, and sprinkle some granola in an even layer over the yogurt ice cream and continue to fill the cups with yogurt ice cream. Then proceed to make the well at the top of the ice cream as described previously.*

Granola

YIELD: 14 OUNCES, USED
BELOW IN THE COOKIE
MIXTURE

Oz	Grams	Name of ingredient
4	120	**Almonds,** whole
5	150	**Oats**
0.5	15	**Sesame seeds**
1.5	45	**Brown sugar**
1	30	**Honey**
2	60	**Canola oil**

→ In a preheated 350°F oven, on a baking sheet lined with parchment paper, toast the almonds for approximately 10–12 minutes, or until fragrant.

→ Remove from the oven and allow to cool.

→ Chop roughly and proceed with the recipe.

→ In a large bowl, combine the toasted almonds, oats, sesame seeds, brown sugar, honey, and oil.

→ Pour the mixture onto a Silpat-lined sheet pan and bake in a preheated 250°F oven for approximately 1 hour, stirring every 10 to 15 minutes to ensure even browning.

→ Let cool and then make the cookie as follows:

Oz	Grams	Each	Name of ingredient	Baker's percentages—Granola mixture at 100%
2	60		Butter	14
2	60		Brown sugar	14
0.16	4.8	1 t.	Vanilla extract	1
2.5	75	Approx 1.5 eggs	Whole large eggs	18
3	90		All purpose flour	21
		½ t.	Baking soda	0.5
		¼ t.	Salt	0.3
14, approximately	420		Granola from above	100
1	30		Dried cranberries	7
1	30		Dried apricots, cut into ½ inch cubes	7
1	30		Dried apples, cut into ½ inch cubes	7

→ In the bowl of an electric mixer, outfitted with the paddle attachment, cream butter until light and fluffy.

→ Add brown sugar and vanilla and mix until blended.

→ Add eggs gradually and mix until emulsified and incorporated. Sift flour, baking soda, and salt.

→ Add granola to the dry ingredients, mix to combine, and then add all to the mixture in the bowl.

→ Mix just until incorporated.

→ Add dried fruits and mix just to distribute evenly throughout the mixture.

→ Spray and line a half-sheet baking pan with parchment paper.

→ Using an offset metal spatula, spread the cookie mixture into an even layer and bake in a preheated 350°F oven for approximately 15 minutes, or until puffed and golden brown.

→ Remove from the oven and allow to cool on a rack.

→ Using a round cookie cutter measuring 2 inches in diameter, cut out 12 rounds of the granola cookie.

→ Set aside until ready to assemble the dessert.

Oz	Grams	Each	Name of ingredient
32	960	2 medium to large	Flesh from **fresh pineapples,** crowns of leaves, eyes and skin removed, cut into 1 inch pieces
4, or as needed	120		**Simple syrup**

→ Puree pineapple with enough simple syrup to a smooth paste.

→ Spread mixture onto two half-sheet pans, lined with Silpats in a thin, even layer. Bake in a preheated 250°F oven for approximately 1 hour 30 minutes.

→ Allow to cool.

→ When ready to serve the dessert, cut each half sheet into 6 rectangles roughly 5 by 5½ inches. Roll each piece into a cornucopia shape. (See photograph on page 122.)

Fruit garnish

YIELD: ENOUGH FOR
12 SERVINGS

Oz	Grams	Name of ingredient
12	360	**Pineapple,** cut into ½ inch cubes
12	360	**Fresh apricot,** cut into ½ inch cubes
12	360	**Raspberries**

Fruit puree garnish and plating sauces

YIELD: ENOUGH FOR
12 GENEROUS SERVINGS

Oz	Grams	Each	Name of ingredient
8 net puree	240	If using fresh berries, approximately 2 pints will yield 8 ounces of puree, after sieving out seeds	**Raspberry puree,** commercially prepared, frozen (these usually contain 10% sugar), and then thawed, or made from fresh berries, pureed and sieved
8 net puree	240	If using fresh apricots, approximately 1 lb fresh fruit will yield 8 ounces of puree, after removing the pits and sieving	**Apricot puree,** commercially prepared, frozen (these usually contain 10% sugar), and then thawed, or made from fresh apricots, pitted and pureed and then pressed through a fine sieve

Raspberry puree and apricot puree are used both as plating sauce and as an accent to the fresh fruit garnishing the tops of each ice cream.

→ If using frozen purees, simply thaw them in the refrigerator and transfer to squeeze bottles.

→ Store in the refrigerator until ready to serve the dessert.

→ If using fresh fruit, puree the fruits separately, passing them through a fine sieve.

→ Pour each into squeeze bottles and store, refrigerated, until ready to serve the dessert.

Assembly and plating

Remove top cups from frozen yogurt ice cream. Place one granola cookie on each of 12 plates. Place a frozen yogurt ice cream on top of the cookie. Fill the indentation in the ice cream cups with the fresh fruit garnish, spooning extra fruit and some raspberry puree on to the plate. Garnish each plate with a cornucopia of pineapple leather.

Hand-Pulled Strudel with Creamy Cheese Filling, Tahitian Vanilla Bean Syrup, and Vanilla Roasted Pears

YIELD: 12 SERVINGS

Hand-pulled strudel with cream cheese filling, Tahitian vanilla bean syrup, and vanilla sautéed pears, warm custard sauce, oven dried pear chip garnish.
In much of Western Europe, perfectly ripened cheese and fruit simply served at the end of a meal is often a substitute for dessert. Borrowing from the sweets traditions of Germany, Austria, and also from much of central and eastern Europe where ultra thin layers of dough are pulled from a well-rested dough based on high gluten flour, this dessert combines the best of both worlds. The cheese in this case is a blend of farmer cheese and cream cheese, and the fruit is in two forms, fresh and then caramelized, and crisped in the form of a slow-baked fruit chip. Floral, fragrant Tahitian vanilla flavors the strudel filling, adds character to the caramelized fruit, and scents both the chilled custard sauce and the warm syrup that is drizzled over the finished pastry.

The order of things:

1. **Make cream cheese filling** for the strudel
2. **Make strudel dough** and allow to rest for 1 to 2 hours at room temperature
3. **Bake the pear chips**
4. **Make vanilla bean custard sauce** and chill until ready to serve dessert
5. **Make vanilla bean syrup,** transfer to squeeze bottle, and chill until ready to serve dessert
6. **Stretch the strudel dough, buttering the surface** to keep from drying out
7. **Fill strudel dough and roll, buttering each exposed surface** as the strudel is being formed
8. **Bake strudel**
9. **Sauté pears** as close to serving time as possible

Equipment list:

Large clean cloth, at least 5 feet square, used as the surface on which to stretch the strudel dough, which facilitates in rolling it once filled, before baking

Silpat to place the thinly sliced pears on before drying in the oven, for the pear chips

Two squeeze bottles, one each for the vanilla bean custard sauce and vanilla bean syrup

Sugar dredger or fine sieve used to sift confectioners' sugar over the strudel after it has been baked

Cheese filling for strudel

YIELD: APPROXIMATELY 44 OUNCES, HALF USED FOR EACH STRUDEL

Ozs	Grams	Each	Name of ingredient	Baker's percentages— Farmer cheese and cream cheese total 100%
4	120		**Farmer cheese,** room temperature	20
16	480		**Cream cheese,** room temperature	80
16	480		**Granulated sugar**	80
0.03	1	⅛ t.	**Salt**	0.1
6.6	200	4	**Large eggs**	33
0.16	4.8	1 t.	**Tahitian vanilla bean paste or extract**	0.8
2	60		**All purpose flour**	10

→ In the bowl of an electric mixer outfitted with the paddle attachment, cream the farmer cheese and cream cheese together with the salt until smooth, scraping the bottom and sides of the bowl frequently to ensure that the mixture is well blended and lump-free.

→ Add the sugar and mix to combine, scraping again.

→ Add the eggs and vanilla and mix until incorporated.

→ Add the flour mixing *just until the flour disappears.*

TIP: *Do not overbeat. This mixture should appear creamy and dense after it is baked in the strudel, not pocked with air holes due to over-aeration.*

Strudel dough

YIELD: APPROXIMATELY 11 OUNCES OF DOUGH

Oz	Grams	Each	Name of ingredient	Baker's percentage	Notes
7	210		**Bread flour,** 12 % protein	100	
0.1	2	½ t.	**Salt**	0.9	
3	90		**Water,** warm	42	
0.5	15	1 T.	**Oil**	7	
0.4	12		**Fresh lemon juice,** from ½ medium-sized lemon	6	
16	480		**Unsalted butter**		To brush the dough when assembling the strudel, before and during baking

→ Place flour and salt into the bowl of an electric mixer outfitted with the dough hook attachment.

→ In a small bowl, combine water, oil, and lemon juice.

→ Add this mixture into the dry ingredients and mix for about 3 minutes at high speed to a smooth silky dough.

→ Remove the dough from the mixing bowl and place it in a lightly oiled bowl, cover the bowl, and place in a warm place for 1 to 2 hours, or until dough is completely rested and soft and feels warm to the touch.

Assembling the strudel

Clarifying the butter

→ While the dough is resting, clarify the butter by placing it into a medium-sized heavy saucepan.

→ Heat the butter until melted, skimming off the white foamy layer on top as it forms.

- Continue to heat, over medium heat, until the foam stops rising and the milk solids layer at the bottom of the saucepan is slightly browned.
- Remove from the heat and allow the butter to sit at room temperature to settle.
- Spoon off the clear yellow liquid, which is the clarified butter, leaving the browned milk solids in the pan.
- Reserve the clarified butter, discarding the milk solids.

Rolling and stretching the dough

- When the dough is ready to use, prepare the work surface by lightly flouring a clean cloth, 5 feet square, which will cover the entire work surface, measuring approximately 22 inches by 44 inches, with a generous overhang.
- Without wrinkling it, roll the dough to a thin even rectangle and then begin stretching the dough by placing the backs of your hands, lightly floured, under the dough and pulling the dough gradually, area by area, until the dough is paper-thin.
- Using scissors or a sharp knife, trim off and discard the thick edges all around the perimeter of the dough. Allow the dough to dry slightly on the top side, turn over to dry briefly on the other side and then using a brush, lightly but evenly butter the surface of the dough.

Middle and Eastern European baking tradition asserts that it should be possible to read a newspaper through the dough if the paper were placed under the dough.

TIP: Wrinkled areas are impossible to stretch thin and lead to tears in the dough when it is being stretched.

Filling and rolling up the dough

- Cut the dough into two equal pieces, each measuring approximately 22 inches square.
- Use half of the filling for each sheet of dough. Deposit the filling 4 inches from the edge of the dough, leaving a margin of 2 inches of unfilled dough at each end of the sheet.
- Roll the dough once to enclose the filling and then fold in the two sides of the dough over the filling, and continue rolling and buttering the exposed surfaces of the dough until the dough has been rolled completely into a tight cylinder, measuring 4 inches by 18 inches.
- Repeat with the other piece of dough.

Baking the strudel

- Place the filled cylinders of dough onto a parchment-lined baking full-sheet pan, butter the surface of the roll again, dock the dough every 2 inches or so with the point of a knife and bake in a preheated 375°F oven approximately 40 minutes, or until the strudels are deep golden brown, brushing the surface of the dough with melted butter, every 10–15 minutes.
- When well browned, remove from the oven and transfer the strudels to a cooling rack. Allow to cool at room temperature.

Vanilla sautéed pears
YIELD: 12 HALF PEARS, ONE PER SERVING

Oz	Grams	Each	Name of ingredient	Notes
48, gross weight, yielding approximately 42 oz after coring		6	Bosc pears	Other varieties such as Comice or Anjou, which are slightly firm when ripe, may be substituted here
4	120		Unsalted butter	
0.5	15		Tahitian vanilla bean paste or	
		1	Tahitian vanilla bean, split	
4	120		Granulated sugar	

→ Cut each of the pears in half, leaving stems attached, if desired, and then remove the cores and set aside.

→ In a heavy wide sauté pan, melt 2 ounces of the butter with the vanilla bean paste or vanilla bean.

→ When foaming, add six of the pear halves, cut side down, in a single layer, and cook over medium heat until lightly browned.

→ Add half of the sugar, continuing to cook the pears, turning once, until evenly browned and slightly caramelized.

→ Remove the finished pears to a parchment-lined sheet pan, and then add the remaining butter to the pan.

→ Add the remaining pears, cut side down, cooking until browned. Sprinkle the remaining sugar evenly over the pears and continue to cook until evenly browned and slightly caramelized.

→ Remove the second batch to the sheet pan and reserve at room temperature if serving within a few hours.

→ If not, refrigerate and remove from the refrigerator a few minutes before serving the dessert to allow the pears to come to room temperature.

Vanilla bean syrup

YIELD: APPROXIMATELY
8 OUNCES, 12 SERVINGS,
EACH MEASURING
⅔ OUNCE

Oz	Grams	Each	Name of ingredient
8	240		**Simple syrup**
0.5	15		**Vanilla bean paste** or
		1	**Tahitian vanilla bean**, split
1	30		**Eau de vie de poire** (clear pear brandy), optional

→ Bring simple syrup and the vanilla bean paste or vanilla bean to the boil. Reduce the heat to a simmer and cook for approximately 5 minutes, or until the vanilla flavors comes through clearly in the syrup.

→ Remove from the heat and cool. Add the eau de vie de poire, if using, and stir to combine.

→ Transfer to a squeeze bottle, covered, and store at room temperature, if using within a few hours.

→ If not, refrigerate and then remove from the refrigerator, placing the bottle over a hot water bath to rewarm.

Vanilla bean custard sauce

YIELD: APPROXIMATELY
24 OUNCES, 12 SERVINGS,
EACH APPROXIMATELY
2 OUNCES

Oz	Grams	Each	Name of ingredient	Baker's percentages— Milk at 100%
16	480		**Whole milk**	100
		1	**Tahitian vanilla bean**, split	
4	120	6	**Egg yolks**, from large eggs	25
4	120		**Granulated sugar**	25

→ In a medium-sized heavy saucepan, place the milk and the vanilla bean and bring to the boil. Reduce the heat and simmer for approximately 5 minutes.

→ Remove from the heat, cover, and allow to infuse for approximately 15 minutes. The vanilla flavor should come through clearly.

→ If not, infuse for a few minutes longer.

→ Remove the vanilla bean and discard. Set aside the infused liquid.

→ In the bowl of an electric mixer outfitted with the whisk attachment, whip the egg yolks and sugar until light.

→ When the whisk is lifted from the bowl, the mixture should fall slowly in a thick ribbon.

- → Reheat the infused milk until hot and then temper it into the egg yolk–sugar mixture.
- → Transfer the mixture to a stainless steel bowl, set over a pan of simmering water (the water should not touch the bottom of the bowl), and cook, stirring with a heat-resistant spatula until the mixture reaches 180°F and coats the back of the spoon.
- → Remove from the heat. Pass the mixture through a fine sieve into a clean stainless steel bowl, set over an ice water bath.
- → Stir to cool quickly and evenly.
- → Transfer to a squeeze bottle, covered, and place in the refrigerator until ready to plate the dessert.

Pear chips
YIELD: 18 CHIPS, ALLOWING FOR EXTRAS IN CASE ANY ARE MISSHAPEN OR OTHERWISE UNUSABLE

Oz	Grams	Each	Name of ingredient
18 slices		From 3, approximately	Thin slices of **fresh pear,** unpeeled from large pears
6	180		**Simple syrup**

- → Holding the fruit upright, stem side up, slice the pears thinly on a mandoline. (Note that the slices closer to the core yield better-shaped chips.)
- → Soak the slices in the simple syrup for approximately 15 minutes.
- → Remove from the syrup and place on a Silpat-lined baking sheet. Bake in a preheated 225°F oven for approximately 45 minutes, or until dry to the touch.
- → Remove from the oven and allow to cool to room temperature.
- → Using a small metal spatula or plastic bowl scraper, carefully release the pear chips from the Silpat.
- → Store them at room temperature in an airtight container, with a tight-fitting lid, outfitted with a piece of limestone or a packet of silica gel, to retain crispness.

Confectioners' sugar garnish

Oz	Grams	Name of ingredient
2	60	Confectioners' sugar

Assembly and plating

Using a dredger or a fine sieve, dust the top of the strudels with sifted powdered sugar. Sauce the plate with a pool of vanilla bean custard sauce. Trim each strudel to a rectangle measuring approximately 18 inches long by approximately 4 inches wide. Cut the 18 inch length into three equal 6 inch rectangular sections. Slice each rectangle into two equal triangles, measuring 4 inches on one side, 6 inches on another, and 7.2 inches on the third side. Stand the slice upright in the center of the sauce, with the 4 inch side down on the plate. Serve with pan-roasted pear half and garnish with a pear chip. Drizzle the strudel with the vanilla bean syrup. Serve immediately.

Ros Malai with Cardamom Milk Sauce and Pistachios in a Nutted Florentine Bowl

YIELD: 12 SERVINGS

Ros Malai, Indian creamy curds, with cardamom milk sauce and pistachios, served in an edible nutted Florentine cookie bowl. A traditional coda to a traditional Indian meal, ros malai, with its rich, creamy consistency and appealing undertone of spice, is a dessert that could cap a meal of almost any ethnicity. Here its presentation in a bowl made of a cross between a florentine and a tuile batter brings it beyond its rustic beginnings. It might also be fairly called "the two textures of milk," one semi-solid (the paneer cheese thickened by an acidic ingredient) and the other, semi-liquid (the plating sauce), thickened by reduction to the consistency of clotted cream. All it takes to make this most low-tech but delicious kind of handmade unripened "cheese," the centerpiece of this dessert, is a large deep saucepan, milk, lemon juice used as a coagulant, a wooden spoon and a fine-meshed piece of cheesecloth with which to strain and compress the resulting soft cheese. Richly fragrant cardamom pods appear in two places here: first in the sugary poaching liquid for the cheese and then in the milk-based sauce, each underscored here by a generous use of fragrant cardamom pods, considered the world's most pricey flavoring (after saffron and vanilla, in that order).

The order of things:

1. **Make the paneer,** drain and compress
2. **Make the spiced sugar syrup** in which the paneer is placed
3. **Make the florentine cookie batter**
4. **Make the milk sauce**
5. **Bake the florentines,** shape into bowls as they are removed from the oven

Equipment list:

Large deep saucepan, with a 4 gallon capacity, in which to cook the paneer

Large double-thickness of cheesecloth to drain and compress the paneer

Small bowl, measuring approximately 3 inches in diameter, used to shape the tuile bowls

Paneer

YIELD: 24–36 QUENELLES, DEPENDING ON SIZE, ENOUGH FOR 12 SERVINGS, 2 TO 3 PIECES FOR EACH SERVING

Lb	Oz	Grams	Each	Name of ingredient	Notes
16 lbs		7.68 kg	2 gal	Whole milk	Lower-fat milk may be used but the resulting cheese may be drier in consistency and will therefore crumble
	6 to 8	180 to 240		Fresh lemon juice, sieved	
	2½	75	36	Whole square sugar cubes, each weighing 2 grams	

- → In a large deep saucepan, cook the milk and lemon juice, stirring constantly with a wooden spoon until the curds rise to the top of the pot.
- → Using a ladle, scoop the curds into a cheesecloth-lined sieve, set over a bowl.
- → Squeeze cheesecloth to remove excess liquid. (The resulting liquid is called *whey*, which may be used as an enrichment in yeast breads, fruit smoothies, or discarded, as desired.)
- → Knead the compressed cheese briefly on a clean surface and form into quenelle shaped ovals, each weighing approximately 1 ounce.
- → Pinch off pieces of the cheese, each weighing approximately ¾ ounce to 1¼ ounce, and wrap the cheese around a sugar cube, making sure that the cheese covers the sugar completely.
- → Set aside, refrigerated, and lightly covered until ready to poach in the sugar syrup below.

Spiced sugar syrup

Oz	Grams	Each	Name of ingredient
		2	Bay leaf
		6	Cardamom pods
7	210		Granulated sugar
32	960		Water

- → In a large saucepan, place the spices, sugar, and water and bring to the boil.
- → Reduce to a simmer and carefully lower the paneer quenelles into the syrup and simmer for about 5 minutes.
- → Allow the quenelles to cool in the syrup, and then using a slotted spoon, carefully remove to a sheet pan lined with absorbent paper.
- → Discard the syrup after poaching the cheese.

Milk sauce

YIELD: APPROXIMATELY
16 OUNCES, 12 SERVINGS,
1⅓ OUNCES EACH

Oz	Grams	Each	Name of ingredient
32	960		Whole milk
		5	Whole pale green-skinned cardamom pods

TIP: *Taste the sauce to be sure that it tastes clearly of the cardamom. If not, continue cooking and/or add a few more cardamom pods, tasting to confirm that the flavor of the spice comes through.*

- → In a heavy saucepan, bring the milk to the boil with the cardamom pods.
- → Reduce the heat to a simmer and cook the liquid to reduce by half, stirring constantly and thoroughly with a flat-edged wooden spoon, scraping the sides and the bottom of the pan frequently to be sure that the mixture is not burning.
- → When satisfied that the flavor of the cardamom comes through clearly, remove the pods from the liquid.
- → When chilled, the mixture should be thick enough to coat the back of a spoon.
- → If it is too thin, simply return the mixture to the heavy saucepan and continue to cook, stirring constantly, until it reduces slightly.
- → Set the mixture over an ice water bath, stirring to cool.
- → Check for thickness when cold.

Pistachio florentine "bowls"

YIELD: 12 BOWLS, EACH
WEIGHING APPROXIMATELY
2¾ OUNCES EACH, VARY-
ING SLIGHTLY FROM COOKIE
TO COOKIE, DEPENDING ON
HOW THICKLY THE BATTER IS
SPREAD

Oz	Grams	Each	Name of ingredient	Baker's percentages—Ground pistachios and flour total 100%
4	120		Granulated sugar	50
4	120		Ground pistachios	50
4	120		All purpose flour	50
8	240		Unsalted butter, at room temperature	100
4	120		Honey	50
8	240	8	Egg whites, from large eggs	100
2, approximately	60, approximately		Pistachios, ground	50

→ Place sugar and pistachio nuts in a food processor and grind until fine but not pasty. Then combine the mixture with the flour. Set aside.

→ In the bowl of an electric mixer, outfitted with the paddle attachment, cream the butter until soft and light. Add the honey and mix until blended. Add the egg whites and mix until incorporated. Finally, add the ground nut-flour mixture and mix just until the nuts and flour are incorporated, scraping the bowl to ensure that the mixture is thoroughly blended.

→ Using a flat metal spatula, spread the batter for four cookies at a time onto Silpat-lined sheet pans, in a thin, but not translucent, layer shaped in a circle, measuring approximately 4 inches in diameter (approximately 2¾ ounces of batter is used for each cookie).

→ Sprinkle ground pistachios on each cookie.

→ Bake one sheet of the cookies at a time in a preheated 375°F oven for approximately 6 minutes.

→ Remove from the oven and immediately, and while still pliable, form each cookie over the bottom outside curve of a small bowl, measuring approximately 3 inches in diameter. You may need to reheat the florentines to soften them enough to curve.

→ Continue baking and shaping until you have made 12 perfectly shaped florentine bowls.

TIP: *Alternatively you may use a tuile template with a round cutout measuring approximately 4 inches in diameter. Place the template on a Silpat set onto the back of a sheet pan and spread the batter through it in a thin but not translucent layer, removing the template and then repeating the process. It's best to bake only a few of these at a time as they need to be warm to be shaped immediately after they are removed from the oven. If the florentines cool before you have shaped all of them, return them briefly to the oven to soften and then shape immediately.*

Garnish

Each	Name of ingredient
12	Pistachios, shelled, roughly chopped
12	Whole or chopped cashews

Plating and assembly

Divide the milk sauce evenly among the 12 portions. For each serving, use approximately 1½ ounces of milk sauce. Pour the sauce into the florentine bowls and place 2 or 3 quenelles of paneer into the sauce. (If desired, reserve a small amount of the sauce for use on the plate.) Garnish with pistachios and cashews. Serve immediately with a spoon, knife, and fork for each serving.

Walnut Torte, Blue Cheese Mousse, Port Sauce, and Puff Pastry Corkscrew with Candied Walnuts

YIELD: 12 SERVINGS

Walnut torte, blue cheese-mascarpone mousse, port gelée on top, port gelée garnish, puff pastry corkscrew decoration, and candied walnuts. Taking cues from a hallowed British tradition of serving blue cheese, usually Stilton, with aged port and walnuts, this dessert includes elements of each in several forms. Here French Roquefort, mellowed with the addition of mild-flavored Italian mascarpone, replaces the Stilton. Stilton and Roquefort, two members of cheese royalty, differ in two important ways. First, Stilton, shaped in a characteristic cylindrical shape, is made solely from cow's milk. It gains its blue veining as a result of the cheese being pierced once with a long needle, allowing oxygen to enter the interior of the cheese, thereby encouraging the growth of natural bacteria that leads to the formation of blue pockets peppered throughout the cheese. Roquefort is made solely from sheep's milk. It gets its blue-veined appearance thanks to the addition of a special mold, *Penicillium roqueforti*, which is added when the cheese is in its curd form, before it has been completely drained of the whey that separates out when the milk has been cultured.

The walnuts here are in two forms, with some ground into the fine-textured flourless torte and others dipped into hot caramel as a crunchy candied garnish. Instead of being sipped, the port is turned into a tender gelée, used in the mirror-like glaze on the top of the mousse and in small cubes, glistening somewhat like rubies, garnishing the plate.

The order of things:

1. **Make quick puff pastry** and chill
2. **Toast the walnuts** for the walnut torte
3. **Make vanilla syrup** to brush onto the tortes
4. **Make the walnut torte batter**
5. **Bake the walnut tortes,** remove from oven
6. **Make blue cheese-mascarpone mousse**
7. **Place cake layer into the bottom of each entremet ring**
8. **Brush the cakes with vanilla syrup**
9. **Pour half of the blue cheese-mascarpone mousse into each prepared mold** and chill
10. **Roll and cut puff pastry into strips for corkscrew decoration** and chill until ready to bake
11. **Make port gelée** and coat the top of each torte with a thin layer of it
12. **Bake the corkscrew puff pastry** decoration and store at room temperature
13. **Cut port gelée into small cubes** for garnishing the plates

Equipment list:

Two round springform molds, measuring 8 inches in diameter by 1 inch tall, for the walnut tortes

Two entremet rings, measuring 8 inches in diameter by 2 inches tall

Two strips of acetate each measuring 25 inches long by 2½ inches wide

One square cookie cutter, measuring 3 inches square to mold the port gelée

Aluminum foil to line the mold above

Toothpicks to stick in to the walnuts before candying them

Rolled-up cloth dish towel to set under one side of the sauce pan of the hot caramel to make it flow into a deep pool, when candying the walnuts

A Styrofoam block, measuring 3 inches by 4 inches by 2 inches tall, to stand the candied walnuts in to allow them to cool and dry after being dipped into the hot caramel

Walnut torte

YIELD: APPROXIMATELY 32 OUNCES, 2 TORTE LAYERS, EACH 8 INCHES IN DIAMETER BY 1 INCH TALL, EACH WEIGHING APPROXIMATELY 16 OUNCES

Oz	Grams	Each	Name of ingredient	Baker's percentages— Walnuts replace flour in this torte and therefore represent 100%
10	1		**Shelled walnuts**	100
14	420	8 or 9	**Large eggs,** separated	140
2	60		**Granulated sugar**	14 This is used when grinding the walnuts
7	210		**Granulated sugar,** divided	35 Half of the sugar is used with the egg yolks and the other half is used with the egg whites
0.16	4.8	1 t.	**Vanilla extract**	2
		Pinch	**Salt**	.3

Vanilla syrup to brush on tortes after baking

Oz	Grams	Each	Name of ingredient
2–3	60–90		**Simple syrup**
0.16	4.8	1 t.	**Vanilla extract**

TIP: *Do not overbeat the egg whites. They should remain "creamy" in order to incorporate them easily without deflating the mixture. If they are overbeaten they will appear mottled and grainy-looking. What might appear underbeaten will stiffen a bit after being taken from the mixer so do not be tempted to whip more air into them at this point.*

→ Prepare two round springform molds, measuring 8 inches in diameter by 1 inch tall, by first spraying them lightly with pan spray.

→ Line the bottoms of each with a round of parchment paper and then lightly spray the molds again with the pan spray.

→ Set aside.

→ In a preheated 350°F oven, toast the walnuts on a parchment-lined sheet pan, for approximately 10 minutes, or until lightly golden and aromatic.

→ Remove from the oven, cool, and then place the nuts into a food processor with the first quantity of granulated sugar (2 ounces) and process until finely ground.

→ Set aside.

→ Separate the eggs, placing the whites into the bowl of an electric mixer, and set aside.

→ Using an electric mixer outfitted with the whisk attachment, beat the egg yolks with half of the second quantity of sugar and vanilla extract until light in color and fluffy in texture.

→ Place the bowl of egg whites onto the electric mixer, outfit it with the whisk attachment, and whip the egg whites with the remaining half of the second quantity of sugar and the salt to soft but shiny peaks.

→ Gently but thoroughly fold the walnuts into the egg yolk mixture.

→ Gently fold in the beaten whites.

→ Immediately pour the mixture into the prepared pans, set the pans onto a sheet pan, and bake in a preheated 350°F oven for approximately 45 minutes, or until a skewer inserted into the center of each torte comes out clean.

→ Remove the tortes from the oven and cool on a rack.

→ Set aside until ready to assemble the dessert.

→ For vanilla syrup, combine the simple syrup and the vanilla in a small bowl and set aside.

Oz	Grams	Each	Name of ingredient
0.8	24	8	**Gelatin sheets**
10	300		**Roquefort cheese,** room temperature
20	600		**Mascarpone,** room temperature
6	180		**Simple syrup**
8	240		**Heavy cream,** whipped to soft peaks

→ Place the gelatin sheets into a small bowl with enough cold water to cover.

→ Allow to soften, and when soft, remove the gelatin from the water, squeezing out excess liquid. Place the squeezed-out gelatin into a small bowl and set aside.

→ In the bowl of an electric mixer outfitted with the paddle attachment, beat the Roquefort and mascarpone until smooth.

→ In a small heavy saucepan, heat the simple syrup until hot, remove from the heat, and then add the bloomed gelatin, stirring until completely dissolved.

→ Allow syrup and gelatin mixture to cool slightly and then add it to the cheese mixture, mixing with the paddle just to incorporate.

→ In the bowl of an electric mixer, outfitted with the whisk attachment, whip the cream to soft peaks and then fold it into the cheese mixture.

→ Set aside.

Assembly

→ Line two entremet rings, measuring 8 inches in diameter by 2 inches tall, each with a strip of acetate 25 inches long by 2½ inches wide.

→ Clip or staple the acetate together where the two ends meet.

→ Place one torte into each of two entremet rings.

→ Brush the tortes lightly with the vanilla syrup just to moisten.

→ Pour half of the mousse mixture into each ring and place the tortes in the refrigerator on a level shelf to set.

→ When set, remove from the refrigerator, place the torte on a level surface, and pour a thin layer of port gelée evenly over the top of the mousse.

Oz	Grams	Each	Name of ingredient
4	12	4	Gelatin sheets
8	240		Simple syrup
4	120		Port

YIELD: APPROXIMATELY
12 OUNCES, ENOUGH FOR
A THIN LAYER ON TOP OF
THE MOUSSES AND ALSO FOR
CUBED GELÉE GARNISH, EACH
CUBE MEASURING ½ INCH ON
ALL SIDES, ALLOWING THREE
CUBES PER SERVING

Prepare the mold for the port gelée cube garnish as follows

→ Wrap the bottom of a square cookie cutter, measuring 3 inches square, with a square of heavy gauge aluminum foil, measuring 5 inches square.

→ Place the mold onto a small sheet pan and set aside.

→ Place the gelatin sheets into a small bowl with enough cold water to cover.

→ Allow to soften, and when soft, remove the gelatin from the water, squeezing out excess liquid.

- → Place the squeezed-out gelatin into a small bowl and set aside.
- → Bloom gelatin until softened.
- → Heat simple syrup until hot.
- → Add the bloomed gelatin and stir to dissolve completely.
- → Add the port and allow the mixture to cool.
- → The mixture should still be flowing.

Coat the tops of each torte as follows

- → Pour a thin layer of the cooled but still flowing mixture on top of each of the tortes, tilting the tortes, if necessary, to coat the tops evenly.
- → Then return the tortes to a level shelf in the refrigerator until ready to serve.

Make the cubed gelée garnish as follows

- → Pour the remaining gelée (rewarm gently over low heat, if necessary, to make the mixture flow) into the prepared square mold to a depth of approximately ½ inch. Place the mold on a level shelf in the refrigerator.
- → Allow to set, and when set, unwrap the foil under the mold and remove the mold.
- → Cut the gelée into thirty-six ½ inch cubes (six rows of six on each side), and store the cubes, refrigerated, until ready to plate the dessert. (You will need three cubes per serving.)

TIP: *Tawny or ruby port works best here as a complement to the veined cheese–based mousse.*

Cinnamon puff pastry corkscrews

YIELD: APPROXIMATELY
1½ POUNDS

Puff pastry dough

Oz	Grams	Each	Name of ingredient	Baker's percentages
10	300		**All purpose flour**	100
10	300		**Unsalted butter, cool,** waxy, not soft or greasy	100
.03	1	Pinch	**Salt**	0.3
5	150		**Ice water**	50

This dough may be made either by hand or by machine, depending on the size of the batch.

Mixing by hand

- → Cut butter into 1½ inch chunks.
- → Place flour and salt into a large bowl.
- → Mix to combine.
- → Add the butter and coat with the flour and salt mixture.
- → Add ice water all at once and lightly mix until the dough coheres into a rough mass. Do not overprocess.
- → Turn the ragged mass of dough out onto a lightly floured surface and tap the dough firmly with a rolling pin to coax the dough into a roughly cohesive shape.
- → Check to be sure that the dough is not sticking to the surface.

Making by machine

- → Using the paddle attachment, mix the flour and salt at low speed to combine.
- → Then add the butter, cut into 1½ inch chunks.

- On slow speed, mix just to coat the butter with the flour.
- With the machine running, add ice water all at once, and briefly mix, turning the machine on and off rather than allowing it to run continuously, just until the dough becomes a rough mass. It is better to underprocess rather than overprocess the dough. The mixer should be turned on and off during this step rather than allowing it to run continuously.

Rolling the dough

- Turn the ragged mass of dough out onto a floured surface and tap firmly with the rolling pin to coax the dough into a roughly cohesive shape.
- Check to be sure that the dough is not sticking to the surface.
- Use a plastic dough scraper frequently to free the dough from the work surface, as necessary, if it is sticking.
- Flour the work surface *lightly* from time to time.
- Once the dough has been rolled to a rough rectangular shape, mentally divide the dough in thirds and fold one third of the dough from the end closest to you toward the middle and the other third over the first third to create a package of dough made up of three thick layers.
- Turn the packet of dough 90 degrees so that the short side is facing you.
- Then roll the dough to lengthen it again to a rectangle measuring roughly 7 inches by 12 inches. Fold in thirds again, turn it 90 degrees so that the short side is facing you again.
- Now roll the dough again to a rectangle measuring roughly 7 inches by 12 inches.
- Chill in between the rolling and folding steps if the dough shows signs of softening or sticking to the work surface.
- Repeat the rolling and folding once more, chilling as needed if the dough shows signs of softening or is being resistant to rolling. (See following pages.)

Making Quick Puff Pastry

Place cold butter, flour, and salt together in the mixing bowl.

Briefly mix the butter, flour, and salt for Quick Puff Pastry, using paddle attachment.

Add ice water just until dough coheres lightly and continue mixing.

Remove the dough from the mixing bowl onto a floured work surface. It will be a rough, shaggy mass, as shown here.

Roll dough out using a floured rolling pin to compress the dough and begin to flatten out large pieces of butter into long, thinner layers.

Continuing the compressing and rolling of the dough so that it coheres into a smooth and roughly laminated dough.

Baked quick puff pastry showing lamination.

→ Chill until firm. (The dough may be refrigerated overnight but for longer storage, freeze it, and thaw when needed in the refrigerator.)

Complete the cinnamon puff pastry corkscrews as follows

Oz	Grams	Each	Name of ingredient
2	60		Cold water
2	60		Granulated sugar
0.06	1.8	1 t.	Ground cinnamon

→ Roll chilled dough on a lightly floured surface to a rectangle measuring approximately 6 inches wide by 12 inches long by approximately ¼ inch thick.

→ Combine the sugar and the cinnamon in a small bowl and set aside.

→ Brush dough lightly with cold water and then coat the top of the dough evenly with cinnamon sugar mixture.

→ Cut the dough lengthwise into ½ inch wide strips, measuring approximately 12 inches in length.

→ Twist each strip several times, holding one end in place to achieve a twisted cookie with four each alternating cinnamon-sugar-coated and uncoated areas along the dough.

→ Place the strips onto a parchment-lined baking sheet and chill to firm.

→ Bake in a preheated 400°F oven for approximately 15 minutes, or until golden brown and fully puffed.

→ Remove from the oven and place on a cooling rack to cool to room temperature.

→ If not serving within a few hours, store in an airtight container until ready to plate the dessert.

→ These are best served within a few hours of baking.

Candied walnuts

Oz	Grams	Each	Name of ingredient
		12	Whole shelled walnuts
6	180		Granulated sugar
3	90		Water
1	30		Corn syrup

→ Place toothpicks into the center bottom of each whole walnut.

→ In a medium-sized heavy saucepan, bring the sugar, water, and the corn syrup to the boil, without stirring.

→ Continue to cook the mixture until golden amber in color.

→ Remove from the heat and carefully prop one side of the bottom of the pan on a rolled-up towel to make the hot caramel flow into a deep pool on the other side of the pan.

→ Dip the nuts into the hot, still flowing caramel and then carefully insert the toothpicks into a Styrofoam block placed onto a parchment-lined baking sheet.

→ If desired, briefly hold the nuts over the parchment until the caramel stops flowing, leaving a thin thread protruding from the end of each nut.

→ Alternatively, simply dip the toothpick-impaled nuts into the caramel and allow them to dry on a Silpat until ready to use.

Assembly and plating

Cut each torte into six even wedges, using a knife dipped into hot water and dried after each cut. Place a wedge of the torte onto the plate, with the wide end toward the front of the plate. Garnish the top of the torte with a candied walnut. Place three cubes of the port gelée in front of, and near the wide end of, the torte, and then place a puff pastry corkscrew to the left of the cake. Serve immediately.

Citrus Walnut Sour Cream Cake

YIELD: 12 SERVINGS

Citrus Walnut Sour Cream Cake with cactus pear sorbet, pink pomelo segments, candied pomelo peel, and candied walnut garnish. Inspired by a refreshing, blushing pink Technicolored Oaxacan drink, a blend of prickly pear juice and horchata, a creamy cinnamon-scented rice-based liquid, this dessert has an unusual and colorful palette of ingredients and textures. A square of a moist, close-grained walnut and citrus-flavored cake, tenderized and enriched with sour cream, anchors the presentation, flanked by a scoop of faintly floral cactus pear sorbet. Complementing the candied pomelo peel whose astringent personality has been mellowed by long cooking in a sugar syrup are pink wedges of the same fruit which, when whole, looks like a grapefruit on steroids. Walnuts appear in a second form here as an adornment on the cake and come coated with crunchy, deep amber-colored caramel. The sour cream–based plating sauce, thinned with a combination of lightly sweetened lemon and orange juice, is a reminder of the creamy inspiration for the dessert.

The order of things:

1. **Make simple syrup for sorbet**
2. **Make cactus pear sorbet**
3. **Make candied pomelo peel**
4. **Filet the pomelo into segments** to be used as garnish
5. **Make candied walnut garnish**
6. **Make citrus soaking syrup**
7. **Make citrus walnut sour cream cake batter and bake**
8. **Make sour cream plating sauce**

Equipment list:

Cooling rack with close-spaced wires to air-dry the candied pomelo peel

12 thin skewers, with a sharp point, used in candying the walnuts for the candied walnut garnish

Square of Styrofoam or floral "oasis," approximately 6 inches by 6 inches by 4 inches square, covered with aluminum foil, for use in allowing the walnuts to drip and dry after being candied

Rectangular baking pan measuring 6 inches by 8 inches by 2 inches deep, to bake the citrus walnut sour cream cake

Cactus pear sorbet

YIELD: APPROXIMATELY
20 OUNCES, 12 SERVINGS,
EACH SERVING APPROXI-
MATELY 1⅔ OUNCES

For simple syrup

Oz	Grams	Each	Name of ingredient
7	210		Granulated sugar
4	120		Water
1	5	1	Lemon zest, grated

To complete the sorbet

Oz	Grams	Each	Name of ingredient
12	360	6	Ripe red-fleshed cactus or prickly pears (*tuna*), or commercially prepared frozen fruit puree, seedless
1.25	38		Fresh lemon juice, sieved
		¼ t.	Vanilla extract

→ Make the simple syrup and let cool.

→ When cool, refrigerate until cold.

→ Then puree the fresh cactus pears with the simple syrup.

→ Pass through a sieve set over a bowl and add the lemon juice and vanilla to the puree. (If using the commercially prepared fruit puree, simply thaw it and proceed as above.)

→ Freeze the mixture in an ice cream machine.

→ Remove ice cream to a container, cover, and store in the freezer until ready to serve the dessert.

Candied pomelo peel and pomelo segments for garnish

YIELD: MORE THAN WHAT IS
USED IN THE 12 SERVINGS
OF THIS DESSERT

Oz	Grams	Name of ingredient
Variable	Variable	Whole large pink-fleshed pomelos
As needed to cover the peel		Water
16	480	Simple syrup
1	30	Corn syrup
4 to 6, approximately	120 to 180, approximately	Granulated sugar

Keeps well, covered, in a cool dry place, for at least 2 weeks due to the high level of sugar, which acts as a preservative.

Note: If pomelos are unavailable, you may substitute pink grapefruits.

→ Using a small sharp knife, cut a thin slice from the top and bottom of the fruit.

→ Then, following the contours of the fruit, remove the peel in wide slices, with a thin layer of white pith attached.

→ Reserve the fruit to be used as garnish when plating the dessert.

→ With the peeled fruit placed securely on a cutting surface, continue removing any additional pith from the fruit and discard the pith.

→ Now, using a small sharp knife, remove the citrus segments in filets between the membranes that hold the fruit together, making the first cut toward the center of the fruit and the next away from the center.

→ Continue this process until all of the filets have been removed.

→ Place the filets in a covered container and refrigerate until ready to serve the dessert.

→ Place the prepared peel into a saucepan filled with water.

→ Bring the water to the boil and then reduce to simmer, cooking for approximately 10 minutes.

- → Remove from the heat and remove the peel from the water.
- → Rinse the peel in cold water and return it to the saucepan with fresh water.
- → Bring again to the boil, reduce to a simmer and cook again for approximately 10 minutes longer.
- → Repeat the rinsing and boiling process once more, cooking the peel, covered with water, until tender.
- → After the last cooking, drain and rinse the peel.
- → Place the now tender peel into a medium-sized heavy saucepan with the simple syrup and cook over low heat until the peel becomes translucent.
- → Remove from the syrup, allow to drain, and then dip into the granulated sugar, coating both sides thoroughly.
- → Allow to dry on a cooling rack, set over a sheet pan and store at room temperature.
- → With a heavy sharp knife, cut the candied peel into thick julienne, measuring approximately 1½ to 2 inches long by approximately about ⅛ inch wide. Use four or five strips per serving.
- → Set aside until ready to plate the dessert.

Candied walnuts as garnish
YIELD: 1 PER SERVING

Oz	Grams	Each	Name of ingredient
		18	Walnut halves
16	480		Sugar
4	120		Water
4	120		Corn syrup

Note: The amount of ingredients shown above yields more than 12 garnishes so that you may select the best, most perfectly shaped and dipped ones to use as garnishes.

- → Place toothpicks securely into the center of the flat back of each walnut half.
- → Place a small square of Styrofoam or floral "oasis," approximately 6 inches by 6 inches by 4 inches square, covered with aluminum foil, onto a baking sheet lined with a Silpat or parchment paper. Set aside.
- → In a small heavy saucepan, bring the sugar, water and corn syrup to the boil.
- → Reduce the heat to medium and continue to cook the syrup until it turns a golden color, about 310°F.
- → Quickly remove the caramel from the heat, prop the saucepan at an angle so that the caramel creates a 2 inch deep pool.
- → Submerge the nuts, one by one, into the pool of caramel, removing them carefully.
- → As the nut is removed from the caramel, carefully the end of the toothpick opposite from the nut into the side of the Styrofoam or oasis, allowing the caramel to drip off the nut in a long thin thread.
- → Allow the dipped nuts to cool without disturbing until ready to garnish the dessert.

Citrus soaking syrup
YIELD: APPROXIMATELY 5 OUNCES

Oz	Grams	Each	Name of ingredient
1.5	45	1 medium lemon	**Fresh lemon juice,** sieved
2, approx	60	1 medium orange	**Fresh orange juice,** sieved
3	90		**Granulated sugar** or Lyle's Golden Syrup

- → Warm juices in a small saucepan over low to medium heat with sugar until sugar dissolves. If using the Lyle's Golden Syrup instead of granulated sugar, be sure to watch it carefully so that it does not burn as it dissolves into the citrus juices.
- → Set aside to cool.

Citrus walnut sour cream cake

YIELD: APPROXIMATELY
46 OUNCES, 12 SQUARE
SLICES, EACH MEASURING
2 INCHES BY 2 INCHES BY
2 INCHES TALL, WEIGHING
SLIGHTLY LESS THAN
4 OUNCES EACH

Oz	Grams	Each	Name of ingredient	Baker's percentages
10	300		**All purpose flour**	100
0.3	10		**Baking soda**	3
0.2	6		**Baking powder**	2
	1	Pinch	**Salt**	0.3
8	240	5	**Large eggs,** separated	80
8	240		**Unsalted butter,** at room temperature	80
4	120		**Granulated sugar**	40
0.25	7	From 1 medium orange	**Fresh orange zest,** finely grated	2
0.25	7	From 1 large lemon	**Fresh lemon zest,** finely grated	2
3	90		**Granulated sugar**	30
4	120		**Walnuts,** finely ground	40
5.65	170		**Sour cream**	57

TIP: *Commercially ground walnuts will yield a finer-grained texture in the resulting cake. If commercially ground walnuts are unavailable, use a food processor to grind the nuts, placing them along with an ounce or so of granulated sugar (additional to what is used in the recipe) and grind, pulsing the machine, scraping the sides of the processor bowl frequently to help prevent the nuts from turning into a paste.*

→ Grease a rectangular baking pan measuring 6 inches by 8 inches by 2 inches deep and then line the bottom and sides of the pan neatly with parchment paper. Spray the parchment paper with pan release spray and set aside.

→ Sift flour, baking soda, baking powder, and salt into a large bowl. Set aside.

→ Separate the eggs placing the yolks in one small bowl and the whites into the bowl of an electric mixer outfitted with the whisk attachment. You should have approximately 3 to 4 ounces of egg yolk and 5 ounces of egg whites.

→ In the bowl of an electric mixer outfitted with the paddle attachment, cream butter until light in color and texture.

→ Add the first quantity of the sugar and blend, scraping the bottom and sides of the bowl to ensure that the mixture is well blended.

→ Add the zest and mix until evenly incorporated.

→ Add the egg yolks gradually, mixing to emulsify, and scraping the bottom and sides of the bowl occasionally.

→ Fold the walnuts and then the sour cream into the cake batter base.

→ Whip the whites with the second quantity of sugar to stiff but shiny peaks. Set aside.

→ Then gently but thoroughly fold the dry ingredients into the batter and finally, fold in the beaten egg whites, scraping the bowl well.

→ Pour the mixture into the prepared baking pan and bake in a preheated 350°F oven for approximately 1 hour, or until the cake tests done.

→ When the cake is done, remove it from the oven and immediately pour half of citrus soaking liquid (above) over the cake, reserving 2 ounces of it to use in the sour cream plating sauce (below), and the remainder to pour over the cake just before serving.

→ Cut the cake into 12 squares, in rows of 3 along the 6 inch side, and in rows of 4 along the 8 inch side, with each serving of cake measuring 2 inches square.

→ Set the sliced cakes on a parchment-lined sheet pan and cover.

→ Store at room temperature if you are serving the dessert on the same day. If not, refrigerate the sliced cake, covered, and bring to room temperature just before serving.

Sour cream
plating sauce
YIELD: APPROXIMATELY
10 OUNCES, 12 SERVINGS,
EACH WEIGHING
APPROXIMATELY ¾ OUNCE

Oz	Grams	Name of ingredient
8	240	Sour cream
2	60	Citrus soaking syrup

→ In a small bowl, combine the sour cream with the citrus soaking syrup, whisking lightly just to blend, without aerating.

→ Assemble and plate the dessert as follows.

Assembly and plating

Place sauce on plate. Place one square piece of cake on sauce. Place several citrus segments, drained of juice, on the plate next to the cake. Place the candied pomelo peel and a candied walnut on top of the cake. Drizzle with additional soaking syrup if desired. Lastly, place a quenelle of cactus pear sorbet to the side of the cake and serve immediately.

Creamsicle in the Round, with Orange Gelée and Vanilla Cream Semifreddo

YIELD: 12 SERVINGS

Three main elements come together in a bowl. Creamsicle in the round, vanilla semifreddo and orange sorbet molded into cones, garnished with a tuile cookie Popsicle stick, set afloat in a sea of citrus gelée. A kid's treat grows up in this fanciful tribute to the winter season's freshest citrus fruits. During the coldest and often dreariest months of the year, when sunshine is in short supply, nature's bounty of citrus fruits (from oranges and tangerines to all of the newly emerging hybrids) bring bright sunny flavor to the table. If statistics are reliable, surprisingly more frozen desserts are consumed during winter than at any other time of the year. Celebrating the fruits of the season, this dessert-in-a-bowl features contrasts both in temperature (the cold, but melt-in-your-mouth, citrus gelée playing against the frozen creamsicle) and in texture, with a vanilla semifreddo enriched with mascarpone and cream juxtaposed with a deliberately icy orange sorbet.

The order of things:

1. **Dry the tangerine peel** at warm room temperature until crisp; **then pulverize**
2. **Make vanilla semifreddo**
3. **Make orange sorbet**
4. **Fill conical molds** with each flavor and freeze
5. **Cut each cone shape** of semifreddo and orange sorbet vertically in half
6. **Re-form the cones** by filling them each with a half cone of semifreddo and a half cone of sorbet and refreeze
7. **Make plain and cocoa-flavored tuile batters**
8. **Bake tuiles**
9. **Make citrus gelée** and pour into serving bowls
10. **Prepare citrus segments garnish**
11. **Decorate edges of the serving bowls** with a dusting of powdered dried tangerine peel

Equipment list:

Two **silicone plaques** each with 12 conical-shaped indentations, each measuring 2¾ inches in diameter at the top by 2½ inches tall, one for the vanilla semifreddo, and the other for the orange sorbet

12 stainless steel or stainless steel–coated **pastry tips** or other small conical shapes to act as place savers in the citrus gelée before serving the dessert

Heavy sheet of acetate, slightly less than ⅛ inch thick

X-ACTO knife used to cut the Popsicle stick shape in the acetate, as a template

Parchment paper cone for piping wood graining cocoa-flavored tuile paste to create the "Popsicle" stick tuile

Vanilla semifreddo

Oz	Grams	Each	Name of ingredient
3	90	2	Whole large eggs
4	120		Granulated sugar
14	420		Mascarpone
0.16	4.8	1 t.	Vanilla extract
11	330		Heavy cream

- Arrange two silicone plaques each with 12 conical-shaped indentations, each measuring 2¾ inches in diameter at the top by 2½ inches tall, onto empty cardboard egg crates or use foil to support the molds so that they are secure and upright.
- Place each plaque onto a sheet pan. Set aside until ready to fill.
- In a stainless steel bowl set over a saucepan of simmering water, whisk the eggs and sugar until the mixture reaches 185°F. The mixture should be light in color, airy and coat the back of a wooden spoon.
- Remove from the heat immediately and place the mixture over an ice water bath to cool it quickly.
- Place mascarpone in another bowl and add the cooled egg-sugar mixture to it, whisking until smooth.
- Mix in the vanilla extract.
- In the bowl of an electric mixer outfitted with the whisk attachment, whip the cream to soft peaks. Do not overbeat.
- Fold the softly whipped cream into the eggs-sugar-mascarpone mixture and pipe the mixture into the 12 conical indentations, being careful not to create air pockets as you fill the molds.
- Freeze until firm.
- After filling the 12 indentations, you may have extra semifreddo. Freeze it either in additional silicone molds or pour it into an acetate sheet–lined rectangular pan and freeze, well covered, for another use.
- Make orange sorbet as follows.

Orange sorbet

Oz	Grams	Name of ingredient
20	600	**Fresh orange juice,** sieved
4	120	**Simple syrup**

TIP: *It is best to halve the semifreddo and the sorbet when they are both well frozen, using a sharp knife, dipped briefly into hot water. If you note signs of melting, place them back into the conical molds and return them to the freezer before proceeding.*

- Combine the juice and syrup and pour the mixture into the bowl of an electric ice cream machine.
- Freeze until semi-firm.
- Once the sorbet is semi-firm, fill the 12 conical-shaped indentations in the second silicone plaque with the sorbet and freeze until firm.
- When both the vanilla cream semifreddo and orange sorbets are frozen, unmold each one at a time. Cut each of the frozen vanilla cream semifreddos in half from top to bottom.
- Cut each of the orange sorbets in half from top to bottom.
- Reassemble the conical shapes by placing one half cone of the vanilla cream semifreddo and one half cone of orange sorbet, side by side in the conical molds.
- Allow to freeze again.
- When they are frozen, remove from molds to trim approximately ⅓ inch from the bottom pointed end of each to allow it to stand firmly in the bowl of gelée.
- Smooth the outside surfaces if needed with a hot knife or spatula.
- Using the point of a knife, make a ½ inch deep slit into the center of the flat side of the Popsicle wide enough to insert the tuile Popsicle stick easily into it.
- Return the Popsicles to the freezer until ready to assemble and serve the dessert.
- Make the wood-grained tuiles as follows.

Oz	Grams	Each	Name of ingredient	Baker's percentages
4	120		Unsalted butter, soft	80
4	120		Granulated sugar	80
4	120	From 4 large eggs	Egg whites	80
4	120		All purpose flour	80
1	30		Cocoa powder	20

Batter for wood-grained tuile Popsicle stick

YIELD: 17 OUNCES, 12 OUNCES PLAIN BATTER AND 5 OUNCES COCOA BATTER

→ In the bowl of an electric mixer outfitted with the paddle attachment, cream the butter until light. Add the granulated sugar and mix until well blended.

→ Add the egg whites and mix until incorporated, scraping the bottom and sides of the bowl as necessary to ensure that the mixture is well blended.

→ Add the flour and mix only until the flour disappears.

→ Set aside one fourth of this mixture and mix the cocoa powder into it to create a brown-colored tuile batter used for creating the "wood grain" design.

Note: Depending on the wood-grain design that you create, you may have extra of the cocoa-flavored tuile batter. Reserve any leftover, refrigerated, for another use.

To make the tuile template

→ Using an X-ACTO knife or box cutter, cut an oblong-shaped opening, 2 inches long by ¾ inch, with rounded edges at one end and a triangular-shaped point at the other, in a heavy (slightly less than ⅛ inch thick) sheet of acetate to act as the template for the tuiles.

→ Cut away excess around the design, leaving about 1½ inches all around, and an elongated piece of the acetate on one side to use as a "handle" to lift the template away from the Silpat when you are laying the batter onto it.

Laying out the tuile batter and then baking it

→ Beginning at one end of a Silpat placed onto an inverted half-sheet pan, position the template onto the Silpat and using a small spatula, spread a thin but not translucent layer of the plain tuile batter into the cut out area.

→ With a back and forth motion, spread the batter evenly.

→ Remove the template and repeat the process, until you have created 12 Popsicle stick shapes.

→ Fill a small parchment cone with the cocoa tuile batter.

→ Cut the end of the cone so that there is a small opening, large enough to allow the batter to be extruded in a thin line.

→ Pipe a little of the mixture onto a spatula or other surface to check the thickness of the line being produced.

→ Once satisfied that it is the right thickness, proceed by piping a wood-grain pattern onto each tuile Popsicle stick on the Silpat. (See photograph on page 152.)

→ Bake the tuiles in a preheated 350°F oven for 8–10 minutes.

→ Bake only until the tuiles feel dry to the touch but not overly browned.

→ Remove from the oven and cool on a rack.

→ When the cookies have cooled, store them in an airtight container, outfitted with a piece of limestone or a packet of silica gel, to help retain their crispness.

TIP: *Be aware that the tuile paste spreads slightly so the thinner the lines piped out to resemble wood graining, the more convincing as a simulation of wood grain the design will be. So when cutting the end of the parchment paper cornet, be sure to snip off just enough to allow the batter to be piped out in a very thin line.*

Citrus gelée

YIELD: APPROXIMATELY
24 OUNCES

Oz	Grams	Each	Name of ingredient
24, approximately	720		**Fresh citrus juice**—the Cara Cara variety, if available, has a pinkish orange colored juice which works well here
As needed			**Sugar,** optional, to taste
.7	21	7 sheets	**Sheet gelatin,** bloomed in cold water

→ Bloom the gelatin sheets in enough water to cover them.

→ When softened, remove from the water and squeeze excess liquid out of the sheets.

→ In a medium-sized heavy saucepan, heat half of the orange juice.

→ Add the bloomed gelatin and stir to dissolve.

→ Add the remaining orange juice and pour this mixture into 12 shallow serving bowls to a depth of about 1 inch.

→ Carefully place these on a perfectly level shelf in the refrigerator.

→ Place a flat-bottomed pastry tip in the center of each bowl to act as a place saver while the gelée sets.

→ When the dessert is served, the pastry tip is removed and then the creamsicle is placed, flat-bottomed side down into the hole left by the pastry tip.

Garnishes

Each	Name of ingredient
4	**Oranges,** peeled, pith and membrane removed

For the filleted citrus garnish

→ Using a sharp knife, cut a thin slice from the top and bottom of each fruit.

→ Using a small sharp knife, remove the skin and pith from the oranges, cutting from top to bottom in a curving motion, following the contour of the fruit.

→ Remove the filets of the fruit by cutting between the thin membranes that separate each wedge.

→ With an in-and-out motion, release the filets of orange by making one cut toward the center of the fruit and the next cut away from the center. The filet should release cleanly from the membrane that holds it in place.

→ Repeat this process until all of the filets have been removed.

→ Reserve in a covered container, refrigerated, until ready to serve the dessert.

Oz	Grams	Name of ingredient
1 to 2, approximately	30 to 60	**Powdered tangerine peel,** made by drying the peel from the fresh tangerines at room temperature, and then once fully dry, powdering it in a spice grinder

→ To prepare dried tangerine peel, remove peel from the fruit and place at room temperature, uncovered, overnight or until dry and brittle.

→ When dry, place the dried rind in a spice grinder and process until the peel is reduced to a fine powder.

→ Pass through a fine sieve, if desired, to remove any larger, more-coarse particles.

→ Keep in an airtight container at cool room temperature for longer storage.

Oz	Grams	Name of ingredient
4, approximately or as needed	120	Corn syrup

Corn syrup to brush on edge to apply the dried tangerine peel garnish

Assembly and plating

When ready to serve, remove the serving bowls from the refrigerator. Using a small pastry brush, paint a thin coat of corn syrup on the edge of each bowl and cover this area lightly but thoroughly with the powdered tangerine peel. In order to ensure a clean precise presentation, be careful not to allow any of the powder to disperse elsewhere in the bowl. Then remove the pastry tips or other conical shaped pieces from the gelée-filled bowls, which were acting as place savers. Position one vanilla cream semifreddo/orange sorbet cone upright into the hole that remains. Carefully place one wood-grained Popsicle stick tuile into the top center of each of the cones. Garnish the bowls with filleted citrus segments. Serve immediately.

Tangerine Dream

YIELD: 12 SERVINGS

Tangerine Dream—candied whole Pixie tangerine, hollowed out, filled with tarragon-scented tangerine sorbet, gratin of tangerine, bitter chocolate bouchon, and hibiscus sauce. Here, tangerines—in this case, of the Pixie variety (other seedless varieties will work as well)—a gift of the winter citrus season wrapped in candied edible package, are featured in one frozen element and one warm one, each of which brings out a different side of the tangerine's personality. When served warm, their sweet and tart duality is accentuated. In the frozen sorbet, the fresh unheated tangerine juice, enlivened with the licorice taste of fresh tarragon, takes on a refreshing intensity and clears the palate between bites of the warmed chocolate bouchon with its truffle center. Having been well cooked in syrup until tender, the confited tangerine shell is more than just a container for the sorbet. It will soften enough at the table when at room temperature for a few minutes to provide a touch of something tangy that bites back just a little. On the plate flows a crimson-colored river of sauce, made from cooking the dried calyxes of the hibiscus flower also known as *jamaica* (pronounced ha-MY-ee-ka). Favored in Mexico as a base for refreshing iced drinks or *aguas frescas*, here it adds another sweet-tart element and a stunning color contrast to the other parts of this dessert.

The order of things:

1. **Prepare the confited tangerines** and store at room temperature, if using the same day; if not, refrigerate, covered and remove from the refrigerator as needed

2. **Prepare the tangerine sorbet** and freeze

3. **Make ganache for centers of bitter chocolate bouchon cakes**

4. **Make bitter chocolate bouchon batter**

5. **Make gratin custard mixture,** assemble gratins and bake; cool and then store in the refrigerator, lightly covered, until ready to serve

6. **Make hibiscus sauce**

7. **Complete the gratin by caramelizing sugar on top of each,** as ordered

8. **Bake bitter chocolate bouchon cakes** *to order*

Equipment list:

Small muffin tins, about 1½ inches in diameter, measured at the top

12 small shallow round gratin dishes, each measuring about 2 inches in diameter by ¾ inch deep

Torch for melting sugar on top of the tangerine gratins

Small serrated-ended spoon, or regular or demitasse-sized teaspoon, for scraping the flesh out of the confited tangerine shells

Confited tangerines

YIELD: 12 CONFITED
TANGERINE SHELLS,
ONE PER SERVING

Lbs	Grams	Each	Name
2	960		Simple syrup
		12	**Medium-sized seedless tangerines,** whole, weighing about 2 oz each

→ In a large wide sauté pan, approximately 3 inches deep, bring the simple syrup to a boil.

→ Reduce to a low simmer and place the tangerines into the syrup.

→ Cook, over low, until the tangerines are tender but not falling apart, about 40 minutes.

→ After cooking, remove the tangerines from the syrup.

→ With a small serrated knife, with the tangerine stem side up, make a horizontal cut all the way through the tangerine, one third of the way down from the top.

→ Then, remove the tops of each tangerine, using a small serrated-ended spoon, gently and carefully scrape the flesh out of the shells and discard what has been scraped out.

→ Reserve both parts of each shell. Refrigerate until ready to fill.

Tarragon-scented tangerine sorbet

YIELD: APPROXIMATELY
14 OUNCES, 12 SERVINGS,
EACH WEIGHING APPROXI-
MATELY 1¹⁄₆ OUNCES

Tarragon-scented simple syrup

Oz	Grams	Each	Name of ingredient
6	180		**Simple syrup**
1	30	8 to 10 approximately	**Fresh tarragon sprigs**

→ In a medium-sized saucepan, combine the simple syrup and tarragon.

→ Bring to the boil and then reduce to a simmer, cooking for 5 minutes.

→ Remove from the heat and cover, allowing the syrup to infuse for 15 minutes.

→ The tarragon flavor should come through clearly. If not, return to the heat and simmer for an additional 5 minutes, then remove the saucepan from the heat, cover, and allow to infuse for an additional 15 minutes.

→ When fully infused, pass the mixture through a fine sieve set over a bowl.

→ Chill the mixture, either in the refrigerator, or over an ice water bath until cold.

To complete the sorbet

Oz	Grams	Each	Name of ingredient
10	300		**Tangerine juice**
4	120		**Simple syrup infused with fresh tarragon**
		12 sprigs, 1½ inches long	**Fresh tarragon** as garnish

→ When the infused syrup (from above) is cold, add the tangerine juice and pour the mixture into the bowl of an electric ice cream machine.

→ Freeze until semi-firm, and then fill the tangerine shells with the mixture, placing on a sheet pan.

→ When all are filled, place the sheet pan into the freezer, place one tangerine shell top onto each tangerine shell, cover the sheet pan, and then freeze until firm.

→ Store in the freezer until ready to serve the dessert.

Oz	Grams	Each	Name of ingredient	Baker's percentages
		48	**Fresh seedless tangerine segments,** any white pith removed	
24	720		**Heavy cream**	100
16	480	24	**Egg yolks** from large eggs	67
0.5 oz	15		**Vanilla extract**	2
12	360		**Granulated sugar**	50
4 to 6	120 to 180		**Granulated sugar** for caramelizing the tops of each gratin	

→ Place 12 small shallow round gratin dishes, each measuring about 2 inches in diameter by ¾ inch deep, on a half-sheet pan.

→ Place 4 tangerine segments in each.

→ In a medium-sized bowl, without aerating, combine the heavy cream, the egg yolks, vanilla, and sugar.

→ Place the sheet pan on the middle rack of the oven.

→ Pull the rack halfway out and then pour the liquid over the segments, without spilling it.

→ Pour hot water into the sheet pan to reach halfway up the sides of the gratin dishes, and then carefully push the oven rack into position.

→ Bake in a preheated 350°F oven for approximately 20 minutes, or until set.

→ Remove from the oven and chill, covered, in the refrigerator until ready to serve.

→ When ready to serve, cover the tops of each gratin with a thin but even layer of granulated sugar and torch to brown slightly and evenly just before serving.

Oz	Grams	Each	Name of ingredient	Baker's percentages
8	240		**58% bittersweet chocolate**	200
4	120		**Unsalted butter**	100
2	60		**Granulated sugar**	50
0.25	7.5		**Tangerine zest**, grated	6
4	120		**All purpose flour**	100
2	60	3	**Egg yolks** from large eggs	50
0.25	7.5		**Baking powder**	6
	1		**Salt**	.8

Oz	Grams	Name of ingredient	Baker's percentages
3	90	**58% bittersweet chocolate**	100
1.25	38	**Heavy cream**	42

TIP: *For best results, be sure the ganache balls are well frozen. This will yield a discernible fudgy mass at the center of the chocolate bouchon cakes.*

→ Finely chop the chocolate and place in a small stainless steel bowl.

→ In a small heavy saucepan, bring the heavy cream to the boil.

→ Pour the hot cream over the chocolate and stir, without aerating the mixture, until melted and smooth.

→ Place over a bowl of ice water, stirring to cool. The mixture should remain soft enough to scoop into 12 small balls.

→ When slightly formed, scoop the mixture into 14 balls, each weighing approximately ⅓ ounce.

→ Place the balls on a parchment-lined sheet pan and place in the freezer to firm, while you complete the bouchon cake batter.

Proceed with the bouchon cake batter as follows

→ In a medium-sized sauce pan, set over a pan of simmering water, melt the chocolate and butter, stirring until smooth.

→ When melted, remove from the heat and add the sugar, tangerine zest, and egg yolks.

→ Into a medium-sized bowl, sift the flour with the baking powder and salt.

→ Add these sifted dry ingredients to the chocolate mixture and gently mix until incorporated.

Prepare the mold for the bouchons as follows

→ Using pan release spray, coat the plaque of 12 small muffin molds, and a mold to hold the additional two bouchons.

→ Then line each cavity with a collar of foil, which protrudes an inch above the top of the molds.

→ Then spray the foil collars.

→ Pipe in a small amount of batter, about 0.5 ounce, and then place a ganache ball into each mold on top of the batter.

→ The batter is enough to make 14 bouchons, which allows for two extra in case any are imperfectly formed or baked.

TIP: *The bouchon cakes are best assembled to order, just before serving, in order for the center ganache ball to remain frozen as the cake is put into the oven*

Hibiscus sauce

YIELD: APPROXIMATELY
6 OUNCES, 12 SERVINGS,
APPROXIMATELY ½ OUNCE
EACH

Oz	Grams	Name of ingredient
2	60	Dried **Hibiscus flowers**
3	90	**Simple syrup**
0.5	15	**Cornstarch**
3	90	**Water**
1	30	**Fresh lemon juice,** sieved
As needed, if needed, to thin the sauce		**Water**

TIP: *If desired, you may reserve the hibiscus flowers to use as garnishes on the plate.*

→ Place hibiscus flowers and simple syrup in a small saucepan.

→ Bring to the boil and then reduce the heat to a simmer.

→ Allow to simmer for 5 minutes, then remove from the heat, cover the saucepan, and allow to infuse for 15 minutes.

→ When infused, pass through a fine sieve, pressing hard on the solids, and then discard them.

→ Reserve the infused liquid.

→ Return the liquid to a clean small saucepan and bring again to a simmer.

→ Add the dissolved cornstarch and water mixture and cook until the mixture thickens slightly and loses any raw cornstarch taste. The sauce should flow easily but not be watery.

→ Remove from the heat and add the lemon juice.

→ Thin with water if necessary.

→ Set the sauce aside until ready to plate the dessert.

	Oz	Grams	Each	Name of ingredient
Optional	3	90		**Granulated sugar**
			12	**Tarragon sprigs**
			12	**Fresh tangerine leaves,** if available

Assembly and plating

Bake the chocolate bouchon cakes in a preheated 400°F oven for 8–10 minutes. (They should be risen but still very moist.) Dip the top of each tangerine shell into granulated sugar to coat, if desired. Onto each plate, place one caramelized gratin, one just-out-of-the-oven chocolate bouchon (if impractical to bake to order, then microwave briefly, just before serving, to refresh the ganache center) and the candied tangerine filled with the tangerine sorbet. Garnish the tangerines with a sprig of tarragon or fresh tangerine leaf, if available. Sauce the plate generously with hibiscus sauce, garnish with a reserved hibiscus flower, if desired, and serve immediately.

Three Textures of Lemon— Curd, Chiffon, and Sorbet

YIELD: 12 SERVINGS

Three textures of lemon—curd, chiffon, and sorbet, garnished with a trio of glassy tuiles, served in three glasses. Three textures—creamy, airy, and icy—are used to showcase the versatility of one ingredient. In winter, when the fresh produce possibilities dwindle to a precious few, the always-reliable lemon handily comes to the rescue. If fragrant, low-acid Meyer lemons are available, by all means use them in the sorbet, adding yet another layer of contrast to the other two elements, made with ordinary tart acidic lemons. Straightforward in preparation, this dessert however requires paying close attention to time and temperature to achieve perfect results. If all of the ingredients are weighed out and gathered in advance, mixing bowls at hand, hot, warm, and iced water baths ready, then the preparations will go smoothly. The three translucent tuile garnishes each add the requisite crunch. Three temperatures— frozen (the sorbet), chilled (the chiffon), and warm (the curd)—add further intrigue.

The order of things:

1. **Make lemon curd**
2. **Make base for lemon chiffon**
3. **Make Italian meringue** for lemon chiffon
4. **Complete lemon chiffon**
5. **Make lemon sorbet**
6. **Make glassy tuile paste** and reserve
7. **Make candied lemon rounds** to garnish the glass tuile cookies
8. **Bake cocoa nib encrusted tuiles**
9. **Bake remaining glassy tuiles,** half of which will be candied lemon garnished and the other half of which will be pistachio encrusted

Equipment list:

Heat-proof glasses in which to serve the lemon curd, if serving warm

Bowls of ice water and hot water to cool and rewarm the chiffon base, as necessary

Pastry bag outfitted with a ½ inch plain tip to pipe out lemon curd into serving glasses

Rectangular pan, measuring approximately 6 inches by 12 inches by ½ inch deep, lined with a sheet of food-grade acetate for the lemon chiffon

Round metal cutter measuring 2 inches in diameter, to cut the glassy tuiles into perfect circles

Lemon curd

YIELD: APPROXIMATELY
36 OUNCES, 12 SERVINGS,
EACH WEIGHING
APPROXIMATELY 3 OUNCES

Oz	Grams	Each	Name of ingredient	Baker's percentages
8	240		**Fresh lemon juice**, sieved	100
10	300	6	**Whole large eggs**	125
10	300		**Granulated sugar**	125
8	240		**Unsalted butter**	100

→ In a stainless steel bowl, whisk together all ingredients over a hot water bath. (The water should not touch the bottom of the bowl.)

→ Cook until thickened, whisking constantly.

→ Remove from the heat, pass through a fine sieve into a bowl and then, if serving cold, set over an ice water bath, stirring occasionally to cool evenly and quickly.

→ When cool, using a pastry bag outfitted with a ½ inch plain tip, pipe the mixture into serving glasses to fill, and allow to set in the refrigerator.

→ If serving warm or hot, if practical, pipe the warm or hot mixture into heat-proof glasses just before serving the dessert and serve while still warm or hot.

Lemon chiffon

YIELD: APPROXIMATELY
28 OUNCES, 12 SERVINGS,
EACH WEIGHING APPROXI-
MATELY 2⅓ OUNCES

Oz	Grams	Each	Name of ingredient
0.8	24	8	**Gelatin sheets**
4 to 5, approximately	120 to 150	7	**Egg yolks** from large eggs
4	120		**Granulated sugar**
4	120		**Fresh lemon juice**, sieved

Italian meringue

Oz	Grams	Each	Name of ingredient
4	120		**Granulated sugar**
4	120		**Water**
7	210	7	**Egg whites** from large eggs
8	240		**Heavy cream**, whipped to soft peaks

→ Place the gelatin sheets in a small bowl with enough cold water to cover them.

→ Allow to soften and when soft, remove gelatin from water, squeezing out any excess liquid. Set aside the squeezed-out gelatin in a small bowl until ready to use.

→ Line the bottom of a rectangular pan approximately 6 inches by 12 inches by ½ inch deep with a sheet of food-grade acetate and set aside.

→ In the bowl of an electric mixer, outfitted with the whisk attachment, whip the egg yolks with the first quantity of sugar until thick and light.

→ When the whisk is lifted out of the bowl, the mixture should fall slowly in a thick ribbon.

→ Transfer the mixture to a stainless steel bowl, set over a pot of simmering water (the water should not touch the bottom of the bowl).

→ Stir, without aerating, until the mixture reaches 180°F and coats the back of the spoon.

→ Remove from the heat and immediately add the lemon juice and the gelatin, stirring until the gelatin melts completely.

→ Set this mixture aside at room temperature and proceed to the next steps.

For the Italian meringue

→ In a medium-sized heavy saucepan, cook the second quantity of sugar with the water, without stirring, until the mixture reaches 242°F.

→ Warm the egg whites briefly over a bowl of hot water.

→ Transfer the whites to the bowl of an electric mixer, outfitted with the whisk attachment, and begin whipping, adding the hot syrup in a thin stream until all of the syrup has been added.

→ Continue to whip the egg whites until fluffy and light.

→ While the whites are whipping, place the bowl of the chiffon base over an ice water bath, stirring to chill evenly.

→ Do not allow the mixture to set.

Completing the lemon chiffon

→ In the bowl of an electric mixer outfitted with the whisk attachment, whip the cream to soft peaks.

→ Fold the whipped cream into the chiffon base and then finally fold in the Italian meringue.

→ Immediately pour the mixture into the prepared pan, smoothing with an offset spatula or plastic bowl scraper.

→ Chill, covered, until firm, and then invert the mixture onto a cutting surface.

→ Using a knife dipped in hot water and dried, cut the mixture into ½ inch wide strips.

→ Dip the knife in hot water again and dry it, and then cut across the strips to create ½ inch square cubes.

→ Gently place the cubes into 12 serving glasses and refrigerate, covered, until ready to serve the dessert.

> **TIP:** It's useful to have a bowl each of hot water and ice water on hand to control the rate at which the mixture is setting. Be careful not to allow the mixture to set before folding the whipped cream, below, into it. If it is setting too quickly, remove the bowl from the ice water bath and place it over the bowl of warm water to re-melt slightly, smoothing it out with a whisk as needed. Then proceed with the next step.

Oz	Grams	Name of ingredient
12	360	**Simple syrup**
6	180	**Fresh lemon juice** from ordinary or Meyer lemons, sieved
1	30	**Grated lemon zest**

Lemon (ordinary or Meyer) sorbet

YIELD: APPROXIMATELY 19 OUNCES, 12 SERVINGS, EACH WEIGHING APPROXIMATELY 1½ OUNCES

→ In a medium-sized bowl, combine the syrup, lemon juice, and zest.

→ Chill until cold and then transfer to the bowl of an electric ice cream machine.

→ Freeze until semi-firm and then, using a small ice cream scoop, scoop the mixture onto a parchment-lined sheet pan.

→ Freeze, covered, until ready to assemble the dessert.

→ Just before serving, fill 12 glasses with equal amounts of the balls of sorbet.

Oz	Grams	Name of ingredient
2	60	**Butter**
4	120	**Corn syrup**
4	120	**Granulated sugar**

Basic glassy tuile batter

YIELD: APPROXIMATELY 10 OUNCES, DIVIDED EQUALLY INTO THREE PARTS, ONE FOR EACH VARIETY OF TUILE GARNISH

→ Place the ingredients in a small heavy saucepan, heat until the butter melts, whisking vigorously to emulsify.

→ Then use one-third of the batter for each of the three different tuile garnishes.

Cocoa nib–encrusted tuiles to garnish the lemon curd

YIELD: 12 COOKIES, EACH 2 INCHES IN DIAMETER

Oz	Grams	Name of ingredient
3, approximately	90	Glassy tuile paste
0.5	15	Cocoa nibs

→ Allow the mixture to cool slightly and then spoon out twelve ½ teaspoonfuls of the batter into mounds, spaced 3 inches apart, onto a Silpat set on the back of a sheet pan.

→ In a preheated 375°F oven, bake the tuiles for 6–7 minutes.

→ Remove from the oven and immediately scatter the cocoa nibs evenly over each cookie.

→ While the tuiles are still warm and flexible, use a round cutter to trim them into perfect circles.

→ Allow to cool and set aside, at room temperature. If not using immediately, store in an airtight container, with a tight-fitting lid, outfitted with a piece of limestone or a packet of silica gel, to preserve crispness. If the tuiles cool before being able to trim them, return them to the oven briefly and then resume trimming while the tuiles are still warm.

→ Just before serving, place a cocoa nib-encrusted tuile on end, on top of each serving of lemon curd.

Candied lemon topped tuiles to garnish the lemon sorbet

YIELD: 12 TUILES, EACH 2 INCHES IN DIAMETER

Oz	Grams	Each	Name of ingredient
		12	Paper-thin lemon slices
6	180		Simple syrup
3	90		Glassy tuile paste from above

→ Bring the syrup to the boil and then reduce to a simmer.

→ Add the lemon slices and cover at the lowest possible simmer until tender but not disintegrating.

→ When the lemon slices are tender, carefully remove them to a cooling rack.

→ Then transfer them to a Silpat-lined sheet pan and bake in a preheated 350°F oven until dry but not browned.

→ Remove from the oven and while the tuiles are still warm and flexible, use a round cutter measuring 2 inches in diameter, to trim them into perfect circles.

→ If the tuiles cool before being able to trim them, return them to the oven briefly and then resume trimming while the tuiles are still warm.

→ Place one candied lemon slice on each cookie.

→ Set aside until ready to serve. If not using immediately, store in an airtight container, with a tight-fitting lid, outfitted with a piece of limestone or a packet of silica gel, to preserve crispness.

Pistachio-
encrusted tuiles
to garnish the
lemon chiffon
YIELD: 12 COOKIES, EACH
2 INCHES IN DIAMETER

Grams	Each	Name of ingredient
3, approximately	90	**Glass tuile mixture**
1	30	**Pistachios,** medium chopped

→ Spoon out twelve ½ teaspoonfuls of the batter into mounds, spaced 3 inches apart, onto a Silpat set on the back of a sheet pan. Scatter pistachios evenly over each cookie.

→ In a preheated 375°F oven, bake the tuiles for 6–7 minutes.

→ Remove from the oven and while the tuiles are still warm and flexible, use a round cutter measuring 2 inches in diameter, to trim them into perfect circles.

→ Set aside until ready to serve.

→ If not using immediately, store in an airtight container, with a tight-fitting lid, outfitted with a piece of limestone or a packet of silica gel, to preserve crispness.

Assembly and plating

If serving the lemon curd warm, then warm it over a hot water bath, and using a pastry bag outfitted with a plain round tip measuring ½ inch in diameter, pipe the mixture into heat-proof glasses (stemmed or not) just before serving. Then place a cocoa nib-encrusted tuile into the hot or warm (or if not practical, cold) lemon curd. Place a pistachio-encrusted tuile into the lemon chiffon and a candied lemon tuile into the lemon sorbet. Serve immediately.

Caramelized Mango Tart with Toasted Coconut Ice Cream, Lime Sorbet, and Dried Mango Tuile

YIELD: 12 SERVINGS

Caramelized mango tart with toasted coconut ice cream, lime sorbet, and dried mango chip tuile and mango fruit leather corkscrew. The best, least-fibrous, and most highly perfumed mangoes appear in late spring to early summer. Coupled with caramel and lime, the natural sweetness of the fruit sparkles in this version, which makes the most of that brief moment when the fruit is at its peak by featuring it in three forms: fresh, which is then caramelized; in a fruit leather; and in a crisp chip. It is no surprise that the coconut is a prime partner as well, sharing the same growing regions around the world. Flaky, buttery quick puff pastry serves as the base for the tart, providing a crisp backdrop for the creamy melting fruit.

The order of things:

1. **Make puff pastry,** chill and rest
2. **Make toasted coconut ice cream and lime sorbet**
3. **Make mango chips and fruit leather**
4. **Roll out pastry and assemble the mango tarts**
5. **Bake tarts**
6. **Cut ice cream and sorbet into desired shapes** and freeze

Equipment list:

Silicone plaque with 12 square indentations, each measuring 2¾ inches square at the top and 2 inches at the bottom.

Rectangular pan, measuring 3 inches by 4½ inches by 1 inch deep, for the toasted coconut ice cream

Rectangular pan, measuring 2 inches by 4½ inches by 1 inch deep for the lime sorbet

Square metal cookie cutter, measuring 1½ inches on each side to cut the ice cream and sorbet

Oz	Grams	Name of ingredient	Baker's percentages
9.6	288	**All purpose flour**	100
9.6	288	**Unsalted butter,** cool, waxy, not soft or greasy	100
	1		0.3
4.8	144		50

This dough may be made either by hand or by machine, depending on the size of the batch.

Mixing by hand

→ Cut butter into 1½ inch chunks.

→ Place flour and salt into a large bowl.

→ Mix to combine.

→ Add the butter and coat with the flour and salt mixture.

→ Then add ice water all at once and lightly mix until the dough coheres into a rough mass.

→ Do not overprocess.

→ Turn the ragged mass of dough out onto a lightly floured surface and tap it firmly with a rolling pin to coax the dough into a roughly cohesive shape.

→ Check to be sure that the dough is not sticking to the surface.

Mixing by machine

→ Using the paddle attachment, mix the flour and salt at low speed to combine.

→ Add the butter, cut into 1½ inch chunks.

→ On slow speed, mix just to coat the butter with the flour.

→ With the machine running, add ice water all at once, and briefly mix, turning the machine on and off rather than allowing it to run continuously, just until the dough becomes a rough mass. It is better to underprocess rather than to overprocess the dough.

Rolling the dough

→ Turn the ragged mass of dough out onto a floured surface and tap firmly with the rolling pin to coax the dough into a roughly cohesive shape.

→ Check to be sure that the dough is not sticking to the surface.

→ Use a plastic dough scraper frequently to free the dough from the work surface, as necessary, if it is sticking.

→ Flour the work surface *lightly* from time to time.

→ Once the dough has been rolled to a rough rectangular shape, mentally divide the dough in thirds and fold one third of the dough from the end closest to you toward the middle and the other third over the first third to create a package of dough made up of three thick layers.

→ Turn the packet of dough 90 degrees so that the short side is facing you. Then roll the dough to lengthen it again to a rectangle measuring roughly 4 inches by 10 inches.

→ Fold in thirds again, turn it 90 degrees so that the short side is facing you again.

→ Now roll the dough again to a rectangle measuring roughly 4 inches by 10 inches.

→ Chill in between the rolling and folding steps if the dough shows signs of softening or sticking to the work surface.

→ Then repeat the rolling and folding once more, chilling as needed if the dough shows signs of softening or is being resistant to rolling. (See process shots on page 143.)

TIP: *Note that, like all pastry doughs, a well-chilled and well-rested puff pastry dough is essential to achieve a delicately layered final product that holds a precise shape well. Also note that each time the dough is manipulated, it needs to be put back into the refrigerator to relax the gluten before proceeding to the next step.*

- → Chill until firm. (The dough may be refrigerated overnight, but for longer storage, freeze it, well wrapped, and then, when needed, thaw slowly in the refrigerator.)
- → Roll the dough to a sheet about ⅓ inch thick and then cut into twelve 3-inch squares.
- → Dock with a fork at ⅓ inch intervals all over the dough.
- → Reserve the squares, refrigerated, on a parchment-lined baking sheet until ready to assemble the tarts.
- → Cover the fruit with the pastry squares and then bake in a preheated 375°F oven for about 20–25 minutes, or until pastry is puffed and golden brown.
- → Allow to cool briefly and then turn the tarts out onto a parchment-lined baking sheet.
- → Keep at room temperature until ready to serve (not for longer than 4 hours).

These are best served the day they are made.

Lime sorbet
YIELD: APPROXIMATELY 22 OUNCES

Oz	Grams	Each	Name of ingredient
10	300	18, approximately	Fresh lime juice, sieved
10	300		Simple syrup
2	60		Fresh lime zest, grated

- → Combine all ingredients and freeze in an ice cream machine until semi-firm.
- → Pour the mixture into a rectangular pan, measuring 2 inches by 4½ inches by 1 inch deep.
- → Freeze covered until firm.

Forming the ice cream-sorbet cubes

- → Remove the coconut ice cream from the freezer.
- → Using a 1½ inch square cookie cutter, cut the ice cream into six uniform squares.
- → Remove the squares from the pan and place on a parchment-lined sheet pan.
- → Return them to the freezer, covered, and then remove the lime sorbet from the freezer.
- → Using the same 1½ inch square cookie cutter, cut the sorbet into six uniform squares.
- → Remove the squares from the pan and place onto a parchment-lined sheet pan.
- → Return to the freezer to firm up as necessary.
- → Cut the squares of ice cream and sorbet on the diagonal, each into 12 triangular shapes.
- → Place one triangular shape of the ice cream into the mold and then place into the mold one triangle of the sorbet, to create 12 two-toned squares.
- → Return the molded ice cream and sorbet to the freezer until ready to plate the dessert.

Mango chips

YIELD: 12 CHIPS

Oz	Grams	Each	Name of ingredient
2	60		**Simple syrup**
		12	Thin slices of **ripe but not mushy mangoes**

→ Peel the mango and slice on a mandoline into ⅛ inch thick slices.

→ Dip in the simple syrup and bake on a Silpat set onto a sheet pan, in a preheated 225°F oven for approximately 1 hour 30 minutes, or until dry to the touch.

→ Remove from the oven, release from the Silpat, and place the chips in a container with a tight-fitting lid, in a single layer, outfitted with a piece of limestone or a packet of silica gel to absorb any moisture.

→ Store at room temperature until ready to plate the dessert.

Preparing the mango for the tarts

Oz	Grams	Each	Name of ingredient
36 net weight, after peel and pit are removed	1080	6	Medium to large **fresh, ripe mangoes**, peeled and sliced into ½ inch thick slices
4, approximately	120		**Fresh lime juice**, sieved, to brush on slices

Caramel syrup for filling bottoms of Silform molds

Oz	Grams	Name of ingredient
4	120	**Brown sugar**
4	120	**Butter**
1	30	**Lime juice**

→ Peel and slice the mango into ½ inch thick oval-shaped pieces.

→ Then slice the ovals into ½ inch wide strips and brush lightly with the first quantity of lime juice.

→ In a small saucepan, combine the brown sugar and butter and heat until butter melts and the sugar dissolves.

→ Add the second quantity of lime juice, stir to blend, and then pour an even amount of the mixture into the bottom of each of 12 square Silform molds, measuring 2¾ inches square at the top and 2 inches at the bottom.

→ The molds used have a square indentation, measuring 1½ inches square, at the bottom that provides the perfect place for the ice cream and sorbet cube when the tart is inverted. Note that the molds will be inverted when serving the dessert so that the top becomes the bottom and the bottom becomes the top.

→ Place fruit slices over the caramel in a compact striped mass, without leaving gaps. Refrigerate them while you prepare the puff pastry.

Note: The molds will be inverted when serving the dessert so that the top becomes the bottom and the bottom becomes the top.

Assembly and plating

Place one tart onto each plate. Place the two-toned ice cream and sorbet square onto the top of the tart. Garnish the top of the tart with a mango chip. Place a corkscrew of mango fruit leather to the side. Serve immediately.

Cherimoya Mousse with Almond-Lime Joconde Base, Lime Compote, and a Cherimoya-Shaped Tuile

YIELD: 12 SERVINGS

Cherimoya mousse, almond-lime joconde base, lime compote, and cherimoya-shaped tuile. Native to the mountains of Peru, the cherimoya has more than a touch of the exotic. The whole fruit looks otherworldly with its pale green skin marked by symmetrical indentations that look like someone had pressed a fingertip into it. Its off-white flesh is studded with off-putting, though easily removable, inedible hard black seeds. Most agree that its flavor seems to be a cross between pineapple, banana, and papaya with undertones of vanilla. When ripe, the fruit is easily bruised and its skin may show signs of darkening. Here coupled with a lime-scented sponge cake and confited lime slices, the mousse, set by cocoa butter rather than gelatin, is pure tropical flavor on a plate. A touch of whimsy is added in the form of a tuile cookie, colored and designed to resemble a cross section of the fresh fruit.

The order of things:

1. **Make almond-lime joconde base**
2. **Make tuile batter**
3. **Make lime compote**
4. **Make cherimoya mousse**

Equipment list:

Silicone plaque with 12 flat-topped heart-shaped indentations, each measuring 2½ inches from the point of the heart to the center of the flat top by 2⅝ inches, measured at the widest point, by 1 inch deep.

Heart-shaped template for the tuile measuring 2½ inches from the point to the center of the flat top, by 2⅝ inches, measured at the widest point

Mandoline to slice the lime for the lime compote

Microplane grater to grate the lime zest for the garnish on the plate

Almond-lime joconde base

YIELD: APPROXIMATELY
22 OUNCES

Oz	Grams	Each	Name of ingredient	Baker's percentages
4	120		**Almond flour**	66
2	60		**All purpose flour**, sifted	34
3, approximately	90	From 5 large eggs	**Egg yolks**	50
2	60		**Granulated sugar**	34
5	150	From 5 large eggs	**Egg whites**	83
2	60		**Granulated sugar** to make meringue	34
0.5	15		**Lime zest**, grated	8.5
2	60		**Butter**, melted	34

→ Sift the almond flour and the all purpose flour together onto a sheet of parchment paper.

→ In the bowl of an electric mixer outfitted with the whisk attachment, whip the egg yolks with the first quantity of sugar until light in color.

→ When the whisk is lifted, the mixture should fall slowly from it in a thick ribbon.

→ Remove the bowl of the yolk mixture from the machine.

→ In a clean mixing bowl outfitted with a clean whisk, beat the egg whites with the second part of the sugar to stiff but shiny peaks.

→ Set aside.

→ Fold the sifted dry ingredients into the egg yolk mixture alternately with the meringue.

→ Thoroughly but gently fold in the melted butter and spread the batter into a greased and parchment-lined or Silpat-lined half-sheet baking pan.

→ Bake in a preheated 375°F oven for approximately 15 minutes, or until lightly golden.

→ Allow to cool. Then using a heart-shaped cookie cutter, measuring 3 inches from point to the indented area between the two humps at the top of the heart by 3½ inches measured at the widest point, cut the cake into 12 pieces to be used as bases for the cherimoya mousse.

→ Cut in rows of four along the long side of the rectangle, and in rows of three along the shorter side of the rectangle, totaling 12 heart-shaped cakes.

Lime compote (or confiture)

YIELD: ENOUGH FOR
12 SERVINGS, 4 TO
5 SLICES EACH

Oz	Grams	Each	Name of ingredient
4 to 5 limes, depending on size		36	**Fresh limes**, thinly sliced on a mandoline
8, approximately	240		**Water** to cover
32	960		**Simple syrup**

TIP: *Choose very thin-skinned (and unblemished) limes for ease of slicing on the mandoline, yielding a more tender cooked fruit for the finished dessert.*

→ Place the limes into a stainless steel bowl.

→ Cover with boiling water and allow to stand until the water is cool.

→ Drain, and then rinse the lime slices in cold water.

→ Place the limes into a medium-sized saucepan with simple syrup.

→ Cook at the barest simmer until tender.

→ When tender, remove from the syrup and place on a fine sieve to drain.

→ Save the cooking liquid to use as plating sauce.

→ Store the lime slices at cool room temperature if using the same day.

→ If not, store, refrigerated, in a single layer in a container with a tight-fitting lid, until ready to use.

→ Use within two days.

Oz	Grams	Each	Name of ingredient
4	120		**Unsalted butter**
4	120		**Granulated sugar**
4	120	From 4 large eggs	**Egg whites,** from large eggs
4.75	143		**All purpose flour**
As needed to color a portion of the tuile batter for the edge of the "cherimoya" tuile			**Green food coloring,** either powder, liquid or paste
0.5 oz approximately, or as needed to color a portion of the tuile batter for the "seeds" of the "cherimoya" tuile	15		**Cocoa powder**

Cherimoya–shaped tuile

YIELD: ENOUGH FOR 12 TUILES, PLUS ADDITIONAL TO ALLOW FOR BREAKAGE, IMPERFECTLY FORMED OR IMPROPERLY BAKED TUILES

→ In the bowl of an electric mixer outfitted with the paddle attachment, cream the butter with the sugar until light and fluffy.

→ Add the egg white and mix to incorporate, scraping the bottom and sides of the bowl to ensure that the mixture is well blended.

→ Add the flour and mix just until flour disappears.

→ Transfer the mixture to a covered container, refrigerate, and let rest for at least an hour, or overnight.

→ Divide the batter into three parts as follows: 6 ounces in one bowl for the base tuiles; 4 ounces for the green-colored outline, and 2¾ ounces for the cocoa-colored batter, used for the "seeds" of the cherimoya.

→ To the 4 ounce portion, add green coloring to obtain a light lime green–colored batter.

→ Place this batter into a pastry bag with a round metal tip measuring ⅓ inch in diameter.

→ To the 2¾ ounce portion, add ½ ounce of cocoa powder to obtain a dark brown colored batter (note that the batter darkens some in baking).

→ Place this batter into a paper parchment decorating cone, seal the top by folding the top left and right corners of the bag toward the middle, and snip ⅛ inch from the bottom point of the bag.

→ To shape the tuiles, use a heart-shaped template measuring 2½ inches from the point to the center of the flat top, by 2⅝ inches, measured at the widest point.

→ Place the template on a Silpat set on the back of a baking sheet and using a metal spatula, spread a thin but not translucent layer of the plain batter.

→ Remove the template and then outline the heart-shaped batter on the Silpat with a thin, even line of green batter.

→ Then, using the cocoa-colored batter, pipe six dots, three on each side of the heart, spaced approximately ⅓ inch apart (see the photograph).

→ Continue laying down the batters for the tuiles, three to four on a Silpat.

→ When you have completed 12 perfect tuiles, bake them in a preheated 375°F oven for 7–10 minutes, or until set but not browned.

→ Remove from the oven and allow to cool on the Silpats.

→ When cool, carefully remove from the Silpat and store in an airtight container with a tight-fitting lid, outfitted with a piece of limestone or a packet of silica gel, to retain crispness. Use the same day or the following day.

TIP: *Note that the colored tuile paste tends to darken slightly after baking, so compensate by making the batter slightly more vividly colored than you wish it to end up.*

Cherimoya mousse

YIELD: APPROXIMATELY
48 OUNCES, 12 SERVINGS
EACH APPROXIMATELY
4 OUNCES; EACH SERVING
IS COMPRISED OF TWO
MOLDS, UNMOLDED, AND
THEN PLACED WITH THE TOP
SIDES FACING EACH OTHER

Oz	Grams	Each	Name of ingredient
11	330	2 to 3, depending on size	**Cherimoya puree** from fresh cherimoyas, peeled, seeded, divided into 4 ounces (120 g) in one bowl, and 7 ounces (210 g) in another bowl
7	210		**Granulated sugar**
2.3	69		**Cocoa butter,** powdered
0.87	26		**Lime juice,** fresh
26	780		**Whipped heavy cream**

→ In a heavy saucepan, set over low heat, heat 4 ounces of cherimoya puree with sugar to 158°F.

→ Add cocoa butter and stir until completely melted.

→ Add remaining cherimoya puree and cool over an ice water bath to 65°F, and then add the lime juice.

→ Remove from ice water bath and let stand at room temperature while the cream is whipped.

→ In the bowl of an electric mixer outfitted with the whisk attachment, whip the cream to soft peaks.

→ Fold the whipped cream into the cooled cherimoya mixture. Pipe the mousse using a pastry outfitted with a plain round tip, measuring ½ inch diameter, into 24 flat-topped heart-shaped Silform molds, measuring 2½ inches from the point to the center of the flat top by 2⅝ inches, measured at the widest point, by 1 inch deep.

→ Using a small metal spatula or plastic bowl scraper, smooth the tops of the mousses.

→ Wrap and freeze

→ Remove from the freezer and unmold the mousses.

→ For each serving, join two mousses, placing the larger faces together, using a small metal spatula dipped in hot water to smooth the seams where they are joined.

→ Set aside in the refrigerator until ready to serve.

Garnish

Each	Name of ingredient
From 2 to 3 limes	**Fresh lime zest,** grated

Assembly and plating

Place a heart-shaped piece of the joconde on the plate. Place the mousse-pointed end facing up, onto the cake. Arrange a few slices of the lime confit to the side of the cake. Spoon a few teaspoonfuls of the cooking liquid next to the cake. Garnish with the cherimoya tuile.

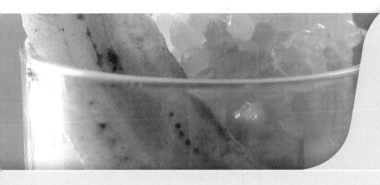

South Asian Coupe—Pandan Panna Cotta, Tapioca, Baby Bananas, and Fresh Pineapple, with Coconut Tuile Garnish

YIELD: 12 SERVINGS

A South Asian bowl: Tapioca with pandan panna cotta, baby bananas in coconut milk, and coconut tuile garnish. This South Asian–inspired dessert clearly illustrates that agricultural products that grow together go together, from tapioca to pandan leaf, and from banana to coconut. Riffing on those desserts in a glass found everywhere on the streets of Southeast Asia, from Thailand to Vietnam to the Philippines (albeit with different names), this dessert gives a contemporary spin to the flavors of this region. Pandan, the large deep-green aromatic leaf from the screw pine tree, with its subtle vanilla aroma and toasty, almost nutty overtones, is used here to flavor and color a tremulous panna cotta. Vanilla syrup scents the slow-cooked tapioca that crowns this dessert. A drizzle of coconut milk, slices of caramelized miniature banana, and a crunchy coconut encrusted tuile cookie complete the tropical experience.

The order of things:

1. **Make vanilla syrup**
2. **Cook tapioca pearls** and let cool, reserve
3. **Make coconut tuile batter**
4. **Make panna cotta** and chill in refrigerator
5. **Bake tuiles**
6. **Prepare baby bananas**

Equipment list:

Oval-shaped **tuile template,** measuring 4¾ inches lengthwise from rounded end to rounded end by 1¾ inches across, measured at the widest point in the center

Rack to separate the serving glasses when storing them in the refrigerator

Tapioca pearls

YIELD: ENOUGH FOR
12 DESSERTS

Oz	Grams	Name of ingredient
4 (dry, before cooking)	120	**Dried tapioca pearls,** small sized
As needed to cover the tapioca		**Water**

Vanilla-flavored simple syrup

Oz	Grams	Name of ingredient
4	120	**Simple syrup**
0.5	15	**Vanilla extract**

TIP: *Cooking tapioca to the right texture involves patience. Changing the cooking water three times to eliminate extra starch is key to yielding tapioca balls that are tender but still offer a bit of resistance when chewed. Removing excess starch is necessary to allow the tapioca to absorb maximum flavor from the vanilla syrup.*

→ Combine the simple syrup and the vanilla extract in a small bowl.

→ Set aside.

→ Place the tapioca and enough water to allow the tapioca to float into a medium-sized heavy saucepan.

→ Bring to the boil, reduce to a simmer, and cook for 15 minutes.

→ Drain, rinse, and place back into the saucepan.

→ Cover again with fresh water, bring to a boil, and then simmer for another 15 minutes.

→ Drain, rinse, and return the tapioca to the saucepan, covering again with fresh water.

→ Bring to the boil, reduce to a simmer, and cook until the pearls are almost translucent. (This process takes approximately 45 minutes in all.)

→ Remove from the pan, rinse under cold water and place into the small bowl of vanilla-flavored simple syrup.

→ Set aside to cool.

→ Refrigerate, covered, until ready to assemble the dessert.

→ Drain the tapioca from the syrup, reserving the syrup for another use, if desired, or use a small amount of it on top of each finished dessert just before serving.

Pandan panna cotta

YIELD: APPROXIMATELY
30 OUNCES, 12 SERVINGS,
2½ OUNCES EACH

Oz	Grams	Each	Name of ingredient	Baker's percentages
8	240		**Pandan leaves,** fresh, if available, or frozen	1.8
32	960		**Heavy cream**	25
8	240		**Granulated sugar**	100
0.6	18	6	**Gelatin sheets**	25
As needed, if desired			**Green food coloring** powder, liquid or paste	

TIP: *Taste the liquid before sieving to confirm that the pandan flavor has strongly infused the cream. If not, infuse for a few more minutes and then taste again.*

TIP: *Alternatively, for visual drama, you can place the glasses into a plastic rack and then set the rack at a 45 degree angle in the refrigerator so that the panna cottas are higher on one side of the glass than the other, leaving an open area for the tapioca pearls and caramelized baby bananas.*

→ Bring the cream to a boil, add pandan leaves and sugar, and simmer for 5 minutes.

→ Remove from the heat, cover, and allow to infuse for approximately 15 minutes.

→ Pass through a fine sieve, pressing hard on the solids. Bloom the gelatin in cold water to cover.

→ Allow to soften and then squeeze out the excess liquid. Add the squeezed-out gelatin to the hot cream mixture and stir to dissolve.

→ If using food color, add a small amount of the mixture to the food coloring, stir to dissolve and then add the part that is colored back to the main part of the mixture.

→ Pour the mixture into twelve clear-glass serving glasses, set onto a sheet pan.

→ The mixture should half fill each glass.

→ Carefully place the sheet pan into the refrigerator on a shelf that is level, and allow the panna cottas to set, about 2 hours.

Caramelized baby bananas

YIELD: 12 SERVINGS

Oz	Grams	Each	Name of ingredient
		12	**Baby bananas,** almost ripe, peeled and cut in half lengthwise
8	240		**Unsalted butter**
6	180		**Muscovado, dark brown sugar, or palm sugar**
2 to 3, approximately	60 to 90		**Water**
8	240		**Coconut milk**

→ Place the butter and brown sugar into a wide sauté pan.

→ Add the halved bananas, about 6 pieces at a time, and sauté just until golden brown and slightly softened.

→ Continue sautéing until all of the bananas have been sautéed.

→ Return the sautéed bananas to the saucepan, add the coconut milk and simmer until slightly thickened, turning the bananas gently to coat all sides evenly.

→ Gently remove the bananas from the pan without bruising or breaking them and set aside in a single layer on a parchment lined baking sheet until ready to assemble the dessert.

→ Store covered at cool room temperature or cover and refrigerate if not serving within a few hours.

Coconut tuile

YIELD: 12 TUILES, PLUS SOME EXTRA IN CASE OF BREAKAGE OR IMPERFECTLY SHAPED COOKIES

Oz	Grams	Each	Name of ingredient	Baker's percentages
2	60		Unsalted butter, room temperature	100
2	60		Granulated sugar	100
2	60	2	Egg whites, from large eggs	100
2	60		All purpose flour	100
1	30		Coconut shards to garnish the tuiles	

→ In the bowl of an electric mixer outfitted with the paddle attachment, cream the butter until light and fluffy.

→ Add the sugar and mix to blend, scraping the bottom and sides of the bowl to ensure that the mixture is well blended.

→ Add the egg whites and flour and mix just until smooth.

→ Allow to rest in the refrigerator for at least 1 hour, or until ready to bake the cookies.

→ With a small metal spatula, spread the mixture in a thin, but not translucent layer, through an oval shaped tuile template, measuring 4¾ inches lengthwise from rounded end to rounded end by 1¾ inches across, measured at the widest point in the center, onto a Silpat-lined baking sheet.

→ Scatter a few coconut shards onto each cookie in a preheated 350°F oven for 7–8 minutes.

→ Remove from the oven and immediately bend the tuiles lengthwise to a rough V shape and allow to cool. (If at any point in the baking and shaping process, the cookies have become too cool and difficult to shape, return them to the oven briefly, remove, and then shape.)

→ Continue depositing the batter to bake a few cookies at a time until all of the batter has been used. Store, until ready to serve the dessert, in an airtight container with a tight-fitting lid, outfitted with a piece of limestone or a packet of silica gel to preserve the cookies' crispness.

For plating

Oz	Grams	Name of ingredient
12	360	**Sweetened condensed milk**
		Reserved vanilla syrup from tapioca above, if desired

Assembly and plating

Place three half bananas roughly upright, in a crisscross pattern, on top of the panna cotta in the glass. Spoon approximately 1½ tablespoons of the tapioca on top of the panna cotta. Drizzle condensed milk and vanilla syrup, if desired, into each glass. Place the glass on a serving plate and garnish with one coconut tuile. Serve immediately.

The Lime in the Coconut— Lime Meringue Tart with Tamarillo Sorbet and Raspberry Sauce

YIELD: 12 SERVINGS

The lime in the coconut—lime meringue tart with tamarillo sorbet, Italian meringue court jester's hat garnish, and raspberry plating sauce. Boldly flavored and boldly shaped, this colorful dessert is a study in sweet and tart flavors. It begins with a sweet and tart lime curd filling placed inside a coconut-flavored short dough shell. Moving to the next element, the tamarillo sorbet garnishing the top of the tart epitomizes the meaning of the words "sweet" and "tart" when used in combination. Most likely native to South America, this oval, satiny-skinned fruit is also aptly called the tree tomato, and is available in two varieties, one brick red on the outside with deep reddish orange flesh, and the other, golden skinned, milder, and sweeter, with a lighter yellow-colored flesh. Both taste like a cross between the tomato (which is botanically a fruit since it contains seeds) and the plum, whose texture it somewhat resembles. As a finishing touch, the Italian meringue in the shape of a jester's hat on top of the lozenge of sorbet, lends a whimsical visual exclamation point to the dessert.

The order of things:

1. **Make lime-coconut short dough** and chill
2. **Make tamarillo sorbet** and freeze
3. **Make lime curd filling** and refrigerate
4. **Make raspberry plating sauce** and refrigerate
5. **Cut tamarillo sorbet into desired shapes** and freeze
6. **Make Italian meringue** for court jester's hat garnish
7. **Within a few hours of serving the dessert, bake meringue and set aside at room temperature**
8. **Assemble** the tart just before serving

Equipment list:

12 bottomless diamond-shaped **metal tart frames** for tart shells, measuring 4 inches from point to point at the widest point, from end to end, by 2⅜ inches on each side by 2 inches tall

Pastry bag outfitted with a plain tip with a ½ inch opening to pipe out meringue garnish

Rectangular container measuring 6 inches by 9 inches and spread the tamarillo sorbet to a depth of approximately ½ inch

Diamond-shaped **metal cookie cutter,** measuring 3⅜ inches along the diamond's length, by 2¼ inches wide, to cut the tamarillo sorbet

Squeeze bottle for the raspberry plating sauce

Lime-coconut short dough

YIELD: APPROXIMATELY 45 OUNCES, 12 SERVINGS, EACH TART SHELL, UNBAKED, WEIGHING APPROXIMATELY 3½ OUNCES

Oz	Grams	Each	Name of ingredient	Baker's percentages
12	360		**Unsalted butter,** room temperature	66
6	180		**Granulated sugar**	33
3	90	4½ approximately	**Egg yolks** from large eggs	17
	9		**Freshly grated lime zest**	2
18	540		**All purpose flour**	100
6	180		**Unsweetened coconut,** finely ground	33
9, approximately	270		**Unsweetened coconut shards**	50

→ In the bowl of an electric mixer outfitted with the paddle attachment, cream the butter until soft and fluffy.

→ Add the sugar and egg yolks and mix to emulsify.

→ Add the lime zest and mix to distribute evenly throughout the dough.

→ Add the flour and finely ground coconut and mix until just incorporated.

→ Do not overmix.

→ Remove from the mixing bowl and place on a lightly floured surface.

→ Knead briefly to compact the dough, removing excess air.

→ Divide the dough into two parts, one part weighing approximately 15 ounces and the other weighing approximately 30 ounces.

→ Wrap each part separately in plastic wrap tightly and refrigerate until firm, about 1 hour.

→ Divide coconut shards into two parts, one weighing 3 ounces and the other weighing 6 ounces and then place each part into a bowl.

→ Set aside.

→ Place 12 diamond-shaped bottomless tart molds, measuring 4 inches from point to point at the widest point, from end to end, by 2⅜ inches on each side by 2 inches tall, onto a parchment-lined sheet pan.

→ Remove both packets of dough from the refrigerator and roll the 15 ounce part onto a lightly floured surface to a rough rectangular shape measuring 8 inches by 12 inches by ¼ inch thick.

→ Carefully lift the dough from the rolling surface and set it aside briefly.

→ Scatter half of the 3 ounce part of coconut shards onto the rolling surface.

→ Place the dough back on top of the coconut-coated surface and then scatter the remainder of the 3 ounce part of the coconut shards onto the top of the dough.

→ Then using the rolling pin, lightly compress the dough to make the coconut shards adhere.

→ From this sheet of dough, cut 12 diamond-shaped pieces using the mold as the cutter. These pieces will be used as the bottoms of the tarts.

→ Place the pieces into the tart molds and set aside.

→ Now divide the 30 ounce piece of dough into two equal parts, rolling each part on a lightly floured surface, to a rectangle measuring 10 inches by 12 inches.

→ Lift the pieces of dough carefully from the rolling surface, set aside briefly, and coat the tops and bottoms of the dough evenly with the coconut shards.

→ Using the rolling pin, lightly compress the dough to make the coconut shards adhere. Repeat the process with the remaining dough and coconut shards.

→ Cut each of the rectangles lengthwise into strips measuring 2 inches by 10 inches (six strips per rectangle) and line the sides of the molds with the strips, pressing them into the bottom corners to seal the bottom to the sides of the dough.

- → Chill the lined molds until cold, about 1 hour.
- → Dock the dough all over, fill each mold with baking weights (rice, beans, or other reusable weights, wrapped in plastic wrap, parchment paper, or foil) and then bake in a preheated 375°F oven for approximately 25–30 minutes, carefully removing the weights from each mold, and then continue baking the tart shells for an additional few minutes to dry out and turn evenly golden brown.
- → When dry and golden brown, remove the tart shells from the oven and place on a cooling rack to cool to room temperature.
- → Set aside until ready to assemble the dessert.

Note: There will be a small amount of dough left over after cutting the 12 diamond-shaped pieces.

Lime curd filling

Oz	Grams	Each	Name of ingredient	Baker's percentages
12	360	7, approximately	Whole eggs	200
12	360		Granulated sugar	200
6	180		Freshly squeezed lime juice, sieved	100
12	360		Unsalted butter	200
1	30		Freshly grated lime zest	8

- → In a large stainless steel bowl, mix all ingredients and set the bowl over a pan of simmering water (the water should not touch the bottom of the bowl).
- → Whisk constantly until the mixture thickens to the consistency of mayonnaise.
- → Remove from the heat and pass through a fine sieve into a clean stainless steel bowl set over a bowl of ice.
- → Cool quickly, stirring occasionally. Remove to a clean container with a tight-fitting lid and refrigerate until ready to assemble the dessert.

Italian meringue jester's hat garnish

YIELD: APPROXIMATELY 11 OUNCES, 12 DECORATIONS FOR TOPS OF TARTS, EACH WEIGHING LESS THAN 1 OUNCE

Oz	Grams	Each	Name of ingredient	Baker's percentages
3	90	3	Egg whites, from large eggs, at room temperature	100
6.25	188		Granulated sugar	208
1.25	38		Water	42
0.5	15		Glucose or corn syrup	17

TIP: These are best piped out and baked within 2 hours of serving the dessert.

- → In the bowl of an electric mixer outfitted with the whisk attachment, beat the egg whites to soft peaks.
- → While the whites are beating, place the sugar, water, and glucose or corn syrup into a heavy small saucepan.
- → Cook the mixture to 240°F, remove from the heat, and immediately add the hot syrup to the whites, continuing to whisk until thick, white, and fluffy, about 15 minutes.
- → Using a pastry bag outfitted with a plain tip with a ½ inch opening, onto the back of a heat-proof pan, pipe 12 decorative pyramids of the meringue, about 1½ to 2 inches in diameter measured at the base pulling the meringue into points like a jester's hat (see photograph on page 188).
- → Torch lightly just before serving the dessert.

Tamarillo sorbet

YIELD: APPROXIMATELY
12 OUNCES, 12 SERVINGS,
EACH WEIGHING 1 OUNCE

Oz	Grams	Each	Name of ingredient	Baker's percentage
8	240		**Tamarillo puree,** from fresh red-skinned tamarillos, peeled and seeded	100
4	120		**Simple syrup**	50
As needed, if needed		1–2 limes	**Freshly squeezed lime juice,** sieved	25

TIP: *Be sure to taste the puree to determine how much of the above-noted simple syrup should be added to it. You may need to balance the sweetness by adding a small amount of fresh-squeezed lime juice, sieved, to the puree before freezing.*

→ In a medium-sized saucepan, combine the tamarillo puree and simple syrup.

→ Heat to the boil and then remove from the heat.

→ Cool over an ice water bath and when cold, place into the bowl of an electric ice cream machine and freeze until almost firm.

→ Remove to a rectangular container measuring 6 inches by 9 inches and spread the sorbet to a depth of approximately ½ inch. (See illustration showing how to cut the sorbet.)

→ Freeze, and then when frozen, cut the sorbet into diamond-shaped pieces, using a diamond-shaped cookie cutter, measuring 3⅜ inches along the diamond's length by 2¼ inches wide (slightly smaller than the tart frames in which the tart shells are baked), cutting in rows of four along the 9 inch side and in rows of three along the 6 inch side, totaling 12 diamonds.

→ Freeze, covered, until ready to serve the dessert.

Raspberry plating sauce

YIELD: APPROXIMATELY
9–10 OUNCES, 12 SERVINGS,
EACH WEIGHING APPROXI-
MATELY LESS THAN 1 OUNCE

Oz	Grams	Name of Ingredient
8	240	**Raspberry puree** (either commercially produced which contains 10 percent sugar), thawed, or made from scratch, from fresh berries, sieved to remove the seeds
As needed		**Simple syrup** to thin

→ In a small bowl, combine the puree with enough simple syrup to thin to a flowing consistency.

→ Transfer the mixture to a squeeze bottle, covered, and store, refrigerated, until ready to plate the dessert.

Assembly and serving

Place a tart on the serving plate at an angle. Squeeze a strip of sauce around the tart. Place a sorbet diamond at an angle horizontally across the top of the tart shell and place the Italian meringue jester's hat garnish on top of the sorbet. Serve immediately.

Verrine of Three Mousses

YIELD: 12 SERVINGS

A verrine of three mousses set into a glass on opposing slants. Seasonal fruits and intense chocolate mousse come together in a geometrically pleasing presentation. This recipe involves the mastery of three important skills basic to the dessert maker's art: the use of gelatin, the making of Italian meringue, and whipping cream to just the right degree of thickness. Piping the mousses one by one into tall fluted serving glasses, in three stages, allowing each of the first two mousses to set before topping off with the third takes some time but the dessert is so visually rewarding that it's well worth the effort. The delicate lacy chocolate tube set on the underplate next to the glass provides elegant textural contrast and acts as an airy, though plate-bound, element that brings the eye from the tall mousse-filled glass back down to the plate. Filled with a garnish of plums, raspberries, and loquats, this bit of décor serves to echo the flavors of the mousses. The tricolored tuile cookie garnish also lends textural and visual counterpoint to the verrine, tinted to echo the colors of the mousses in the glass.

The order of things:

1 **Make the two fruit purees: loquat and plum** and set aside

2 **Complete the loquat and raspberry-plum mousses**

3 **Make chocolate mousse**

4 **Make tuile batter,** divide into three equal parts and then color one with cocoa powder and the other two with food coloring

5 **Begin to make the lacy chocolate tube** by tempering chocolate

6 **Pipe out tempered chocolate** onto twelve squares of acetate and shape to form tubes

7 **Lay out tuile batter** on a Silpat and bake

Equipment list:

Bowls of ice and cool water and warm and hot water to place under the mousses to control their temperature, before piping them into the serving glasses

Paper cornets to pipe out tempered chocolate for the lacy chocolate tubes

Stemware rack to hold the 12 tall glasses into which the mousses will be piped

Acetate sheets to form the lacy chocolate tubes

Parchment sheet with shape for tuile drawn on it, to set underneath the Silpat, and to use as a guideline, before piping out the batter for the tricolor tuiles

Mousses

YIELD: APPROXIMATELY 40 OUNCES, 12 SERVINGS, 3⅓ OUNCES EACH

Loquat mousse

Oz	Grams	Name of ingredient	Notes
16	480	Loquat puree	If unavailable, substitute apricot puree
1.67	50	Simple syrup	

Italian meringue

Oz	Grams	Name of ingredient
8	240	Granulated sugar
2	60	Water
3.5	105	Egg whites, at room temperature

Add to the Italian meringue

Oz	Grams	Each	Name of ingredient
0.67	20	6	Sheet gelatin
As needed to soak the sheet gelatin			Water

Add to the above mixture

	Oz	Grams	Name of ingredient
Whipped cream for loquat mousse	13	390	Heavy cream

→ Make Italian meringue.

→ First, in a small heavy saucepan, set over medium heat, cook sugar and water without stirring to 240°F.

→ While the sugar and water are cooking, place egg whites into the bowl of an electric mixer outfitted with the whisk attachment.

→ When the sugar syrup has reached temperature, add it in a stream to the whites and beat until stiff and cooled.

→ While the meringue is being beaten, bloom gelatin in water.

→ When the gelatin has softened, remove from the water and squeeze out excess water.

→ Heat the loquat puree and add bloomed gelatin to the hot puree.

→ In a clean bowl of an electric mixer outfitted with the whisk attachment, whip the cream to soft peaks and fold into the puree, alternating with the Italian meringue.

→ Keep at cool room temperature until ready to pipe the mousse into the glasses.

Raspberry-Plum mousse

YIELD: APPROXIMATELY 39 OUNCES, 12 SERVINGS, 3¼ OUNCES EACH

	Oz	Grams	Name of ingredient
Plum Puree	8	240	Fresh red-fleshed plums, pitted
	8	240	Raspberry puree, either fresh and sieved to remove seeds, or commercially prepared, seedless, thawed (the commercially prepared puree contains 10% sugar)
		As needed, if needed	Simple syrup

→ Puree the plums in a food processor and then pass the puree through a fine sieve, pressing hard on the solids.

→ Reserve the sieved puree, discarding any of the puree that does not come through the sieve, and combine the sieved puree with the raspberry puree.

→ Adjust sweetness level as desired by adding small amounts of simple syrup, if you wish, tasting as you go, bearing in mind that the Italian meringue will add sweetness to the final mousse.

→ Proceed with the recipe for the raspberry-plum mousse by making an Italian meringue as follows.

Oz	Grams	Name of ingredient
7.67	230	Granulated sugar
2	60	Water
3.5	105	**Egg whites,** at room temperature

Add to the Italian meringue

Oz	Grams	Each	Name of ingredient
0.67	20	6	**Gelatin sheets**
As needed to soak the sheet gelatin			**Water**

Add to the above mixture

	Oz	Grams	Name of ingredient
Whipped cream for raspberry-plum mousse	13	390	**Heavy cream**

→ In a small heavy saucepan set over medium heat, cook the sugar and water without stirring to 240°F.

→ While the sugar and water are cooking, place egg whites into the bowl of an electric mixer outfitted with the whisk attachment.

→ When the sugar syrup has reached temperature, with the machine running, add the syrup in a stream to the whites and beat until stiff and cooled.

→ While the meringue is being beaten, bloom the gelatin in water.

→ When the gelatin has softened, remove from the water and squeeze out excess water and set aside.

→ Heat the plum-raspberry puree and add the bloomed gelatin to the hot puree.

→ In a clean bowl of an electric mixer outfitted with the whisk attachment, whip the cream to soft peaks and fold into the puree alternating with the Italian meringue.

→ Keep at cool room temperature until ready to pipe the mousse into the glasses.

Eggless chocolate mousse

YIELD: APPROXIMATELY
26 OUNCES, 12 SERVINGS,
2 $\frac{1}{6}$ OUNCES EACH

Oz	Grams	Name of ingredient
10	300	**68% high-quality couverture chocolate**
8	240	**Heavy cream** for ganache
8	240	**Heavy cream** for whipping and folding into mousse

→ In a medium-sized heavy saucepan, bring the first quantity of the cream to the boil.

→ Place chopped chocolate into a heat-proof stainless steel bowl.

→ Pour the hot cream over the chocolate and stir, without aerating, to blend until all of the chocolate has melted.

→ If pieces of unmelted chocolate remain, place the bowl over a hot water bath and stir just until fully melted. Do not heat over 90°F.

→ Set aside to cool but not set at room temperature.

→ In the bowl of an electric mixer outfitted with the whisk attachment, beat the second quantity of heavy cream to soft peaks and gently fold this cream into the cooled ganache mixture.

→ Keep at cool room temperature until ready to pipe the mousse into the glasses.

Tri-color tuiles

YIELD: ENOUGH BATTER
TO MAKE 12 TUILES,
WITH EXTRA IN CASE OF
BREAKAGE OR IMPERFECT
SHAPING OR BAKING

Oz	Grams	Name of ingredient	Baker's percentages
3	90	**Unsalted butter,** room temperature	80
3	90	**Egg whites**	80
3	90	**Confectioners' sugar**	80
3.75	113	**All purpose flour**	100

→ In the bowl of an electric mixer outfitted with the paddle attachment, cream the butter until light and fluffy.

→ Add the confectioners' sugar and mix to combine, scraping the bottom and sides of the bowl to ensure that the mixture is well blended.

→ Add the flour and mix just until it disappears.

→ Divide the batter into three equal parts (approximately 4¼ ounces each) and place each part into a small bowl. Prepare the three different colored batters as follows:

	Grams	Name of ingredient
For the chocolate tuile paste, add:	3	**Unsweetened cocoa,** sifted
For the pink tuile paste, add:	As needed	**Powdered or paste coloring to make** *pink*, added to tuile paste
For the orange tuile paste, add:	As needed	**Powdered or paste coloring to make** *orange*, added to tuile paste

→ In the bowl of an electric mixer outfitted with the paddle attachment, cream the butter until light and fluffy.

→ Add the confectioners' sugar and mix to combine, scraping the bottom and sides of the bowl to ensure that the mixture is well blended.

→ Add the flour and mix just until it disappears.

→ Divide the batter into three equal parts (approximately 4¼ ounces each) and place each part into a small bowl. Prepare the three different colored batters as follows.

To fill glasses

→ Place a box of 12 serving glasses, each with its own compartment, divided by corrugated cardboard, at a 60 degree angle (use rolled-up towels or cardboard to create the wedge on which you position the box of glasses to create the angle).

→ Fill a pastry bag with the chocolate mousse and then pipe 2 ounces of it into each of 12 glasses.

→ When piped into the glass, the top line of the chocolate mousse should be nearly *parallel* to the flat surface on which you have set up the box.

→ Place the box and its wedge on a level shelf in the refrigerator to allow the first layer to set. Rotate the box 180 degrees, set it again at the same 60 degree angle and pipe 2 ounces of the second mousse (raspberry-plum) into each of the glasses. Again, the top line of the raspberry-plum mousse should be *parallel* to the flat surface on which you have set up the box.

→ Place the box on a level shelf in the refrigerator, at a 60 degree angle, using the same rolled-up towels or cardboard to create the wedge on which you position the box to create the angle.

→ When the second mousse is fully set, remove the box and the wedge from the refrigerator.

→ With the glasses perfectly vertical, pipe 2 ounces of the last mousse (loquat) into each glass, filling the glasses to the rim.

→ Return the glasses, perfectly vertical, to a level shelf in the refrigerator to set, keeping the glasses refrigerated until ready to serve the dessert.

Note: Depending on the serving glasses used for the dessert, the amounts of mousse will vary. Therefore, you may have excess mousse. If so, reserve for another use.

Lacy tubes
chocolate décor
YIELD: 12 LACY TUBE-
SHAPED CONTAINERS TO
HOLD THE FRUIT COMPOTE,
AS GARNISH ON THE PLATE

Oz	Grams	Name of ingredient
12	360	**Chocolate couverture,** tempered, or nontempering chocolate coating, melted and maintained at 90°F

→ Cut 12 squares of food-grade acetate, each measuring 4 inches by 4 inches.

→ Using a paper cone filled with the melted tempered chocolate or nontempering coating, pipe out thin lines of chocolate in a close crosshatch design on the top side of the acetate.

→ Then carefully bring two opposite corners of the acetate together and tape to secure.

→ Allow to dry and set and then carefully remove the acetate.

→ Place the chocolate tubes on each plate. Use the amounts of fruit for the filling, as shown below.

Oz	Grams	Each	Name of ingredient
12 , each weighing approximately 2 ounces, net weight after peeling and pitting	360, approximately	6	**Loquats**
12, each weighing approximately 2 ounces, net weight after peeling and pitting	360, approximately	6	**Fresh plums,** yellow- or red-fleshed variety
8 to 9	240 to 270	36	**Fresh raspberries**

→ Cut each of the loquats, peeled, and pitted, and the plums, peeled and pitted, into six small pieces each, for a total of 36 pieces of each fruit.

→ Use three pieces of each per serving, plus three raspberries for each serving inside of the chocolate tube.

→ Carefully combine the cut fruit and the whole raspberries in a small bowl.

Fresh or canned apricots, pitted, may be substituted here for the loquats, if unavailable.

Assembly and plating

Place one tall-stemmed glass on each of 12 serving plates, place a lacy chocolate tube next to the base of the glass and then place an equal amount of the filling into each chocolate tube. Position one tuile, as per the photograph, in the top of each glass of mousse. Serve immediately.

Warm Feijoa Soufflé with Clove-Scented Cream and Jasmine Tea-Scented Syrup

YIELD: 12 SERVINGS

Warm Feijoa (pineapple guava) soufflé with clove-scented cream and jasmine tea–scented syrup, with feijoa chip tuile. Sometimes erroneously called the pineapple guava, the feijoa is a member of the myrtle family, related to eucalyptus, bay rum, clove, and allspice. Native to South America and highly fragrant, the fruit sports a somewhat bitter dark green skin, which is removed before processing the fruit for any application. The flesh is dense and highly aromatic and lends itself to other bold flavored accompaniments. Here it stars in an egg white–lightened soufflé. Without benefit of egg yolks or a flour-thickened roux, this soufflé sings clearly of the highly aromatic fruit. Simply peeled and then pureed, the dense and granular feijoa, when cooked, here becomes a silky puree, lightened with softly beaten egg whites and perfumed with vanilla bean, another tropical flavoring. Served with a clove-infused whipped cream and the floral infusion of the night blooming jasmine, this dessert is like a delicate *pas de trois*, in which a warm just-out-of the-oven soufflé meets the cold clove-scented cream and then encounters a crisp thin tuile in a back-and-forth sashay of temperatures and textures that is perfectly satisfying. Other than late summer and the dead of winter, this gossamer dessert can grace dessert list menus for much of the year. Available from spring to early summer, and again from fall to early winter, the feijoa has hints of pineapple, strawberry, and grape but is a thing apart, waiting to be discovered as the kiwi of the new millennium. You heard it here first.

The order of things:

1. **Make feijoa chip tuile** and let rest for one hour
2. **Prepare feijoa puree**
3. **Make jasmine tea syrup**
4. **Make soufflé base immediately before baking,** for best volume
5. **Bake the tuiles**
6. **Not more than one hour before serving the dessert, whip the clove-scented cream** to serve as the accompaniment to the soufflé
7. **Bake the soufflés to order**

Equipment list:

Heat-proof ramekins or soufflé dishes, each measuring 3½ inches at the top, tapering down to approximately 1 inch diameter at the bottom, with 6 ounce capacity

Tuile template, with 12 circle-shaped cutouts, each measuring 2⅝ inches in diameter

Metal pastry tip measuring approximately ¼ inch in diameter to cut holes into the warm tuiles after baking to resemble the cross section of the feijoa fruit

Small ramekin for the jasmine tea-scented syrup

Small pitcher for the clove-scented cream

Note: The soufflé base and the accompaniments to the soufflé (the cream, tea syrup, and tuile) may all be prepared in advance but the egg whites, which make the soufflés rise, must be whipped just before folding into the soufflé base; allow approximately 20 minutes from the time the egg whites are beaten and folded into the prepared soufflé base to when the baked soufflés are ready to serve.

Feijoa puree

YIELD: APPROXIMATELY
22 OUNCES, ENOUGH FOR
12 SOUFFLÉS

Oz	Grams	Each	Name of ingredient
22 , gross weight of the fruit before peeling; 16, net weight after peeling	660, gross weight; 480, net weight	8	**Feijoas,** peeled
6	180		**Simple syrup**
		1	**Vanilla bean,** split

TIP: *Taste to confirm that the vanilla flavor is coming through clearly here. If not, allow the fruit to infuse longer.*

→ Peel and chop the feijoas into ¾ inch pieces.

→ In a medium-sized heavy saucepan, bring the simple syrup and the vanilla bean to the boil.

→ Reduce to a simmer and cook for an additional 5 minutes.

→ Remove from the heat, cover, and allow the liquid to infuse.

→ The flavor of the vanilla should come through clearly.

→ Remove the vanilla bean, reserve for another use, and then add the feijoa to the syrup.

→ Cook over low heat until tender.

→ When tender, remove from the heat and allow to cool.

→ Puree the fruit until smooth using a food processor or an immersion blender.

Note: You will need approximately 18 ounces of puree to make 12 servings of the soufflé. Therefore, there will be extra puree remaining after making the 12 portions of soufflés; reserve for other use, freeze, or serve on the side in a small ramekin as an additional adornment for the soufflé.

Feijoa soufflé

YIELD: 12 SOUFFLÉS

To prepare ramekins or other small dishes for the soufflé

Oz	Grams	Each	Name of ingredient	Baker's percentages Fruit puree at 100%
3	90		**Unsalted butter,** room temperature	
1.5	45		**Granulated sugar** to coat baking dish for 4 molds	8
18	540		**Feijoa puree** (from recipe above)	100
7.5	225		**Egg whites,** at room temperature	45
	3		**Salt**	.5
	3		**Cream of tartar**	.5
		1 T.	**Pure vanilla bean paste**	3

→ Coat twelve 6 ounce capacity bowl-shaped footed ramekins (or other heat-proof ramekins or serving dishes of similar size and capacity, as desired), each measuring 3½ inches at the top, tapering down to approximately 1 inch diameter at the bottom with butter and then sprinkle with granulated sugar.

→ In the bowl of an electric mixer, outfitted with the whisk attachment, whip the egg whites with salt and cream of tartar to soft peaks.

→ Fold the whites, along with the vanilla bean paste, into the fruit puree and then gently, without deflating the mixture, fill the prepared molds.

→ Using the point of a small knife, make a trench around the edge of the mold one half inch from the edge and bake the soufflés in a preheated 375°F oven for about 20 minutes, or until risen and golden brown.

→ Remove from the oven, cut a small hole in the center of the soufflé, pour in the clove-scented cream, and serve immediately.

→ Serve the soufflés with small pitchers of jasmine tea–scented syrup and additional clove cream to be poured, as desired, over the soufflé.

Note: For maximum lightness, it's best to prepare the soufflés to order.

Oz	Grams	Name of ingredient	Note
8	240	**Simple syrup**	
1	30	**Peel of lemon, in strips,** 3 inches long	
	12	**Premium quality, naturally flavored jasmine tea, made from black tea leaves**	See Sources on page 00

→ In a small heavy saucepan, bring the simple syrup and lemon peel to the boil.

→ Add the tea and simmer for 2 minutes.

→ Remove from the heat and pass the mixture through a fine sieve into a bowl.

→ Transfer to a squeeze bottle, covered, and refrigerate until ready to assemble the dessert.

TIP: *Use only the colored portion of the peel, removing the white pith under the skin before infusing.*

TIP: *Taste to confirm that the tea and lemon flavors come through clearly. If the flavor is too faint, allow to infuse longer and then pass the mixture through a fine sieve.*

Clove-scented
whipped cream

YIELD: 10 OUNCES,
12 SERVINGS, APPROXI-
MATELY ¾ OUNCE PER
SERVING

Oz	Grams	Each	Name of ingredient
		6	**Whole cloves**
10	300		**Heavy cream**

→ In a medium-sized heavy saucepan, bring the cream to the boil with the cloves.

→ Remove from the heat, cover the saucepan, and allow the mixture to infuse for 15 minutes.

→ The flavor of the cloves should come through clearly.

→ If not, allow to infuse for a few minutes longer.

→ Then pass the mixture through a fine sieve into a bowl and chill, covered, until ready to whip.

→ Within one hour of serving dessert, place the infused cream into the bowl of an electric mixer outfitted with the whisk attachment and whip to soft peaks and reserve, covered in a bowl, in the refrigerator.

Feijoa chip tuile

YIELD: 12 TUILES, EACH
MEASURING APPROXIMATELY
2⅜ INCHES IN DIAMETER,
WEIGHING ⅓ OUNCE EACH

Oz	Grams	Each	Name of ingredient	Baker's percentages
1	30		**Unsalted butter,** room temperature	100
1	30		**Granulated sugar**	100
1	30	From 1 large egg	**Egg white,** from large egg	100
1	30		**All purpose flour**	100

→ In the bowl of an electric mixer outfitted with the paddle attachment, cream the butter with the sugar until light and fluffy.

→ Add the egg white and mix to incorporate, scraping the bottom and sides of the bowl to ensure that the mixture is well blended.

→ Add the flour and mix just until it disappears.

→ Transfer the mixture to a container and allow to rest in the refrigerator at least an hour before using.

- → Remove from the refrigerator and, using a tuile template with 12 circle cutouts, each measuring 2⅝ inches in diameter, spread a thin but not translucent layer of the paste through the template onto a Silpat placed on the back of a sheet pan.

- → Remove the template and bake the tuiles in a preheated 375°F oven for approximately 5–7 minutes, or until lightly golden brown around the edges.

- → Remove from the oven and immediately using the bottom end of a metal pastry tip measuring approximately ¼ inch in diameter, cut four small "eyes" out of each tuile (see photograph) to mimic the seed pod of the feijoa fruit.

- → Place the perforated tuiles onto a slightly curved surface such as a rolling pin to give a gentle curve to the tuile.

- → Allow to cool and set aside, at room temperature.

- → If not using immediately, place the tuiles in a single layer in a container with a tight-fitting lid, outfitted with a piece of limestone or a packet of silica gel, to preserve crispness. These are best served within a few hours of baking.

Spread the tuile batter onto a Silpat through a tuile template, before baking.

Place baked tuile cookies onto rolling pin to cool slightly in a curved shape.

Cut four holes in the center of each tuile, while still warm and then curving them over a rolling pin to cool completely.

Assembly and plating

Fifteen minutes before serving, bake the soufflés as above and then just before serving pour some of the clove-scented cream into the hole that has been made in the center of the soufflé, and serve with a pitcher of the jasmine tea syrup and remaining clove cream on the side. Garnish the soufflé with the feijoa tuile and serve immediately.

A Bunch of Grapes

YIELD: 12 SERVINGS

A wine chaudeau, served warm with three different grape flavored sorbets, accompanied by a small caramel raisin tartlet. Highlighting the different flavor profiles of the commonly available grape, this dessert places fruit front and center for a multilayered textural experience. The contrasting temperatures in the elements of the dessert play a major role here, from the sabayon-inspired chaudeau, served warm, to the palate-cleansing frozen cluster of grape sorbets. The caramel raisin tartlet is interposed between the warm and the frozen components of the dessert, acting as a bridge between the two, and providing a multitextured element in its own right, with its pleasantly sandy-textured lemony dough and chewy raisin filling, held together by the creamiest of caramels and a rich custard filling as the bed for the raisins.

The order of things:

1. **Make the sorbets** and freeze
2. **Make the short dough** and refrigerate
3. **Line tart pans with short dough** and bake
4. **Make the wine chaudeau,** cool and refrigerate
5. **Make lemon custard filling**
6. **Fill and bake tartlets**
7. **Make caramel** for caramel raisin filling
8. **Press mixture into molds**
9. **At least one hour before serving the dessert, cut triangles of sorbet as base for three sorbets and freeze, and then scoop sorbets** and place on frozen sorbet triangles and freeze
10. **Make Isomalt garnishes**

Equipment list:

Melon baller, ¾ inch in diameter by approximately ⅜ inch deep

12 equilateral **triangle-shaped molds or cookie cutters,** measuring 3 inches on each side by 1 inch deep to form the sorbet "grape clusters"

12 small **barquette-shaped tart pans,** each measuring 4 inches long by 1¾ inches wide by ½ inch deep

12 **dowels or wooden spoon handles** to shape Isomalt tendrils

12 **heat-proof wine glasses** to serve the chaudeau

Concord grape sorbet

YIELD: APPROXIMATELY
5 OUNCES

Oz	Grams	Name of ingredient	Baker's percentages
7.5 (yields approximately 3.5 oz of grape puree and juice)	225 gross wt, yielding 105 grape puree and juice	**Concord grapes,** seeds removed	100
1	30	**Simple syrup**	28
0.5	15	**Lemon juice**	14

→ Puree the seeded grapes in a food processor.

→ Pass the mixture through a fine sieve, pressing hard on the solids and discarding them, reserving the liquid.

→ Bring the resulting grape puree and simple syrup to a boil. Remove from the heat, transfer to a bowl set over an ice water bath and cool, stirring occasionally.

→ Once cool, transfer the mixture to the refrigerator until cold.

→ When cold, remove from the refrigerator and add the lemon juice, stir to combine, and then freeze in an ice cream machine.

→ Remove from the machine, and place the frozen mixture into a container, covered. Store in the freezer until ready to assemble the dessert.

If concord grapes are unavailable, substitute bottled Concord grape juice, and proceed to step 3 of the recipe.

Pink and red grape sorbet

YIELD: APPROXIMATELY
18 OUNCES

Oz	Grams	Name of ingredient	Baker's percentages
20 (yields approximately 11.75 oz grape juice, after pureeing and sieving)	600 gross wt, yielding 352 grape juice, after pureeing and sieving	Combination of **seedless pink and red grapes**	100
6	180	**Simple syrup**	51
1	30	**Lemon juice**	9

TIP: *Although the recipes for the three sorbets below recommend specific types of grapes to use, feel free to choose among whatever varieties are available in your area.*

→ Puree the grapes in a food processor and then pass through a fine sieve, pressing hard on the solids and discarding them, reserving the liquid.

→ Bring the resulting grape puree and simple syrup to a boil. Remove from the heat, transfer to a bowl set over an ice water bath and cool, stirring occasionally.

→ Once cool, transfer the mixture to the refrigerator until cold.

→ When cold, remove from the refrigerator and add the lemon juice, stir to combine, and then freeze in an ice cream machine.

→ Remove from the machine, and place the frozen mixture into a container, covered. Store in the freezer until ready to assemble the dessert.

→ Puree the grapes in a food processor and then pass through a fine sieve, pressing hard on the solids and discarding them, reserving the liquid.

→ Bring the resulting grape puree and simple syrup to a boil. Remove from the heat, transfer to a bowl set over an ice water bath and cool, stirring occasionally.

→ Once cool, transfer the mixture to the refrigerator until cold.

→ When cold, remove from the refrigerator and add the lemon juice, stir to combine, and then freeze in an ice cream machine.

→ Remove from the machine, and place the frozen mixture into a container, covered. Store in the freezer until ready to assemble the dessert.

Oz	Grams	Name of ingredient	Baker's percentages
36 (yields approximately 20 oz of sieved puree)	1080 gross wt, yielding 600 sieved puree	Green grapes	100
10	300	Simple syrup	50
1	30	Lemon juice	5

→ One hour before assembling the sorbet "grape clusters," place two half-sheet pans into the freezer. On one of the pans, place 12 equilateral triangle-shaped molds or cookie cutters, measuring 3 inches on each side by 1 inch deep, set onto a sheet of parchment paper.

→ Remove from the freezer and quickly spoon 2 ounces of the green grape sorbet into each of the 12 triangles, compressing the mixture and then smoothing the tops of each with a small metal spatula. Return the sheet pan to the freezer. When fully frozen, remove from the freezer, unmold and return again to the freezer.

→ Remove the second frozen sheet pan from the freezer and place on a work surface. Using a melon baller, ¾ inch in diameter by approximately ⅜ inch deep, scoop 24 balls of each sorbet (two each of the three flavors, totaling six per serving) to resemble grapes and place them on the sheet pan.

→ Return them to the freezer to firm. Then remove from freezer to soften slightly (in order to allow them to adhere to the triangular-shaped bases of green grape sorbet) and then immediately place two of each flavor onto each of the 12 frozen triangular sorbet bases. Freeze, covered, until ready to serve.

Oz	Grams	Each	Name of ingredient	Baker's percentages
3.6	108		Unsalted butter	64
1.85	55		Granulated sugar	33
1.67	50	1	Large egg	29
0.5	15	From 3 medium-sized lemons	Grated lemon zest	.2
5.6	168		All purpose flour	100

→ In the bowl of an electric mixer outfitted with the paddle attachment, cream the butter until soft and light. Add the sugar and mix until blended.

→ Add the egg and the grated lemon zest and mix again until incorporated, scraping the bottom and sides of the bowl to ensure a well-blended mixture.

→ Add the flour and mix only until it disappears. Scrape the dough onto a lightly floured surface and knead briefly to densify.

→ Wrap and chill in the refrigerator until firm. Remove from the refrigerator and on a lightly floured surface, roll the dough to a thickness of ⅛ inch.

→ Line 12 barquette-shaped tartlet molds, each measuring 4 inches long by 1¾ inches wide by ½ inch deep. Chill the tarts until the dough is firm.

→ Then in a preheated 375°F oven, bake the tart shells, docked and lined with parchment paper or plastic wrap filled with rice, beans, or other weights, for approximately 10–12 minutes, or until light brown.

→ Reduce the oven temperature to 350°F. Cool, unmold, and place onto the parchment-lined sheet pan and set aside.

Wine chaudeau

YIELD: APPROXIMATELY
40 OUNCES, 12 SERVINGS,
EACH WEIGHING 3⅓ OUNCES

Oz	Grams	Each	Name of ingredient	Baker's percentages
32	960		Whole milk	100
		One, 3 to 4 inches long	Cinnamon stick	
	5		Freshly grated nutmeg	0.5
		1	Vanilla bean, split	
0.25	7.5	1–2 medium-sized limes	Lime zest	0.8
7	210	4	Whole large eggs	22
3	90		Granulated sugar	9
4	120		Sweet muscat wine	13

TIP: *The Muscat grape with its numerous clonal varieties and skin varying from pale yellow to a deep purple, almost black color, translates beautifully into sweet highly aromatic dessert wines. It is also used in wines that are dry, still, sparkling, and fortified with extra alcohol. France has its well-deservedly famous sweet fortified Muscat de Beaumes-de-Venise (15% alcohol), and Italy its sparkling Moscato d'Asti (5.5 to 8% alcohol). Given that these wines pair well with ice cream, it is not surprising that they would work well to flavor the warm, creamy chaudeau here. Feel free, though, to experiment here using other wines.*

→ In a large heavy saucepan, place the milk, spices, vanilla, and lime zest and bring to the boil. Reduce to a simmer and cook for approximately 5 minutes.

→ Remove from the heat, cover the saucepan, and allow the mixture to infuse. The flavor of the spices, vanilla, and lime should come through clearly. Pass the mixture through a fine sieve into a stainless steel bowl and set aside.

→ In the bowl of an electric mixer outfitted with the whisk attachment, whip the eggs and sugar until thick and light. When the whisk is lifted from the bowl, the mixture should flow slowly in a thick ribbon.

→ Reheat the milk along with the muscat wine and temper it into the eggs and sugar mixture in the bowl. Place the bowl over a saucepan of simmering water (the water should not touch the bottom of the bowl), and cook, stirring without aerating, until the mixture reaches 180°F and coats the back of the spoon.

→ Remove immediately from the heat and pour into heat-proof glasses to serve. If making in advance, refrigerate, and then reheat gently over a warm water bath and then serve.

Lemon custard filling

YIELD: APPROXIMATELY
14 OUNCES, ENOUGH FOR
12 BARQUETTE TARTLETS

Oz	Grams	Each	Name of ingredient	Baker's percentages
2	60		Lemon juice, sieved	50
4	120		Granulated sugar	100
4	120	6	Egg yolks from large eggs	100
4	120		Heavy cream	100

→ In a small bowl, whisk together the sugar and egg yolks until smooth. Add the lemon juice and whisk again until incorporated. Then stir in the heavy cream.

→ Pour equal amounts of this mixture into each of the 12 prebaked tart shells.

→ Carefully place the sheet pan into the oven set at 350°F and bake the tartlets for approximately for 10–12 minutes or until custard is set. Avoid browning the filling (reduce the oven temperature further, if needed).

→ Cool the tartlets and set aside.

You may have some excess filling left. After the first few minutes of baking, it may be possible to pour more of any excess filling into each tart; after that, if there is any remaining, discard or reserve for another use.

Oz	Grams	Name of ingredient	Baker's percentages
3	90	Granulated sugar	100
3	90	Heavy cream	100
6		Dark raisins	100
6		Golden raisins	100

→ In a small heavy saucepan, cook the sugar, stirring until melted and lump-free, to a golden amber color, about 300–310°F.

→ While the sugar is cooking, heat the heavy cream in a small heavy saucepan until hot.

→ When the sugar is properly colored, carefully pour in the hot cream, stirring to combine. Remove from the heat and set aside.

→ In a small bowl, combine the raisins and the still-warm caramel.

→ Pack the mixture into 12 barquette-shaped Teflon-coated molds (molds of other shapes, such as rounds, squares, or triangles would work here equally well) or molds that have first been sprayed lightly with pan release spray.

→ Allow to set and unmold onto the custard-filled baked tartlets. Set aside until ready to serve.

Isomalt tendrils or coils

Oz	Grams	Name of ingredient
6	180	Isomalt
	As needed	**Green food coloring powder, liquid or paste**

→ Spray 12 wooden dowels or handles of wooden spoons (each ⅝ inch diameter) with pan release spray and set them aside.

→ In a small heavy saucepan, melt the Isomalt. Add the color and stir to color evenly.

→ With a small spoon, drizzle a ⅛ to ¼ inch thick line of Isomalt, about 10 inches long onto a Silpat set onto a sheet pan.

→ Wait about 2 seconds, and when the Isomalt just starts to set, pick it up and wrap tightly onto the wooden dowels or spoon handles.

→ Allow to cool and carefully remove the tendrils or coils to a clean Silpat to store until ready to assemble the dessert.

Assembly and plating

Fill a heat-proof wine glass with the warm chaudeau. Place raisin tart on the plate. Position the bunch of sorbet grapes onto the plate so that it is leaning on the tart. Place an Isomalt tendril across the bunch of sorbet grapes and serve the dessert immediately.

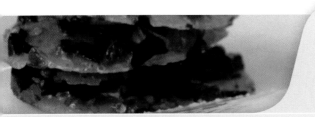

Caramelized Banana Mousse with Cocoa Nib Tuiles

YIELD: 12 SERVINGS

Caramelized banana mousse with rum syrup, cocoa nib tuiles, and roasted dried banana corkscrew on a base of sliced caramelized bananas. In a perfect marriage of flavors and textures, where the perfume of ripened bananas in three components here joins the intense notes of caramel and rum, this heart-shaped mousse plated vertically knows no season. In the dead of winter, when the palette of fresh fruits is more limited, pastry artists can turn to the tropical banana. Rum in the plating sauce complements the bananas perfectly, providing further proof that ingredients that share the same *terroir* (encompassing numerous factors such as climatic and soil conditions of the growing region) harmonize beautifully on the plate and on the palate. Cacao nibs, made from the roasted broken bits of cacao beans, all of which are grown in a band 20 degrees north and south of the equator, give crunch and an appealing bite to the delicate tuiles that share the plate with the mousse.

The order of things:

1 **Make the roasted dried banana corkscrews**

2 **Make banana mousse** and freeze

3 **Make cocoa nib tuile batter** and let cool at room temperature to thicken before baking

4 **Make rum caramel syrup pasting sauce**

5 **Bake tuiles**

6 **Cut mousse into heart-shaped portions**

7 **Slice and sauté the bananas just before serving**

Equipment list:

Rectangular-shaped pan (lined at the bottom with a sheet of food-grade acetate) measuring 8 inches by 14 inches by 1½ inches deep

Acetate sheet to line pan for mousse

Heart-shaped cutter for mousse, measuring 3½ inches at the widest point, by 2⅝ inches measured from the point of the heart to the indentation between the two lobes at the top of the heart

Small round cookie cutters to cut tuiles

Wooden dowels for dried banana corkscrews

Caramelized banana corkscrews as garnish

YIELD: 12 FINISHED GARNISHES

Oz	Grams	Each	Name of ingredient
12	360	3 to 4, approximately	**Medium-sized bananas,** peeled
16	480		Simple syrup
		2	**Ascorbic acid (vitamin C) tablets,** 500 mg each, finely powdered, to help prevent the bananas from browning

→ Heat the simple syrup and then add the powdered ascorbic acid and stir to dissolve.

→ Allow the mixture to cool and pour into a shallow rectangular pan.

→ Slice the bananas lengthwise, into ¼ inch thick slices, measuring about 5 inches to 6 inches in length and then place the sliced bananas carefully into the syrup

→ Allow to stand for 5 minutes (each slice should weigh about 1 ounce before baking).

- → Carefully remove the banana slices from the syrup and place them on a Silpat-lined half-sheet baking pan.
- → Bake in a preheated 225°F oven for approximately 45 minutes, or until the bananas feel dry to the touch.
- → Remove from the oven and using a small metal spatula or plastic scraper, carefully release the banana slices from the Silpat and immediately roll each of them in a tight corkscrew shape around a wooden dowel, approximately ¼ inch in diameter.
- → Place the banana-wrapped dowels onto a clean Silpat and allow to cool and dry.
- → Store at room temperature.

Cocoa nib tuiles

YIELD: THIRTY-SIX ⅓ OUNCE
TUILES, 3 PER SERVING

Oz	Grams	Name of ingredient	Baker's percentages
3.3	100	Corn syrup	100
3.3	100	Granulated sugar	100
3.3	100	Unsalted butter	100
3.3	100	Cocoa nibs	100

- → In a small heavy saucepan, bring the sugar and the corn syrup to a boil.
- → Add the butter, continue cooking until melted and then remove from the heat.
- → Whisk the mixture to emulsify, and when emulsified, stir in the nibs.
- → Pour the mixture onto a Silpat set on a half-sheet pan and chill. Divide the chilled batter into thirty-six ⅓ ounce portions for each tuile.
- → Place onto a Silpat-lined baking sheet, leaving about 2 inches in between each circle of batter.
- → Bake in a preheated 375°F oven for about 5 to 7 minutes.
- → Remove from the oven, and before the cookies cool and harden, use a 1 to 1¼ inch cookie cutter to cut out perfect round shapes, if desired, and then allow to cool.

Rum caramel syrup plating sauce

YIELD: APPROXIMATELY
5 OUNCES, 12 SERVINGS,
EACH WEIGHING SLIGHTLY
LESS THAN ½ OUNCE

Oz	Grams	Name of ingredient	Baker's percentages
4	120	Simple syrup	100
2	60	Water	50
1	30	Dark rum	25

- → Bring the simple syrup and water to the boil.
- → Continue to cook without stirring until the sauce turns a rich golden brown, approximately 320° F.
- → Remove from the heat and stir in the rum, mixing to combine.
- → Set aside at room temperature until ready to plate the dessert.

Oz	Grams	Each	Name of the ingredient	Baker's percentages
0.25	7.5	2.5	Sheet gelatin	1.5
16	480		Ripe bananas, chopped.	100
2	60		Unsalted butter	12
4	120		Brown sugar	24
	1	Pinch	Salt	
1.5	45		Water	9
12	360		Heavy cream	75
0.16	4.8	1 t.	Vanilla extract	1

Banana mousse

YIELD: APPROXIMATELY
2 POUNDS, 7 OUNCES

The skins of the bananas should be just starting to become spotted with black specks indicating the degree of desired ripeness.

Bloom the gelatin as follows

→ Place the gelatin into a bowl large enough to cover it completely with cold water.

→ Allow to soften and when soft, remove the gelatin and squeeze out excess liquid.

→ Discard the liquid and place the squeezed-out gelatin into a small bowl and reserve.

Continue preparing the mousse as follows

→ In a large heavy sauté pan, melt the butter.

→ Add the bananas, brown sugar, and salt, and cook until the bananas are tender and well coated with the butter–brown sugar mixture.

→ Add bloomed gelatin to the bananas in the pan, and stir to melt completely.

→ Remove the mixture from the sauté pan and then puree it along with the water in a food processor until smooth.

→ Allow to cool slightly, to approximately 80–85°F.

→ While the banana puree is cooling, place the cream and vanilla into the bowl of an electric mixer outfitted with the whisk attachment, and whip to soft peaks.

→ Remove from the machine and fold the whipped cream into the banana puree.

→ Pour the mixture into a rectangular-shaped pan (lined at the bottom with a sheet of food-grade acetate) measuring 8 inches by 14 inches by 1½ inches deep.

→ Freeze until firm.

→ When frozen, cut the mousse using a heart-shaped cutter, measuring 3½ inches at the widest point, by 2⅝ inches measured from the point of the heart to the indentation between the two lobes at the top of the heart.

→ Cut in rows of three along the 8 inch side of the rectangular and in rows of four on the 14 inch side of the rectangle. You should have 12 heart-shaped mousses.

→ As you cut the mousses, remove them from the pan and place them on a parchment-lined half-sheet baking pan.

→ Cover and return to the freezer until ready to plate the dessert.

TIP: *The butter and brown sugar used to sauté the bananas lend the requisite complexing flavor to the fruit, working well to give the mousse its mellow, round personality.*

Sliced sautéed bananas

YIELD: 12 SERVINGS,
APPROXIMATELY 24 OUNCES,
EACH SERVING WEIGHING
APPROXIMATELY 2 OUNCES

Oz	Grams	Each	Name of ingredient
8	240		Unsalted butter
8	240		Brown sugar
20	600	5 to 6 medium-sized bananas	Medium-sized just ripe bananas, peeled, halved across the middle of the banana, and then sliced lengthwise.

The skins of the bananas should be just starting to become spotted with black specks.

→ In a medium-sized heavy sauté pan, melt the butter, stir in the brown sugar, and continue stirring until mostly dissolved.

→ Then gently add the banana slices, one by one, in a single layer, being careful not to break them.

→ Sauté gently until the butter and brown sugar have coated the banana slices evenly.

→ Using a fork or perforated spatula, remove the bananas from the pan and place on a parchment-lined baking sheet until ready to plate the dessert.

Assembly and plating

Just before serving the dessert, allow the banana mousse to soften slightly at room temperature. Fan three sautéed banana slices with the rounded ends pointing forward on each plate. Place one slightly softened mousse, set on one of its flat sides, with the point of the heart facing you, just covering the cut ends of the banana slices. Spoon slightly less than ½ ounce of rum caramel syrup plating sauce on the bananas, allowing it to flow onto the plate. Place three cocoa-nib tuiles toward the back of the plate, where the mousse and the bananas meet. Garnish the top of the heart-shaped mousse with a banana corkscrew and serve immediately.

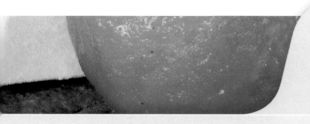

Caramel Poached Pear Tart

YIELD: 12 SERVINGS

Caramel poached pear tart with bourdaloue cream, vanilla ice cream triangles, and cassis-flavored short dough boulettes cookie garnish. While few food historians can agree on the origin of the name of this classic French tart, one popular theory goes like this. Louis Bourdaloue was a 17th century Paris preacher who frequently bought baked goods from a stall outside of his church. The baker eventually moved to more permanent digs, founding a bakery that ultimately became Patisserie Bourdaloue, in homage to the cleric, where the original rendition of this tart became a specialty. Here the tart is deconstructed in a modernized version and there's no denying that all will say "Amen" when tasting its combination of elements (pears, caramel, almond, hazelnut, and vanilla). Its season is fall, suggesting the colors of the leaves as they change: the coppery colored caramel, the bronzed golden brown pastry, the pale purple outside of the miniature cookies, and the flecks of festive gold leaf on the pear stem. There is textural variety here too. Despite long cooking, the pears retain a bit of their pleasantly granular quality echoed by the characteristic sandy texture in the short tart crust and cookies. The bourdaloue cream offers a slightly moist chewiness and the ice cream provides a welcome silky, melt-in-your-mouth creaminess.

The order of things:

1. Make hazelnut short dough and chill.
2. Prepare pears in caramel.
3. Make bourdaloue filling and assemble tart.
4. Bake tart
5. Make cassis flavored boulettes dough and chill
6. Make vanilla ice cream and freeze. Once frozen, cut into triangles and store in freezer.
7. Bake boulettes and allow to cool.
8. Glaze baked tarts.
9. Dust the boulettes with confectioner's sugar coating.

Equipment list:

Bottomless rectangular tart forms, measuring 3¹¹⁄₁₆ by 4³⁄₁₆ inches

Triangular cutter, measuring 3 inches on each side by 2⅝ inches tall to cut ice cream

Hazelnut short dough

YIELD: ENOUGH DOUGH FOR 12 RECTANGULAR TARTS, EACH MEASURING 3¹¹/₁₆ INCHES BY 4³/₁₆ INCHES BY 1 INCH HIGH, EACH WEIGHING APPROXIMATELY 3 OUNCES

Oz	Grams	Each	Name of ingredient	Baker's percentages
10	300		Unsalted butter	67
5	150		Granulated sugar	33
2.6	75	4	Egg yolks from large eggs	17
15	450		All purpose flour	100
	3		Salt	.6
3	150		Hazelnuts, toasted, skinned, and then finely crushed	33

→ In the bowl of an electric mixer outfitted with the paddle attachment, cream the butter until light. Add sugar and beat until well blended.

→ Add egg and mix to incorporate, scraping the bottom and sides of the bowl to ensure that the mixture is well blended. Add flour, salt, and crushed hazelnuts, mixing only until the flour disappears.

→ Remove the dough from the mixer and knead briefly on a lightly floured surface to combine.

→ Flatten into a ½ inch thick disk, wrap well, and chill in the refrigerator until firm.

→ Place 12 rectangular tart forms onto a parchment-lined baking sheet.

→ On a lightly floured surface, roll the dough to a rectangle measuring 18 inches by 21 inches by ¼ inch thickness.

→ Cut rectangular pieces of dough each measuring 5¼ inches by 6 inches, in rows of three along the 18 inch side and in rows of four along the 21 inch side.

→ Slide a thin, long metal spatula under the dough to release it from the surface as needed.

→ Carefully pick up the cut pieces of dough, one at a time, and line each of the tart forms, pressing the dough against the bottom and sides of the mold to form a precise shell.

→ Place the sheet pan in the refrigerator to chill the dough until it is firm again.

While the shells are chilling, prepare the pears in caramel as follows

If you are serving this dessert the same day it is baked, the unbaked shells may be stored at room temperature, covered, while the pears are cooking in caramel. Alternatively, if serving the dessert on the next day, the shells may be held refrigerated overnight.

Pears in caramel

YIELD: 12 PEARS, ONE PER SERVING

Lbs	Oz	Each	Name of ingredient
4 lb, approximately		12, approximately 5.5 oz each, when weighed whole, before peeling, whole with core intact	Whole ripe but not overripe or mushy Bosc variety pears; if unavailable, other varieties may be used: Packham, Taylor's Gold, French butter, or less preferably, Bartlett or Anjou
	2		Fresh lemon juice, sieved
	16		Water

→ Mix lemon juice and water in a large bowl.

→ Peel the pears, without bruising, keeping the stems intact and place them into the acidulated water until ready to cook.

Lb	Oz	Each	Name of ingredient
4			Sugar
2			Water
	8		**Trimoline,** invert sugar syrup
1			**Unsalted butter,** cut into tablespoon-sized pieces
	32		**Heavy cream**
		6 each, split	**Vanilla beans**

Note that there will be caramel left after serving this dessert. Reserve, refrigerated, either for another batch, or for another use. It could also be used as a sauce for a poached pear, served with vanilla ice cream.

→ Cook sugar, water, and Trimoline in a large, wide, heavy saucepan until deep golden brown, or when it reaches approximately 340°F.

→ Add cream and vanilla beans and cook, stirring constantly, until smooth. Add the butter, piece by piece, whisking to keep the mixture emulsified.

→ Add the pears in a single layer and cook over low to medium heat, turning them occasionally to color them, and cook them evenly until tender but not mushy. This process may take as long as two-and-a-half to three hours, over very low heat.

→ Cooking the caramel on low heat ensures that the pears will remain intact. When the pears are tender but not mushy and deeply colored, remove them carefully, without denting or bruising them, to a parchment-lined baking sheet. Using a corer, remove the cores starting at the bottom of the fruit, leaving the stem intact. Discard the cores.

→ Reserve the cooking liquid to use as plating sauce.

For best color and texture, it is best to use the pears on the same day that they are cooked.

Ozs	Grams	Each	Name of ingredient	Baker's percentages
3.1	100		**Unsalted butter**	100
3.1	100		**Sugar**	100
2	60	(3 egg yolks)	**Egg yolks**	60
3.1	100		**Almond flour**	100
0.3	10		**Dark Rum**	10
0.3	10		**Vanilla extract**	10
	2		**Almond extract**	2

→ In the bowl of an electric mixer outfitted with the paddle attachment, beat the butter and sugar together until smooth.

→ Add the egg yolks and then blend in the almond flour.

→ Add rum, vanilla, and almond extracts and mix lightly until combined. Set aside.

Vanilla ice cream

YIELD: EQUILATERAL TRIANGLES, EACH MEASURING 3 INCHES ON A SIDE, 2⅝ INCHES HIGH, AND APPROXIMATELY ¾ TO 1 INCH THICK

Oz	Grams	Each	Name of ingredient
12			Whole milk
		2 each	Madagascar vanilla beans, split
4			Egg yolks
3			Granulated sugar
		1	Salt
6			Heavy cream

→ In a medium-sized heavy saucepan, bring the milk and vanilla beans to a simmer. Remove from the heat, cover the pan and allow to infuse for 30 minutes.

→ Remove vanilla beans, rinse, and dry, and reserve for another use. In the bowl of an electric mixer outfitted with the whisk attachment, beat egg yolks and sugar to thick ribbon stage.

→ The mixture should fall off the whisk slowly in a thick ribbon.

→ Reheat milk and temper half of it into the egg and sugar mixture.

→ Add the remaining milk and then cook the mixture over medium heat, stirring with a wooden spoon constantly, without aerating, until the mixture reaches 185°F.

→ Remove from the heat and stir in the salt and mix to dissolve. Pass through a fine sieve into a stainless steel bowl set over an ice bath.

→ Cool quickly, stirring occasionally, and when cold stir in the cream and transfer the mixture to the bowl of an electric ice cream machine.

→ Freeze until semi-firm and then pour out the mixture into a rectangular pan, measuring approximately 9 inches wide by 10 inches tall, spreading it out evenly, using an offset spatula or plastic bowl scraper.

→ Freeze until firm again and then cut into 12 uniform triangles, using a triangular-shaped cookie cutter, measuring 3 inches on each side by 2⅝ inches tall.

→ With the 10 inch side of the rectangle facing you, start from the top left corner edge, roughly ½ inch in from that corner, and cut one triangle with the point of the triangular cutter facing you.

→ Then moving to your right, cut another triangle and then another.

→ You can now cut two more triangles from the areas left between the first and second triangles and the second and third triangles, this time with the point of the triangle facing away from you.

→ Repeat the process to yield five more triangles in the next row, starting 3⅛ inches down from the top left corner of the rectangle.

→ After cutting these five triangles, repeat the process again, starting again 5¾ inches from the top left corner of the rectangle.

→ You will have 15 equal triangles of ice cream, 12 of which will be used for this dessert. The extras may be set aside for another use or take the place of any that are imperfectly shaped. Keep the triangles frozen, covered, and remove from freezer just before serving the dessert.

Cassis-flavored short dough boulettes

YIELD: APPROXIMATELY
4 OUNCES, ENOUGH FOR
3 BOULETTES PER SERVING,
EACH COOKIE WEIGHING
APPROXIMATELY 4 GRAMS

Oz	Grams	Name of ingredient	Baker's percentages
2		**Confectioners' sugar,** to coat the cookies after baking	
		Purple (or red and blue combined) powdered food coloring combined with cassis powder, as needed	
1	28	**Unsalted butter**	66
0.5	14	**Granulated sugar**	33
0.5	14	**Whole egg**	33
1.5	42	**Almond flour or finely ground almonds**	100
0.25	8	**Cassis powder;** dehydrated raspberries, powdered, may be substituted here	

→ Combine the confectioners' sugar, cassis powder and purple coloring and set the mixture aside.

→ In the bowl of an electric mixer, cream the butter with the sugar until well blended. Add the egg and mix to incorporate.

→ Add the almond flour and cassis powder and mix until absorbed. Remove the dough from the mixer, compress, wrap, and refrigerate until firm.

→ Remove from the refrigerator and pinch off pieces of the dough, each weighing approximately 4 grams.

→ Round the dough and place on a parchment-lined baking pan.

→ Bake in a preheated 350°F oven for approximately 20 minutes, or until dry and baked through.

→ Remove from the oven and immediately dredge the cookies in the confectioners' sugar mixture.

→ Store at room temperature until ready to plate the dessert.

Glaze to finish the tarts

YIELD: APPROXIMATELY
6 OUNCES

Oz	Name of ingredient
4	Apricot or clear glaze
2–3	Water

Garnish

Oz	Name of ingredient
	Gold leaf, if desired
24	**Caramel sauce,** from above

Optional flavoring

Oz	Name of ingredient
1–2	**Eau de vie de poire Williams** (clear pear brandy)

Assembling and baking the tart

Pipe a ½ inch thick layer (generous 1 oz per tart) of Bourdaloue filling into the chilled tart molds lined with tart dough. Bake in a preheated 350°F oven until the filling is set and lightly golden. Do not overbake or the filling will be dry. Remove from oven and place onto a cooling rack.

In a small heavy saucepan, bring the apricot or clear glaze to the boil, stirring to smooth. Allow the glaze to cool slightly to egg-white consistency and then using a pastry brush, glaze the top of the tarts in a thin, even layer. Reheat as necessary over low heat to re-liquefy to complete the glazing of all the tarts.

With an apple corer, small sharp knife or melon baller, carefully remove the cores from the pears, starting at the bottom of the pear. Discard the cores. Place the cored pears, standing upright, pointed side up, on top of the filling. Place each tart on a serving plate. Place one each of the vanilla ice cream triangles on each tart, beside and slightly behind the pears. Affix a small amount of gold leaf to the stem of each pear. Garnish the plate with three cassis-flavored short dough boulettes and spoon some caramel sauce in front of the tart, approximately 2 ounces per serving. The caramel may be flavored lightly with *eau de vie de poire* Williams, pear brandy, if desired.

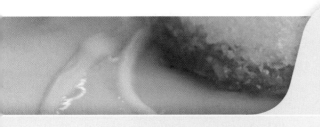

Pineapple Upside Down Cake

YIELD: 12 SERVINGS

Pineapple upside down cake, lavender honey ice cream, rum syrup, and crème anglaise, with a pineapple-lavender French macaroon garnish. Using a classic American comfort dessert as a point of departure, this version of pineapple upside down cake is the epitome of balance, both literally and figuratively. A see-saw–like baton of lavender honey ice cream is poised horizontally and seemingly precariously on top of the cake. Lavender is used in two forms in the ice cream; in its crème anglaise base, which is infused with dried lavender flowers, and in the honey itself, made in Provence, France, where these and many other flowers are grown for the perfume and cosmetics industry. Rings of sweet-tart fresh tropical pineapple are bathed in a dark brown sugar and butter syrup at the bottom of the mold with the fine-grained pound cake above, absorbing some of the molasses sweetness of the syrup as well. The rum-based plating sauce, with its own burnt sugar notes, adds another element of the tropics. Once again, crunch and cream go hand in hand in the French-style macaroons, redolent of pineapple and lavender.

The order of things:

1 **Make crème anglaise** and chill

2 **Make lavender honey ice cream,** using chilled crème anglaise, and freeze

3 **Make crème anglaise** for plating sauce and chill

4 **Make buttercream**

5 **Make the smear to line the bottom of the molds for the cakes; then make the pineapple upside down cakes**

6 **Make batter for macaroon cookies, pipe out and bake,** then cool

7 **Cut frozen ice cream into baton shapes** and reserve in freezer

8 **Make rum syrup** for plating sauce and chill

9 **Temper white chocolate** and hold

Equipment list:

Round metal cookie cutter, measuring approximately 1⅜ inches in diameter, to trim the pineapple rounds

12 **thimble-shaped molds,** each measuring 2¾ inches diameter at the top wider end, 1¾ inches diameter at the smaller end by 2½ inch high for cakes

Paper cornets to pipe out white chocolate onto plates

Rectangular pan measuring 4½ inches by 8 inches lined with a sheet of food-grade acetate, for the ice cream **OR**

Heavy stainless steel caramel bars used to create the mold in which the ice cream will be placed to freeze before cutting into thin rectangular batons

Upside down pineapple cake

YIELD: APPROXIMATELY
30 OUNCES, 12 SERVINGS,
EACH WEIGHING
APPROXIMATELY
2½ OUNCES

Oz	Grams	Each	Name of ingredient	Baker's percentages
4.8, approximately, for 12 cored rings	144		**Fresh pineapple,** peeled and cored, from one large pineapple	
8	240		**Unsalted butter,** room temperature	100
8	240		**Granulated sugar**	100
8.3	250	5	**Large eggs**	104
0.5	15	1 T.	**Vanilla extract**	6
8	240		**Cake flour**	100
.17	5	1 t.	**Baking powder**	2
	2		**Salt**	.8

For the smear in the base of the molds

YIELD: ENOUGH TO
COAT THE BOTTOMS
OF 12 MOLDS

Oz	Grams	Each	Name of ingredient	Baker's percentages
3	90		**Unsalted butter**	100
3	90		**Muscovado or dark brown sugar**	100
.03	1	½ t.	**Freshly grated nutmeg**	1

Prepare the pineapple for the cake as follows

→ Remove the crown of leaves from the pineapple and discard it.

→ Peel and core the pineapple, discarding the peel.

→ Turn the pineapple on its side on a cutting surface and using a serrated knife, slice it into ½ inch thick rounds.

→ Using a round cookie cutter, trim each slice into a circle, measuring approximately 1⅜ inches in diameter.

→ Each slice should weigh about 0.40 ounce.

→ Reserve any leftover pineapple for another use.

Prepare the cake as follows

→ In the bowl of an electric mixer fitted with the paddle attachment, beat the butter until creamy, fluffy, and light in color.

→ Add sugar and beat until the sugar has nearly dissolved.

→ Add the eggs and vanilla extract, beating until smooth.

→ Sift cake flour, baking powder, and salt and then gently but thoroughly fold into the cake base.

→ For smear in the base of the molds, in the bowl of an electric mixer outfitted with the paddle attachment, cream the butter with the brown sugar until light and fluffy.

→ Add nutmeg and mix to distribute evenly.

→ Then coat the bottom of twelve Silform thimble-shaped molds, each measuring 2¾ inches diameter at the top wider end, 1¾ inches diameter at the smaller end by 2½ inch high with a thin layer of this mixture.

→ Place the prepared rings of fresh pineapple into the molds, on top of the butter mixture.

→ Pour the cake batter over the pineapple, rap the mold against a hard surface to settle the batter and remove any air bubbles.

- Place the plaque of molds onto a sheet pan and bake in a preheated 325°F oven for approximately 40 minutes, or until the cake is fully risen and golden brown, and is done when a skewer inserted in the center of the cake tests dry.

- Allow to cool.

- Unmold the cakes by inverting the plaque onto a parchment-lined sheet pan.

- Remove the plaque and then using a serrated knife, level the bottoms of each of the 12 cakes, removing any bulge, as needed, to create flat-bottomed thimble shaped cakes.

- Set aside, covered, until ready to assemble the dessert.

Oz	Grams	Each	Name of ingredient	Baker's percentages
16	480		Whole milk	100
4	120		Lavender honey	25
2.6	78	4	Egg yolks from large eggs	16
1.4	42		Dried lavender flowers	9
8	240		Heavy cream	50

Lavender honey ice cream

YIELD: APPROXIMATELY 24 OUNCES, 12 SERVINGS, EACH WEIGHING APPROXIMATELY 2 OUNCES

Prepare the pan for the ice cream in one of two ways, as follows

- Line a rectangular pan measuring 4½ inches by 8 inches with a sheet of acetate.

- Set aside.

- **Alternatively,** place four metal bars on the back of a sheet pan, with an acetate sheet on it.

- Arrange the bars to create a rectangle measuring 4½ inches by 8 inches by 1 inch deep.

- Set the prepared pan aside in the freezer until ready to fill.

Prepare the ice cream as follows

- In the bowl of an electric mixer outfitted with the whisk attachment, whip the egg yolks with the lavender honey until the honey is dissolved and the mixture is thick.

- In a medium-sized heavy saucepan, scald the milk with the dried lavender flowers and then simmer for 5 minutes more.

- Remove from the heat, cover, and allow to infuse for 30 minutes. The flavor of the lavender should come through clearly here.

- Pass the mixture through a fine sieve, discarding the lavender flowers.

- Reheat the resulting lavender-infused milk and then temper it into the egg yolks and honey mixture, mixing without aerating.

- Transfer the mixture to a stainless steel bowl set over a saucepan of simmering water. (The water should not touch the bottom of the bowl.) Cook, stirring with a wooden spoon, without aerating, until the mixture reaches 180°F and coats the back of the spoon.

- Remove from the heat, pass through a fine sieve, cool over an ice water bath, stirring occasionally, and when cool, add the heavy cream.

- Transfer the mixture to the bowl of an electric ice cream machine and freeze until semi-firm.

- When semi-firm, remove from the freezer and transfer the mixture either into the prepared rectangular pan or onto the back of the sheet pan prepared with the metal caramel bars, smoothing the top of the mixture with an offset spatula or plastic scraper.

- Freeze, covered, until firm.

- When firm, remove from the freezer and cut the ice cream into thin batons, each measuring 4 inches long by ¾ inch wide, cutting in rows of 2 on the 8 inch side and rows of 6 on the 4½ inch side.

- → If at any time during the cutting process the ice cream begins to soften, return it immediately to the freezer and then, when firmed, resume the cutting.
- → As the ice cream is cut, remove the batons from the pan, placing them on a parchment-lined sheet pan.
- → Return to the freezer, covered, until ready to plate the dessert.

Rum syrup

YIELD: APPROXIMATELY
9 OUNCES, 12 SERVINGS,
EACH WEIGHING
¾ OUNCE

Oz	Grams	Name of ingredient	Baker's percentages
8	240	**Simple syrup** (a mixture of equal parts by weight of granulated sugar and water, boiled until the sugar dissolves)	100
1	30	**Dark rum**	12

- → In a small bowl, combine the syrup and the rum and transfer the mixture to a squeeze bottle, and cover it.
- → Store in the refrigerator until ready to assemble the dessert.
- → Rewarm as needed to re-liquefy just before using to sauce the plate.

Crème anglaise as sauce for the plate

YIELD: APPROXIMATELY
20 OUNCES, 12 SERVINGS,
EACH WEIGHING 1⅜ OUNCES

Oz	Grams	Each	Name of ingredient	Baker's percentages
12	360		**Whole milk**	100
5	150	From 8 eggs	**Egg yolks** from large eggs	42
4	120		**Granulated sugar**	33
		1	**Vanilla bean,** split	

TIP: *By agitating the egg yolks and sugar mixture by beating until thick, the sugar is being broken down into smaller particles and almost dissolves, leading to a silky-textured, uniformly smooth crème anglaise.*

- → In the bowl of an electric mixer outfitted with the whisk attachment, whip the egg yolks and sugar until light in color and thick.
- → When the whisk is lifted from the bowl, the mixture should flow slowly in a thick ribbon.
- → Transfer the mixture to a stainless steel bowl and set aside.
- → In a medium-sized heavy saucepan, bring the milk along with the vanilla bean to the boil. Reduce to a simmer and cook for 5 minutes.
- → Remove from the heat, cover, and allow the mixture to infuse. The flavor of the vanilla should come through clearly here.
- → Remove the vanilla bean (wash and reserve for another use).
- → Reheat the infused liquid and then temper a small amount of it into the egg yolk–sugar mixture.
- → Place this mixture over a pan of simmering water (the water should not touch the bottom of the bowl).
- → Cook, stirring with a wooden spoon, without aerating, until the mixture reaches 180°F and it coats the back of the spoon.
- → Remove from the heat, pass through a fine sieve into a stainless steel bowl set over a bowl of ice water, and cool quickly, stirring occasionally.
- → When cold, pour the mixture into a squeeze bottle, cover, and refrigerate the bottle until ready to assemble the dessert.

Grams	Each	Name of ingredient
8	240	White chocolate couverture or nontempering white chocolate coating

If using white chocolate couverture, temper as follows

→ Heat ⅔ of the white chocolate couverture in a stainless steel bowl over simmering water.

→ Melt it, stirring occasionally, until it reaches 122°F.

→ When it reaches this temperature, remove from the heat and add the remaining one-third of the chocolate to lower the temperature of the chocolate to 81°F.

→ Stir constantly during this process to encourage the production of many small cocoa butter crystals that will lead to a good temper for the chocolate.

→ Then carefully rewarm to 86°F.

→ Maintain over a warm water bath at this prescribed temperature.

→ To test to see if the chocolate is in temper, dip the corner of a small piece of parchment paper in the chocolate and then place the parchment pieces on a work surface.

→ If the chocolate is in temper, it should dry within minutes and break cleanly when the paper is folded. It also should not melt readily when touched.

If using non-tempering white chocolate

→ Chop the white chocolate coating and place each piece into a stainless steel bowl, set over a water bath of simmering water.

→ Stir to melt and keep warm so that the coating flows easily.

Oz	Grams	Name of ingredient	Baker's percentages
	12 g—Start with approximately 20 g, since you will most likely be discarding some unpulverized lumps, which would reduce the yield to the desired 12 grams	**Freeze dried pineapple,** powdered in a small blender, sieved to remove any large lumps; discard any lumps	11
3.8	114	**Almond flour,** finely ground	100
7	210	**Confectioners' sugar**	210
3	90	**Egg whites,** room temperature	78
1.75	53	**Granulated sugar**	46

Pineapple lavender French macaroons

YIELD: APPROXIMATELY 36 MACAROONS, WEIGHING APPROXIMATELY ½ OZ. EACH

To make the macaroons, prepare the baking pan as follows

→ Draw thirty-six 1⅞ inch diameter circles onto a sheet of parchment paper.

→ Place this template onto the back of a half-sheet pan.

→ Place the dried pineapple into a spice grinder or small blender to pulverize.

→ Then press the powder through a fine sieve and set aside.

→ Preheat the oven to 325°F.

TIP: *Allow the cookies to dry at room temperature for approximately 15 minutes before placing the sheet pans into the oven. This helps to create a smooth well rounded top surface on the macaroons.*

- Into a medium-sized bowl, sift the almond flour, confectioners' sugar, and dried pineapple powder together, pressing the mixture through the sieve to yield as much as possible. The mixture should have no lumps.

- In the bowl of an electric mixer outfitted with the whisk attachment, beat the egg whites with the granulated sugar until thick and stiff, about 10 minutes.

- Using a wide spatula, thoroughly but gently fold the beaten whites into the dry mixture. Place the mixture into a pastry bag outfitted with a plain pastry tip, measuring ½ inch in diameter.

- Using the pastry bag, pipe out 36 equal mounds of batter onto the parchment-lined baking sheets, using the template underneath as your guide.

- When piping, place the end of the pastry tip at a 45 degree angle to the baking sheet and pipe circles for each cookie without moving the bag, to create an even, rounded shape.

- Rap the sheet to settle the cookie batter lightly.

- Bake for approximately 12 minutes. The ideal macaroon should look puffed with a slightly grainy "foot" of the mixture around the perimeter of the base of each cookie. Allow to cool and then assemble the cookies.

Lavender butter cream

YIELD: APPROXIMATELY 15 OUNCES

Oz	Grams	Each	Name of ingredient	Baker's percentages
6	180		**Simple syrup**	100
1	30		**Dried lavender**	16
2.6	78	4	**Egg yolks** from large eggs, warmed to approximately 90°F	43
8	240		**Unsalted butter**	133
Few drops, as needed			**Lavender-colored food coloring**	

- Heat simple syrup with dried lavender to a simmer.

- Allow to simmer for about 5 minutes and then remove from heat.

- Allow the lavender to infuse for approximately 15 minutes and then pass the mixture through a fine sieve, discarding the lavender flowers.

- Return the sieved infused syrup to a heavy saucepan and heat to 236°F.

- Place egg yolks in the bowl of an electric mixer outfitted with the whisk attachment.

- Beat the yolks until thick and light, and with the machine running pour the hot syrup in a thin stream into the egg yolks.

- Continue beating until the mixture is light in color and cool.

- Add the butter in tablespoon-sized pieces.

- Add color and mix until evenly colored.

- Set mixture aside at room temperature until ready to fill the macaroons.

Assembling the macaroons

→ For each cookie garnish, lay out three similar-sized macaroons.

→ Pipe a small dollop of lavender butter cream on two of the three macaroons.

→ Start with one butter cream–topped cookie as the bottom, rounded side down.

→ Place the second butter cream–topped cookie on top of the first one, press gently to compact, and then complete the stack by placing the third macaroon on top of the second, rounded side up.

Assembly and plating

Over a double boiler, melt the tempered white chocolate or non-tempering white chocolate coating, until fluid. Allow to cool briefly and fill parchment paper cones with the mixture. Using a parchment paper decorating cone filled with the tempered white chocolate or non-tempering white chocolate coating, pipe out two circles onto the plate, which touch at the back of the plate, the smaller one 3 inches in diameter and the larger one 5 inches in diameter. Allow the chocolate to set and reserve the plates in a cool place until ready to complete the presentation of the dessert. Using squeeze bottles, one filled with rum syrup and the other one filled with crème anglaise, carefully fill the smaller circle with rum syrup and the larger one with crème anglaise. Carefully center one of the pineapple upside down cakes onto the circle of rum sauce and then place a baton of lavender honey ice cream onto the cake. Place a pineapple lavender macaroon to the right of the cake. Serve immediately.

Broiled Fresh Figs, Goat Cheese–Mascarpone Crema with Sweet Basil Sauce and Pine Nut Tuile

YIELD: 12 SERVINGS

Caramelized fresh figs, goat cheese–mascarpone crema, sweet basil sauce, pine nut tuile. A fruit known in antiquity, figs were enjoyed by the ancient Romans who knew both the fresh and dried variety and took advantage of the inherent sweetness of the fruit at a time when processed sugar itself was a rare luxury. In the United States, the fresh fig market is small compared to the quantities of dried figs that are sold for use in the cookie making industry. There is no clearer announcement that high summer has arrived than featuring a fig-based dessert on the menu. With their succulent honeyed interior, fresh figs are particularly well suited to treating simply—the less manipulated, the better. Here, lobes of the fresh fruit are quickly pan seared in butter and honey and arranged around a mound of a mild-flavored mixture of mascarpone and goat cheese. Completing the quartet of elements are two more entries from the Mediterranean pantry: pine nuts and basil. Usually more at home in a savory pesto, here the pine nuts stud a crisp cookie garnish that falls somewhere between a lacy florentine and a brittle. The basil appears in a sweetened syrup that dots the plate.

The order of things:

1. **Make pine nut tuile batter** and keep at room temperature until ready to bake (if baking within a few hours); if not, refrigerate and then bring to room temperature before spreading the batter through a template on to a Silpat, then bake

2. **Make sweet basil sauce, prepare goat cheese–mascarpone crema** and refrigerate

3. **Bake tuiles**

4. **Caramelize the figs**

Equipment list:

Leaf-shaped tuile template with cutouts measuring approximately 4 inches long by 1½ inches wide measured across the leaf at the widest point for the pine nut tuiles

Squeeze bottle for saucing the plates

For alternate presentation of the goat cheese–mascarpone crema: silicone plaque with 12 demispherical indentations, each measuring 2 inches in diameter

Caramelized fresh figs

YIELD: 12 SERVINGS, ONE LARGE FIG EACH

Oz	Grams		Name of ingredient
18	340	12	*Large* **fresh figs**, ripe, either purple- or green-skinned variety
2	60		**Unsalted butter**
2, approximately	60		**Sugar or honey**

→ From the stem end, using a small sharp knife, separate each fig into five equal "petals."

→ In a heavy saucepan, melt the butter and sear each petal, turning once to brown both sides, adding sugar and honey.

→ Caramelize briefly and then remove them from the pan. The fig petals should remain intact and should have a golden color on each cut side. Set aside.

TIP: *Alternatively, a torch may be used to caramelize the figs after they have been sautéed, if you would like the figs to have a deeper, more caramelized color.*

Goat cheese-mascarpone crema

YIELD: 12 SERVINGS, EACH 1¾ OUNCES

Filling for figs

Oz	Grams	Name of ingredient
11	330	**Fresh soft goat cheese**
8	240	**Mascarpone**
2	60	**Simple syrup**

TIP: *Instead of piping the mixture free form into coiled pyramids for a rustic presentation, if desired, the mixture may be piped into small demispherical silicone molds and then frozen for easy removal. Once frozen, remove from the molds, place the crema mounds onto a parchment-lined sheet pan and refrigerate until ready to serve the dessert.*

→ In the bowl of an electric mixer outfitted with the paddle attachment, cream the goat cheese and mascarpone until well blended. Add simple syrup and continue blending until well incorporated.

→ Refrigerate mixture until ready to plate the dessert.

Fresh sweet basil sauce

YIELD: APPROXIMATELY 5 OUNCES, 12 SERVINGS, LESS THAN ½ OUNCE PER SERVING

Oz	Grams	Name of ingredient
1.2	36	**Fresh basil leaves,** washed and dried gently
4	120	**Simple syrup**

→ Blanch basil leaves in boiling water just until they brighten in color.

→ Drain immediately, place briefly in ice water to set the color.

→ Remove from ice water, gently squeeze out excess moisture and place in the bowl of a food processor or blender with simple syrup.

→ Process until small flecks of basil leaf remain.

→ Transfer the mixture to a squeeze bottle, covered, and refrigerate until ready to plate the dessert.

Pine nut tuiles

YIELD: 12 SMALL LEAF-SHAPED COOKIES, EACH MEASURING APPROXIMATELY 4 INCHES LONG BY 1½ INCHES WIDE MEASURED ACROSS THE LEAF AT THE WIDEST POINT, EACH WEIGHING APPROXIMATELY 1 OUNCE

Oz	Grams	Each	Name of ingredient	Baker's percentages
2.7	81		**Heavy cream**	270
2.7	81		**Honey**	270
0.66	20		**Corn syrup**	67
4	120		**Granulated sugar**	400
	1	Pinch	**Salt**	3
1	30		**All purpose flour**	100
1½ total, using approximately 2 to 3 g of pine nuts for **each** tuile	45		**Pine nuts,** toasted in preheated 350°F oven, until golden brown, about 5 minutes	150

TIP: *It's important here to spread the batter in an even layer on the Silpat for even baking.*

→ In a small heavy saucepan, bring cream, honey, corn syrup, and sugar to a boil.

→ Remove from heat, stir in salt and flour, and deposit each cookie onto the back of a Silpat-lined baking sheet, using a leaf-shaped template measuring approximately 5 inches long (from point to point) by 1½ inches wide, measured across the leaf at the widest point.

- Sprinkle pine nuts evenly over each cookie. Bake in a preheated 375°F oven for approximately 5 minutes, or until bubbling and golden brown. Remove from oven, allow to cool briefly, and then curve over a rolling pin, nutted side facing the rolling pin (see photograph).

- Cool completely and store in airtight container, outfitted with a piece of limestone or a packet of silica gel to help preserve the cookies' crispness, until ready to serve.

Assembly and plating

Using a pastry bag outfitted with a ½ inch diameter rosette tip, at the center of each plate, pipe out goat cheese–mascarpone crema in a 2 inch tall rosette. Position the five fig "petals" evenly around the base of the crema, placing each petal at an angle so that the fig resembles a flower with slightly upturned petals. Using a squeeze bottle, pipe small dots of the sweet basil syrup in between each "petal." Gently insert one point of the pine nut tuile into the back of, and arching over, the crema, nutted side facing the front of the plate. Serve immediately.

Fresh Rhubarb Tatin with Ginger Ice Cream and Strawberry Rhubarb Sauce

YIELD: 12 SERVINGS

Fresh rhubarb tart "Tatin," on a base of filo dough, with a hole in middle, supported by a cone of ginger ice cream, served with strawberry sauce. Two old maids, living in the mid-19th century to early in the 20th, who ran the Hotel Tatin in the small town of Lamotte-Beuvron, about 24 miles from Orleans, France, and immortalized the hotel and perhaps themselves in the process with their unintentionally upside-down caramelized apple tart, spawned a whole series of imitators down to the present day. As a kind of homage to the inventors, this tart in its modern presentation is baked likewise with its pastry on top, using filo here instead of the more rustic short dough of the original, and rhubarb instead of apples, baked below in a buttery brown sugar coating. This dessert calls for precision both in the cutting of the fruit and the layering and cutting of the pastry dough to yield a geometrically balanced design. A crème anglaise–based ice cream is flavored with two forms of ginger, fresh and candied, and acts as a whimsical and tasty support for the tart, which is suspended about halfway up the sides of the ice cream. Strawberry, rhubarb's favorite sidekick, appears in a puree on the plate.

The order of things:

1. **Make ginger ice cream and fill plastic pastry bags** with the mixture to freeze into conical shapes
2. **Prepare rhubarb**
3. **Prepare filo dough**
4. **Assemble the rhubarb tarts** and bake
5. **Make strawberry sauce**

Equipment list:

Twelve 10 inch tall **clear plastic disposable pastry bags,** which will be cut down to bags measuring 6 inches tall and 4½ inch across the top, to shape the ice cream

Twelve 32 ounce **disposable plastic containers** each measuring 5⅝ inches tall, used to suspend the ice cream filled pastry bags, while freezing

Thin skewers, 6 to 8 inches long

Heavyweight round metal cutters, one measure 6 inches in diameter, and the other measuring 1½ inches in diameter

Two **silicone plaques** each with 6 indentations, each measuring 6 inches in diameter

Pastry brushes to brush melted butter on the filo sheets

Squeeze bottle for strawberry plating sauce

Small metal spatula and vessel containing hot water to use when smoothing out the surface of the ginger ice cream "cones"

Ginger ice cream

YIELD: APPROXIMATELY
54 OUNCES, 12 CONES,
EACH WEIGHING APPROXI-
MATELY 4½ OUNCES

Oz	Grams	Each	Name of ingredient
4	120		**Crystallized ginger,** cut into ¼ inch cubes
24	720		**Whole milk**
		3	**Whole Madagascar vanilla beans,** split
2	60		**Fresh gingerroot,** peeled and sliced into thin coins
8	240		**Egg yolks**
6	180		**Granulated sugar**
12	360		**Heavy cream**
		3	**Salt**

→ Using a heavy chef's knife, chop the crystallized ginger into ¼ inch cubes.

→ Set aside until ready to add to the finished ice cream.

→ In a medium-sized heavy saucepan, bring the milk, vanilla beans, and gingerroot to a simmer.

→ Cover the pan and allow to infuse for 30 minutes.

→ Pass the mixture through a fine sieve to remove the vanilla beans and gingerroot.

→ Retrieve the vanilla beans, rinse, and dry, and reserve for another use.

→ Discard the gingerroot.

→ In the bowl of an electric mixer outfitted with the whisk attachment, beat the egg yolks and the sugar to thick ribbon stage.

→ Reheat the milk and temper half of it into the egg and sugar mixture.

→ Add the remaining milk and then cook the mixture over medium heat, stirring with a wooden spoon constantly, without aerating, until it reaches 185 degrees F.

→ Stir in the salt and mix to dissolve.

→ Remove from the heat and pass through a fine sieve into a stainless steel bowl set over an ice bath.

→ Cool quickly, stirring occasionally, and when cold, freeze the mixture in the bowl of an electric ice cream machine.

→ When almost firm, remove from the ice cream machine, stir in chopped crystallized ginger.

→ Place the mixture into a rectangular container and freeze while you prepare the molds for the ice cream.

Preparing the molds

→ Remove the top 3½ inches from each of twelve 10 inch tall clear plastic disposable pastry bags by making a cut across the bag parallel to the top opening of the bag, yielding a pastry bag measuring approximately 6½ inches from the point of the bag to the top of the bag. The open end of the bag should now measure approximately 4¼ inches wide.

→ With the point of a thin wooden skewer, make a hole, ½ inch down from the top of the pastry bag, at the center point of the top of each bag, through both layers of plastic and then open the bags.

→ Insert the skewer through the two holes that you have just made and suspend each bag onto a 32 ounce disposable plastic container measuring 5⅝ inches tall, resting the skewer on the top edge of the container.

→ Tape the skewer to the container to secure it at the two points where it touches the top of the container.

→ Place the 12 containers on a full sheet pan.

→ Remove the ice cream from the freezer and allow it to soften slightly.

→ Then fill the pastry bags with the ice cream, compacting it as much as possible so that there are no air pockets.

→ Place the sheet pan of ice cream-filled pastry bags into the freezer until ready to finish the dessert.

TIP: *Fresh gingerroot should have a taut unblemished skin and be firm to the touch with no soft or bruised areas. Shriveling is a sign of less than pristinely fresh gingerroot, which often has an off or weak flavor.*

*Fresh rhubarb
cooked in butter
and brown sugar*

YIELD: 12 SERVINGS, EACH WITH
4 TO 5 OUNCES OF FRUIT

Oz	Grams	Name of ingredient
50–60, approximately	1500–1800, approximately	**Fresh rhubarb,** cut into sticks, about ½ inch wide by 2¼ inches long
8–10, approximately	240–300, approximately	**Unsalted butter**
12	360	**Brown sugar**

→ Wash and dry the rhubarb.

→ Cut off the top 1 inch of each stalk of rhubarb.

→ Cut each stalk into 2¼ inch lengths ½ inch thick. You will need approximately 30 pieces cut this size for each tart.

→ Set aside the cut fruit, covered with a damp paper towel, until ready to assemble the tart.

Oz	Grams	Each	Name of ingredient
		18	**Rectangular sheets of filo dough,** each measuring 12 inches by 17 inches
0.5	15		**Ground cinnamon**
0.25	7.5		**Ground ginger**
6	180		**Granulated sugar**
8, approximately	240		**Butter,** melted

→ Remove the filo dough from the plastic package and unroll the dough into one flat stack, with the long edge that measures 17 inches facing you.

→ Keep the filo covered with a lightly damp towel at all times, to prevent drying out. In a medium-sized bowl, mix the cinnamon, ginger, and sugar until uniform in color and set aside.

→ Remove one sheet of filo from the stack and lay it on your work surface, long side facing you.

→ Brush the dough *evenly but lightly* with melted butter.

→ Place another sheet on top of the first, brushing with butter, and then sprinkle a light coating of the spice and granulated sugar mixture on the dough.

→ Continue layering, buttering, and sprinkling with the spice and sugar mixture until you have created a stack of six sheets. (For each stack, the spice mixture is used once again, after you have placed the fourth layer of filo on the stack.)

→ Repeat this process twice more to yield three stacks of filo, six sheets each.

→ Using a round cookie cutter measuring 6 inches in diameter, rotating the cutter, right to left and left to right, cut four rounds of filo from each of the six-layered stacks.

→ Use a small sharp knife to complete the cuts, as needed. From each stack, you will have a strip measuring approximately 5 inches by 12 inches left over.

→ Reserve for another use.

→ Using a 1½ inch round cookie cutter cut a hole in the center of each filo round and remove it. Discard or reserve for another use.

→ In a small saucepan, melt the butter and brown sugar, stirring to combine.

→ Pour a small amount of this mixture into each of the twelve 6 inch round cavities of the silicon plaques, coating the bottom of the indentation thinly but completely. (Each silicon plaque has six indentations so you will need two plaques to yield 12 finished tarts.)

→ Keep the mixture warm as you arrange the rhubarb into the silicone plaque as follows.

TIP: *Depending on how lightly (or heavily) you brush each layer of filo with butter, you may find that you will need somewhat more than the 8 ounces called for.*

Assembling and baking the rhubarb/filo component

→ Place the rhubarb pieces into the 6 inch round cavities of each of two Silicone plaques (six cavities per plaque for a total of 12), arranging them closely together like the spokes of a wheel, covering the bottom of each cavity with a single layer of the rhubarb and leaving the center open, measuring 1½ inches in diameter.

→ Brush the fruit evenly with the remaining butter–brown sugar mixture.

→ Place six filo rounds onto the rhubarb arranged in each of the plaques. Then brush the tops of each round of filo generously with melted butter.

→ Place each of the silicone plaques carefully onto a full sheet pan and bake in a preheated 400°F oven for approximately 25 minutes. The pastry dough should be golden brown and the rhubarb should be tender but not disintegrating.

→ Remove from the oven and place the sheet pans on a cooling rack and store at room temperature until ready to assemble the dessert. (If serving the next day, refrigerate the tarts and allow to come to room temperature or, if you prefer, warm the tarts to order briefly in a 350°F oven until warm, about 10 minutes.)

Strawberry sauce for plating

YIELD: APPROXIMATELY 12 OUNCES, 12 SERVINGS, EACH WEIGHING APPROXIMATELY 1 OUNCE

Oz	Grams	Name of ingredient
16	480	Fresh strawberries
4	120	Simple syrup

→ In a food processor, puree the strawberries with the syrup until smooth.

→ Pass through a fine sieve to remove seeds and any bits of unpureed pulp.

→ Pour into a squeeze bottle and set aside, covered, in the refrigerator until ready to plate the dessert.

Assembly and plating

Just before plating each dessert, remove the plastic container containing the pastry bag of ginger ice cream from the freezer. Remove the skewers from the pastry bag and peel off the pastry bag. Place the cone onto a parchment-lined baking pan. With a small knife dipped in hot water, trim the base of the cone, as needed, so that it stands perfectly vertical on the sheet pan. Using a small spatula dipped in hot water, smooth rough areas, if any, on each cone of ice cream.

Invert the silicone plaques onto a parchment-lined full-sheet pan to remove the rhubarb tarts from the plaque.

Center one cone of ice cream on each serving plate. Carefully place one tart over the ice cream, balancing it so that it is parallel to the surface of the plate. The tart should rest at a point 3¼ inches from the base of the cone (or approximately half way from the top of the cone and the bottom of the cone). Beginning at the left back side of the cone and keeping approximately equidistant ½ inch from the base of the cone, pipe a series of five dots of strawberry sauce, becoming progressively larger as you move toward the front of the plate, with the last and largest dot of sauce adjacent to the front of the cone of ice cream. Serve immediately.

Persimmon Pudding

YIELD: 12 SERVINGS

Fall quartet: Persimmon pudding, persimmon sorbet, persimmon chips, and persimmon carpaccio, set onto a square filo stack. This dessert gives the persimmon, an undeservedly neglected fruit, its day in the sun during its peak from fall to winter. Thought to be Chinese in origin and revered in Japan, two kinds of the fruit, the heart-shaped Hachiya (which must be used when fully ripe and very soft), and the somewhat flattened, round Fuyu, the nonastringent variety (which may be eaten when still hard, almost like a crisp apple), are used in four forms: pureed and baked into a pudding, frozen into a sorbet, sliced thinly as a base for the dessert, and oven dried into a chip. At its best, the fruits have a mild but sweet flavor, which is complemented by the warm aroma of cinnamon, used here in two forms: as a ground flavoring for the pudding and in whole stick form to flavor the caramel sauce that tops the dessert. Contrasts of texture abound here. The creamy sorbet contrasts with the crunchy filo layers on the plate and with the shatteringly crisp translucent fruit chip. The soft, juicy, thin slices of fruit in the persimmon "carpaccio" work well against the crisp filo as well. Dates and currants provide spots of sweetness in the overall custardy softness of the pudding.

The order of things:

1. **Make persimmon chips**
2. **Make persimmon sorbet**
3. **Make persimmon pudding**
4. **Prepare filo bases**
5. **Make cinnamon caramel**
6. **Bake filo bases** within two hours of serving the dessert, for maximum crispness and freshness
7. **Slice persimmons** for persimmon "carpaccio" to order just before serving

Equipment list:

Mandoline to slice persimmons for persimmon chips and for persimmon "carpaccio"

Silicon plaque with 12 heart-shaped indentations, each measuring 2½ inches from the point to the flat top by 2½ inches measured at the widest point, from side to side, by 1 inch deep

Pastry brush to brush melted butter on the layers of filo dough

Squeeze bottle to deposit cinnamon caramel onto plate

Oz	Grams	Each	Name of ingredient
8, approximately	240, approximately	2	**Persimmons,** whole, unpeeled
3	90		**Simple syrup**

Persimmon chips

YIELD: ENOUGH CHIPS FOR 12 SERVINGS, ALLOWING FOR EXTRAS IN CASE ANY OF THE CHIPS ARE MISSHAPED OR OTHERWISE UNUSABLE

→ Using a mandoline, slice the persimmons across the fruits to reveal a star-shaped pattern, making the slices thin enough to be translucent but not so thin as to break at the edges.

→ Place the slices into a small bowl.

→ Pour the simple syrup over them and allow to soak for a few minutes.

TIP: *With their flattened round shape and the fact that they may be eaten when still hard, the Fuyu variety will yield more uniform-sized chips and they will be easier to slice.*

TIP: *It may take a few passes of the fruit over the mandoline blade before finding just the right setting to produce slices of the proper thickness.*

→ Remove the slices carefully from the syrup and place them on a Silpat-lined baking sheet.

→ Bake in preheated 250°F oven for approximately 50 minutes, or until somewhat dry to the touch, rotating the sheet pan as needed to ensure even drying.

→ Remove from the oven and allow to cool at room temperature.

→ When cool, using a small spatula, if necessary, carefully release the chips from the Silpat and place them in a single layer, or layered with sheets of parchment between the layers, in an airtight container with a tight-fitting lid, outfitted with a piece of limestone or a packet of silica gel, to retain crispness.

→ Store at cool room temperature until ready to use.

Persimmon sorbet

YIELD: APPROXIMATELY
24 OUNCES, 12 SERVINGS
EACH WEIGHING 2 OUNCES

Oz	Grams	Each	Name of ingredient
19 net weight, after peeling	570 net weight after peeling	3	**Persimmons**
5	150		**Simple syrup**
0.5	15		**Fresh lemon juice,** sieved
		1	**Salt**

→ Peel the persimmons and remove the large brown inedible seeds, as necessary.

→ Puree the fruit in a blender or food processor with the simple syrup, lemon juice, and salt.

→ Transfer the mixture to an electric ice cream machine and freeze until semi-firm.

→ Remove from the machine and spoon the mixture into fill 12 flat-topped heart-shaped Silform molds, of the same dimensions as used above for the persimmon puddings, smoothing the tops with a metal spatula or plastic bowl scraper.

→ Cover the plaque of molds and freeze until firm.

→ Unmold when frozen and place the sorbet hearts onto a parchment-lined sheet pan, covered well.

→ Store in the freezer until ready to plate the dessert.

Persimmon pudding

YIELD: ENOUGH FOR
24 FLAT-TOPPED HEART-
SHAPED MOLDS, USING
2 PER SERVING, APPROXI-
MATELY 1½ OUNCES EACH

Oz	Grams	Each	Name of ingredient
2.5	75		**All purpose flour**
	5		**Baking powder**
	3		**Ground cinnamon**
	1.5		**Salt**
3.5	105		**Dates,** pitted and coarsely chopped
2	60		**Dried currants**
14	420	3 to 4, approximately	**Persimmon puree**
9	270	5 to 6, approximately	Large whole eggs
3	90		Muscovado or dark brown sugar
3.5	105		Unsalted butter, melted and browned

→ Sift the flour, baking powder, cinnamon, and salt onto a sheet of parchment paper, and set aside.

→ Soak dates and currants in hot water to cover, 3–4 minutes. Drain and set aside.

→ Peel and puree the persimmons.

→ In a small bowl, whisk together the eggs and brown sugar.

TIP: *Use fully ripe persimmons for best flavor. The heart-shaped Hachiya variety works best here, but the flatter Fuyu variety, if ripened until very soft, may be used instead.*

- In a small heavy saucepan, melt the butter, cooking it until it browns. Do not burn.
- Remove from the heat, skimming off any foam as necessary.
- Cool slightly and whisk the melted butter into the eggs and brown sugar mixture.
- Fold in the persimmon puree, the dates, and the currants.
- Then finally, fold in the sifted dry ingredients, mixing just to combine.
- Fill 24 heart-shaped Silform molds, each measuring 2½ inches from the point to the flat top by 2½ inches measured at the widest point, from side to side, by 1 inch deep.
- Place each plaque of molds into a water bath and bake in a preheated 350°F oven for approximately 20–30 minutes, or until the puddings test done when a skewer inserted in the middle comes out clean. Do not overbake.
- Remove from the oven, allow to cool to room temperature, and then remove the plaques from the water baths.
- When fully cool, refrigerate until ready to plate and serve the dessert.

Baked filo bases for the pudding

YIELD: 12 PIECES, EACH MEASURING APPROXIMATELY 3 INCHES ON EACH SIDE, ONE PER SERVING

Oz	Grams	Each	Name of ingredient
4	120		**Unsalted butter,** melted
2	60	4	**Rectangular sheets of filo,** each measuring 12 inches by 17 inches

TIP: *These are best baked within a few hours of serving the dessert. They may be stacked and buttered and stored on the parchment-lined sheet pan up to a day before baking.*

- In a small heavy saucepan, melt the butter, skimming off and discarding the white foam as it rises to the top.
- Keep the butter warm.
- Place one filo sheet onto a work surface, with the long side facing you.
- Brush the sheet with a light coating of melted butter.
- Stack three more sheets, one at a time, brushing melted butter between each layer.
- Brush the top sheet of the stack with melted butter.
- Cut the resulting stack of filo sheets into two equal rectangles each measuring 8½ inches by 12 inches.
- Stack one rectangle on top of the other one, creating a stack eight layers thick.
- Cut this eight-layer rectangle into 12 equal-sized pieces, three along the 9 inch side by four along the 12 inch side. Each resulting piece should measure slightly less than 3 inches square. Place the pieces on a sheet pan, lined with parchment paper.
- Not more than 2 hours before serving the dessert, bake the filo bases in a preheated 375°F oven for approximately 10 minutes, or until golden brown and puffed.
- Remove from the oven, placing the pan on a cooling rack.
- Store the baked filo pieces at room temperature until ready to plate the dessert.

Cinnamon caramel

YIELD: 12 SERVINGS, 1 OUNCE EACH

Oz	Grams	Each	Name of ingredient
6	180		**Heavy cream**
		3	**Cinnamon sticks,** approximately 3 inches long each
6	180		**Granulated sugar**

→ In a medium-sized heavy saucepan, bring the cream and cinnamon sticks to a boil.

→ Reduce the heat to a simmer and cook for 5 minutes.

→ Remove from the heat, cover the pan, and allow the cream to infuse for approximately 15 minutes. The flavor of the cinnamon should come through clearly.

→ If not, allow the mixture to infuse for a few minutes longer.

→ Remove the cinnamon sticks and discard, reserving the infused liquid.

→ Reheat the infused liquid and keep it warm.

→ In a medium-sized heavy saucepan, cook the sugar to an amber color.

→ Immediately add the warmed cream and the salt, stirring to combine. (Note that the mixture will bubble up while adding the cream, so be careful.)

→ Remove the pan from the heat and allow to cool to room temperature.

→ When cooled, transfer the mixture to a squeeze bottle and, if not using immediately, store, refrigerated, until ready to plate the dessert.

→ Rewarm the sauce over a hot water bath to re-liquefy before using.

Persimmon "carpaccio"

YIELD: 12 SERVINGS, 8 TO 10 SLICES PER SERVING

Oz	Grams	Each	Name of ingredient
24 net weight approximately	720 net weight	6	Medium to large **Fuyu persimmons,** peeled

TIP: *Here, note that the Fuyu variety is used for the "carpaccio" since the fruit must be firm enough to hold its shape when slicing on the mandoline, and this variety is ripe and sweet even when it is still rather firm.*

→ Peel the persimmons and slice into thin but not translucent slices using a mandoline with the flat side facing the blade.

Assembly and plating

Overlap the slices of the persimmon "carpaccio" in a circle, measuring approximately 5 inches in diameter, at the center of the plate. Brush the fruit lightly with simple syrup (a mixture of equal parts of granulated sugar and water, boiled until dissolved, and then cooled.) Place a baked filo square centered on top of the persimmon "carpaccio." Place persimmon pudding, wider side down, onto the filo square. Place an unmolded persimmon sorbet heart on top of the pudding, narrower side down. Place a second persimmon pudding, wider side down, on top of the sorbet. Drizzle the top of the pudding with the warmed cinnamon caramel and garnish with a persimmon chip. Serve immediately.

Raspberry Chiffon Cake with Lychee Sorbet and Raspberry Gelée

YIELD: 12 SERVINGS

Raspberry chiffon cake with lychee sorbet, raspberry gelée, fresh raspberries, lychees, and rose-scented syrup. From early summer to early fall, fresh lychees, native to south China and now grown in Hawaii and Florida, deliver their perfumed punch. Inside what appears to be an impenetrable spiked shell, the pearly white fruit fairly drips with juice, somehow tasting how fragrant roses smell. (A rosewater-flavored plating sauce used here amplifies that impression.)

Once its hard inedible brown seed is removed, the fruit yields easily to the bite and is used here pureed as the basis for a pure white sorbet. Like roses, grown on thorny stems, raspberries have a unique intoxicating fragrance strong enough to complement rather than compete with lychee. The berry is used here in four forms: first, in the cake which is flavored with pulverized dried raspberries; next, in the puree, which soaks the cake; then, in the jewels of gelée that garnish the plate, and act as a melt-in-the-mouth bed for the layers of cake and sorbet; and finally, in the crown on top of the cake, alternating with the bright white lychees.

The order of things:

1. **Make lychee sorbet** and freeze
2. **Make raspberry chiffon cake**
3. **Make raspberry sauce** to brush onto cake
4. **Make raspberry gelée** and refrigerate to set
5. **Make rose-scented syrup**

Equipment list:

Quarter-sheet pan, measuring 9½ inches by 13 inches

12 **rectangular cutters or molds,** each measuring 3¼ inches by 3¹¹⁄₁₆ inches to cut cake and sorbet, and then used to shape after being assembled

Truffle cutters or other small decorative geometric cutters to cut the raspberry gelée

Pastry brush to brush raspberry sauce onto raspberry chiffon cake

Squeeze bottle for the rose-scented syrup

Raspberry chiffon cake

YIELD: APPROXIMATELY 24 OUNCES, ENOUGH FOR 24 TRIANGLES EACH MEASURING 3¹¹/₁₆ BY 1⅝ INCHES BY 4 INCHES, USING 2 TRIANGLES PER SERVING

Oz	Grams	Each	Name of ingredient	Baker's percentages
4	120		**Cake flour**	63
2.4	72		**All purpose flour**	37
0.36	11	2 t.	**Baking powder**	6
		1½ T.	**Dried raspberry powder**	4
		⅓ t.	**Salt**	0.9
4	120	6	**Egg yolks**	62
7	120		Granulated sugar	109
6	180	6	**Egg whites**	93
3	90		Granulated sugar	47
2.4	72		**Vegetable oil**	38
5	150		**Water**	78
0.25	7.5	1½ t.	**Vanilla**	4
As needed			**Red food coloring,** powdered, liquid or paste, to yield a pink-colored cake, if desired	

→ Prepare the baking pan.

→ Spray a quarter-sheet pan measuring 9½ inches by 13 inches, with pan release spray.

→ Line the bottom of the pan with parchment paper.

→ Spray the paper lightly with the pan release spray and set aside.

→ Sift the two kinds of flour, baking powder and raspberry powder onto a sheet of parchment paper and set aside.

→ In the bowl of an electric mixer, outfitted with the paddle attachment, mix the egg yolks, the first quantity of sugar, oil, water, and vanilla (and food color, if using) to a smooth batter, and gently fold the sifted dry ingredients into this mixture.

→ In the bowl of an electric mixer outfitted with the whisk attachment, whip the egg whites to a froth.

→ Then gradually add the second quantity of sugar to the whites, whipping to stiff shiny peaks.

→ Gently but thoroughly fold the whites into the cake base.

→ Pour the batter into the prepared pan and bake in a preheated 350°F oven for 35 minutes, or until the cake springs back when lightly touched in the middle.

→ Remove from the oven and allow to cool on a cooling rack.

→ When cool, cut as follows, placing the cut pieces on a parchment lined sheet pan:

→ Using a rectangular cutter measuring 3¼ inches by 3¹¹/₁₆ inches, cut the cake into rectangles, in rows of two along the 9½ inch side and in rows of three along the 13 inch side.

→ Then cut each resulting rectangle into two equal rectangles by cutting the rectangle in half, beginning at the 3¼ inch side and cutting across to the opposite side.

→ Then cut each half into two equal triangles, starting the cut at the top left corner of the rectangle and cutting across to the opposite corner.

→ Repeat with the other rectangles, resulting in 24 triangles of equal size.

→ The triangles should each measure approximately 3¹¹/₁₆ at the base by 1⅝ inches tall by 4 inches for the hypoteneuse. You will need two triangles of the cake per serving.

→ Make the raspberry glaze as follows and brush the top surfaces and edges of each triangle with an even coat.

→ Set aside, refrigerated, until ready to assemble the dessert.

Oz	Grams	Name of ingredient
8	240	Raspberry puree
As needed		Simple syrup

→ Place the raspberry puree into a medium-sized bowl and add enough simple syrup to make the liquid into a paintable consistency.

→ If not using immediately, cover and refrigerated until ready to proceed.

Oz	Grams	Each	Name of ingredeint
0.3	9	3	Gelatin sheets
8	240		Raspberry puree
3	90		Simple syrup

→ Place the gelatin sheets in to a small bowl with enough cold water to cover.

→ Allow to soften and when softened, remove from the water, squeezing out excess.

→ Place the squeezed-out gelatin into a small bowl and set aside.

→ In a small heavy saucepan, heat the raspberry puree with the simple syrup.

→ Add the gelatin to the hot raspberry puree–syrup mixture.

→ Stir until it is fully dissolved.

→ Pour the mixture into a shallow rectangular mold or pan, measuring 6 inches by 8 inches.

→ Carefully place on a level shelf in the refrigerator and chill until set.

→ Reserve refrigerated until ready to plate the dessert.

Lychee sorbet
YIELD: APPROXIMATELY
22 OUNCES, 24 TRIANGLES,
EACH WEIGHING SLIGHTLY
LESS THAN 1 OUNCE, 2 TRI-
ANGLES PER SERVING

Oz	Grams	Each	Name of ingredient
16	480		Fresh lychee puree or commercially prepared frozen puree, thawed
6	180		Simple syrup
0.08	2.5	½ t.	Rosewater

→ Line the bottom of a quarter sheet pan, measuring 9½ inches by 13 inches by approximately ¾ inch deep, with food-grade acetate and set aside.

→ In a medium-sized bowl, combine all of the ingredients and mix until well blended.

→ Chill until cold.

→ Then transfer the mixture to an electric ice cream machine and freeze until semi-firm.

→ Transfer the mixture to the prepared quarter-sheet pan and smooth the top using an offset spatula or plastic bowl scraper.

→ Cover tightly and freeze until ready to cut into triangles.

If the sorbet begins to soften during the cutting process, return it to the freezer immediately to refirm.

Cutting the sorbet

→ Using a rectangular cutter measuring 3¼ inches by 3¹¹⁄₁₆ inches by approximately 1 inch tall, cut the sorbet into rectangles, in rows of two along the 9½ inch side and in rows of three along the 13 inch side.

→ Cut each rectangle in half, beginning at the 3¼ inch side and cutting across to the opposite side.

→ Then cut each half into two equal triangles, starting the cut at the top left corner of the rectangle and cutting across to the opposite corner.

→ Cut all of the other rectangles in the same way, to yield 24 triangular pieces of sorbet. The triangles should each measure approximately 3¹¹⁄₁₆ inches at their base by 1⅝ inches tall by 4 inches for the hypoteneuse. You will use two triangles of the sorbet per serving.

Garnishes

Fruits

Each	Name of ingredient
24	**Fresh lychees, or canned lychees, peeled and pitted, well drained**
24	**Fresh raspberries**

→ If using fresh lychees, peel by pressing near one end to break the shell and then carefully removing it in pieces.

→ When peeled, make a small cut to free the hard seed and then discard it.

Rose syrup

YIELD: APPROXIMATELY
8 OUNCES

Oz	Grams	Each	Name of ingredient
0.25	7.5	1½	**Rosewater**
8	240		**Simple syrup**
0.5	15		**Fresh lemon juice,** sieved

→ In a small bowl combine the rosewater, simple syrup, and lemon juice.

→ Transfer the mixture to a squeeze bottle and set aside, covered, in the refrigerator until ready to plate the dessert.

TIP: *An alternative to chopping the gelée would be to use small truffle cutters or other decorative cutters to create jewels of a uniform shape such as circles, diamonds, or triangles (or a combination of several shapes), if desired.*

TIP: *The cake and sorbet stacks may be assembled in advance of serving. Compress the layers by fitting the stacks into rectangular molds, each measuring approximately 3¼ inches by 3¹¹⁄₁₆ inches, placing them horizontally onto a parchment-lined sheet pan, covered, and stored in the freezer. After being frozen, remove the stacks from their molds and trim if necessary to align all of the edges. Return to the freezer until a few minutes before serving so that the cake may thaw slightly before being served.*

Assembly and plating

Chop the raspberry gelée into rough ½ inch jewels and reserve, chilled.

Scatter a semicircle of the gelée in the front of each plate. Place one triangle of cake on the plate with the 3¹¹⁄₁₆ inch side down. Stack one triangle of lychee sorbet on top of the cake with the 3¹¹⁄₁₆ inch side facing up. Complete the stack using another layer composed of cake and sorbet.

Garnish the top layer of sorbet with two each fresh lychees and fresh raspberries. Drizzle a small amount of the rose syrup onto the raspberry gelée in front of the cake. Serve immediately.

Rustic Quince Tart with Buttery Almond Cake, Mascarpone Cream, and Pomegranate Sauce

YIELD: 12 INDIVIDUAL TARTS

Rustic quince tart with buttery almond cake base in a whole-wheat crust, served with a drift of mascarpone cream and rose-pomegranate sauce, and a crystallized rose-petal garnish. Simple in execution but complex in flavor, this rustic tart choreographs a quintet of entries from the Mediterranean dance card: quince, an underutilized fruit, red wine, rose in syrup and petal forms, mascarpone, and pomegranates. The buttery almond cake layer baked inside of a rustic whole-wheat short dough is shown off to good advantage peeking through the curved notches cut into the tart shell. Poaching the quince in a vanilla-scented red wine syrup adds another layer of flavor to a fruit that taste somewhat like a highly perfumed pear when ripe. With this treatment, it takes on an intense cerise color, which contrasts nicely with the paler pink of the plating sauces and the bright white of the mascarpone cream garnish.

The order of things:

1. **Crystallize rose petals** and set aside at room temperature
2. **Poach quince and reserve poaching liquid** for plating sauce
3. **Make whole-wheat tart dough** and chill until firm
4. **Make almond cake batter**
5. **Fill tart shells with cake mixture, top with poached quince, and bake tarts**
6. **Reduce poaching liquid** for plating sauce
7. **Make rose-pomegranate syrup**
8. **Prepare mascarpone cream**

Equipment list:

Small brush for brushing the rose petals with egg white mixture when crystallizing

Round metal cutter, measuring 5 inches in diameter, to cut tart dough

Round metal cookie cutter, measuring 2¼ inches in diameter, to cut notches out of tart dough

Two silicone plaques with six 4 inch round cavities (tapering to 3½ inches on the bottom, in which to bake the tarts, **or**

one Silicone plaque with twelve 4 inch round cavities (tapering to 3½ inches on the bottom), in which to bake the tarts, **or 12 bottomless tart rings,** measuring 4 inches in diameter

Two squeeze bottles for saucing the dessert, one for the red wine sauce and the other for the rose-pomegranate syrup

Red wine–poached quince

YIELD: APPROXIMATELY
24 OUNCES, 12 SERVINGS,
EACH SERVING WEIGHING
APPROXIMATELY 2 OUNCES

Oz	Grams	Each	Name of ingredient
8	240		Dry red wine
		1, split lengthwise	Vanilla bean
8	240		Granulated sugar
8	240		Water
20	600	3	**Fresh quince,** peeled and quartered, woody cores removed

TIP: *Cooking times for quince vary from fruit to fruit. For best results, source fragrant fruits that tend to become meltingly tender but not fall apart.*

→ In a medium-sized, heavy, nonreactive saucepan, bring the wine, water, sugar, and vanilla bean to the boil.

→ Reduce to a simmer, add the quince, and cook for approximately 45 minutes, over low heat, or until tender but not disintegrating.

→ Cool the fruit in the syrup.

→ Reserve the syrup for the plating sauces below.

→ Remove to a shallow rectangular container, covered, and refrigerate until ready to assemble the tart.

Whole wheat tart dough

YIELD: ENOUGH FOR
12 TART SHELLS, MEA-
SURING APPROXIMATELY
4 INCHES IN DIAMETER
AFTER BAKING, EACH SHELL
WEIGHING 2¼ OUNCES

Oz	Grams	Each	Name of ingredient	Baker's percentages
12	360		Whole wheat flour	100
	2		Salt	4
0.12	3.4	¾ t.	Cinnamon	0.9
8	240		Butter	66
4	120		Granulated sugar	33
2	60	3	Egg yolks, from large eggs	17
0.12	3.6	¾ t.	Vanilla extract	.6

→ In a large bowl, mix flour, salt, and cinnamon together.

→ In the bowl of an electric mixer outfitted with a paddle attachment, cream the butter until smooth and light.

→ Add sugar and mix until blended.

→ In a small bowl, whisk egg yolks and vanilla and then add to the butter and sugar mixture, mixing to incorporate, scraping the bottom and sides of the bowl to ensure that the mixture is well blended.

→ Add the flour and mix just until it disappears.

→ Remove the dough to a lightly floured surface and knead briefly to densify.

→ Wrap well in plastic wrap and chill until firm, about one hour.

→ On a floured surface, roll the dough to a ¼ inch thickness.

→ Using a 5 inch round cutter, cut the dough into 12 rounds.

→ Reroll as necessary to yield 12 rounds.

→ Place the rounds on a parchment-lined baking sheet and using a cookie cutter measuring 2½ inches in diameter, and positioning it 1⅛ inches in from the outer edge of the circle, cut four half circles out of each round of tart dough, starting at the top of the round, designated as the 12 o'clock position for the first cut. Work around the circle clockwise, to the 3 o'clock position, the 6 o'clock position, and finally the 9 o'clock position, for the second, third, and fourth cuts.

→ Reserve the cutout pieces of dough for another use.

→ Chill the notched rounds of dough again while you set up the baking pans or molds.

- → Place one silicone plaque with six 4 inch round indentations , tapering to 3½ inches on the bottom, on each of two half-sheet pans **or** one plaque with twelve 4 inch round indentations on one full-sheet pan.
- → Alternatively, use 12 metal bottomless ring molds, measuring a diameter of 4 inches by ¾ inch high and place six molds on each of two parchment-lined half-sheet pans or 12 molds on one full-sheet pan.
- → When lining the molds, be sure to center the dough before pressing it into mold.
- → Chill the shells until ready to bake.
- → Make the almond cake filling as follows.

Almond cake filling for tarts

YIELD: APPROXIMATELY 18 OUNCES, ENOUGH TO FILL 12 TARTS, EACH WEIGHING APPROXIMATELY 1½ OUNCES

Oz	Grams	Each	Name of ingredient	Baker's percentages: Flour and almond meal total 100%
3.3	100	2	Large eggs	63
1.75	53		All purpose flour	34
	5	1 t.	Baking powder	3
3.5	105		Almond meal, unblanched	66
3.5	105		Unsalted butter, room temperature	66
4.75	142		Granulated Sugar	89

- → In a small bowl, break up the eggs until yolks and whites are well mixed and set aside.
- → Sift the flour, baking powder, and almond meal and set aside.
- → In the bowl of an electric mixer outfitted with the paddle attachment, cream the butter until light and fluffy.
- → Add sugar and mix until well incorporated, scraping the sides and bottom of the bowl occasionally to ensure that the mixture is well blended.
- → Add the eggs in a steady stream and mix until absorbed.
- → Add the sifted dry ingredients to the above mixture.
- → Scrape the bottom and sides of the bowl again to be sure that the mixture is smooth and well blended. Set aside.
- → Pipe the cake mixture to a height of about ½ inch in each pastry-lined mold.
- → Top with quartered quince and then bake the tarts in a preheated 375°F oven for about 30 minutes, or until the pastry is well browned and the cake has risen.
- → Cool completely and unmold from the silicone plaques or remove the tart rings.

Mascarpone cream

YIELD: APPROXIMATELY 14 OUNCES, 12 SERVINGS, EACH WEIGHING APPROXIMATELY 1 GENEROUS OUNCE

Oz	Grams	Name of ingredient
4	120	Heavy cream
2	60	Granulated sugar
8	240	Mascarpone

- → In the bowl of an electric mixer outfitted with the whisk attachment, whip the cream with the sugar to soft peaks.
- → In a medium-sized bowl, whip the mascarpone briefly to soften and then gently fold the whipped cream into the mascarpone.
- → Reserve the mixture in the refrigerator until ready to plate the dessert.

Red wine sauce

Oz	Grams	Name of ingredient
20, approximately, from above	600	**Red wine from poaching liquid** above
1	30	**Fresh lemon juice**, sieved

→ Pass the poaching liquid through a fine sieve and transfer to a medium-sized heavy saucepan.

→ Cook over high heat, to reduce to a coating consistency.

→ Watch carefully so that the mixture does not burn.

→ Remove from the heat and allow the sauce to cool.

→ Stir in the lemon juice and transfer the liquid to a squeeze bottle.

→ Refrigerate, covered, until ready to use.

→ When removed from the refrigerator, the sauce may need to be heated over a water bath to re-liquefy.

Rose-pomegranate syrup

YIELD: APPROXIMATELY
16 OUNCES, 12 SERVINGS,
EACH WEIGHING APPROXI-
MATELY 1⅓ OUNCES

Oz	Grams	Each	Name of ingredient
2, approximately	60	From ½ large fresh pomegranate	**Fresh pomegranate juice**
12, approximately	360		**Simple syrup**
1	30		**Rosewater**
1	30		**Fresh lemon juice**, sieved

TIP: *Rosewaters vary in intensity of flavor from brand to brand so add sparingly to the syrup, tasting as you go, to achieve just the right hint of floral flavor.*

If unavailable, commercially produced frozen pomegranate puree, thawed, may be substituted in the same amount. Taste the puree for sugar content and reduce the amount of simple syrup accordingly, if necessary.

→ Roll the pomegranate on a work surface to release the juice from the seeds inside of the fruit.

→ Set a fine sieve over a medium-sized bowl.

→ Carefully cut the fruit in half and holding it over the sieve, squeeze out the juice surrounding each of the seeds.

→ In a medium-sized heavy saucepan, bring the simple syrup to the boil. Cool to lukewarm and then add the rosewater, the lemon juice, and the freshly squeezed pomegranate juice.

→ The sauce should be just barely pink, slightly tart, and flavored subtly with rose.

→ Add more simple syrup, if desired, to adjust the color and flavor balance.

→ Place the sauce into a squeeze bottle, covered, and set aside, refrigerated, until ready to plate the dessert.

Oz	Grams	Each	Name of ingredient
		36, approximately	**Fresh rose petals,** organic and unsprayed
2 to 3, approximately	60 to 90	2 to 3	**Egg whites** from large eggs
			or
			2 T. meringue powder dissolved in approximately 2 T. water to make a thin paintable mixture
7	210		Granulated sugar

→ Gently wash and dry the rose petals.

→ In a small bowl, beat the egg whites or, if using instead, the mixture of meringue powder and water.

→ Dip petals quickly into the mixture and then sprinkle the petals with the granulated sugar.

→ Set aside on a fine-meshed cooling rack to dry at room temperature.

TIP: *For best results, allow the rose petals to dry overnight, or at least for 4 hours in advance of serving. Once dry, they may be stored in an airtight container, outfitted with a packet of silica gel or a piece of limestone, to keep dry.*

Assembly and plating

Coat half of the center of the plate with the rose-pomegranate syrup. Place a tart half-way over the sauce and then encircle the first sauce with a rough line of the red wine sauce, brushing some of this sauce on the pieces of quince as a glaze. Place a dollop of mascarpone cream on top of the tart, allowing it to flow onto the sauced plate. Garnish the sauced areas of the plate with crystallized rose petals, if desired, and serve immediately.

Strawberries and Cream Mousse Afloat over a Mint Mojito, with Lime Wafer

YIELD: 12 SERVINGS

Strawberries and cream mousse afloat over a frozen mint mojito granita, with sugar cane sorbet, and a lime-scented wafer with mint fondant filling, garnished with a mint *pâte de fruit* leaf. With their affinity for mint and cream, strawberries are the anchor for this pastel-colored dessert, which is layered not only visually, but from the taste and texture points of view as well. Cuba's national drink, the mojito, composed of muddled fresh mint leaves, lime juice, often some fresh raw sugar cane juice (*guarapo*), and rum, is the inspiration for the frosty white layer of the dessert, which is pale only in color but vibrantly and potently flavored, like its cocktail counterpart. Where sugar cane grows, rum is widely produced so it's no surprise that the two ingredients often end up in the same glass. The fresh sugar cane juice adds an almost perfumed honeydew melon taste to the third layer of the dessert. If the fresh cane juice is unavailable, a reasonable facsimile of it, which is more widely available, is dehydrated sugar cane juice in a convenient canned powdered form, ready to be reconstituted with water. The fourth and last layer of this dessert in a glass is the apple-based mint *pâte de fruit*, leaf shaped and in line to banish the fresh mint leaf from the dessert plate forevermore. A thin, buttery, lime-flavored sandwich cookie filled with a minty fondant lends more cream and crunch to the whole ensemble.

The order of things:

1. **Make mint mojito granita and sugar cane juice sorbet** and freeze
2. **Make strawberries and cream mousse** and freeze
3. **Make cookie dough for lime-scented wafers** and chill
4. **Make *pâte de fruit*** and allow to dry at room temperature
5. **Roll out cookie dough and bake**
6. **Make mint fondant filling** for cookies
7. **Fill and assemble lime-scented wafers**

Equipment list:

Silicone plaque with 12 conical shaped indentations, each measuring 2 inches in diameter by 2 inches high

Round cookie cutter, measuring 2 inches in diameter, to cut sugar cane juice sorbet

Rectangular pan, measuring 4 inches by 6 inches, for mint mojito granita

Heavy metal caramel bars, 12 inches long by ⅝ inches wide, for the mint *pâte de fruit* mixture

Leaf-shaped cookie cutter, measuring 2 inches long by 1 inch wide, measured at the widest point, to cut the *pâte de fruit*

Pastry bag outfitted with a small plain tip or rose petal tip, to pipe onto the wafer cookies before sandwiching them together

Strawberries and cream mousse

YIELD: 12 SERVINGS, MADE IN A SILICONE PLAQUE WITH SMALL CONICAL INDENTATIONS, EACH MEASURING 2 INCHES IN DIAMETER BY 2 INCHES HIGH

Oz	Grams	Name of ingredient
5	150	**Strawberry puree,** divided (if using commercially prepared frozen fruit purees, thaw out—these contain 10% sugar by weight so omit the simple syrup below)
1, approximately	30	**Simple syrup** to taste if using *unsweetened* fresh or frozen berries, pureed
1	30	**Powdered cocoa butter** (Mycryo brand was used in the recipe)
3	90	**Crème fraiche**
9	270	**Heavy cream,** whipped to soft peaks

→ In a small heavy saucepan, heat 3 ounces of the puree to 100°F, adding the simple syrup now if using unsweetened fresh or frozen berries.

→ Add the cocoa butter and stir to melt thoroughly.

→ Add the remaining 2 ounces of the strawberry puree and set aside over an ice bath to cool and thicken slightly. Do not allow the mixture to set completely.

→ In the bowl of an electric mixer outfitted with the whisk attachment, beat the crème fraiche and heavy cream to soft peaks.

→ Fold crème fraiche–whipped cream mixture into strawberry mixture gently but thoroughly.

→ Pour into 12 conical-shaped indentations on a silicone plaque and freeze.

→ Place the serving glasses into the freezer to chill.

Mint mojito granita

YIELD: 12 SERVINGS, EACH WEIGHING SLIGHTLY MORE THAN ¾ OUNCE

Oz	Grams	Name of ingredient
8	240	**Fresh mint leaves**
4	120	**Fresh lime juice,** strained
4	120	**Simple syrup**
2	60	**Rum**

→ In a food processor, blend all of the ingredients until liquefied.

→ Pass through a fine sieve and then freeze in a rectangular pan, measuring 4 inches by 6 inches, covered, until frozen hard.

Sugar cane juice sorbet

YIELD: 12 SEMICIRCLES, EACH WEIGHING APPROXIMATELY 1⅓OZS

Oz	Grams	Name of ingredient
18	540	**Freshly squeezed sugar cane juice**
2	60	**Simple syrup**
.5	15	**Fresh lime juice,** sieved

TIP: *Freshly squeezed sugar cane juice is available in Latin American, Hispanic, and Southeast Asian markets in most major American cities. If unavailable in your area, you may substitute 8 ounces of Sucanat, though not as flavorful or refreshing (dehydrated sugar cane juice dissolved in enough cold water to make a thin liquid), in approximately 10 ounces of water.*

→ Combine freshly squeezed sugar cane juice (or dehydrated sugar cane juice powder dissolved in water), simple syrup, and fresh lime juice in a bowl.

→ Pour the mixture into the bowl of an electric ice cream machine and freeze until almost firm.

→ Remove to a container, pour into a rectangular form, measuring 4 inches by 6 inches, to a depth of about 1 inch, cover, and freeze until ready to assemble the dessert.

→ When the sorbet is almost fully frozen, using a 2 inch diameter round cookie cutter, cut into 6 rounds, in rows of three on the 6 inch side and rows of two on the 4 inch side.

→ Halve each round, yielding 12 semicircles. Place the semicircles onto a sheet pan and cover.

→ Keep frozen until ready to assemble the dessert.

Lime-scented
wafers

YIELD: 24 BATON-SHAPED
COOKIES, EACH MEASURING
3 INCHES LONG BY ¾ INCH
WIDE, BY ⅓ INCH THICK,
TWO PER SERVING

Oz	Grams	Each	Name of ingredient	Baker's percentages
8.5	255		All purpose flour	100
		½ t.	Baking soda	.9
		¼ t.	Salt	0.5
4	120		Unsalted butter	47
7	210		Granulated sugar	82
1.67	50	1	Whole large egg	20
0.5	15		Lime zest, grated	6
0.08	2.4	½ t.	Vanilla extract	0.9
2	60		Granulated sugar, for sprinkling onto each strip of cookie dough	

→ Sift the dry ingredients together and set aside.

→ In the bowl of an electric mixer outfitted with the paddle attachment, cream the butter until light and fluffy.

→ Add the sugar and mix to blend, scraping the bottom and sides of the bowl to ensure that the mixture is well blended.

→ Add the egg and mix again until the mixture is emulsified, scraping the bowl occasionally to be sure that all of the ingredients are well distributed and incorporated.

→ Add the lime zest and vanilla and mix just until blended.

→ Add the dry ingredients and mix only until they disappear into the mixture.

→ Remove the mixture to a sheet of plastic wrap or parchment paper and flatten the mixture into a rough rectangle.

→ Wrap tightly and refrigerate until firm, about 30 minutes.

→ When the dough is chilled and firm, roll it on a lightly floured surface into a rectangle, measuring 4½ inches by 12 inches, approximately ⅓ inch thick.

→ With the 12 inch side facing you, cut the dough as follows:

→ Beginning at the 4½ inch side, and ¾ of an inch below the top left corner of the dough, make the first of five parallel cuts the length of the dough, yielding six strips of dough, each ¾ inch wide by 12 inches long.

→ Then cut the dough along the 12 inch side, make the first of three cuts, moving from left to right with the first cut 3 inches from, and parallel to, the 4½ inch side on your left.

→ Make the two other cuts, 3 inches apart, yielding 24 rectangular shaped pieces of dough, each measuring 3 inches long by ¾ inch wide.

→ Carefully place the rectangles of dough onto a Silpat lined baking sheet and sprinkle lightly with the granulated sugar.

→ Bake in a preheated 350°F oven for approximately 18 minutes. Do not overbake; the cookies should be just barely browned.

→ Remove from the oven and allow to cool.

→ Cover to keep fresh until ready to assemble.

→ These will be trimmed to even batons, sandwiching a mint filling in between two cookies.

Mint syrup

Oz	Grams	Name of ingredient
3.35	100	Fresh mint leaves, stems removed, washed and dried
6	180	Simple syrup

Depending on how much the mint leaves absorb, you may have more syrup than the filling requires (Save any extra for another use, in drinks, as a moistening syrup brushed onto cake layers, or as a drizzle over fresh fruit.)

Fondant base for filling

Oz	Grams	Name of ingredient
4, approximately	120	**Confectioners' sugar,** sifted
4	120	**Unsalted butter,** room temperature
2, approximately	60	**Mint syrup** (from above)

→ Make the mint syrup by placing the mint leaves and the simple syrup into a small saucepan.

→ Bring to the boil and then reduce to a simmer, cooking for 5 minutes.

→ Pass the mixture through a fine sieve, discarding the mint leaves and reserving the liquid.

→ Allow to cool and set aside.

→ Sift the confectioners' sugar and set aside.

→ In the bowl of an electric mixer, outfitted with the paddle attachment, cream the butter.

→ Add the confectioners' sugar and mix until smooth, scraping the bottom and sides of the bowl to ensure that the mixture is well blended.

→ Gradually add 2 ounces of the mint syrup, beating until the mixture is smooth but still remains thick.

→ The filling should hold a shape.

→ If not, add more sifted confectioners' sugar.

→ Reserve the mixture at room temperature, if you are ready to fill the cookies.

→ If not, refrigerate, and then bring to room temperature to soften before filling the cookies.

→ For each finished cookie, you will need two baked rectangles. You will have 24 cookies in all, two for each finished sandwich cookie.

→ Just before serving, using a pastry bag outfitted with a small plain tip or rose petal tip, pipe out an even, thin layer of the mixture onto 12 of the 24 cookies.

→ Assemble the cookies by placing the unfilled ones on top of the filled ones, pressing gently to sandwich the cookies together.

TIP: *When making a short dough, cream the butter until small tails of butter appear on the paddle when it is lifted from the bowl, but do not over-aerate since the final product should be densely buttery, firm and rich but not overly airy and therefore crumbly.*

Mint pâte de fruit

YIELD: 12 LEAVES, EACH MEASURING 2 INCHES LONG BY 1 INCH WIDE, MEASURED AT THE WIDEST POINT

Oz	Grams	Each	Name of ingredient
7	210		**Green apples**
0.75	23		**Granulated sugar**
0.16	4.8		**Pectin powder**
7	210		**Granulated sugar**
1.5	45		**Glucose**
	3		**Citric acid**
		Few drops	**Peppermint flavoring**
		Few drops	**Green food coloring**
4	120		**Granulated sugar,** to coat the finished *pâte de fruit*

- → Peel and core the apples.
- → Chop into rough ½ inch cubes.
- → In a medium-sized heavy saucepan, cook the fruit with just enough water so that it does not burn, until soft, stirring occasionally.
- → Remove from the heat and puree in a food processor until smooth.
- → In a small bowl, combine the first quantity of sugar with the pectin powder and mix until the pectin is evenly distributed throughout the sugar.
- → Set aside.
- → Onto a Silpat set onto a work surface, create a thin rectangle, measuring 2 inches wide by 12 inches long, by ⅝ inches high, by arranging four heavy metal *caramel* bars, 12 inches long by ⅝ inches wide as follows.
- → Place two of the bars parallel to each other, 2 inches apart.
- → Place the other two bars, parallel to each other, one each at the narrow end of the rectangle that you are forming, to close off the rectangle.
- → In a clean medium-sized heavy saucepan, bring the pureed fruit and the sugar-pectin mixture to a boil, stirring to be sure that the pectin and sugar mixture is well dissolved into the fruit.
- → Add the second quantity of sugar and bring to a rolling boil, stirring constantly.
- → Add glucose and boil again, stirring constantly.
- → Bring the mixture to 225°F.
- → Immediately add the citric acid and stir until dissolved.
- → Add the peppermint flavoring and coloring, as desired, and pour mixture immediately into the rectangle created by the caramel bars, spreading quickly to an even thickness, before the mixture cools.
- → Allow to cool completely and then cut into leaf shapes, using a leaf-shaped cookie cutter, measuring 2 inches long by 1 inch wide, measured at the widest point.
- → Dip the leaf-shaped *pâte de fruit* into the granulated sugar to coat well on all sides and set aside at cool room temperature until ready to garnish the dessert.

Assembly and plating

When ready to serve the dessert, grate the frozen mint mojito mixture with a fork or large-holed grater into each well-chilled glass to fill the glass to a height approximately two-thirds of the way up the sides. Place a cone of strawberry and cream mousse into each glass, flat side up, pointed side down. Depending on the height of the glass, there will be a space between the mousse and the frozen mint mojito mixture. Place a half round of the sugar cane juice sorbet on top of each glass. Garnish with the mint *pâte de fruit* leaf. Place a lime wafer sandwich on the plate below each glass and serve the dessert immediately with long spoons.

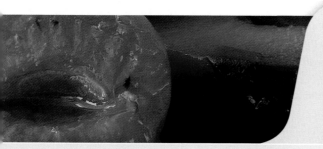

Tea-Poached Plums, Earl Grey Tea–Orange Ice, Amaretti Cookie Garnish with Tea Syrup

YIELD: 12 SERVINGS

Tea-poached plums, Earl Grey tea–orange ice, and amaretti cookie garnish and tea syrup. Here the brightness of all-year-round citrus pairs with the bergamot orange-scented Earl Grey tea that flavors a granita-like ice. Taking advantage of the abundance of stone fruits and the ever widening array of hybrids throughout the summer, this dessert trumps eating these fruits simply out of hand by poaching them in a tea-scented liquid. Tender but still slightly toothy, the fruit contrasts nicely with the ice, the texture of billowy snow. If filled with a layer of meltingly tender Earl Grey tea ganache, the chewy yet crisp cookies accompanying the dessert set up another layer of textural contrast.

The order of things:

1. **Make Earl Grey tea–orange ice,** place into the freezer and scrape frequently to yield a fluffy, granular texture
2. **Poach plums**
3. **Pack the tea-orange ice into molds and freeze**
4. **Make amaretti cookies**
5. **Make Earl Grey tea ganache**
6. **Fill the cookies**

Equipment list:

Fine sieve, used to remove the tea leaves from the tea infusion for the sorbet

Plain round decorating tip, measuring approximately ½ inch diameter, used to pipe the ganache filling for the amaretti cookie garnish

Silicone plaque with 12 demispherical indentations, each measuring 3 inches in diameter by 2 inches deep, to mold the tea-orange ice

Oz	Grams	Each	Name of ingredient
Approximately 48 to 60 ounces gross weight, before removing the pits. It is difficult to estimate the net weight of the fruit, given that the pit size varies from fruit to fruit and hybrid to hybrid.	1440 to 1800 gross weight	12	Purple plums
Approximately 2 to 3 oz each before pitting for a total gross weight of approximately 12 to 15	360 to 540 gross weight	6	Apricots
OR			
Approximately 2 to 3 oz each before pitting for a total gross weight of approximately 12 to 15		6	Apriums
It is difficult to estimate the net weight of the fruit, given that the pit size varies from fruit to fruit and hybrid to hybrid.			
32	950		Simple syrup
	15		Good quality, whole leaf Earl Grey tea leaves

Tea-poached plums (or a combination of plums, apriums, and apricots, as desired)

YIELD: 12 SERVINGS, 3 HALF FRUITS EACH SERVING

TIP: *Instead of the combination and amounts of fruits shown here, you may use instead the same total weight, composed of a combination of plums, and apricots, or a combination of the hybrids now currently available such as plumcots, apriums, or pluots, choosing whichever fruits have the most flavor.*

→ Pit the fruits and discard pits.

→ Place simple syrup and tea leaves into a medium-sized heavy saucepan.

→ Simmer to infuse, about 15 minutes.

→ Pass the poaching liquid through a fine sieve.

→ Rinse and dry the saucepan and return the sieved liquid to the cleaned saucepan.

→ Add the fruit to the liquid in the saucepan and simmer for approximately 30 minutes, or until slightly tender but not mushy.

→ Allow to cool to room temperature in the liquid and set aside until ready to plate the dessert.

Earl Grey tea–orange ice

YIELD: 12 APPROXIMATELY
1 OUNCE SERVINGS

Oz	Grams	Name of ingredient
4	120	**Simple syrup**
0.5	15	**Good quality, whole leaf Earl grey tea leaves,** naturally scented
12	360	**Fresh orange juice,** sieved

→ In a medium-sized saucepan, bring the simple syrup to a boil.

→ Add the tea leaves and infuse, simmering, for about 2 minutes.

→ Remove from the heat, cover the saucepan, and allow the mixture to infuse for approximately 10 minutes.

→ Then pass the liquid through a fine sieve.

→ Add orange juice to the sieved liquid and cool.

→ Once cool, place the mixture into a wide shallow stainless steel pan.

→ Place the pan into the freezer and allow the mixture to freeze until slushy.

→ Scrape with a fork frequently until the ice freezes, producing a mixture that is uniformly granular in texture.

→ Spoon or scoop the granular mixture into a plaque with 12 demispherical indentations, each measuring 3 inches in diameter by 2 inches deep, compacting them slightly, and keep frozen and covered until ready to serve the dessert.

Amaretti cookies

YIELD: APPROXIMATELY
3 DOZEN COOKIES, EACH
WEIGHING APPROXIMATELY
½ OUNCE

Oz	Grams	Each	Name of ingredient	Baker's percentages Almond flour at 100%
8.8	264		**Almond flour**	100
8.75	263		**Granulated sugar**	100
0.16	4.8	1 t.	**Almond extract**	2
3	90		**Egg whites**	34
7	210		**Confectioners' sugar,** used to dip the cookies while shaping	

→ Combine almond flour and granulated sugar in a large bowl.

→ Add almond extract and egg whites and stir until smooth.

→ The mixture can be rolled in confectioners' sugar and then molded in a silicone plaque with small pyramid, oval, or round indentations, or rolled in confectioners' sugar and formed by hand into rough small pyramid shapes that have been dimpled symmetrically four times around the outside edge of the cookie, pulling the center up a bit as you dimple the sides.

- → Alternately, the cookie mixture may be formed into ½ inch diameter balls, flattened slightly and encrusted lightly with pearl sugar.
- → Once formed, bake the cookies in a preheated 375°F oven for approximately 6 minutes or until golden brown.
- → If you wish, you may sandwich two each of either of the two shapes of cookies together to enclose a filling of Earl Grey tea truffle ganache, prepared as follows.

Earl grey tea ganache

YIELD: ENOUGH TO FILL 12 PAIRS OF AMARETTI COOKIES

Oz	Grams	Name of ingredient	Baker's percentages: Chocolate at 100%
	15	**Good quality, whole leaf Earl Grey tea leaves,** naturally scented	8
3	90	**Heavy cream**	67
6	180	**58% dark chocolate,** finely chopped	100

- → Place the chocolate in a heat-proof bowl.
- → Place tea leaves and heavy cream into a small heavy saucepan.
- → Bring the mixture to a boil, then reduce to a simmer and simmer for 5 minutes.
- → Remove from heat, cover the saucepan, and allow the mixture to infuse for approximately 15 minutes.
- → Then pass the liquid through a fine sieve, pressing hard on the solids, into the bowl of chopped chocolate.
- → Stir with a spoon without aerating until the mixture is smooth.
- → Set aside to cool, and if necessary, place over a bowl of ice briefly to firm slightly.
- → Place the mixture into a pastry bag outfitted with a plain round tip, measuring approximately ½ inch diameter, and pipe out enough to barely cover the flat side of each of 12 cookies.
- → Pair each of these cookies with one of the remaining 12 cookies, pressing gently, to make a sandwich.
- → Set aside in a cool place until ready to serve the dessert.

Assembly and plating

Place two plum halves side by side and a half of an apricot or Aprium in front of the plums on each of 12 serving plates. Surround the fruits with the poaching liquid. Place a demisphere of Earl Grey tea–orange ice centered on the plum halves, and serve a small plate of amaretti cookies set on the main dessert plate or beside it.

Warm Souffléed Pancake with Nectarines and Peche de Vigne (Red Peach) Ice Cream, with Red Wine Sauce and Crème Fraiche

YIELD: 12 SERVINGS

Warm souffléed pancakes with pan sautéed nectarines, *peche de vigne* (red peach) ice cream and red wine sauce, with crème fraiche garnish. Dripping with juice, nectarines and peaches mingle their highly aromatic personalities in this dessert. Inspired by the glories of the stone fruit season, this dessert makes use of the red-fleshed *peche de vigne*, which imparts a rosy glow to the ice cream. The true variety's origins date back to the several-hundred-years-old practice in the Coteaux du Lyonnais wine growing region where winemakers planted peach trees at the end of their rows of vines. Planted as an early alert system to show any signs of sickness or infestation in the vineyard, the peach is now produced in orchards and many red-fleshed hybrids exist whose parentage is probably traceable to those original trees.

Pairing a warm just-from-the-oven pancake with hot, slightly caramelized sautéed nectarines and icy cold, creamy ice cream, this dessert provides a set of temperature and taste contrasts for the palate. The tart-sweet red wine sauce ties things together and acts as a nod to the long-ago origins of the fruit that flavors the ice cream. If true *peche de vigne* varieties are unavailable, look for other red-fleshed peaches at farmers markets, sometimes called Indian blood peaches, a favorite in the southern United States, dating back to the time of Thomas Jefferson.

The order of things:

1 **Make peche de vigne ice cream**
2 **Make *beurre noisette***
3 **Prepare nectarines**
4 **Make pancake batter base**
5 **Make red wine sauce**
6 **Form quenelles of crème fraiche** as a garnish for each dessert as it is ordered
7 **Finish pancake batter by adding whipped egg whites** for each serving as it is ordered

Equipment list:

A **silicon plaque** with 12 conical indentations, each measuring 3 inches in diameter at the top by 2½ inches tall, for the peche de vigne ice cream

Clean, empty, cardboard egg crates to support the conical indentations so that they stand perfectly vertical

Nonstick ovenproof pan, 5 to 6 inches in diameter, in which to cook the souffleed pancakes

Souffléed pancake batter

YIELD: APPROXIMATELY
60 OUNCES, 12 SERVINGS,
APPROXIMATELY 5 OUNCES
EACH

Oz	Grams	Each	Name of ingredient	Baker's percentages
22	660	13	**Large eggs,** separated	169
13	390		**Whole milk**	100
6	180		**Granulated sugar,** divided	46
6	180		**Unsalted butter,** melted	46
0.5	15	1 T.	**Vanilla extract**	4
		6 t. from 6 medium-sized oranges	**Orange zest,** grated	
		3 t. from 3 medium-sized tangerines	**Tangerine zest**	
	5	3 t. from 3 medium-sized lemons	Lemon zest	
13	390		All purpose flour	100
.18	5.4	1½ t.	Baking powder	1
.15	4.5	¾ t.	Salt	1

TIP: *If tangerines are unavailable, double up on either the orange or lemon zest.*

TIP: *For maximum lightness, it is best to fold the beaten egg whites into each portion of the pancake batter base as the dessert is ordered.*

→ Separate the eggs.

→ Place the whites in one small bowl and the yolks into a large bowl.

→ Add the milk and half of the granulated sugar to the yolks and mix until blended, without aerating.

→ Add the vanilla and the citrus zests and mix to combine.

→ Sift the flour, baking powder, and salt into a bowl.

→ Add the liquids gradually to the dry ingredients.

→ The pancake batter base should be prepared and held at this point and divided into twelve 5 ounce portions, for each serving of the dessert.

→ Just before baking the pancake, for each portion place 1 ounce of the whites and ¼ ounce of the remaining sugar into the bowl of an electric mixer, outfitted with the whisk attachment and whip the mixture to soft peaks.

→ Fold the beaten whites into single serving portion of the batter.

→ Immediately pour the batter into a nonstick ovenproof pan, 5 to 6 inches in diameter, first sprayed lightly with pan spray.

→ Bake in a preheated 400°F oven for approximately 15 minutes, or until puffed and golden brown.

→ While the pancake is baking, just before serving, sauté the nectarines as follows.

Preparing the nectarines

Oz	Grams	Each	Name of ingredient
6	180		**Brown butter** (*beurre noisette*)
42 net weight	1260	12, one nectarine per serving, approximately 3.5 oz, pitted	**Fresh nectarines,** pitted and sliced into wedges approximately ½ inch thick
12	360		**Granulated sugar**
Few drops for 12 portions of fruit			**Pure almond extract**

→ In a small heavy saucepan, melt the butter, removing the foam that rises to the surface.

→ Continue cooking until the butter turns a golden nut brown. Do not burn.

→ Carefully spoon off the browned *beurre noisette* from the pan into a bowl and reserve, leaving behind the burnt milk solids in the bottom of the saucepan that are to be discarded.

- → For each portion, place 1½ t. of the *beurre noisette* into a heavy, nonstick skillet.
- → Add 1 ounce of sugar and 3½ ounces of the sliced nectarines to the pan and sauté until the fruit is slightly brown and tender, but *not* mushy.
- → Add a drop of the almond extract and stir to combine.
- → Remove from the pan and set aside to serve.
- → As needed, repeat the process to continue to cook the fruit for each serving as above.

Red peach ice cream (peche de vigne)

YIELD: APPROXIMATELY 30 OZ, 12 SERVINGS, EACH WEIGHING 2½ OUNCES

Oz	Grams	Name of ingredient
14	420	**Fresh red peach puree,** or commercially prepared *peche de vigne* red peach puree, frozen, thawed
4	120	**Simple syrup**
8	240	**Heavy cream**
4	120	**Whole milk**
	1	**Salt**

- → Combine all of the ingredients in a large bowl, mix well, and then transfer to an electric ice cream machine.
- → Freeze until semi-firm.
- → Transfer the ice cream from the machine to fill 12 conical molds, each measuring 3 inches in diameter at the top by 2½ inches tall, smoothing the tops of the molds with a metal spatula or plastic bowl scraper.
- → Place the plaque of conical molds, pointed side down, onto clean, empty, cardboard egg crates to support the molds so that they stand perfectly vertical.
- → Place the egg crates containing the molds onto a sheet pan, cover the molds, and freeze until fully frozen.
- → When frozen, unmold the ice cream and place onto a parchment-lined sheet pan.
- → Cover well and freeze until ready to plate and serve the dessert.

Red wine reduction sauce

YIELD: APPROXIMATELY 16 OZ.

Oz	Grams	Name of ingredient
32	960	**Dry red wine**
4, approximately	120, approximately	**Granulated sugar**

Garnishes

Oz	Grams	Name of ingredient
2	60	**Confectioners' sugar**
4–5 oz	120 to 150	**Crème fraiche**

- → In a nonreactive medium-sized heavy saucepan, bring the wine to the boil.
- → Simmer until the wine has lost its biting alcoholic overtones.
- → Add the sugar and cook until the sugar dissolves.
- → Continue cooking to reduce the liquid to a thin syrup, adding more sugar, to taste, as desired.
- → Remove from the heat, cool to room temperature, and transfer the mixture to an airtight container, refrigerated, until ready to serve the dessert.

Assembly and plating

Scatter a few slices of cooked nectarine on the center of each plate. Place one warm pancake on top of the fruit. Sprinkle confectioners' sugar sparingly over the pancake. Garnish with the remaining fruit. Top with a conical serving of the red peach ice cream. Sauce the plate with a drizzle of red wine sauce. Finally place a quenelle of crème fraiche beside the pancake and serve immediately.

A Duo of Cream Puffs

YIELD: 12 SERVINGS

A duo of cream puffs, lemon, and espresso fillings, with a frilly skirt of filo garnish for the top puff, divided horizontally by a cocoa tuile with a powdered sugar edge, sauced with lemon curd sauce. Espresso and lemon have been inextricably linked, but Italians who earn the bragging rights to claim that they invented espresso are adamant that serving a cup of espresso with anything other than a bit of sugar is purely an American affectation. They maintain that if the coffee is made with quality beans, properly roasted, and properly ground, and the drink "pulled" properly using a fine-tuned espresso machine, then there's no need for lemon peel to mask the true flavor of the coffee since it's the coffee that espresso aficionados want to taste. Here pairing the two flavors, coffee and lemon, is conscionable and even desirable given the intervening elements of caramel, two kinds of crusty buttery-browned pastry and chocolate. The architecture of this gravity-defying dessert appeals to the rational minded. A sturdy espresso cream filled puff is set on a plate adorned with tart and zesty lemon curd sauce, then surmounted by a bittersweet thin chocolaty wafer and finally topped with yet another puff, this one filled with a starch-free lemon curd, the ultimate buttery distillation of the ubiquitous citrus fruit. A bit of caramel crackles on the bottom puff and a shatteringly crisp frill of well-browned filo tops the upper puff. Whether the layers are demolished by the over-eager hand of someone who thinks that all foods are finger foods, or the dessert is caused to tumble more ceremoniously thanks to the ministrations of a knife and fork—in either case, the result is pure heaven on the plate.

The order of things:

1. **Make pâte à choux dough** and pipe it out onto parchment-lined baking sheets for puffs and bake the puffs
2. **Make lemon filling**
3. **Make espresso filling**
4. **Make chocolate tuile batter** and rest
5. **Prepare filo "skirts"** by stacking the dough, brushing with melted butter, and then cutting to circles of graduated diameters
6. **Bake filo rounds**
7. **Bake chocolate tuiles**
8. **Fill the puffs**
9. **Make caramel** and dip the tops of twelve of the puffs into it, then set aside the dipped puffs
10. **Assemble the desserts** just before serving

Equipment list:

Pastry bag, outfitted with a round plain tip, measuring ½ inch in diameter

Three round metal cutters, one each measuring 2 inches, 2½ inches and 3 inches in diameter

A **muffin pan** with twelve 2-inch diameter muffin cavities, the backs of which will be used to shape the filo "skirts" before baking

Tuile template with cutout circles 4½ inches in diameter

Pâte à choux dough

YIELD: 24 PUFFS, 1.3 OUNCES EACH, ALLOWING TWO 2½ INCH DIAMETER PUFFS PER SERVING, TOTALING 12 SERVINGS

Oz	Grams	Each	Name of ingredient	Baker's percentages
9	270		Water	128
4.5	135		Unsalted butter	64
		¼ t.	Salt	.7
1	30		Granulated sugar	14
7	210		All purpose flour	100
11	330	6 to 7	Whole large eggs	157

Finished baked dimensions: large 2½ inch diameter circle

→ Make the pate a choux dough as follows:

→ Place the water, butter, salt and sugar into a heavy medium sized saucepan.

→ Over high heat, bring the mixture to the boil, stirring with a wooden spoon until the butter is fully melted.

→ Reduce the heat to medium and add the flour all at once, stirring until the mixture is thick and resembles mashed potatoes.

→ Remove from the heat and transfer the mixture to the bowl of an electric mixer, outfitted with the paddle attachment.

→ Place the eggs into a bowl and mix until the yolks and whites are mixed.

→ Allow the cooked mixture to cool to 140°F, and when it is at that temperature add the eggs in a thin stream, mixing on medium speed until well absorbed and the mixture is smooth.

→ Place the cream puff pastry into a pastry bag, outfitted with a plain round tip, measuring ½ inch in diameter.

→ Pipe the mixture in even rounds onto a parchment paper–lined sheet pan creating a base circle, approximately 2 inches in diameter, and building two more tightly coiled circles on top of the base circle.

→ Using a finger dipped in warm water, smooth out the dough, eliminating any protruding points or irregularities before baking.

→ Bake the puffs in a preheated 400°F oven for 15 minutes, or until puffed.

→ Reduce the oven temperature to 375°F and bake for an additional 10 minutes.

→ Remove from the oven when fully puffed and golden brown.

→ Set on a cooling rack to cool and then using a sharp serrated knife, cut twelve of the puffs horizontally to remove the top half of each of them. (The top halves of these puffs may be discarded or reserved for another use.) These open-topped puffs will be filled with the lemon curd filling.

→ When assembling the dessert, the baked filo skirts will replace the top halves of the puffs that have been removed.

→ Examine the other twelve puffs and using a sharp serrated knife, trim off any points that will interfere with being able to balance the chocolate tuile cookie securely on top of them. (See photograph.)

→ Then set these puffs aside to be dipped in caramel as instructed below.

Filo dough "skirt" to decorate the upper cream puff of the construction

YIELD: 12 "SKIRTS"

Oz	Grams	Each	Name of ingredient
3	90	6 sheets	**Filo dough** rectangles, measuring 12 inches by 17 inches
12 to 16	360 to 480		**Unsalted butter,** melted

Each sheet weighs approximately 0.5 ounce

→ Make two stacks of three sheets of filo each, brushing the surface of the bottom sheet with a thin layer of melted butter.

→ Repeat the layering and buttering using two more sheets of filo.

- For each of the twelve filo "skirts," using round metal cutters, cut the stacked dough into twelve circles each of 2 inches, 2½ inches and 3 inches in diameter, using cookie cutters to cut the dough by firmly pressing down on the cutter and rotating it back and forth until the dough has been cut through. (Note that after all of the stacks of circles have been cut out, you will have a piece of leftover dough, measuring approximately 10 inches by 13 inches that may be saved for another use).
- To build the "skirts," start with the twelve 3 inch stacks of circles.
- Lightly brush melted butter on the top layer of each of these stacks and then center the twelve 2½ inch diameter stacks of circles on top of the first ones.
- Brush the top layer of that stack lightly with melted butter and then finally center the 2 inch diameter stacks of circles on top of the 2½ inch ones.
- Place these 9-layer stacks, graduating from largest at the bottom, to smallest at the top, on the back of each of twelve 1½ inch diameter muffin cavities, protruding up from an inverted muffin plaque, lightly and gently crimping the stacks around the edges of the stacks before baking. (See process photographs.)
- Place the plaque onto a half-sheet baking pan and bake in a preheated 375°F oven for approximately 10 minutes, or until lightly golden.
- Remove from the oven and move the baked puffs from the muffin cups to a cooling rack to cool to room temperature.
- Make the two fillings as follows.

TIP: *When working with filo dough, be sure to keep the surface of the dough covered with a slightly damp cloth or paper towel. The objective here is to keep the dough damp enough to remain flexible but not so wet that the layers stick together, making it impossible to remove sheets intact from the stack of pastry layers. When buttering the sheets, brush gently but thoroughly, making sure that the entire sheet is evenly buttered all the way out to the edges of the dough.*

Brush filo sheets with melted butter and then stack them, to build a stack of three sheets.

Cut stacks of filo with three different-sized round cutters.

Place stacks of filo rounds on the back of an inverted muffin tin before baking, starting with the largest filo round on the bottom and the smallest filo round on the top for the stack. Lightly crimp the edges of the skirt to conform to the shape of the muffin cup.

Filo "skirt" after baking.

Espresso pastry cream filling for puffs

YIELD: APPROXIMATELY 17 OUNCES, ENOUGH TO FILL 12 PUFFS WITH SLIGHTLY LESS THAN 1½ OUNCES EACH

Oz	Grams	Each	Name of ingredient
10	130		Whole milk
		1	Vanilla beans, split
2	60		Whole eggs
2.5	75		Granulated sugar
1	30		Cornstarch
0.5	15		Coffee extract
1.5	45		Unsalted butter
	1	Pinch	Salt

→ Place the milk and the vanilla bean into a medium-sized heavy saucepan.

→ Bring to the boil, reduce heat to simmer for 5 minutes and then remove from the heat.

→ Cover the saucepan and let the liquid infuse for 15 minutes.

→ Pass the mixture through a fine sieve, reserving the vanilla bean, washed and dried, for another use.

→ Reserve the liquid.

→ In a small bowl, whisk the eggs, granulated sugar, and cornstarch together until smooth.

→ Return the infused milk to the saucepan and reheat.

→ Temper half of the hot liquid into the egg mixture in the bowl, whisking to combine until smooth.

→ Pass the liquid through a fine sieve into the saucepan with the remaining milk in it. Return to the stove and cook the mixture, whisking, until it thickens. Remove from the heat and add the coffee extract, the butter and the salt, whisking until smooth.

→ Scrape the mixture out of the saucepan into a stainless steel bowl, set over an ice water bath, and cool quickly, stirring occasionally.

→ When cool, transfer the mixture to a pastry bag, outfitted with a round plain tip, measuring ½ inch in diameter.

→ Fold the top of the bag over and place the bag into the refrigerator until ready to fill the puffs.

Lemon curd filling for puffs

YIELD: 30 OUNCES, ENOUGH TO FILL 12 PUFFS WITH APPROXIMATELY 1¾ OUNCES

Oz	Grams	Each	Name of ingredient
13.2	396		Whole eggs
9.6	288		Unsalted butter
7.2	216		Granulated sugar
1.2	36		Fresh lemon juice, sieved
	5	1 medium-sized lemon	Fresh lemon zest, grated

→ In a medium-sized stainless steel bowl, set over a saucepan of simmering water (the water should not touch the bottom of the bowl), whisk all of the ingredients together, cooking until the mixture thickens to a mayonnaise consistency.

→ When thickened, remove from the heat, pass through a fine sieve set over a heatproof bowl, pressing hard on the solids, reserving the curd and discarding the solids left in the sieve.

→ Remove 9 ounces of the sieved curd for the plating sauce and place this portion into a medium-sized bowl and set aside.

→ Transfer the remaining curd to a stainless steel bowl, set over an ice water bath, and stir until cool.

→ When cool, transfer this portion of the mixture to a pastry bag, outfitted with a round plain tip, measuring approximately ½ inch in diameter.

→ Fold the top of the bag over to seal and place the bag into the refrigerator while you complete the following sauce.

Oz	Grams	Name of ingredient
3, approximately	90	Simple syrup
9	270	Lemon curd from above

→ In a medium-sized bowl, whisk the simple syrup into cooled lemon curd, adding more syrup, if necessary to thin the curd so that it flows easily as a plating sauce.

Chocolate Tuile Garnish

YIELD: APPROXIMATELY 12 OUNCES OF TUILE BATTER, ENOUGH FOR 12 TUILE COOKIES, EACH MEASURING 4½ INCHES IN DIAMETER, PLUS ADDITIONAL ALLOWING FOR BROKEN OR OTHERWISE IMPERFECT COOKIES

Oz	Grams	Each	Name of ingredient
2.5	775		All purpose flour
0.5	15		Unsweetened cocoa powder
3	90		Unsalted butter, room temperature
3	90		Granulated sugar
3	90	3	Egg whites, from large eggs

→ Sift the flour and cocoa into a bowl and set aside.

→ In the bowl of an electric mixer, outfitted with the paddle attachment, cream the butter and sugar until light.

→ Add the egg white and mix to blend, scraping the bottom and sides of the bowl to ensure a well-blended mixture.

→ Add the sifted dry ingredients, mixing only until they disappear.

→ Using a small offset spatula, using a tuile template with circles 4½ inches in diameter cut out of it, spread a thin but not translucent layer of batter onto a Silpat, placed on an inverted half-sheet baking pan.

→ Bake the tuiles in a preheated 375°F oven for approximately 6 minutes.

→ Place a circle of parchment measuring 4 inches in diameter over the center of each tuile.

→ Sift confectioners' sugar through a fine sieve onto the edges of the cookie.

→ Carefully remove the parchment template and repeat the process to make the remaining tuiles until all of the tuile paste has been used.

Oz	Grams	Name of ingredient
8	240	Granulated sugar
4	120	Water

→ In a small, heavy saucepan, cook the sugar and water together, without stirring, until the mixture turns a golden amber color, approximately 300° to 310° F.

→ Immediately set the edge of the pan from which the handle extends onto a folded towel so that the caramel pools in one side of the pan.

→ Carefully but quickly dip the tops of twelve puffs into the caramel to coat lightly.

→ Immediately place the puffs, dipped side up, onto a cooling rack, placed on a parchment-lined sheet pan.

→ Allow to cool.

→ Reheat the caramel, if necessary (if it cools and hardens), to complete the dipping of all of the puffs.

Assembly

It is best to fill the puffs just before assembling the dessert. When ready to fill the puffs, remove the two pastry bags from the refrigerator, one filled with the espresso pastry cream and the other filled with the lemon curd. Insert the tip of the bag into the bottom center of each caramel-dipped puff and fill each with approximately 1.5 ounces of the espresso pastry cream. Fill each of the open-topped puffs with approximately 1.75 ounces of the lemon curd. Set aside the puffs until ready to plate.

Plating

Squeeze out the thinned lemon curd onto each dessert plate. Then center one of the espresso pastry cream–filled puffs on the sauce. Balance a chocolate tuile on each puff and then place one of the lemon curd–filled puffs on top of the tuile. Carefully place a filo "skirt" on the top puff, allowing some of the lemon curd filling to show, and serve the dessert immediately.

Blancmange with a Nutted Almond Tuile and Roasted Apricots

YIELD: 12 SERVINGS

Blancmange, crowned by an almond tuile, garnished with caramelized apricots.
With its ancestry traceable to medieval Europe, blancmange—meaning "white food" in French—was made from shredded chicken breast, rice, and almonds or almond milk. In later years, it became a mixture of milk, thickened with cornstarch and sweetened, and often festively colored, and therefore no longer white. Here, the cornstarch thickening is replaced by gelatin. And the chicken and rice have been left in the savory kitchen. With its subtle but noticeable almond flavor, this tender, almost quivering pudding, pairs neatly with dead-ripe fresh apricots in season. (Look for the rapidly disappearing Royal Blenheim variety, sometimes called Royal from its French origins and sometimes called Blenheim from its English parentage. Though not as picture-perfect as others on the market, whatever they're called, these fruits more than make up in "apricot" flavor what they might lack in looks. They often have a slightly greenish tinge, which is *not* in their case a sign of under ripeness.) Accentuating the fruit's honeyed lushness is a caramel sauce flavored with honey. A crisp crown of an almond-studded tuile cookie adds sharp contrast to the creamy ensemble below it.

The order of things:

1. **Infuse the milk** for the almond blancmange
2. **Complete the blancmange,** and store for use later that day or the next day
3. **Make almond tuile batter** and let rest
4. **Make caramelized apricots**
5. **Pipe out almond tuile batter and bake**
6. **Shape the warm tuiles** and store
7. **Make honey caramel sauce**

Equipment list:

Silicone plaque with fluted round indentations, each measuring 3 inches in diameter at the top (which will become the bottom of the blancmange when served), 1½ inches on the bottom (which will become the top when served) by 1½ inches deep

Paper parchment cone to pipe out tuile batter

Parchment paper template to place under the Silpat on a baking sheet to act as a guide when piping the tuile batter

Almond blancmange

YIELD: 12 MOLDED
DESSERTS, EACH WEIGHING
APPROXIMATELY
3.4 OUNCES

Oz	Grams	Each	Name of ingredient
18	540		**Blanched almonds**, either slivered or whole
4.5	135		**Water**
9	270		**Whole milk**
	13.5	4.5	**Gelatin sheets**
18	540		**Heavy cream**
8	240		**Granulated sugar**
0.33 oz	10		**Kirsch** (clear cherry brandy)

TIP: *With its faintly almond extract character, kirsch, also known as kirschwasser, marries beautifully with the almonds that flavor (and then are sieved out of) the base of the blancmange.*

→ In a mortar and pestle, or using a food processor, process the almonds with 4.5 ounces water and the milk.

→ Strain the liquid through a fine sieve, pressing hard on the solids and discarding them, reserving the liquid.

→ In a small bowl, place the gelatin sheets and enough cold water to cover them. When the gelatin softens, remove it and squeeze out excess liquid.

→ Set aside the squeezed out gelatin in a small bowl.

→ In a medium saucepan, heat the cream and sugar, stirring, without aerating, until the sugar is dissolved.

→ Dissolve the gelatin in the hot cream mixture.

→ Stir in the almond liquid.

→ Add the kirsch and stir to blend.

→ Place a Silform plaque of fluted molds onto a sheet pan.

→ The molds should each measure 3 inches in diameter at the top (which will become the bottom of the blancmange when served), 1½ inches on the bottom (which will become the top when served) by 1½ inches deep.

→ Fill the molds with the blancmange liquid (approximately 3.4 ounces for each mold) and carefully place the sheet pan on a **level** shelf in the refrigerator.

→ Chill until set, about 2 hours.

→ When set, lightly cover with plastic wrap or a sheet of parchment paper.

→ These may be made the day in advance of serving and stored in the refrigerator, covered, until serving.

Almond tuile crowns

YIELD: WEIGHTS OF EACH
NEST ARE VARIABLE, BUT
AVERAGE APPROXIMATELY
.75 OUNCE

Oz	Grams	Name of ingredient	Baker's percentages
1.25	45	**Almonds,** sliced and lightly toasted	Use approximately 3 grams of the almonds for each cookie
2	60	**Unsalted butter,** room temperature	85
2	60	**Granulated sugar**	85
2	60	**Egg whites**	85
2.4	70	**All purpose flour**	100

Use approximately 3 grams of the almonds for each cookie.

→ In a preheated 350°F oven, toast the almonds on a parchment lined baking sheet, for approximately 5 to 7 minutes, or until fragrant and light golden brown.

→ Remove from oven and set aside.

- In the bowl of an electric mixer, outfitted with the paddle attachment, cream the butter and the sugar until light.
- Add the egg white and mix to incorporate, scraping the bottom and sides of the bowl to ensure that the mixture is well blended.
- Add the flour and mix just until flour disappears.
- Transfer the mixture to a covered container, refrigerate, and let rest, for at least an hour, or overnight.
- Draw a rectangle, measuring 5 inches by 6 inches onto a sheet of parchment paper.
- Place it under a Silpat set onto the back of a baking sheet.
- Using the template as a guide, pipe the chilled batter, inside of the rectangle, creating a free-form, open lacy pattern, made up of interlocking circles, making sure that every line connects with another, and keeping the thickness of the circles uniform throughout. (See process shot.)
- Scatter almonds evenly on the batter and bake in preheated a 375°F oven for about 6 minutes, or until evenly light brown, rotating the baking sheet as or if needed to ensure even baking.
- Remove from the oven, and using a thin flat spatula or plastic bowl scraper, loosen the cookie from the Silpat and shape it by balling it up gently, gathering the outer edges of the cookie, inward and down, keeping the nutted side facing out.
- Place the tuile nests into a Silform plaque with thimble-shaped cavities to support them as they cool.

As with any tuile batter-based cookie, it is best to bake and form these a few at a time as they need to remain warm to be flexible enough to shape. If they cool and harden before they are formed, return them briefly to the oven to soften and then shape. If using within a few hours of baking, store at room temperature, uncovered. For longer storage, place the tuile nests carefully into a deep container with a tight-fitting lid, outfitted with a piece of limestone or a package of silica gel to keep them dry and crisp. These are best served the day they are made.

Pipe the tuile batter onto Silpat in an open interlocking design.

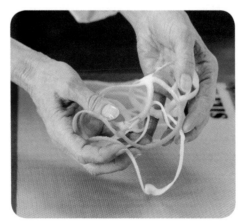

Gently shape the still warm baked tuile design as a sculptural garnish for desserts.

Caramelized apricots

YIELD: 24 HALVES, 2 HALVES
PER SERVING

Oz	Grams	Each	Name of ingredient
24, net weight (pit and skin removed)	720	12	**Apricots,** whole, fresh, peeled, if desired
4	120		**Granulated sugar**
0.04	1.2	¼ t.	**Almond extract**

TIP: *If the apricots are ripe, the peel should release easily from the fruit **without** needing to blanch them briefly in boiling hot water.*

→ Halve apricots, removing and discarding the pits.

→ Combine granulated sugar and almond extract.

→ Dip the apricot halves into sugar mixture and place under a salamander or torch until lightly golden.

→ The fruit should show signs of some slight blackening.

→ Reserve until ready to serve.

Honey caramel sauce

Oz	Grams	Name of ingredient
12	360	**Sugar**
4	120	**Water**
2, approximately	60	**Hot water**
2	60	**Strong flavored honey** like buckwheat or lavender

→ Place the sugar and the first quantity of water into a medium-sized heavy saucepan.

→ Cook, without stirring, until the mixture turns a deep golden color.

→ Add the hot water and cook to dissolve the caramel.

→ Then add the honey, boiling to thicken slightly.

→ Keep warm and use as a plating sauce.

→ If not using immediately, cool and place in a squeeze bottle, cover, and refrigerate.

→ When ready to use, rewarm the sauce over a hot water bath to re-liquefy before using.

Assembly and plating

Place the blancmange onto the plate. Place two apricot halves to the side of, and behind, the blancmange. Drizzle the apricots with the honey caramel sauce. Arrange a tuile nest on top of the blancmange and serve immediately.

Root Beer Ice with Tahitian Vanilla Ice Cream, Ginger and Chocolate Wafer Cookie with Vanilla Buttercream Filling

YIELD: 12 SERVINGS

Root beer ice "float" with Tahitian vanilla bean ice cream and ginger and chocolate sandwich cookie with buttercream filling. A bit of soda fountain nostalgia colors this fanciful and generous-sized construction. Perfect for the kid in everyone, this frozen dessert combines crunch and cream in a sophisticated combination of flavors that are at once familiar and yet new. Crunchy comes three times in the forms of the icy root beer shell, the thin short dough layers of the cookie, and the sugar straw; creamy appears twice, once in the ice cream and again in the creamy simple buttercream that sandwiches the two different-flavored cookies together. The sweetness of root beer has been toned down slightly with fresh lime juice and the vanilla ice cream is complexed by using not just any vanilla, but the floral, mellow, Tahitian variety. (The most flavorful vanilla beans should be flexible, soft, and highly fragrant, indicating freshness.) The accompanying sandwich cookie with its own spicy notes and creamy textured filling echoes the intensely aromatic flavor profile of the "float" itself.

The order of things:

1 **Make the root beer ice,** and mold in 5 ounce paper cups, using the 3 ounce paper cups as place savers for the vanilla ice cream; freeze

2 **Make the vanilla ice cream,** freeze until semi-firm but still pipeable, and pipe into the paper cups or other molds, then freeze

3 **Make the dough for the ginger thins** and chill

4 **Make the dough for the chocolate thins** and chill

5 **Make the vanilla buttercream**

6 **Bake the ginger and the chocolate thins** and allow to cool

7 **Make the caramel straws** and store in an airtight container, outfitted with a piece of limestone or a packet of silica gel

8 **Fill the cookies and make cookie sandwiches,** using one ginger thin and one chocolate thin for each serving

9 **Peel away the paper cup molds, assemble the "floats,"** and freeze until ready to plate the dessert

Equipment list:

Twelve 5 ounce liquid capacity paper cups as molds, measuring 3¾ inches tall, 2 inches in diameter at the base, and 2¾ inches at the top

Twenty-four 3 ounce paper cups, measuring 2¾ inches tall, 1¾ inches in diameter at the base, and 2½ inches at the top, used as place savers and molds for the piped-out vanilla ice cream topping the "float"

Parchment cone to pipe out the filling for the sandwich cookies

Root beer ice

YIELD: APPROXIMATELY 80 OUNCES, 12 SERVINGS, 6½ OUNCES EACH

Oz	Grams	Name of ingredient
72	2160	**Good-quality natural root beer soda,** opened and allowed to stand at room temperature to lose its effervescence
6	180	**Simple syrup**
3	90	**Fresh lime juice,** strained

→ Combine the root beer, simple syrup, and lime juice.

→ Freeze in an electric ice cream machine until almost firm.

→ Using twelve 5 ounce liquid capacity paper cups as molds (measuring 3¾ inches tall, 2 inches in diameter at the base, and 2¾ inches at the top), line each with a half-inch thick layer of the mixture.

→ Place a 3 ounce paper cup (measuring 2¾ inches tall, 1¾ inches in diameter at the base, and 2½ inches at the top) inside of each of the twelve 5 ounce liquid capacity cups and press to compact the root beer ice mixture.

→ Freeze until firm.

→ Make Tahitian vanilla bean ice cream, as follows.

Tahitian vanilla bean ice cream

YIELD: APPROXIMATELY 50 OUNCES, 12 SERVINGS, 4 OUNCES EACH

1. In a medium-sized heavy saucepan, bring the milk and vanilla beans to a simmer.

2. Cover the pan and allow to infuse for 30 minutes. The flavor of the vanilla should come through clearly.

3. Remove the vanilla beans, rinse and dry, and reserve for another use.

4. In the bowl of an electric mixer outfitted with the whisk attachment, beat the egg yolks and the sugar to thick ribbon stage.

5. When the whisk is lifted out of the bowl, the mixture should flow slowly in a thick ribbon from it.

6. Transfer the mixture to a stainless steel bowl.

7. Reheat the milk and temper half of it into the egg and sugar mixture in the bowl.

8. Add the remaining milk and then cook the mixture set over a hot water bath (the water should not touch the bottom of the bowl), stirring with a wooden spoon constantly, without aerating, until the mixture reaches 185°F.

9. When the mixture reaches temperature, immediately remove from the heat and pass through a fine sieve into a stainless steel bowl.

10. Stir in the salt and mix to dissolve.

11. Set the mixture over an ice water bath.

12. Cool quickly, stirring occasionally, and when cold, freeze the mixture in the bowl of an electric ice cream machine.

13. When almost firm, remove from the ice cream machine and place into a large piping bag.

14. Pipe the mixture into each of twelve 3 ounce paper cups (or other molds), measuring 1¾ inches in diameter at the bottom, beginning at the bottom with a round circle, repeating the same circle until you have created a cylinder tall enough to fill the root beer ice "glasses."

15. Finish piping, gradually reducing the size of the circles to create a swirled pyramid shape that will protrude from the top of the "glass."

16. Freeze the molded ice cream until ready to finish the dessert.

TIP: *Keeping vanilla beans fresh and flexible is best accomplished by burying them in a tightly closed container filled with granulated sugar. After a few days, the vanilla will perfume the sugar, producing a by-product that is always good to have around a pastry kitchen, and the beans themselves will remain pliable and fresh.*

Ginger thins

Oz	Grams	Each	Name of ingredient	Baker's percentages
2	60		**Unsalted butter,** room temperature	50
.5	15		**Molasses**	13
2	60		**Granulated sugar**	50
1	30	1	**Egg white** from one large egg	25
4	120		**All purpose flour**	100
		¼ t.	**Baking soda**	1
		1 t.	**Ground ginger**	2
	3	Generous pinch	**Salt**	2

Sandwich cookies

YIELD: APPROXIMATELY
9 OUNCES, 12 DIAMOND-
SHAPED COOKIES, EACH
WEIGHING APPROXIMATELY
¾ OUNCE

Egg wash

Oz	Grams	Each	Name of ingredient
1.3	39	2	**Egg yolks** from 2 large eggs
As needed to thin the egg yolk for the egg wash			**Water**

Crystallized ginger garnish for ginger thins

Oz	Grams	Name of ingredient
3–4	120–160	**Crystallized ginger,** cut into ⅛ inch square cubes

→ In the bowl of an electric mixer outfitted with the paddle attachment, cream the butter until light and fluffy.

→ Add molasses and granulated sugar.

→ Mix until well blended, about 3 minutes.

→ Sift flour, soda, ginger, and salt into a medium-sized bowl and set aside.

→ Add the egg white to the butter mixture and mix until just combined, scraping the bottom and sides of the bowl well.

→ Add the dry ingredients and mix only until they disappear.

→ Remove from the mixer and flatten into a ½ inch thick rectangle.

→ Wrap and chill until firm.

→ When cold and firm, roll the dough on a lightly floured surface to a thickness of approximately ⅛ inch.

→ Cut into twelve diamond shapes, measuring 2 to 2½ inches on each side, and place the diamonds on a silpat.

→ Mix egg yolk and enough water to make an egg wash the consistency of paint.

→ Brush the tops of the cookies **lightly** with egg wash and arrange 5 cubes of ginger randomly on the top of each cookie. Bake in a preheated 350°F oven for approximately 8 minutes.

→ Watch these carefully, as they burn easily.

Chocolate thins

YIELD: APPROXIMATELY
12 OUNCES, 12 DIAMOND-
SHAPED COOKIES, ONE PER
SERVING

Oz	Grams	Each	Name of ingredient	Baker's percentages
2	60		70% bittersweet chocolate, cut into small pieces	50
2	60		Unsalted butter	50
2	60		Granulated sugar	50
1.67	50	1	Large egg	42
		½ t.	Vanilla extract	4
4	120		All purpose flour	100
	3	Generous pinch	Salt	0.03

Egg wash

	Oz	Grams	Name of ingredient
	1.2	36	Egg yolks
	As needed to thin the egg yolk for the egg wash		Water

→ Place chocolate and butter into a medium-sized stainless steel bowl.

→ Set the bowl over a pot of simmering water.

→ Stir until melted and remove from heat.

→ In the bowl of an electric mixer outfitted with the paddle attachment, beat sugar, egg, and vanilla extract until the mixture is slightly thickened and lighter in color. Add the melted chocolate and butter mixture and stir with a wooden bowl until combined.

→ Combine the flour and salt in a small bowl and then at low speed, add this mixture to the chocolate mixture, stirring just until the dry ingredients disappear. Remove from the mixer and flatten into a ½ inch thick rectangle.

→ Wrap and chill until firm.

→ On a lightly floured surface, roll the dough to a thickness of approximately ⅛ inch.

→ Chill again and then cut the dough into 12 diamond-shaped pieces, to match the vanilla diamonds above, measuring 2 to 2½ inches on each side.

→ Chill until firm again.

→ Mix egg yolk and enough water to make an egg wash the consistency of paint.

→ Brush the tops of the cookies **lightly** with egg wash and then bake in a preheated 350°F oven for approximately 8 minutes.

→ Watch these carefully, as they burn easily.

→ Cool and set aside.

→ Prepare vanilla buttercream as follows.

Vanilla buttercream

YIELD: APPROXIMATELY
6 OUNCES

Oz	Grams	Each	Name of ingredient
2	60		Unsalted butter, room temperature
4	120		Confectioners' sugar, sifted
0.5	30	1 T.	Vanilla extract

→ In the bowl of an electric mixer outfitted with the paddle attachment, cream the butter until light and fluffy.

→ Add sugar and vanilla extract, and beat until smooth, scraping the bottom and sides of the bowl occasionally.

- Remove from the mixing bowl and fill a parchment paper cone with the mixture.
- Using the parchment paper cone, deposit a thin layer slightly less than a ¼ inch thick of the buttercream on each of 12 chocolate diamonds.
- Gently, spread the buttercream neatly and evenly almost to the edge of each cookie. (Being thin, these cookies are fragile and therefore break easily.)
- Carefully top each with a ginger wafer.
- Press the "sandwich" lightly to force the buttercream to ooze evenly and slightly out of the sides of the cookie.
- Set the cookies aside in a cool place until ready to serve.
- If the cookies are refrigerated, remove from the refrigerator a few minutes before serving, as they are best served at cool room temperature.

Caramel sugar "straws"

YIELD: ENOUGH FOR 12 STRAWS

Oz	Grams	Name of ingredient
8	240	Granulated sugar
4	120	Water
1	30	Corn syrup

- Bring sugar, water, and corn syrup to a boil.
- Cook to a light amber color, without stirring approximately 300°F.
- Pour the mixture onto a Silpat into twelve 10–12 inch-long straw shapes.
- When cool enough to handle, using two hands, one at each end of the straw, twist the straws to make each into a corkscrew shape. (Reheat as needed to make them flexible in a preheated 300°F oven.)
- These may be cut down to whatever length you desire.
- Set aside in a container with a tight-fitting lid, outfitted with a piece of limestone or a package of silica gel, to help keep these dry until ready to serve the dessert.

Assembly and plating

Cut or carefully tear the paper cups away from the root beer ice "floats" and remove the place-saver 3 ounce cups set into the top of each "float." Place the vanilla bean ice cream swirls into each of the root beer ice "floats." Carefully position the sugar straws, set at a 45 degree angle, at the back of the "float" between the ice cream and the root beer ice. Place one completed root beer ice onto each plate. Garnish with one sandwich cookie in front of, and to the right of, the root beer "float." Allow the ice to soften slightly on the plate before serving. Serve immediately with long-handled spoons and a knife, to facilitate breaking the ice up into manageable bites.

Sesame Chiffon Cake with Sesame Halvah Mousse and Orange Sections

YIELD: 12 SERVINGS

Sesame chiffon cake with orange stencil paste garnish, sesame halvah mousse, orange sections, orange blossom sauce, black and white sesame tuile, orange syrup. Here two seemingly disparate flavors marry well. One is orange, which is used in three forms; first, in a plating sauce and moistener brushed on the cake, next, as a fresh fruit garnish, and last, as a visual grace note in the form of the blossoms from the orange tree. The blossoms are obviously seasonal and region-specific, and though not widely available, worth seeking out. (In February, like clockwork, when the rest of the United States can be blanketed with the white stuff, the Southern California night air is perfumed with the scent of the white multipetaled flowers.) Bottled commercially made orange flower water is a fairly representative distillation of the flavor and aroma of the fresh blossoms but cannot take the place of the fresh flowers just picked from the tree. The second dominant flavor in this dessert, sesame, also appears in two forms here: first, in a halvah- or sesame paste-based mousse and then, as a black and white stippling on the crisp tuile cookies.

The order of things:

1. **Make the orange stencil paste,** lay out on Silpat, placed on the back of a half-sheet pan, comb to create a decorative design, and freeze
2. **Make the sesame chiffon cake**
3. **Place the Silpat with the stencil paste into a half-sheet pan and pour the sesame chiffon cake batter over the paste, and bake the cake immediately**
4. **Pour out remaining cake batter into second Silpat-lined half-sheet pan and bake**
5. **Make halvah mousse** and freeze
6. **Make the tuile batter** and rest
7. **Cut the halvah mousse** into rounds and place the rounds onto a parchment lined sheet pan; freeze
8. **Bake the tuiles**
9. **Make the orange syrup**
10. **Prepare the citrus filets** as garnish

Equipment list:

Two half-sheet pan-sized **Silpats**

Plastic or metal **cake comb** with evenly spaced "teeth," each measuring ³⁄₁₆ of an inch

Metal cookie cutter, 3 inches in diameter, to cut the chiffon base to be used for the base of the mousse cakes

Acetate sheet to line the pan for the mousse

Round metal cookie cutter, measuring 2 inches in diameter, to cut the mousse

Tuile template, with cut outs measuring 3 inches in diameter, for the black and white sesame tuiles

Prepare the orange stencil paste *first,* and lay it out onto the Silpat as described below, freeze it, and while it is freezing, make the sesame chiffon cake as follows:

Orange stencil paste garnish for cake

YIELD: A GENEROUS AMOUNT TO CREATE A DESIGN ON A HALF-SHEET PAN-SIZED CHIFFON CAKE

Oz	Name of ingredient	Baker's percentages
2	**Unsalted butter**	83
2	**Granulated sugar**	83
2	**Egg white**	83
2.4	**All purpose flour**	100
As needed to achieve the desired color	**Orange paste coloring** (or red paste coloring mixed with yellow paste coloring)	

→ Have two half-sheet pans ready to use.

→ Line one with parchment and spray it lightly with pan release spray.

→ Set aside.

→ The second pan is lined with a Silpat sheet *after* the sheet has been embossed with the stencil paste.

→ In the bowl of an electric mixer outfitted with the paddle attachment, cream butter until light.

→ Add sugar and mix until well blended.

→ Add egg whites and mix until incorporated.

→ Add flour and mix only until the flour disappears, scraping the sides and bottom of the bowl, occasionally, during the mixing process.

→ Add food coloring and mix one more time to incorporate well, scraping as needed, to ensure that the paste is evenly colored throughout.

→ Place the Silpat on your work surface in front of you, with its short side facing you.

→ Using a long flat metal icing spatula, spread a thin but not transparent layer of the paste onto the Silpat.

→ As you face the Silpat, beginning at the upper left hand corner, use a plastic or metal cake comb with evenly spaced "teeth," each measuring 3/16 of an inch, held at a 45 degree angle, to scrape off the paste in one continuous curving motion, leaving behind wavy lines of the paste, removing excess paste as you go.

→ Moving to your right, as you face the Silpat, repeat the scraping process.

→ Repeat once again on the last third of the Silpat.

→ Note that, depending on the width of the cake comb, it may be possible to create the design in two steps rather than three.

→ Carefully pick up the Silpat and place it into a half-sheet pan. Then place the sheet pan into the freezer for about 30 minutes, or until the stencil paste design is frozen solid. Now make the sesame chiffon cake.

You may have extra stencil paste, which may be refrigerated for up to 3 weeks and used for another purpose

This batter is divided into two parts, each baked in its own half-sheet pan; one third of the batter is used for the stencil paste sheet, and two thirds of the batter is used for the round cake bases

Using a toothed cake comb, create a pattern through the colored stencil paste laid onto a Silpat. Freeze stencil paste until it is completely frozen.

Pour the sponge cake batter over the frozen stencil paste pattern.

Carefully spread the sponge cake batter in an even layer over the stencil paste pattern and bake according to recipe directions.

Invert the Silpat onto a work surface, carefully pulling the Silpat from the cake to reveal the pattern.

Sesame chiffon cake

YIELD: APPROXIMATELY 46 OUNCES, YIELDING TWO HALF-SHEET PAN-SIZED CAKES, ONE THIN AND ONE THICK

Oz	Grams	Each	Name of ingredient	Baker's percentages— Cake flour and all purpose flour total 100%
6	180		Egg yolks	48
6.5	195		Cake flour	96
6	180		All purpose flour	52
		1 T.	Baking powder	48
		1 T.	Sesame seeds	4
		½ t.	Salt	3
10	300		Egg whites	0.8
16 total: 12 to yolks; 4 to whites	480; 360 to yolks; 120 to whites		Sugar, divided	80
3	90		Vegetable oil	32
1	30		Sesame oil	24
8	240		Water	8
0.5	15	1 T.	Vanilla	64
				4

TIP: *When beating the egg whites for the cake, be sure not to overbeat, as they will become broken, granulated, and difficult to incorporate easily into the cake base, deflating the batter and leading to a leaden cake.*

→ Sift dry ingredients and set aside.

→ Mix egg yolks, 12 ounces sugar, oils, water, and vanilla to a smooth batter.

→ When the mixture is smooth, using a spatula, gently fold dry ingredients into the egg yolk base.

→ In another bowl of the electric mixer outfitted with the whisk attachment, beat the egg whites to a froth, adding the remaining 4 ounces sugar gradually, whisking until stiff but shiny peaks form.

→ Using a spatula, gently fold whites into the cake.

→ Remove the sheet pan with frozen stencil paste from the freezer and carefully pour one third of the sesame chiffon cake batter from above over it, using an offset metal spatula or thin plastic bowl scraper to spread the batter evenly over the paste.

→ Pour the remaining batter into the second half-sheet pan prepared from above.

→ In a preheated 350°F oven, bake both cakes for approximately 20–30 minutes, or until they spring back when pressed lightly in the middle.

→ Note that the thinner cake covering the stencil paste may bake slightly faster. Check this cake for doneness after 15 minutes. (If done, remove it from the oven. If not, continue baking for another few minutes or until it tests done.)

→ At this point, the other, thicker cake should be left in the oven for a little more time to continue baking.

→ When both cakes have been removed from the oven, allow them to cool and proceed as follows.

1. Cut the stencil paste embossed cake lengthwise into twelve 11 inch long by ¾ inch wide strips, which will be used to wrap around the 3 inch diameter rounds of chiffon cake used as the base for the dessert.

2. Set aside the strips of cake until ready to assemble the dessert. (You will have some leftover stencil paste-embossed cake, to be reserved for another use, if desired).

3. Using a cookie cutter 3 inches in diameter, cut the second and thicker cake into 12 rounds. Set aside the rounds, covered, until ready to assemble the dessert.

Oz	Grams	Each	Name of ingredient
	7	2⅓	Sheet gelatin
7	210		Plain halvah, broken into roughly ½ inch pieces
1	30		Tahini (sesame paste)
4	120		Simple syrup
2	60		Hot water
16	480		Heavy cream, whipped to soft peaks

→ In a small bowl, place gelatin sheets in cool water and then set aside to soften.

→ Bring sugar syrup to the boil, remove from the heat, and then add bloomed gelatin, stirring to dissolve.

→ Cover the saucepan to keep the mixture warm.

→ Place halvah and tahini into the bowl of a food processor and run the machine until the mixture is smooth and well blended.

→ Fold the still-warm gelatin and sugar syrup mixture into the halvah; add hot water and process to smooth.

→ While allowing the mixture to cool to room temperature, in the bowl of an electric mixer outfitted with the whisk attachment, beat the cream to soft peaks.

→ Fold the cream into the halvah mixture.

→ Pour the mousse into an acetate sheet-lined half-sheet pan and refrigerate until set.

→ When set, using a round cookie cutter, measuring 2 inches in diameter, cut the mousse into 12 rounds.

→ Set aside, covered, in the refrigerator on a parchment-lined sheet pan until ready to assemble the dessert.

TIP: Ethnic food stores selling Middle Eastern products are a good source for both the halvah and the tahini ingredient.

Oz	Grams	Each	Name of ingredient
1	30		Unsalted butter, room temperature
1	30		Confectioners' sugar
1	30		Egg whites
1.25			All purpose flour
.16	5	1 t.	Vanilla extract
0.50 white sesame seeds 0.50 black sesame seeds	15 grams of each		Sesame seeds—white and black as garnish

→ In the bowl of an electric mixer outfitted with the paddle attachment, cream the butter until light.

→ Add the confectioners' sugar and continue mixing until well blended, about 5 minutes.

→ Add the egg white and mix until incorporated, scraping the bottom and sides of the bowl with a spatula as needed.

→ Add the vanilla extract and mix briefly to combine.

→ Add the flour and mix until it disappears into the batter.

→ Place a Silpat onto the back of an inverted half-sheet pan.

→ Then place a tuile template, with cut-outs measuring 3 inches in diameter, onto the Silpat.

→ Using a small metal spatula or plastic bowl scraper, spread a thin but not transparent layer of batter onto the Silpat, scraping off excess.

- → Remove the template, leaving behind uniform circles of tuile paste on the Silpat.
- → Sprinkle the tuile batter circles lightly but evenly with sesame seeds, using the white sesame seeds on one half of the circle and the black sesame seeds on the other half.
- → Bake the tuiles in a preheated 350°F oven for approximately 7–10 minutes or until set, but not overly brown.
- → When lightly golden brown and set, remove from the oven and allow to cool.
- → With a small sharp knife, trim a ½ inch wide piece from the bottom edge of each cookie to create a flat bottom to facilitate balancing the cookies firmly on the halvah mousse. (See photograph on page 298.)
- → To retain crispness, store the cookies in an airtight container, outfitted with a piece of limestone or a packet of silica gel.
- → Store at room temperature until ready to serve the dessert.

Orange syrup—to be brushed on tops and sides of the rounds of sesame chiffon cake used as the base of the dessert

YIELD: APPROXIMATELY 8 OUNCES

Oz	Grams	Name of ingredient
6	180	**Orange juice,** freshly squeezed and sieved
1	30	**Grated orange zest**
0.33	10	**Orange blossom water**
To taste		**Simple syrup**

- → In a small bowl, whisk together, juice, zest, orange blossom water, and simple syrup until well blended.
- → Reserve, covered and refrigerated, until ready to assemble the dessert.

For the filleted citrus garnish

YIELD: ENOUGH FOR APPROXIMATELY 36 FILLETED SEGMENTS, 12 GARNISHES, THREE PER SERVING

Each	Name of ingredient
From 4 medium to large oranges	**Orange segments,** peel and pith removed, separated in to segments, freed from the membranes holding the orange together

- → Using a sharp knife, cut a thin slice from the top and bottom of each orange.
- → Then using the same small sharp knife, remove the skin and pith from the oranges, cutting from top to bottom in a curving motion, following the contour of the fruit.
- → Remove the filets of the fruit by cutting between the thin membranes that separate each wedge.
- → With an in-and-out motion, release the filets of orange by making one cut toward the center of the fruit and the next cut away from the center. The filet should release cleanly from the membrane that holds it in place.
- → Repeat this process until all of the filets have been removed.
- → Reserve in a covered container, refrigerated, until ready to serve the dessert.

Each	Name of ingredient
36, 3 per plate	**Fresh orange blossoms,** if available

Assembly and plating

Brush the orange syrup on the rounds of sesame chiffon cake to moisten. Place one round of cake on each of 12 plates. Brush the sides of the round cake again lightly with syrup. Wrap one orange stencil paste–designed strip of chiffon cake around each of the 12 circles of cake, pressing to secure them. Place a round of halvah mousse, upright at the back of the circle of cake. Garnish the tops of the cake with overlapping orange filets, around the mousse, to fill in the top of the cakes. Garnish each mousse with a sesame seed encrusted tuile. Spoon a little more of the orange syrup onto each plate, garnishing the plates with three fresh orange blossoms, as desired.

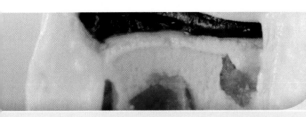

Three Textures of Meringue

YIELD: 12 SERVINGS

Three textures of meringue—homemade graham cracker, topped with two flavors of marshmallows, bittersweet chocolate ganache center, all encased in an Italian meringue, torched, crisp meringue shard garnish, served with warmed strawberry sauce. Somewhat a cross between a campfire s'more and a Mallowmar cookie in reverse since here the chocolate is on the inside, this dessert evokes memories of childhood in each layer. Showcasing the versatility of meringue in three forms—light and crunchy, slightly chewy and gelatinized, and soft with a caramelized torched edge—this construction is truly a study in textures, demonstrating how treating two basic ingredients, egg whites and sugar, differently, yields dramatically different results. Although it's preferable to make this when highly flavored strawberries are in season for the puree and pieces that are used to flavor one of the marshmallow layers, the frozen variety of the fruit will suffice, making this an all-year-round treat. Serving this on a bed of warmed strawberry plating sauce accentuates the fruity perfume of the berries, making this dessert not only a treat for the eyes but also for the nose.

The order of things:

1. **Make crisp meringue shards,** allow to bake at low temperature, and then set aside at room temperature until ready to serve the dessert
2. **Make graham cracker dough** and chill
3. **Make strawberry puree** to flavor half of the marshmallow mixture
4. **Make two marshmallow mixtures** and allow to dry at room temperature
5. **Make bittersweet chocolate ganache** and let cool
6. **Bake graham crackers,** cool, and then cut
7. **Make Italian meringue**

Equipment list:

Round metal cookie cutter, measuring 3 inches in diameter, to cut the graham cracker bases

Two baking pans each measuring 7½ inches by 10 inches, for the marshmallows

Round metal cookie cutter, measuring 2½ inches in diameter, to cut 12 round marshmallows of each flavor

Torch to brown the Italian meringue covering the dessert

Crisp meringue shards to be used as garnishes on top of the completed dessert

Oz	Grams	Each	Name of ingredient	Baker's percentages— Egg whites at 100%
4	120	4	**Egg whites,** from large eggs, room temperature	100
8	240		**Granulated sugar,** divided	.8
		1	**Cream of tartar**	200

→ In the bowl of an electric mixer outfitted with the whisk attachment, beat the egg whites until soft peaks form.

→ Gradually add half of the sugar into the beaten whites and continue to beat until stiff peaks form.

→ Remove from the mixer and fold in the remaining sugar and then using an offset spatula, spread the mixture into an even layer, approximately ½ inch thick, into a half-sheet pan, parchment lined and lightly sprayed with pan release spray.

→ Bake the meringue in a preheated 200–210°F oven, for approximately 45 minutes, until dry and crisp but not browned.

→ Check on the progress of the baking, reducing the oven temperature, if needed, to slow the drying out process so that the meringue does not brown.

→ When dry, remove from the oven and store at room temperature, uncovered.

Graham crackers

YIELD: 12 COOKIES, EACH MEASURING APPROXIMATELY 3 INCHES IN DIAMETER, WEIGHING 1 OUNCE EACH

Oz	Grams	Each	Name of ingredient	Baker's percentages— Bread flour, cake flour, and whole wheat flour total 100%
3	90		**Bread flour**	43
3	90		**Cake flour**	43
1	30		**Whole wheat flour**	14
1	30		**Dark brown sugar**	1
		½ t.	**Baking soda**	
		¼ t.	**Salt**	0.6
		½ t.	**Cinnamon,** ground	0.5
		½ t.	**Ginger,** ground	43
3			**Unsalted butter,** room temperature	14
		½ T.	**Honey**	3
0.5	15	1 T.	**Vanilla**	7
As needed to thin the dough slightly			**Water**	

→ Sift dry ingredients, including salt and spices, and set aside.

→ In the bowl of an electric mixer outfitted with the paddle attachment, cream the butter with brown sugar and honey until smooth.

→ Mix in the vanilla and then dry ingredients, mixing only until the dry ingredients disappear.

→ Add water if needed to thin slightly.

→ Remove the dough from the mixing bowl to a lightly floured surface and knead briefly.

→ Gather the dough into a rough ball, flatten slightly, wrap it, and then refrigerate until well chilled.

- → On a lightly floured surface, roll the chilled dough to a thickness of approximately ¼ inch.
- → Using a 3-inch diameter round cookie cutter, cut 12 cookies and place them on a parchment-lined baking sheet.
- → Gather up the scraps of dough and reroll as needed to produce additional cookies.
- → Dock each cookie with a skewer or the point of a knife, at ½ inch intervals, and then chill to refirm before baking.
- → Bake in a preheated 375°F oven for about 15 minutes, or until set and just lightly browned.
- → Remove from the oven and place the cookies on a wire cooling rack.
- → Reserve until ready to assemble the dessert.

For strawberry marshmallows

Oz	Grams	Name of ingredient
4	120	**Strawberry puree with small chunks of fresh strawberries in it,** thawed
2	60	**Fresh or frozen strawberries,** thawed, cut into ¼ inch to ⅓ inch pieces

- → In a small bowl, combine the strawberry puree and the pieces of fresh strawberry.
- → Add this mixture to half of the marshmallow base set aside from above.

Preparing the pans for the marshmallows

Oz	Name of ingredient
As needed	**Confectioners' sugar,** placed in a medium-sized bowl, to dip the cookie cutter into when cutting the marshmallows

- → Line two shallow baking pans each measuring 7½ inches by 10 inches with parchment paper and then spray the paper lightly with pan release spray.
- → Set aside.

Marshmallow base
YIELD: APPROXIMATELY 24 OUNCES

Oz	Grams	Each	Name of ingredient
0.5	15	5	Gelatin sheets
4	120		Cold water
14	420		Granulated sugar
5.33	160		Corn syrup
2	60		Water
4	120	4	Egg whites, from large eggs, room temperature
		¼ t.	Salt
0.5	15	1 T.	Vanilla extract

- → In a small bowl, place the gelatin and enough water to cover it.
- → Allow the gelatin to soften, remove from the water, and squeeze excess water out of it.
- → Set aside the squeezed-out gelatin.
- → In a heavy saucepan, combine sugar, corn syrup, and water.

- → Cook the mixture to 240°F without stirring.
- → In the meantime begin to beat the egg whites and salt to a foam in the bowl of an electric mixer outfitted with the whisk attachment.
- → With the machine running, pour the boiling syrup over the egg whites in the bowl.
- → Immediately add the bloomed gelatin and the vanilla and continue whipping the mixture, using the whisk attachment, until light and fluffy but still slightly warm.
- → Spread approximately 15 ounces of the mixture into one of the prepared pans, smoothing the top.
- → To the remaining marshmallow mixture (approximately 9 ounces), add the mixture of strawberry puree and fresh (or frozen and thawed) strawberry pieces, from above.
- → Spread this mixture into the second prepared pan.
- → Each of the pans should be filled to a height of approximately ½ inch.
- → Allow the mixtures to set.
- → Then, using a round cookie cutter, measuring 2½ inches in diameter, cut 12 round marshmallows from each, dipping the cutter into a bowl of sifted confectioners' sugar before and after each cut, cutting in rows of three on the 7½ inch side, and in rows of four on the 10-inch side, for a total of 12 of each flavor.
- → Set the marshmallows aside, covered lightly so that they do not dry out.
- → Reserve any extra for another use.

Dividing the marshmallow base mixture unevenly into two parts allows the final yields to remain equal since the smaller part is augmented by the strawberry puree and tiny chunks mixture and the other remains plain.

Bittersweet chocolate ganache

YIELD: 12 OUNCES,
12 SERVINGS, 1 OUNCE EACH

Oz	Grams	Name of ingredient
6	180	65% dark chocolate couverture, chopped
6	180	Heavy cream

- → Place chocolate into a heat-proof stainless steel bowl.
- → In a heavy saucepan, heat heavy cream until boiling.
- → Pour hot cream over the chocolate and stir gently to combine just until smooth and well blended.
- → Set aside until ready to use.

Italian Meringue

YIELD: APPROXIMATELY
18 OUNCES, 12 SERVINGS,
1½ OUNCES EACH

Oz	Grams	Name of ingredient
12	360	Granulated sugar
2	60	Corn syrup
8	240	Egg whites at room temperature

TIP: *This mixture is stable and may be kept at cool temperature (60–70°F) for approximately an hour before serving the dessert. Given that it's quick to make, it would be preferable to make it just before completing the assembly of the dessert, if practical, since as it stands, the meringue loses its desirable creamy softness.*

- → In the bowl of an electric mixer outfitted with the whisk attachment, beat the egg whites until frothy.
- → At the same time, in a heavy saucepan, heat the granulated sugar and corn syrup to 242°F.
- → With the machine running, pour the hot syrup over the frothy egg whites and whisk until they are thick, glossy, and smooth.
- → Set aside and then place in a pastry bag to coat the outside of the dessert as described below.

Oz	Grams	Name of ingredient
12	360	**Fresh strawberries,** sweetened to taste with granulated sugar, and pureed, or thawed frozen commercially prepared fruit puree (this usually contains 10% sugar by weight)
As needed		**Granulated sugar,** if using fresh strawberries instead of a frozen commercially prepared fruit puree

Assembly and plating

Warm the strawberry sauce in a stainless steel bowl set over a pan of simmering water. Keep warm on low heat. For each dessert, build the layers as follows. Spoon or pipe using a pastry bag outfitted with a plain ½ inch diameter tip, a small round of ganache on the center of the graham cracker. Place a vanilla marshmallow onto the ganache and press lightly to seat the marshmallow firmly onto the graham cracker. Then pipe enough ganache to cover the top of the vanilla marshmallow and place the strawberry marshmallow on top of it, pressing lightly to compact the stack. Then pipe the Italian meringue around the marshmallow stack, and using a small metal spatula, smooth the sides. Finally, pipe a series of concentric circles as a garnish on top of the meringue construction, ending in a point. Torch the sides and top of the meringue lightly and then place crisp free-form.

Topsy-Turvy Gateau St. Honore—Pistachio, Raspberry, and Chocolate Fillings

YIELD: 12 SERVINGS

Topsy-turvy Gateau St. Honore—pistachio, raspberry, and chocolate fillings, with three puffs, puff pastry disc, and caramel décor. A classic is remade here with a slightly Neapolitan tinge in its flavoring. A disk of crisp puff pastry seems to float over a trio of three different flavored pastry cream rosettes, balanced on a caramel-dipped cream puff. Pistachio, raspberry, chocolate, and caramel all figure in this reinterpretation of the quintessential French pastry. Textural variety abounds here with the custardy density of the puff's fillings and pyramidal rosettes on the plate contrasted by the crisp and airy puff pastry layers and the crunchy caramel topping on the base puff. Adding another element of crunch, a whirlpool-shaped caramel garnish tops the construction. Although the parts may be made in advance, to retain maximum crispness, the completed construction is best assembled within a few minutes, or at most an hour, before serving.

The order of things:

1 **Make the quick puff pastry** and chill

2 **Make pâte à choux dough, pipe out into puffs, and bake**

3 **Make custard fillings** for the puffs

4 **Make fondant icings** for the puffs

5 **Make caramel** and keep warm (reheating as and if needed)

6 **Dip 12 of the larger sized puffs and make caramel décor**

7 **Fill the puffs and assemble the dessert** as close to serving time as possible

Equipment list:

Round metal cutter, measuring 5 inches in diameter, to cut the completed puff pastry dough before baking

Fork or rolling docker to prick the dough before baking

Pastry bag outfitted with a plain tip measuring ½ inch in diameter to pipe out the pate a choux puffs

Three pastry bags, each outfitted with a rosette-shaped opening, measuring ½ inch in diameter, one for each flavor of filling, to fill puffs and to pipe out rosettes on the plates

Heat-proof gloves, used when piping out the hot caramel designs

Heat-proof pastry bags, used when piping out the hot caramel designs

Heat-proof pastry bag outfitted with a metal tip with a ¹⁄₁₆ inch opening

Quick puff pastry

YIELD: APPROXIMATELY 2½ POUNDS

Lb	Oz	Grams	Name of ingredient	Baker's percentages
1		480	**All purpose flour**	100
1		480	**Unsalted butter**, cool, waxy, not soft or greasy	100
		1	**Salt**	.2
	8	240	**Ice water**	50

This dough may be made either by hand or by machine, depending on the size of the batch.

Mixing by hand

→ Cut butter into 1½ inch chunks.

→ Place flour and salt into a large bowl.

→ Mix to combine.

→ Add the butter and coat with the flour and salt mixture.

→ Add ice water all at once and lightly mix until the dough coheres into a rough mass. Do not overprocess.

→ Turn the ragged mass of dough out onto a lightly floured surface and tap the dough firmly with a rolling pin to coax the dough into a roughly cohesive shape.

→ Check to be sure that the dough is not sticking to the surface.

Mixing by machine

→ Using the paddle attachment, mix the flour and salt at low speed to combine.

→ Add the butter, cut into 1½ inch chunks.

→ On slow speed, mix just to coat the butter with the flour.

→ With the machine running, add ice water all at once, and briefly mix, turning the machine on and off rather than allowing it to run continuously, just until the dough becomes a rough mass. It is better to underprocess rather than overprocess the dough. The mixer should be turned on and off during this step rather than allowing it to run continuously.

Rolling the dough

→ Turn the ragged mass of dough out onto a floured surface and tap firmly with the rolling pin to coax the dough into a roughly cohesive shape.

→ Check to be sure that the dough is not sticking to the surface.

→ Use a plastic dough scraper frequently to free the dough from the work surface, as necessary, if it is sticking.

→ Flour the work surface *lightly* from time to time.

→ Once the dough has been rolled to a rough rectangular shape, mentally divide the dough in thirds and fold one third of the dough from the end closest to you toward the middle and the other third over the first third to create a package of dough made up of three thick layers.

→ Turn the packet of dough 90 degrees so that the short side is facing you.

→ Then roll the dough to lengthen it again to a rectangle measuring roughly 7 inches by 18 inches.

→ Fold in thirds again, turn it 90 degrees so that the short side is facing you again.

→ Now roll the dough again to a rectangle measuring roughly 7 inches by18 inches.

→ Chill in between the rolling and folding steps if the dough shows signs of softening or sticking to the work surface.

→ Repeat the rolling and folding once more, chilling as needed if the dough shows signs of softening or is being resistant to rolling. (See process shots on page 143.)

- → Chill until firm. (The dough may be refrigerated overnight but for longer storage, freeze it and thaw, when needed, in the refrigerator.)
- → Remove the well-chilled dough from the refrigerator and divide it into two equal pieces, each weighing approximately 20 ounces.
- → Roll each piece to a thickness of approximately ⅓ inch and, using a sharp knife and a firm deliberate cutting motion, trim each to a neat rectangle measuring 12 inches by 15 inches.
- → Cut 12 circles of dough, each measuring 5 inches in diameter, six from each piece, in rows of two along the 12 inch side, and in rows of three along the 15 inch side. (Reserve any leftover dough, well wrapped and frozen, for another use.)
- → Place six rounds onto each of two parchment paper-lined half-sheet pans.
- → Chill the dough again until firm, remove from the refrigerator and then dock the dough all over, at 1-inch intervals, using the tines of a fork, or a rolling docker.
- → In a preheated 400°F oven, bake the rounds of dough for approximately 30 minutes, or until they are golden brown and fully puffed.
- → During the baking, rotate the sheet pans, front to back, back to front, to facilitate even baking. Do not underbake this dough or it will be soggy.
- → When fully baked, remove from the oven and move the baked rounds of dough to a cooling rack to cool.
- → Store at room temperature while you make the pâte à choux as follows.

Pâte à choux— cream puff pastry

YIELD: APPROXIMATELY 54 OUNCES, THIRTY-SIX 1 INCH PUFFS AND TWELVE 1½ TO 2 INCH PUFFS

Oz	Grams	Name of ingredient	Baker's percentages
18	540	Whole large eggs	158
15	450	Water	131
7.5	235	Unsalted butter	68
1.5	45	Granulated sugar	13
0.17	5.1	Salt	1
11.4	342	All purpose flour	100

- → In a medium bowl, whisk the eggs to combine and set aside.
- → In a large heavy saucepan, bring the water, butter, sugar, and salt to a rapid boil.
- → Add the flour all at once, stirring the mixture with a wooden spoon, until it has thickened to the consistency of mashed potatoes and leaves a film on the bottom of the pan.
- → Remove from the heat and allow to cool to lukewarm.
- → Transfer the mixture to the bowl of an electric mixer outfitted with a paddle attachment, and beat, adding the eggs in a steady stream until incorporated before adding more.
- → Transfer the mixture to a pastry bag outfitted with a plain tip measuring ½ inch in diameter and pipe the mixture, onto a parchment-lined full-size baking sheet, in 36 uniform 1 inch round puffs, spaced about 2 inches apart, in three rows of 8 puffs each, alternated with two rows of 6 puffs each, in between, parallel to the long side of the pan.
- → Refill the pastry bag as needed.
- → On a separate parchment-lined half-sheet pan, in three rows of four puffs each, pipe out the remaining choux paste in puffs measuring approximately 1½ to 2 inches in diameter. (These large puffs will serve as the base for the dessert, and are dipped in golden caramel to add crunch and color to the base.)
- → Bake both sheets of the puffs in a preheated 425°F oven for 10 minutes.
- → After the puffs have inflated, reduce the heat to 375°F and continue baking until the puffs are golden brown. (Note that the larger puffs may need to bake for a few more minutes longer than the smaller ones.)

- Five minutes before removing them from the oven, using a small sharp knife, make a slit in the side of each puff, to allow excess moisture to escape, resulting in crisper puffs.
- Remove from the oven and allow to cool on a rack.
- Fill one-third of the puffs each with one of the following pastry cream fillings: pistachio, raspberry, and chocolate. Continue filling until you have an equal number of puffs filled with the three different fillings.
- Set the filled puffs aside and then dip the puffs in the appropriate fondant icing, with the flavor of the fondant corresponding to the flavor of the fillings.

Custard fillings
YIELD: APPROXIMATELY 20 OUNCES, FILLING FOR 12 PUFFS

Pistachio filling

Oz	Grams	Each	Name of ingredient
8	240		**Whole milk**
1.3	45		**Granulated sugar**
5	150	3	**Whole large eggs**
0.8	2.4		**Cornstarch**
4	120		**Pistachio paste**
1.3	39		**Unsalted butter**

- In a small heavy saucepan, bring the milk and sugar to the boil.
- In a small bowl, combine eggs and cornstarch, whisking until smooth.
- Temper half of the hot milk mixture into the egg mixture and then whisk until smooth.
- Add this tempered mixture to the milk mixture remaining in the saucepan and cook over medium heat, whisking constantly, until thick. (No raw starch taste should remain.)
- Add the raspberry puree, the butter, and the cocoa butter and stir to incorporate, scraping the bottom and sides of the pan to ensure that the mixture is well blended.
- Transfer the mixture to a bowl set over an ice water bath, stirring to cool quickly, and then place it into a container, cover it, and chill in the refrigerator until ready to fill the puffs.

Raspberry Filling
YIELD: APPROXIMATELY 21 OUNCES, FILLING FOR 12 PUFFS

Oz	Grams	Each	Name of ingredient
8	240		Whole Milk
1.3	39		Granulated sugar
5	150	3	Whole large eggs
.5	16		Cornstarch
4	120		**Fresh seedless raspberry puree** or commercially produced frozen seedless raspberry puree, thawed
2.3	70		**Unsalted butter**

- In a small heavy saucepan, bring the milk and sugar to the boil.
- In a small bowl, combine eggs and cornstarch, whisking until smooth.
- Temper half of the hot milk mixture into the egg mixture and then whisk until smooth.
- Add this tempered mixture to the milk mixture remaining in the saucepan and cook over medium heat, whisking constantly, until thick. (No raw starch taste should remain).
- Add the raspberry puree and the butter and stir to incorporate, scraping the bottom and sides of the pan to ensure that the mixture is well blended.
- Transfer the mixture to a bowl set over an ice water bath, stirring to cool quickly, and then place it into a container, cover it, and chill in the refrigerator until ready to fill the puffs.

Oz	Grams	Each	Name of ingredient
8	240		Whole milk
1.3	39		Granulated sugar
5	150	3	Whole large eggs
0.5	15		Cornstarch
4	120		High-quality **58–60% chocolate couverture** (use thin coins or chop the chocolate into small pieces)
0.16	4.8	1 t.	Vanilla extract
1.3	39		Unsalted butter

→ In a small heavy saucepan, bring the milk and sugar to the boil.

→ In a small bowl, combine the eggs and cornstarch, whisking until smooth.

→ Temper half of the hot milk mixture into the egg mixture and then whisk until smooth.

→ Add this tempered mixture to the milk mixture remaining in the saucepan and cook over medium heat, whisking constantly, until thick. (No raw starch taste should remain.)

→ Add the chocolate, the vanilla, and the butter and stir to incorporate, scraping sides and bottom of the saucepan to ensure that the mixture is well blended.

→ Transfer the mixture to a bowl set over an ice water bath, stirring to cool quickly, and then place it into a container, cover it, and chill in the refrigerator until ready to fill the puffs.

Pistachio fondant-style icing

Oz	Grams	Each	Name of ingredient
2.5, approximately	75		**Confectioners' sugar**, sifted
3.5	105		**Hot water** to thin
		2 t.	**Pistachio paste**

→ Sift the confectioners' sugar first into a bowl and then add the hot water to it, stirring with a whisk to make a paste.

→ Add the pistachio paste and mix to blend to a uniform color. The icing should flow enough to coat the puffs with a thin layer but not be so liquid as to flow off of the puffs.

→ Adjust the consistency by adding more confectioners' sugar or water, as necessary.

Raspberry fondant-style icing

Oz	Grams	Each	Name of ingredient
3.5 approximately; you might need as much as ¼ oz more for proper flowing consistency	105		**Confectioners' sugar**, sifted
0.5	15		**Dried raspberry powder**
1.6	48	8 t.	**Hot water**
0.67	20	4 T.	**Powdered cocoa butter** (Mycryo is one brand) Melted in microwave or over double boiler, stirring to melt evenly

TIP: *It is best to use commercially made raspberry powder. Dehydrated pure fruit powders are intense in flavor and a little goes a long way. If unavailable, freeze-dried fruits may be pulverized using a spice grinder, small food processor, or in a mortar and pestle—but do not overprocess, as the powders tend to clump or agglomerate, making them difficult to distribute evenly in a fondant icing.*

- → Sift the confectioners' sugar with the dried raspberry powder into a bowl.
- → Add the hot water and the melted cocoa butter.
- → Mix until blended.
- → Then add the corn syrup.
- → The icing should flow enough to coat the puffs with a thin layer but not be so liquid as to flow off of the puffs.
- → Adjust the consistency by adding more confectioners' sugar or water, as necessary.

Chocolate fondant-style icing

YIELD: ENOUGH TO COAT 12 PUFFS, APPROXIMATELY A SCANT ½ OUNCE FOR EACH

Oz	Grams	Each	Name of ingredient
4 approximately	120		**Confectioners sugar,** sifted
0.17	5.1	2 t.	**Powdered cocoa butter,** melted (Mycryo is one brand)
1	30		**58% dark chocolate couverture,** melted

- → Sift the confectioners' sugar into a bowl.
- → Melt the powdered cocoa butter in a microwave set on high for about 5 seconds, stirring frequently, or over a double boiler, stirring to melt evenly.
- → Add it and the melted chocolate to the sugar, stirring to a smooth consistency. The icing should flow enough to coat the puffs with a thin layer but not be so liquid as to flow off of the puffs.
- → Adjust the consistency by adding more confectioners' sugar or water, as necessary.

Caramel for puffs and for décor

YIELD: ENOUGH TO COAT 12 PUFFS; USE AS AN ADHESIVE WHEN ASSEMBLING THE DESSERT, AND TO MAKE 12 GARNISHES

Oz	Grams	Name of ingredient
10	300	**Granulated sugar**
2	60	**Water**
1	30	**Corn syrup**

- → In a small heavy saucepan, bring the sugar, water, and corn syrup to the boil without stirring.
- → Cook to golden caramel stage (approximately 318°F), remove from heat, and dip each of the 12 larger puffs in the caramel to coat the tops and part of the sides.
- → Coat each of the caramel disks with a thin layer of the liquid caramel and set aside.
- → Reserve some caramel to be reheated to use as adhesive to join the base puff to the puff pastry disk and to secure the top puffs to the puff pastry disk when assembling the dessert.
- → Reheat the caramel and, wearing heat-proof gloves, pipe out the hot caramel through a heat-proof pastry bag outfitted with a metal tip with a ¹⁄₁₆ inch opening (alternatively, you may use a paper parchment cone cut with a ¹⁄₁₆ inch opening) onto a Silpat-lined sheet pan to create 12 whirlpool-shaped flat caramel designs. (See photograph on page 312.)
- → Reheat the caramel as needed but do not burn or it will taste bitter.
- → If necessary, make another batch of the caramel to complete the process.
- → Set aside the designs at cool room temperature, uncovered, until ready to assemble the dessert.
- → The designs are best made within 2 hours of serving the dessert.

Assembly and plating

For each serving, using a pastry bag outfitted with a plain tip, with a rosette opening measuring ½ inch in diameter, fill three puffs, one puff per filling. Dip the puffs in the corresponding fondant icings. Dip one larger puff into golden, still-flowing caramel, for each dessert. Place one caramel-coated larger-sized puff on the center of each plate. On each plate, using a pastry bag, pipe one rosette of each filling around the puff, spacing the rosettes equidistant from each other and from the center puff, within a circle roughly equivalent to the diameter of the puff pastry disk. Reheat the caramel and apply a dab of it on the center of the bottom side of the pastry disk. Center the disk on the bottom puff and hold for a few seconds until the caramel cools and dries. Then carefully place one of each smaller puffs on the disk of pastry. Position them in a triangular arrangement and place them above the rosette of pastry cream corresponding to the color and flavor of its fondant decoration, balancing the puffs so that the disk remains parallel to the plate. Garnish the dessert with the caramel décor, as desired.

Chocolate Chestnut Cloud

Chocolate Chestnut Cloud, dark chocolate ganache, on a bed of chocolate chestnut cream, whipped cream. Here crunch and cream come together in a celebration of winter. Textural contrast is key, with the slightly crusty exterior of the cake playing against the fudgy interior, all of which is set off against a soft bed of two different creams under the cake. Chestnut is used in three different parts of the recipe here. Chestnut flour stands in for cake flour in the flourless cake. Sweetened chestnut puree flavors the cream, which acts as the base for the plated dessert. Lending a festive air to the ensemble is a whole candied chestnut surmounted by a square of gold leaf–embossed tempered chocolate. A fourth form of chestnut, sweetened pureed chestnut piped into a mound of spaghetti-like strands, is suggested as an option to be used as a piped-out decoration to the side of the cake.

The order of things:

1. **Make chocolate chestnut cake**
2. **Make dark chocolate ganache**
3. **Make whipped cream** as base for chocolate chestnut cream
4. **Complete chocolate chestnut cream**
5. **Make square tempered chocolate**
6. **Make the candied chestnuts,** if not using commercially prepared ones

Equipment list:

Silicone plaque with square indentations, each measuring 2¾ inches square (which will become the bottom when the dessert is served), by 2¼ inches square on the bottom of the mold by 1¼ inches high, with a 1½ inch square depression in the center of the bottom of each cavity (which will become the top of the dessert when served)

Two pastry bags, each outfitted with a plain tip, measuring ½ inch in diameter, one each for the chocolate chestnut cream and plain whipped cream

Sheet of **food-grade acetate** for the chocolate decorations

Small, sharp knife or X-ACTO knife to cut the square tempered chocolate decorations

Small brush to apply the gold leaf design on the chocolate decorations

Pastry bag with a tip with a small opening to pipe out the optional chestnut puree "spaghetti"

Chocolate chestnut cake

YIELD: APPROXIMATELY
45 OUNCES, 12 SERVINGS,
EACH WEIGHING
3¾ OUNCES

Oz	Grams	Each	Name of ingredient	Baker's percentages
10	300	6	Large eggs	107
10	300		Granulated sugar, divided	107
16	480		60% dark chocolate couverture	172
.5	15		Vanilla extract	5
	2		Salt	.7
9.3	279		Chestnut flour	100

→ Place a plaque of square Silform molds on a baking sheet.

→ The top of each cavity should measure 2¾ inches square (which will become the bottom when the dessert is served), by 2¼ inches square on the bottom of the mold by 1¼ inches high, with a 1½ inch square depression in the center of the bottom of each cavity (which will become the top of the dessert when served).

→ Spray the molds lightly with pan release spray and set aside.

→ Separate the eggs, placing the yolks in a medium-sized stainless steel bowl and the whites into the bowl of an electric mixer outfitted with the whisk attachment.

→ Place the egg yolks and half of the sugar in a metal bowl set over a saucepan of simmering water (the water should not touch the bottom of the bowl) and whisk constantly until the mixture reaches 110°F.

→ Remove from the heat, add the vanilla and the salt.

→ Transfer to the bowl of an electric mixer outfitted with the whisk attachment, and whip until the mixture triples in volume and lightens in color.

→ When the whisk is lifted from the bowl, the mixture should fall slowly in a thick ribbon.

→ Place the bowl of egg whites onto the electric mixer and whip them with the remaining half of the sugar to soft, shiny peaks.

→ Set aside.

→ Place the chocolate in a metal bowl over a saucepan of simmering water and stir until fully melted.

→ Cool slightly.

→ Fold the chocolate into the yolk mixture.

→ Then gently fold or stir in the chestnut flour just to combine.

→ Finally, fold the egg whites into the mixture.

→ Fill each cavity with an equal amount of the batter. The batter will rise above the tops of the mold but will deflate some while cooling.

→ Bake in a preheated 350°F oven to approximately 20 minutes. Do not overbake. The cakes should be firm but moist.

→ Remove from the oven.

→ Place the plaque on a cooling rack and reserve at room temperature until ready to assemble the dessert.

→ Trim, if needed, to level the tops of the cakes, which will become the bottoms of the cakes when served.

→ Make dark chocolate ganache as follows.

Oz	Grams	Name of ingredient
3	120	**60% dark chocolate couverture**, chopped
3	120	**Heavy cream**

Dark chocolate ganache for filling the cavities of each cake, and for flavoring the chocolate chestnut cream

YIELD: APPROXIMATELY 6 OUNCES

→ Chop the chocolate and place into a stainless steel bowl.

→ In a small, heavy saucepan, bring the cream to the boil.

→ Remove from the heat and pour the hot cream into the chocolate, stirring, without aerating, until the chocolate has melted and the mixture is perfectly smooth.

→ Set aside until ready to plate the dessert.

→ Store at cool room temperature if using within a few hours.

→ If not, refrigerate covered, and then remove from the refrigerator, placing the ganache over a hot water bath to re-liquefy just before ready to use.

Oz	Grams	Name of ingredient
12	360	**Heavy cream**

Whipped cream to be used in chocolate chestnut cream and as plain

→ In the bowl of an electric mixer outfitted with the whisk attachment, whip the cream to soft peaks.

→ Remove from the machine and divide the cream into two equal parts, placing each part in a small bowl.

→ The first half of the cream will be used for the chocolate chestnut cream below.

→ Place the second half into a pastry bag, outfitted with a plain tip, measuring ½ inch in diameter.

→ Fold the top of the bag to seal and set aside in the refrigerator until ready to plate the desserts.

Oz	Grams	Name of ingredient
6	180	**Softly whipped cream** from above
3.5	105	**Chestnut puree**
2.25	68	**Chocolate ganache** from above

Chocolate chestnut cream

YIELD: APPROXIMATELY 12 OUNCES, 12 SERVINGS, 1 OUNCE EACH

→ Add the chestnut puree into whipped cream.

→ Then gently fold in 2 ounces of the chocolate ganache.

→ Place into a pastry bag, outfitted with a plain round tip, measuring ½ inch diameter.

→ Seal the top of the pastry bag and refrigerate, covered, until needed.

Gold leaf–decorated chocolate square

YIELD: ENOUGH FOR 12 GARNISHES AND ALLOWS FOR EXTRAS IN CASE A FEW BREAK, ARE MISSHAPEN, OR OTHERWISE UNUSABLE

Tempering chocolate

→ If tempering the chocolate, heat ⅔ of it in a stainless steel bowl set over simmering water.

→ Melt it, stirring occasionally, until it reaches 122°F.

→ When it reaches this temperature, remove from the heat and add the remaining one third of the chocolate to lower the temperature of the chocolate to 81°F.

→ Stir constantly during this process to encourage the production of many small cocoa butter crystals that will lead to a good temper for the chocolate.

→ Carefully rewarm the chocolate to 90°F, which is the temperature at which the chocolate should be held when ready to spread out onto acetate for the decorations.

→ To test to see if the chocolate is in temper, dip the corner of a small piece of parchment paper in the chocolate and then place the parchment on a work surface.

→ If the chocolate is in temper, it should dry within minutes and break cleanly when the paper is folded. It also should not melt readily when touched.

Although the following decorations require only 4 ounces of tempered chocolate, it is impractical to temper such a small amount. Therefore, increase the amount of chocolate to 16 ounces and proceed with the tempering discussed above, and then use 4 ounces of it to spread onto the acetate sheet to make the chocolate squares for the garnish.

Oz	Grams	Each	Name of ingredient
4	120		**Chocolate couverture,** tempered, or non-tempering chocolate coating
.5	15		**Clear alcohol** such as vodka or gin
		Two square sheets, each measuring roughly 2 inches square	**Gold leaf**

→ Onto a sheet of food-grade acetate, spread a thin but not translucent layer of the tempered chocolate couverture or non-tempering chocolate coating.

→ Just before the chocolate dries, use a sharp knife or X-ACTO knife to cut 1 inch squares.

→ Release from the acetate and place the squares carefully onto a parchment -lined baking sheet.

→ In a small bowl, combine the alcohol and gold leaf.

→ Using a small brush, gently brush a thin layer of the gold leaf "paint" onto the chocolate squares.

→ Allow to dry and then carefully place one on the center of the serving of cake. (See photograph on page 320.)

(See photograph on page 320.)

TIP: *Candied chestnuts may be made from scratch by cutting an X in the flat side of each chestnut with a sharp knife and then roasting the nuts on a sheet pan in a preheated 350°F oven until the cut areas of the shell curl, and the nuts have a fragrant aroma. Remove the chestnuts from the oven, allow them to cool slightly and them peel off and discard the skins and the inner "hairy" covering of the nut. Place the nuts in a vanilla-scented simple syrup (equal parts of water and granulated sugar boiled until the sugar dissolves, flavored with a vanilla bean, split lengthwise, per quart of syrup). Cook in the syrup at a low simmer, about 30–45 minutes, until the chestnuts are tender but not disintegrating. Allow to cool in the syrup and then remove to drain. Be sure to roast extra chestnuts, because you may find some of them to be moldy inside of their shell, and therefore unusable.*

Candied chestnuts for garnish, one for each serving

Each	Name of ingredient
12, 0.5 oz each, approximately	Whole candied chestnuts

Oz	Grams	Name of ingredient
6	180	Sweetened, canned puree of chestnut
As necessary to thin slightly, to make the mixture easily pipeable, but not so thin that it will lose its shape after being piped		Simple syrup

Optional garnish: Sweetened chestnut "spaghetti"

Assembly and plating

Pipe enough of the reserved ganache to the cavity in the top of the cake.

Pipe alternating stripes of the chocolate chestnut cream and plain whipped cream, adjacent to each other, in the center area of the serving plate. Place the cake at an angle on top of the stripes of cream. Garnish the top of the cake with candied chestnut and the gold leaf–decorated chocolate square. Optionally, using a pastry bag with a tip with a small opening, pipe out a mound of thin spaghetti-like strands of the sweetened chestnut spaghetti to the side of the cake.

Crepe Cake Marjolaine Layered with Hazelnut, Coffee, and Chocolate Creams

YIELD 2 CREPE CAKES, EACH SERVING 6; TOTAL SERVINGS: 12

Crepe cake layered with hazelnut, coffee and chocolate creams, hot ganache plating sauce, and *sarments noisette* (chocolate twigs) garnish. This dessert borrows some of its inspiration from the patriarch of modern French gastronomy, Fernand Point, chef-owner of La Pyramide in Vienne, France, who created *la marjolaine*, a layered nutted meringue with almonds, hazelnuts, and chocolate. Instead of tender nutted meringue, the layers here are thin custardy crepes, and in addition to the hazelnuts and chocolate in the original, coffee introduces another layer of flavor.

Key points to consider are the following: allow the crepe batter to rest for a few hours to yield tender rather than tough and chewy crepes; be precise when dosing out the batter in the crepe pan so that all crepes are uniform in size; and lastly, use thin and uniform amounts of filling between each layer to produce a precise, visually stunning dessert. Note that the crepes may be made in advance of the day when the dessert is served, and then refrigerated for a day or for longer storage (up to a month), frozen, well wrapped, with squares of parchment paper in between each one so that they do not stick together, until ready to assemble the dessert.

The order of things:

1. **Make crepe batter** and let rest for a few hours before making the crepes
2. **Make pastry cream base** for the hazelnut, coffee and chocolate cream fillings for the crepe cake
3. **Make the ganache** and refrigerate, reheating it before serving the dessert
4. **Temper chocolate** for the chocolate twigs
5. **Make crepes**
6. **Assemble crepe cake**

Equipment list:

Nonstick crepe pan, with a diameter of 9 inches

Crepe batter

YIELD: APPROXIMATELY 50 CREPES, ROUGHLY 9 INCHES IN DIAMETER, EACH CREPE WEIGHING APPROXIMATELY 1¼ OUNCES

Oz	Grams	Each	Name of ingredient	Baker's percentages
24	720		Whole milk	300
16	480	9–10	Whole large eggs	200
8	240		Unsalted butter, melted	100
2	60		Granulated sugar	25
8	240		All purpose flour	100
		½ t.	Salt	1
0.5	15		Vanilla extract	6
As needed			Water to thin batter	

→ In a large stainless steel bowl, whisk milk, eggs, and butter until combined.

→ Add sugar and whisk again.

→ Add flour and salt, sifted, mixing just until the batter is smooth.

→ Add vanilla and whisk to incorporate.

→ Rest batter, covered, for 2 hours in the refrigerator.

→ Whisk again briefly before using.

→ Using a nonstick 9 inch crepe pan, ladle or spoon 1 ounce of crepe batter into the pan while tilting it to help coat the pan evenly.

→ If the batter does not flow easily, gradually add water to thin.

→ When the edges of the crepe begin to brown lightly, carefully turn the crepe over and allow to cook for about 10 seconds.

→ Invert pan and remove the crepe, depositing it onto a parchment lined sheet pan.

→ As you stack the finished crepes, place a square piece of parchment paper in between each layer.

→ Continue making crepes until all of the batter is used. (You may have more crepes than you will need to construct the two crepe cakes. The crepes keep well, refrigerated or frozen, well wrapped, with the squares of parchment paper in between each crepe, until ready to assemble the crepe cake.)

→ Make the pastry cream base and then the three fillings immediately after, as follows.

Pastry cream

YIELD: APPROXIMATELY 60 OUNCES, DIVIDED INTO THREE FLAVORS

Oz	Grams	Each	Name of ingredient	Baker's percentages— Milk at 100%
24	720		Whole milk	100
		2	Vanilla beans, split	.1
12	360		Granulated sugar, divided	50
20	600		Whole eggs	83
4	120		Cornstarch	10
8	240		Unsalted butter	33

→ Place the milk, vanilla beans, and half of the sugar in a medium-sized heavy saucepan.

→ Bring to the boil, reduce to a simmer, and cook for 5 minutes.

→ Remove from the heat, cover the saucepan, and allow the mixture to infuse for 15 minutes.

→ Taste to be sure that the vanilla flavor comes through clearly. If not, reheat the liquid briefly, remove from the heat, cover the saucepan, and allow to infuse for a few more minutes.

- When the liquid is well infused, remove the vanilla bean, rinse and dry, and reserve for another use.
- Set aside the infused liquid.
- In a stainless steel bowl, whisk the eggs, the remaining half of the sugar, and cornstarch in a bowl until light and smooth.
- In a heavy, nonreactive saucepan, bring the infused milk and remaining sugar to the boil.
- Temper the eggs mixture with about 2 cups of the hot milk, whisking until smooth.
- Add this tempered mixture to the remaining milk in the saucepan, whisking until the mixture thickens to the consistency of mayonnaise.
- Keep whisking until the mixture is completely smooth.
- Add butter and then divide into three equal parts.
- For the chocolate pastry cream, add chocolate, whisking until the chocolate melts and the mixture is smooth once again.
- For the hazelnut cream, add the hazelnut paste, whisking until smooth.
- For the coffee pastry cream, add the instant coffee dissolved in the coffee liqueur.

Chocolate pastry cream

Oz	Grams	Name of ingredient	Baker's percentages— Pastry cream at 100%
20, approximately	600	**Pastry cream** from above	100
9	270	**High-quality 70% dark couverture chocolate**	45

- Add the melted chocolate to the still warm pastry cream, whisking as needed to smooth, and set aside until ready to assemble the dessert.

Hazelnut pastry cream

Oz	Grams	Name of ingredient	Baker's percentages
20, approximately	600	**Pastry cream** from above	100
6	180	**Hazelnut paste**	30

- Whisk the pastry cream and hazelnut paste together in a medium-sized bowl, and set aside until ready to assemble the dessert.

Coffee pastry cream

Oz	Grams	Name of ingredient	Baker's percentages
20, approximately	600	**Pastry cream** from above	100
1	30	**Instant coffee powder**	5
1	30	**Coffee liqueur** such as Kahlua or Tia Maria	5

- In a small bowl, dissolve the coffee powder in the coffee liqueur.
- In a medium bowl, combine this liquid with the pastry cream, whisking until smooth.
- Set aside until ready to assemble the dessert.

Oz	Grams	Name of ingredient
16	480	**Tempered dark chocolate,** chopped, or non-tempering chocolate coating, melted and maintained at 90°F over warm water
4	120	**Hazelnuts,** toasted in a 350°F oven, skins removed, and then finely chopped

If using tempered chocolate, temper the chocolate as follows

→ Heat ⅔ of the chocolate in a stainless steel bowl over simmering water.

→ Melt it, stirring occasionally, until it reaches 122°F.

→ When it reaches this temperature, add the remaining one third of the chocolate to lower the temperature of the chocolate to 81°F.

→ Stir constantly during this process to encourage the production of many small cocoa butter crystals that will lead to a good temper for the chocolate.

→ Then carefully rewarm the chocolate to 90°F, which is the temperature at which the chocolate should be held when spreading it out on a marble or stainless steel work surface to create the twigs (*sarments*).

→ To test to see if the chocolate is in temper, dip the corner of a small piece of parchment paper in the chocolate and then place the parchment on a work surface.

→ If the chocolate is in temper, it should dry within minutes and break cleanly when the paper is folded. It also should not melt readily when touched.

→ If using non-tempering coating chocolate, melt it over a water bath and then proceed as below.

Now proceed with the making of the chocolate twigs (*sarments noisette*)

→ Spread the tempered (or non-tempering) chocolate in a thin layer on a marble or clean and dry stainless steel work surface.

→ Sprinkle half of the nuts over the chocolate and then using a wide palette knife, held at a 70 degree angle, using short strokes, immediately scrape the surface of the chocolate, in the direction away from you, to yield 3 inch long twig-shaped pieces, rolling the chocolate over onto itself as you scrape the chocolate from the work surface.

→ Continue scraping to create chocolate twigs until the work surface is clean.

→ If needed, you can remelt the tempered chocolate, without heating it beyond 90°F so that it remains in temper, and repeat the process of spreading it out on the work surface, scraping to create the twigs as discussed above. (If you are using non-tempering chocolate coating, it, too, may be reheated until it is liquid and then may be poured out onto the work surface to repeat the scraping process.)

→ Garnish the twigs with more chopped hazelnuts as follows.

Final garnishing of the twigs

→ Using a paper parchment cone, pipe out a thin stream of melted tempered (or non-tempering) chocolate over the twigs (*sarments*), sprinkle with the remaining nuts and set the twigs (*sarments*) aside at cool room temperature until ready to plate the dessert.

TIP: *Other than the chocolate and hazelnut fillings, the crepe cake may be layered with lightly sweetened and vanilla-flavored whipped cream, fresh raspberries, candied kumquats, and fresh filets of blood orange, and then garnished with either the hot ganache (as shown above) or a fruit coulis, or several fruit coulis made from the fruits that you are using inside of the cake.*

Oz	Grams	Name of ingredient	Baker's percentages—Chocolate at 100%
8	240	**High-quality 70% dark chocolate couverture,** finely chopped	100
8	240	Heavy cream	100

→ In a heavy saucepan, bring cream to the boil.

→ Place chocolate into a heat-proof stainless steel bowl and then pour heated cream over chocolate and stir gently until smooth and completely melted.

→ Set aside until ready to plate dessert.

→ Reheat over a double boiler until hot and then place on plates just before serving.

Assembly and plating

Spoon a pool of heated ganache on the right side of each plate. Slice each crepe cake into 6 even wedges. Place one wedge of the crepe cake on each plate. Place 5 or 6 of the sarments noisette, piled in a crisscross fashion, on top of each slice. Serve immediately.

Dark Milk Chocolate Mousse

YIELD: 12 SERVINGS

Dark milk chocolate mousse with croquantine layer, peanut sponge, salted peanut Florentine, tamarind sauce. Taking a page from the Thai book of flavors, this dessert incorporates two ingredients commonly used in the savory cuisine of that Southeast Asian country: peanuts and tamarind. The first, an element from the New World (thought to have been domesticated in South America in 2000 BCE), was brought to Asia by the Spanish and Portuguese almost three-and-a-half millennia later, in the 15th century, where it was incorporated as a thickener and sauce base in the cuisines of China and much of Southeast Asia. (Given Americans' insatiable taste for peanut butter, contrary to what one might think, on the agricultural side, the United States trails way behind India and China, which are the largest growers of peanuts.) A side note: Peanuts are not in fact nuts, but rather legumes, grown underground, unlike true nuts, which are tree fruits botanically speaking.

Tamarind, the second Southeast Asian ingredient used here, is a slightly curved large seeded pod from a tree native to India. It is often found paired with the peanut in Thai sweet and sour sauces, and used widely in diverse parts of the world as a souring agent in sauces, stews, soups and beverages from Mexico to the Middle East. Here the sweet-tart fruit becomes a bracing saucy accent on the plate. This dessert would aptly follow an Asian-inflected meal.

Peanut adds texture here to the sponge cake base and the hollow peanut-encrusted tower of crisp florentine that garnishes the mousse. Peanut in its spreadable form is used as an important flavoring in the thin, crunchy chocolate croquantine that separates the two layers of the creamy, dark milk chocolate mousse.

The order of things:

1. **Make the peanut sponge and bake**
2. **Make the croquantine and chill**
3. **Make the dark milk chocolate mousse and refrigerate**
4. **Place a piece of sponge into each mold**
5. **Make the salted peanut florentine cookie batter and refrigerate**
6. **Pipe two layers of the mousse into the molds separated by a layer of croquantine and refrigerate**
7. **Bake and shape the florentines**
8. **Make tamarind sauce and refrigerate** until ready to serve the dessert, rewarming (and/or adding small amounts of hot water) to liquefy just before plating the dessert

Equipment list:

24 metal 8-sided faceted **square cutters,** 2¼ inches on each side by ½ inch thick, 12 to use as molds for the mousses and 12 to use as the forms around which the salted peanut florentines will be shaped

Pastry bag outfitted with a plain metal tip, measuring ½ inch in diameter to pipe mousse into molds

Peanut sponge cake

YIELD: ONE QUARTER SHEET, WHICH YIELDS 12 PIECES OF CAKE, CUT USING A FACETED SQUARE, 2¼ INCHES ON EACH SIDE BY ½ INCH THICK

Oz	Grams	Each	Name of ingredient	Baker's percentages— Cake flour and ground peanuts total 100%
8, approximately	240		Eggs	50
4	120		Granulated sugar	100
2	60		Peanuts, finely ground	50
2	60		Cake flour	50
	2		Salt	2
0.16	4.8	1 t.	Vanilla extract	4
2	60		Unsalted butter, melted	50

Note: You may double this recipe to yield one half-sheet pan, yielding enough cake for 24 mousse bases, freezing the extra cake, well wrapped, for future use.

→ Prepare a quarter sheet pan, approximately 8 inches by 12 inches. Spray the bottom of the pan with pan release spray, and then line the bottom with a piece of parchment paper. Set aside.

→ Warm eggs and sugar over a bain marie until 110°F.

→ Remove to the bowl of an electric mixer and, using the whisk attachment, beat the mixture until light in color and tripled in volume.

→ Combine the ground peanuts, cake flour, and salt.

→ Sift the mixture and then fold gently into the egg base, adding the vanilla and melted butter as you fold. Handle gently to avoid deflating.

→ Pour the batter immediately into the prepared pan, and bake in a preheated 375°F oven for approximately 15 minutes.

→ Using a faceted square bottomless mold, cut the cake into 12 pieces, in rows of four along the 11 inch side and in rows of three on the 8 inch side. (Reserve cake that is left in between each cut, for another use).

→ Place the molds onto a parchment-lined sheet pan and place one piece of cake into the bottom of each mold.

→ Set aside and make the croquantine.

Croquantine layer

YIELD: APPROXIMATELY 9 OUNCES, 12 SERVINGS, ¾ OUNCE EACH

Oz	Grams	Name of ingredient
1.5	45	Unsalted butter
4	120	Milk chocolate, melted
1	30	Smooth peanut butter, room temperature
2.5	75	Commerically prepared croquantine flakes, or corn-based flaked cereal

TIP: *If on hand, well-baked puff pastry, broken up into flakes may be substituted here for a buttery and slightly more coarse-textured croquantine. However, note that the puff pastry flakes may not remain as crisp as commercially prepared croquantine flakes.*

Low-sodium and reduced sugar peanut butter or natural health food store varieties work well here.

→ Place the milk chocolate and butter into a medium-sized stainless steel bowl.

→ Set the bowl over a saucepan of simmering water.

- → Stir to melt and then add the peanut butter.
- → Stir to emulsify and then fold in the croquantine flakes.
- → Remove from the heat and pour the mixture onto a Silpat, spreading it into a rough rectangle, measuring approximately 8 inches by 11 inches by ¼ inch thick.
- → Allow to set in the refrigerator almost completely and then perforate with the edge of the mousse mold to mark the desired finished shape in rows of four along the 11 inch side and in rows of three along the 8 inch side.
- → When completely cool, cut all the way through and set aside in the refrigerator to re-firm.
- → Make the milk chocolate mousse as follows.

Oz	Gram	Each	Name of ingredient
16	480		Dark milk chocolate 41%
8	240		Heavy cream
	3	1 sheet	Sheet gelatin
6	180		Heavy cream, softly whipped

Dark milk chocolate mousse

YIELD: 12 FACETED SQUARE MOUSSES, EACH MEASURING 2¼ INCHES ON EACH SIDE BY 1½ INCHES TALL, EACH SERVING WEIGHING APPROXIMATELY 2½ OUNCES

- → Chop the milk chocolate into small pieces and place into a heat-proof bowl.
- → In a small heavy saucepan, bring the cream to the boil.
- → Remove from the heat and pour the hot cream over the chocolate, stirring, without aerating, to melt into a smooth ganache.
- → Place the gelatin in a bowl large enough to submerge the sheets in cold water.
- → Allow to soften until most of the water has been absorbed and the gelatin is soft but not disintegrating.
- → Squeeze out excess liquid, if any, and add the squeezed-out gelatin to the still warm ganache. (If the ganache is not warm, reheat it gently over a hot water bath until warm).
- → Allow the mixture to cool to 70°F.
- → In the bowl of an electric mixer outfitted with the whisk attachment, whip the second quantity of cream to medium stiff peaks and gently but thoroughly fold it into the cooled milk chocolate ganache mixture. (Note: It is best to use the mousse immediately, before it sets completely.)
- → Using a pastry bag outfitted with a plain tip measuring ½ inch in diameter, quickly pipe the mousse into each mold halfway up the sides of the mold.
- → Using a small spatula, carefully pick up the piece of croquantine and ease it onto the layer of mousse in each mold. (If the cut pieces of croquantine break, simply place the broken pieces in a single layer into the molds.)
- → Fill the molds with the remaining mousse, gently tap the sheet pan of molds against the countertop to densify and remove any air bubbles, and then freeze.

Salted peanut florentine cookie

YIELD: APPROXIMATELY 13 OUNCES, ENOUGH FOR 12, PLUS ADDITIONAL ALLOWING FOR BREAKAGE, OR MISSHAPED OR OTHERWISE IMPERFECT COOKIES

Oz	Grams	Each	Name of ingredient	Baker's percentages Sugar and corn syrup total 100%
4	120		Granulated sugar	88
0.5	15		Corn syrup	12
4	120		Unsalted butter	88
1	30		Heavy cream	22
4	120		Peanuts, coarsely chopped	88
0.16	4.8	1 t.	Vanilla extract	3
0.1	3	½ t.	Salt	2

→ In a medium-sized heavy saucepan, bring the sugar, corn syrup, butter, and heavy cream to 190 to 200°F.

→ Remove from the heat, whisk to emulsify, add the peanuts, vanilla, and salt.

→ Spread the mixture in twelve ½ inch wide strips on a Silpat.

→ Bake in a preheated 375°F oven for approximately 8 to 10 minutes. (Note that these will spread to approximately 1 inch in width.)

→ Remove from oven and immediately drape the cookies without delay over the sides of the mousse mold.

→ Trim while still hot into strips measuring 8 inches long by 2 inches wide and gently curve over the faceted square metal mold used for the mousses, measuring 2¼ inches on each side to form into a curved "bracelet" shape. (See photograph on page 332.)

→ Allow to cool on the mold, and when cool, carefully remove and store at cool room temperature (60 to 70°F), standing upright and well spaced on a parchment- or Silpat-lined baking sheet.

→ If not using immediately, store upright in a deep container with a tight-fitting lid outfitted with a piece of limestone or a packet of silica gel to help retain crispness.

Tamarind sauce

YIELD: APPROXIMATELY 9 OUNCES, 12 SERVINGS, ¾ OUNCE EACH

Oz	Gram	Name of ingredient
6	180	Tamarind pulp, seedless
3 to 4 depending on tartness of the tamarind	90 to 120	Simple syrup

→ In a small heavy saucepan, bring the tamarind pulp and simple syrup to a boil, whisking until smooth.

→ Remove from the heat, pass through a fine sieve set over a small bowl, pressing hard on the solids.

→ Add water as needed to make a thick but still flowing mixture.

→ Transfer to a squeeze bottle, covered, and refrigerate until ready to plate the dessert.

→ It may be necessary to rewarm the sauce or add small amounts of hot water to make it flow before using.

Assembly and plating

Unmold the mousse and center it on a plate. Squeeze out a comma-shaped swath of sauce starting at the left back of the mousse, and moving in a counterclockwise direction toward the front center of the mousse. Place a bracelet of salted peanut florentines on top of the mousse, pressing gently into the mousse to secure. Serve immediately.

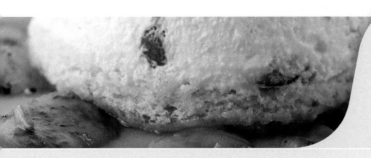

Nougat Glacé with Roasted Peaches and Darjeeling Tea Sauce

YIELD: 12 SERVINGS

Nougat glacé with sautéed caramelized peaches, genoise base, and Darjeeling tea sauce. Since the early 1700s, nougat has been made in the city of Montélimar in southeastern France. (Spain's *turron* and Italy's *torrone* are related confections, with equally long histories.) Traditionally a mixture of honey or sugar syrup, beaten egg whites, nuts, and sometimes preserved fruit, the combination of crunch and air lends itself to a lightened interpretation here with whipped cream as the enrichment. Going one step further, the whole mixture is frozen and shaped in a demispherical mold, set on a tea syrup–soaked genoise. Instead of fruits inside, the frozen nougat is garnished with a necklace of caramelized sautéed peaches whose flavor echoes the characteristically fruity essence of some of the best Indian Darjeeling teas, often called "the champagne of teas." Using a combination of well-roasted pistachios, almonds, and hazelnuts amplifies the nutty splendor of this traditional treat served up in a new guise.

The order of things:

1. **Make the genoise cake** and cool
2. **Roast the nuts** for the nougat glacé
3. **Caramelize the nuts**
4. **Make the Italian meringue**
5. **Complete the nougat glace** and freeze in molds
6. **Make the Darjeeling tea sauce**
7. **Blanch and then sauté the peaches;** then either store them in the refrigerator in until serving time (reheating them just before serving the dessert), or sauté to order just before assembling each dessert before it is served

Equipment list:

Round metal cookie cutter measuring 3 inches in diameter, cut 12 rounds from the cake to cut the cake bases for the nougat glacé

Silicon plaque with twelve demispherical indentations, each measuring 3 inches in diameter by 2 inches deep for the nougat glacé

Genoise cake layer as base for the nougat

YIELD: ONE HALF SHEET CUT INTO 12 CIRCLES, EACH MEASURING 3 INCHES IN DIAMETER, EACH WEIGHING APPROXIMATELY 1½ TO 2 OUNCES

Oz	Grams	Each	Name of ingredient	Baker's percentages
6	180		Cake flour	100
	1.5		Salt	0.8
12	360	7	Large eggs	200
6	180		Granulated sugar	100
0.25	7.5	1½ t.	Vanilla extract	4
3	90		Butter, melted and warm, not hot	50

→ Sift flour and salt three times, depositing the mixture onto a sheet of parchment and set aside.

→ Place the eggs and sugar into a stainless steel bowl set over a pan of simmering water (the water should not touch the bottom of the bowl).

→ Heat the mixture, whisking constantly, until it reaches 110°F.

→ Transfer the mixture to the bowl of an electric mixer outfitted with the whisk attachment.

→ Whip until light in color and tripled in volume.

→ Fold the sifted dry ingredients gently into the egg base, adding the vanilla and melted butter as you fold.

→ Handle carefully to avoid deflating.

→ Pour the batter immediately into a parchment-lined and greased half-sheet pan, and bake in a preheated 375°F oven for approximately 15 minutes.

→ Remove from the oven to a cooling rack and store, at room temperature, if using the same day, covered, until ready to assemble the dessert.

→ If not using the same day, refrigerate, covered, and use within two days.

→ Trim the cake to a rectangle measuring 9 inches by 12 inches.

→ Using a cookie cutter measuring 3 inches in diameter, cut 12 rounds from the cake.

→ Reserve any extra cake for another use.

→ Set aside the cake rounds and proceed to make the nougat glacé.

Nuts for nougat glacé

Oz	Grams	Each	Name of ingredients
7 gross weight, yielding approximately 5 ounces after skins are removed	210, yielding net weight of 150		Whole roasted almonds, pistachios, filberts, roughly chopped
0.16	4.8	1 t.	Unsalted butter

→ Roast nuts on a baking sheet for 20 minutes in preheated 375°F oven.

→ Remove as much of the skins of the nuts as possible by rubbing them in a clean towel, or against the mesh of a screen sieve.

→ Set aside the nuts.

→ Place the nuts in a heat-proof bowl, coat the bowl with the melted butter, and set aside.

Oz	Grams	Name of ingredient
3	90	Granulated sugar
1	30	Water
5, approximately	150	Roasted and skinned nuts

→ In a small heavy saucepan, cook the sugar and water, without stirring, to a golden amber color.

→ Remove from the heat and pour the caramel over the nuts in the buttered bowl. Toss to coat.

→ Immediately pour the mixture onto a Silpat and allow to cool.

→ Process the caramelized nuts in a food processor to a coarse powder and set aside at room temperature.

→ Make an Italian meringue as follows.

Oz	Grams	Each	Name of ingredient
4	120	4	Egg whites, from large eggs, room temperature
3	90		Granulated sugar, divided
3	90		Honey
1	30		Corn syrup

→ In the bowl of an electric mixer outfitted with the whisk attachment, whip the egg whites with 1½ ounces of the sugar to a foam.

→ In a small heavy saucepan, combine the remaining sugar, honey, and corn syrup and cook without stirring to 248°F.

→ With the mixer running, pour the hot syrup in a thin stream into the frothed egg whites and beat until cool.

Oz	Grams	Name of ingredient
16	480	Heavy cream
0.12	3.6	Vanilla extract
0.06	1.8	Almond extract

→ In another bowl, set onto an electric mixer outfitted with a clean whisk attachment, whip the heavy cream and vanilla and almond extracts to soft peaks.

Completing the frozen nougat glacé

→ Gently fold nuts and heavy cream into the meringue base and mold in Silforms.

→ Rap the sheet pan to remove any air pockets.

→ Place thin sheet of genoise over the tops of each molded nougat glacé and freeze. This makes enough for 12 demisphere molds, each measuring 3 inches in diameter by 2 inches deep.

→ There will be a small amount left over.

→ Reserve the leftover for another use or fill two additional molds as desired.

→ Top each molded frozen nougat glacé with a round of cake.

→ Freeze until ready to plate and serve the dessert.

→ Prepare the sautéed caramelized peaches as follows, either earlier in the day and then refrigerating them and bringing them to room temperature, or warming them briefly in a hot oven to take the chill off just before serving or sauté to order just before serving the dessert.

Sautéed caramelized peaches

Lb	Oz	Grams	Each	Name of ingredient
3, net		1440	12	Ripe but not soft **peaches,** blanched, and peeled, pitted, and halved
	6	180		**Unsalted butter**
			1	**Vanilla bean,** split and scraped
			As needed, using approximately 1 T. per single-layered batch in the sauté pan	**Granulated sugar**

→ Plunge the peaches into a pot of boiling water for just long enough so that the skins may be easily removed.

→ Peel and halve them, removing and discarding the pits.

→ Cut each into 6 to 8 wedges, depending on the size of the fruit.

→ In a heavy sauté pan, place 2 tablespoons of butter and the vanilla bean.

→ Heat until the butter is melted.

→ Cooking the peaches in batches, add 12 wedges to the pan, adding approximately 1 tablespoon of sugar per batch.

→ Cook until the peaches are caramelized, removing them to a parchment-lined baking sheet.

→ Continue cooking the peaches until all have been cooked.

→ Allow the peaches to cool and then set aside.

TIP: *Peaches vary wide in taste profile, from candy sweet to sweet/ tart and from floral to slightly acidic, with lemony undertones. It pays, therefore, to taste as many varieties (preferably from farmers markets or roadside stands in your area) as available before choosing. Perhaps even a combination of different varieties would contribute to a pleasantly complex overall flavor impression in this dessert.*

TIP: *Depending on the natural sweetness of the peaches, you may not need to use any granulated sugar here, when sautéing. Taste the fruit before it is cooked and then after it has been sautéed in the vanilla scented butter to decide.*

Darjeeling tea sauce

Oz	Grams	Name of ingredient	Notes
	15	High-quality whole leaf **Darjeeling tea**	See sources for teas on page 389
8	240	**Simple syrup**	
2	60	**Fresh lemon juice,** sieved	

→ Place the simple syrup into a medium-sized saucepan.

→ Add the tea leaves and bring the syrup to the boil. Immediately remove from the heat, cover the pan, and allow to infuse for approximately 5 minutes.

→ The tea flavor should come through clearly. If not, infuse for a few minutes longer.

→ Pass the mixture through a fine sieve and stir in the lemon juice.

→ Set aside until ready to plate the dessert.

TIP: *Since the flavor profiles of Darjeeling vary widely from estate to estate, season to season, and year to year, it is a good idea to taste a few different teas before settling on the one to use here to flavor the sauce. Matching the right tea with the peaches is key to creating a harmonious blending of flavors in this dessert.*

Assembly and plating

Center one nougat glacé on a plate. Surround with wedges of the sautéed caramelized peaches, to resemble the petals of a sunflower. Drizzle the tea syrup on the peaches, allowing some of it to mask the plate lightly. Serve immediately.

TIP: *A way to add one more layer of complexity to this dessert would be to sauté the peaches right before serving so that they are still warm, contrasting against the frozen nougat glace. If this is not practical, an easier way to introduce another temperature contrast would be to heat the tea syrup and drizzle it while warm over the peaches. In either case, serve the dessert immediately.*

Praline Napoleon with Fine Layers of Feuilletage Stacked Horizontally, with Espresso Sauce

YIELD: 12 SERVINGS

Praline napoleon cube with fine layers of feuilletage stacked horizontally, with thin chocolate sheets on the sides, espresso sauce in a small chocolate cup, and lemony caramel sauce dots as garnish on the plate. The flavor of good butter, toasted caramelized almonds, chocolate, lemon, caramel, and espresso all come together here in this new elegant take on the napoleon, that classic warhorse of the French patissier's repertoire. Here, running counter to the adage that less is more, more is more. Every element is detectable when tasting all of them together.

As with any flaky pastry, this one is at its best when filled and assembled as close to serving time as practical. Its cube shape suggests a gift which when unwrapped reveals what's inside. What's inside is a suave praline-flavored pastry cream in which the flavor of deeply roasted almonds and caramel support each other. Using good-quality dark chocolate couverture for the sidewalls of the napoleon cube and for the cup, which holds an intensely coffee-flavored sauce, pays off. However, in order to provide a true chocolate lover's experience here, perfecting the art of chocolate tempering is required. Lemon plays against caramel in the plating sauce and work together with the pinch of salt to make the sauce taste less sweet.

There's a well-orchestrated symphony of textures to appreciate here with the delicate snap of properly tempered chocolate contrasted by the creaminess of the praline filling. The two sauces add silky smooth touches in a dialogue with the delicately crunchy pastry.

The order of things:

1. **Make puff pastry** and chill
2. **Temper chocolate, if using, and make chocolate sheets** for sidewalls of the napoleon cubes and the chocolate cups for espresso sauce
3. **Make praline** and then powder it
4. **Make praline mousse**
5. **Make espresso sauce**
6. **Make lemony caramel**
7. **Bake puff pastry** and cut into layers as directed below
8. **Assemble napoleon cubes**

Equipment list:

Polycarbonate candy mold with 32 small cup-shaped cavities, each measuring approximately 1¼ inches in diameter by 1 inch deep

Thermometer to monitor the temperature of the chocolate during the tempering process, if tempering

Shiny food-grade acetate sheets

X-ACTO knife to cut chocolate sheets into squares as sidewalls for napoleon cubes

Puff pastry

YIELD: APPROXIMATELY
2½ POUNDS

Lb	Oz	Grams	Name of ingredient	Baker's percentages
1		480	**All purpose flour**	100
1		480	**Unsalted butter,** cool, waxy, not soft or greasy	100
		1	**Salt**	1.5
	8	240	**Ice water**	50

This dough may be made either by hand or by machine, depending on the size of the batch.

Mixing by hand

→ Cut butter into 1½ inch chunks.

→ Place flour and salt into a large bowl.

→ Mix to combine.

→ Add the butter and coat with the flour and salt mixture.

→ Then add ice water all at once and lightly mix until the dough coheres into a rough mass. Do not overprocess.

→ Turn the ragged mass of dough out onto a lightly floured surface and tap the dough firmly with a rolling pin to coax the dough into a roughly cohesive shape.

→ Check to be sure that the dough is not sticking to the surface.

Rolling the dough

→ Turn the ragged mass of dough out onto a floured surface and tap firmly with the rolling pin to coax the dough into a roughly cohesive shape.

→ Check to be sure that the dough is not sticking to the surface.

→ Use a plastic dough scraper frequently to free the dough from the work surface, as necessary, if it is sticking.

→ Flour the work surface **lightly** from time to time.

→ Once the dough has been rolled to a rough rectangular shape, mentally divide the dough in thirds and fold one third of the dough from the end closest to you toward the middle and the other third over the first third to create a package of dough made up of three thick layers.

→ Turn the packet of dough 90 degrees so that the short side is facing you.

→ Then roll to lengthen it again to a rectangle measuring roughly 7 inches by 18 inches.

→ Fold in thirds again and turn it 90 degrees so that the short side is facing you again.

→ Now roll the dough again to a rectangle measuring roughly 7 inches by 18 inches.

→ Chill in between the rolling and folding steps if the dough shows signs of softening or sticking to the work surface.

→ Then repeat the rolling and folding once more, chilling as needed if the dough shows signs of softening or is being resistant to rolling. (See process shots on page 143.)

→ Chill until firm. (The dough may be refrigerated overnight, but for longer storage, freeze it, well wrapped, and thaw in the refrigerator when needed).

→ Remove the well-chilled dough from the refrigerator and divide it into three equal pieces, each weighing approximately 13 ounces.

→ Roll each piece to a thickness of approximately ¼ inch and using a sharp knife and a firm deliberate cutting motion, using a ruler as a guide, trim each to a neat rectangle measuring 2 inches by 14 inches.

TIP: *Alternatively, you may roll the piece of dough, uncut to a rectangle measuring approximately 14 inches wide by 36 inches long and then cut it into three equal pieces.*

→ Place each sheet of piece on a parchment-lined half-sheet pan.

→ Chill again until firm, remove from the refrigerator, and then dock the dough all over, at 1 inch intervals, using the tines of a fork, or a rolling docker.

→ Place a sheet of parchment on top of each sheet of dough and then compress each of the sheets of dough with two half-sheet pans to keep the dough from puffing unevenly.

→ In a preheated 375°F oven, bake the sheets of dough with the weights in place until they are golden brown.

→ Check the progress of the baking after the first half hour.

→ Then check again every 5 minutes or so, to be sure that the dough is browning evenly.

→ Rotate the sheet pans, front to back, back to front, to facilitate even baking.

→ After the first approximately 35 minutes, remove the weights and the sheets of parchment on top of the dough and allow the dough to continue to bake for another 15 minutes or so, until it is evenly golden brown throughout.

→ Do not underbake or the dough will be soggy and difficult to cut neatly.

→ When fully baked, remove from the oven and move the baked sheets of dough to a cooling rack to cool.

→ Store at room temperature while you make the praline mousse as follows.

TIP: The key to tender, flaky, layered puff pastry lies in allowing the dough to rest in the refrigerator so that the gluten developed in manipulating the dough may be relaxed, after it has been rolled out to final thickness before baking. Well-chilled dough rises more evenly and the resulting dough will be tender as desired, not chewy.

Almond praline

Praline mousse

YIELD: APPROXIMATELY 14 OUNCES

Oz	Grams	Name of ingredient
8	240	**Slivered almonds,** blanched
2	60	**Granulated sugar**
2	60	**Corn syrup**
4	120	**Water**

→ Place the almonds on a half-sheet pan.

→ Place the pan into a preheated 350°F oven and roast the almonds until light golden brown.

→ Remove from the oven and transfer the almonds to a medium-sized stainless steel bowl.

→ In a medium-sized heavy saucepan, bring to the boil the granulated sugar, corn syrup, and water.

→ Cook, over medium to high heat, without stirring, to 240°F.

→ Remove from the heat and then pour the hot syrup over the toasted almonds in the bowl. Mix quickly but thoroughly and pour the syrup-coated almonds onto a Silpat, placed on to a half sheet baking pan. (See process shots.)

→ Bake in a preheated 350°F oven for about 10–12 minutes, or until golden brown.

→ Remove from the oven, cool, and then immediately pulverize the praline in a blender or food processor to a fine powder.

→ Store in airtight covered glass jar or plastic container with a tight-fitting lid, until ready to use.

→ Reserve for another use, covered, in a container with a tight-fitting lid, and store at room temperature.

Note that you will have more praline powder than is required for the mousse below.

The mousse

YIELD: APPROXIMATELY
26 OUNCES, 12 SERVINGS, A
GENEROUS 2 OUNCES EACH

Oz	Grams	Each	Name of ingredient
0.20	6	2	**Gelatin sheets**
8	240		**Whole milk**
2	60		**Granulated sugar,** divided
2.68	80	4	**Egg yolks,** from large eggs
1	30		**Cornstarch**
0.04	1.2	⅛ t.	**Vanilla extract**
0.16	4.8	½ t.	**Almond extract**
	1	Pinch	**Salt**
6	180		**Heavy cream,** softly whipped
6	180		**Praline powder,** from above

→ Place the gelatin sheets into a small bowl and cover with cold water.

→ Allow the gelatin to soften and when soft, remove from the water, discard the water, and squeeze out excess liquid.

→ Return the squeezed-out gelatin to the bowl and set aside.

→ In a medium-sized heavy saucepan, bring the milk and half of the sugar to the boil and lower the heat to a simmer.

→ Meanwhile, in a medium-sized mixing bowl, beat the egg yolks, remaining sugar, and the cornstarch until smooth and thick, scraping the sides and bottom of the bowl to ensure that the mixture is well blended and lump-free.

→ Add half of the hot milk into the egg yolk-sugar-cornstarch mixture and whisk to combine.

→ Add this mixture to the remaining milk in the saucepan and cook over medium heat, whisking constantly, until the mixture thickens.

→ Remove from the heat and add the bloomed gelatin, stirring to dissolve.

→ When cool, add the vanilla and almond extracts and the salt.

→ In the bowl of an electric mixer outfitted with the whisk attachment, beat the cream to soft peaks.

→ Fold the cream and the praline powder into the cooled custard mixture and set aside until ready to assemble the dessert.

→ If not using immediately, place the mixture into a bowl, covered, and refrigerate.

→ When ready to assemble the dessert, remove from the refrigerator and allow the mixture to soften a bit before using.

→ Set aside 10 ounces of this mousse to be used on the outside of the cubes of napoleon in a thin layer as an "adhesive" with which to secure the chocolate sidewalls discussed below.

Espresso sauce

YIELD: 12 GENEROUS
SERVINGS

Oz	Grams	Name of ingredient
8	240	**Brewed espresso coffee**
2	60	**Granulated sugar**
0.5	15	**Cornstarch**
2	60	**Water**

→ In a small heavy saucepan, bring the coffee and sugar to the boil, stirring to make sure that the sugar is fully dissolved.

→ Reduce the heat and keep the mixture warm.

- → In a small bowl, dissolve the cornstarch and water and add this mixture to the coffee mixture in the saucepan.
- → Over medium heat, stirring constantly, cook the mixture until the sauce thickens and loses any raw cornstarch taste.
- → Allow to cool and then place the sauce into a squeeze bottle, covered, and refrigerate until ready to plate the dessert.
- → You may need to set the sauce over a hot water bath to re-liquefy before using.

Note that you may have more sauce than you will be able to fit in the chocolate cups. If so, reserve for another use.

Oz	Grams	Name of ingredient
10	300	**Dark chocolate couverture,** tempered, melted or non-tempering chocolate coating, melted

Chocolate cups to contain the espresso sauce, used as a garnish on the plate

YIELD: 12 PLUS ADDITIONAL ALLOWING FOR BREAKAGE OR IMPERFECT CUPS

- → If using couverture, temper it as follows.
- → If tempering the chocolate, heat ⅔ of it in a stainless steel bowl over simmering water.
- → Melt it, stirring occasionally, until it reaches 122°F.
- → When it reaches this temperature, remove from the heat and add the remaining one third of the chocolate to lower the temperature of the chocolate to 81°F.
- → Stir constantly during this process to encourage the production of many small cocoa butter crystals that will lead to a good temper for the chocolate.
- → Then carefully rewarm the chocolate to 90°F, which is the temperature at which the chocolate should be held to fill the polycarbonate molds for the chocolate cups.
- → To test to see if the chocolate is in temper, dip the corner of a small piece of parchment paper in the chocolate and then place the parchment on a work surface. If the chocolate is in temper, it should dry within minutes and break cleanly when the paper is folded. It also should not melt readily when touched.
- → When the chocolate has been tempered, using a ladle or squeeze bottle filled with the chocolate, line a polycarbonate candy mold with 32 small cup-shaped cavities, measuring approximately 1¼ inches in diameter by 1 inch deep, with a thin layer of the chocolate.
- → Allow the chocolate to stay in the mold for a few minutes before inverting the mold over the bowl of tempered chocolate to allow excess to run out.
- → Place the mold, still inverted onto a parchment-lined sheet pan.
- → Allow to set at room temperature, and when fully dry, rap the mold firmly against a hard surface to release the cups from the mold.
- → Reserve any extras at cool room temperature for future use.
- → Alternatively, but less preferably, instead of using tempered couverture, you may use non-tempering chocolate coating to avoid the need to temper and follow the same steps as above to create the chocolate cups for the espresso sauce, or use commercially made chocolate cups to contain the espresso sauce.

This amount of chocolate yields more chocolate cups than you will need for the 12 servings that this dessert yields, but it's a good idea to make extras in case any break or are otherwise improperly formed.

Lemony caramel sauce

YIELD: 12 SERVINGS, APPROXIMATELY 1 OUNCE EACH

Oz	Grams	Each	Name of ingredient
8	240		Heavy cream
	10	From 2 medium sized lemons	Lemon zest
8	240		Granulated sugar
4	120		Water
	1	Pinch	Salt

→ In a small heavy saucepan, bring the cream and lemon zest to the boil, reduce to a simmer, and cook for 5 minutes.

→ Remove from the heat, cover, and allow the cream to infuse for about 15 minutes.

→ Taste to confirm that the lemon flavor comes through clearly in the cream.

→ If it does, pass the liquid through a fine sieve.

→ Discard the zest and reserve the liquid.

→ In a medium-sized heavy saucepan, bring the sugar and water to the boil.

→ Reduce the heat and stir to be sure that the sugar is fully dissolved.

→ Continue cooking, without stirring, until the mixture turns an amber or golden color. To avoid a bitter taste, do not overcook the caramel.

→ Immediately add the lemon-infused cream and stir, carefully, to combine. (Note that the mixture will bubble up and give off steam so stand back from the stove briefly until the bubbling subsides.)

→ Continue to cook the mixture over medium heat, stirring constantly until smooth. Stir in salt to dissolve and remove from the heat and allow to cool.

→ Then transfer the liquid to a squeeze bottle, covered, and refrigerate until ready to assemble the dessert.

→ When ready to use the sauce, you may need to set the squeeze bottle into a hot water bath to re-liquefy, keeping it warm during the service of the dessert.

Chocolate squares as sidewalls on napoleon cube

YIELD: 48 TWO INCH SQUARES, 4 USED PER SERVING, ALLOWING FOR BREAKAGE OR SQUARES THAT ARE IMPERFECT IN ANY WAY

Oz	Grams	Name of ingredient
12	360	Tempered chocolate, or non-tempering chocolate coating

TIP: The chocolate will pick up the shine and any markings or scratches from the acetate sheet so be sure that the acetate is unused and in perfect condition.

→ Using either tempered chocolate or melted non-tempering chocolate coating, using an offset spatula, spread out a thin layer of it into a rectangle measuring slightly larger than 12 inches by 16 inches onto a piece of shiny food-grade acetate, set onto a flat, clean surface.

→ Be conscious to avoid creating any holes or overly thin spots when you spread out the chocolate onto the sheet.

→ Place a second sheet of acetate over the chocolate, weight the four corners of the acetate sheet to prevent the chocolate from curling.

→ Allow to dry and then remove the sheet pan and carefully peel away the top acetate sheet.

- → Using an X-ACTO knife or small knife and a ruler, score the chocolate into 48 two inch squares, in rows of six squares on the shorter side and rows of eight squares on the longer side.
- → You will need four squares per dessert for a total of 48 squares.
- → You may wish to make some extra squares to allow for breakage or to replace squares that are less than perfect in any way.

TIP: *When handling tempered chocolate, it is best to wear thin gloves to avoid imprinting any fingerprints on the chocolate, which would mar its shiny surface.*

TIP: *Alternatively, you may pour a curved swath of sauce onto the plate, starting at the back left corner of the cube and ending just to the left of the chocolate cup.*

Assembly and plating

Trim the puff pastry to create three equal squares measuring slightly more than 10½ inches on each side. (Reserve the trimmings for another use.) Spread one third of the praline mousse onto the first square. Place the second square onto the praline mousse and press lightly to compact the layers slightly. Spread the second half of the praline mousse on top of the second square and then place the final square of puff pastry on top of the praline mousse. You now have a square made up of 3 multileaved layers of pastry and 2 layers of praline mousse. The stack should be no taller than 1¾ inches since it is sized to fit within the four 2 inch square sidewalls of chocolate, made above. If necessary, using a serrated knife, trim the stack horizontally by taking off a few layers of the bottom puff pastry. Place the stacked and filled square of pastry onto a parchment-lined sheet pan and refrigerate to firm, about 30 minutes. Remove from the refrigerator, and using a serrated knife, cut the puff pastry square into 36 squares, measuring 1¾ inches on each side. Set aside. These cubes will be turned on their sides so that the many fine layers of pastry are highly visible.

Turn the squares on their sides and spread a thin layer of the reserved praline mousse on all four sides of the napoleon cube. Pressing lightly and carefully, secure a chocolate sidewall to each side of the cube. Place the completed cube on the plate. Set a chocolate cup to the right of, and in front of, the cube, and fill it with flowing but cool espresso sauce. Starting at the back left corner of the cube, pipe a series of 5 increasingly larger dots of the lemony caramel sauce, equidistant from each other, working toward the front of the cube with the last and largest dot positioned just to the left of the chocolate cup filled with espresso sauce. Serve immediately.

Chocolate Semolina Pudding with Spiced Coffee Syrup

YIELD: 12 SERVINGS

Chocolate semolina pudding with clove-scented crème anglaise, spiced coffee syrup, espresso granita, cocoa nib tuiles, and softly whipped cream. Resting ethereally on the plate, this study in textures is something like a cross between the most down-home mud pie and an elegant warm soufflé. Composed mostly of fine melted chocolate but lent structure with a few eggs and some ground walnuts, it gets its pleasantly gritty texture from semolina, the granular, high-protein wheat flour from which the best pasta is made. Two complementary plating sauces merge here in an explosion of coffee and spice. Divergent temperatures collide when the comfort of warm pudding meets the shock of icy granita. It may be counterintuitive, but the accompanying whipped cream actually helps to give the impression of lightness to an otherwise rich dessert. This airy pudding seems to levitate from plate to espresso spoon to mouth with only the slightest nudge from the person behind it.

The order of things:

1. **Brew the coffee** for the semolina puddings **and the espresso** for the granita
2. **Complete the puddings,** bake and set aside
3. **Make the espresso granita**
4. **Make the cocoa nib tuile batter** and let cool
5. **Make the clove-scented crème anglaise plating sauce**
6. **Bake the tuiles**
7. **Make the spiced coffee syrup plating sauce**
8. **Make the whipped cream**

Equipment list:

Twelve timbale (thimble shaped), or other molds, with 3 to 4 ounce capacity

Grater with ¼ inch sized holes to grate the espresso granita

Chocolate semolina pudding

YIELD: APPROXIMATELY
26 OUNCES, TO FILL
12 SHALLOW TIMBALE
MOLDS OR MUFFIN CUPS

Oz	Grams	Each	Name of ingredient	Baker's percentages— Chocolate at 100%
2, approximately or as needed	60		**Unsalted butter,** to coat molds	
2, approximately, or as needed	60		**Granulated sugar,** to coat molds	
6	180		**Fine-quality bittersweet chocolate**	100
4	120		**Unsalted butter**	67
4	120		**Strong brewed liquid coffee,** made from properly roasted whole coffee beans, ground just before using	67
3	90		**Semolina flour**	50
0.15	4.5		**Baking powder**	3
	1		**Salt**	.5
5	150	3	**Large whole eggs**	83
2.45	74		**Granulated sugar**	41
1.5	45		**Ground walnuts**	25

TIP: *Brewing coffee from properly roasted beans of high quality and freshness (10 grams of ground coffee for each 1¼ ounces of water) is key to the powerful flavor of the pudding. Stale or flavorless beans will not yield memorable results. It pays to source coffee beans wisely by casting a wide net in your market area for importers and roasters who specialize in procuring beans of high quality, and roast on premises in small batches.*

→ Preheat oven to 350°F.

→ Coat twelve 3 to 4 ounce capacity timbale (thimble shaped), or other molds of similar capacity, with butter and then coat with an even sprinkling of sugar, shaking out excess.

→ Place chocolate and butter into a medium-sized stainless steel bowl.

→ Set the bowl over a saucepan of simmering water and melt, stirring occasionally until smooth.

→ When melted, remove from the heat.

→ Add coffee and set aside.

→ Sift semolina, baking powder, and salt and set aside.

→ Place eggs and sugar in the bowl of an electric mixer outfitted with the whisk attachment.

→ Beat until in texture and lemony colored.

→ Blend in chocolate butter mixture and stir to combine.

→ Fold in dry ingredients and the nuts and mix just until smooth.

→ Pour into prepared molds.

→ Bake until tests done, approximately 20–30 minutes.

→ Do not overbake, or the puddings will be dry.

→ These are best served slightly warm.

→ Unless it is practical to bake these to order, it is best to underbake them slightly since they will be warmed before serving.

Clove-scented crème anglaise

YIELD: APPROXIMATELY
12 OUNCES, 12 SERVINGS,
1 OUNCE EACH

Oz	Grams	Each	Name of ingredient
8	240		**Whole milk**
		12	**Whole cloves**
3	90	4.5	**Egg yolks** from large eggs
2	60		**Granulated sugar**

- In a medium-sized heavy saucepan, bring the milk and cloves to the boil, reduce the heat and simmer for 5 minutes.
- Remove from the heat, cover, and allow to infuse for 15 minutes.
- Taste to confirm the strength of the infusion. If it is weak, continue to infuse.
- Once satisfied that the clove flavor comes through clearly here, pass the mixture through a fine sieve set over a stainless steel bowl.
- Discard the cloves, reserving the liquid.
- In the bowl of an electric mixer outfitted with the whisk attachment, beat the egg yolks and sugar until light in color and ribbony in texture. (If properly mixed, the mixture should fall slowly from the whisk in a thick ribbon.)
- Reheat the infused liquid and add half of it to the egg yolks and sugar mixture in the mixing bowl.
- Mix briefly to combine and then add this tempered mixture to the milk remaining in the saucepan.
- Cook the mixture, stirring constantly without aerating, until it reaches 180°F and coats the back of a spoon.
- Pass the mixture through a fine sieve into a stainless steel bowl, set over an ice water bath, and stir frequently to cool quickly.
- When cold, transfer the mixture to a container, with a tight fitting lid, and refrigerate until ready to plate the dessert.

Spiced coffee syrup

YIELD: APPROXIMATELY 8 OUNCES, 12 SERVINGS, ⅔ OUNCE EACH

Oz	Grams	Each	Name of ingredient
8	240		Strong brewed coffee
3.5	105		Granulated sugar
		6	Cloves
		1	**Whole cinnamon stick,** about 3 inches long
		1 t.	Cornstarch
1	30	2 T.	Cold water

Cornstarch slurry to thicken, if desired.

- In a medium-sized heavy saucepan, bring all ingredients to a boil, reduce heat, and then simmer for 5 minutes.
- Strain through fine sieve.
- Return the sieved mixture to a clean, medium-sized heavy saucepan and reduce, over medium heat, to a slightly thickened consistency.
- Alternatively, add the cornstarch slurry and cook until the sauce thickens and the raw taste of the cornstarch disappears.
- Remove from the heat, allow to cool, and place in a container, covered.
- Refrigerate until serving time.

Espresso granita

YIELD: APPROXIMATELY
10 OUNCES, FOR
12 SERVINGS, GENEROUS
¾ OUNCE PER SERVING

Oz	Grams	Name of ingredient
8	240	**Espresso** (or strong brewed coffee)
2	60	**Simple syrup**

TIP: *Don't be tempted to sweeten the coffee more than shown in the recipe, because too much sugar will prevent the granita from freezing properly, the intensity of coffee flavor will be muted, and the amount of sugar is calculated to achieve the desirable icy texture (more sugar would lead to a creamier sorbet, rather than granita, texture). Taken as a whole, the elements of the dessert work well together to balance the overall sweetness level of the dessert.*

→ In a medium-sized bowl, combine the coffee and the simple syrup.

→ Place the mixture into the bowl of an electric ice cream maker and freeze until firm.

→ Remove the mixture to a shallow hotel pan and freeze.

→ Using a grater with ¼ inch sized holes, scrape the mixture to produce a fluffy, icy, and granular-textured mass.

→ Store in a container with a tight-fitting lid and freeze until ready to serve.

Cocoa nib tuiles

YIELD: 11 OUNCES BATTER,
ENOUGH FOR 24 TUILES
SLIGHTLY LESS THAN
½ OUNCE EACH

Oz	Grams	Name of ingredient	Baker's percentages Sugar and glucose (or corn syrup) total 100%
3	90	**Granulated sugar**	50
3	90	**Glucose or corn syrup**	50
3	90	**Unsalted butter**	100
2	60	**Cocoa nibs**	33

→ In a medium-sized heavy saucepan, bring the sugar, syrup, and butter to a boil.

→ Remove from the heat, and then using a whisk, emulsify the mixture.

→ Stir in the nibs and mix until well distributed throughout the batter.

→ Allow the batter to cool until it thickens, about 15 minutes.

→ Since these must be shaped while warm, it is best to bake a few at a time.

→ Divide the batter into 12 equal portions.

→ Deposit four portions of the batter onto a Silpat, spacing them 3 inches apart.

→ Bake in a preheated 375°F oven for 8–10 minutes, rotating pan if the tuiles are baking unevenly.

→ The batter will spread in the oven and bubble up.

→ When set, remove from the oven and then shape as desired.

→ Continue baking the tuiles, four at a time, until all of the batter is used up.

→ Store at room temperature, in a single layer, in containers, with a tight-fitting lids, each outfitted with a piece of limestone or a packet of silica gel, to retain crispness.

Oz	Grams	Name of Ingredient
12	360	Heavy cream

Assembly and plating

Place chocolate semolina pudding on the plate, off center. Spoon a pool of crème anglaise, in front and to the left of the pudding. Drizzle a thin thread of spiced coffee syrup onto the crème anglaise. Garnish the top of the pudding with two cocoa nib tuiles. Carefully mound the shaved espresso ice into a small espresso cup. Mound whipped cream in another espresso cup next to the first one. Serve immediately with espresso spoons, if desired.

Sticky Rice Cooked in Fresh Coconut Milk, with Alphonso Mango, on Steamed Ginger Pudding, with Candied Ginger Florentine

YIELD: 12 SERVINGS

Sticky rice cooked in fresh coconut milk, steamed ginger pudding, frozen mango lassi, candied ginger and coquito encrusted florentine garnish, mango compote garnish, and ginger syrup plating sauce. Thought to be a native of India where hundreds of varieties flourish, the mango is grown in tropical climates from Brazil to Mexico, Hawaii to Florida, and from India to Thailand. Taking advantage of the fully flavored, highly perfumed Alphonso and Kesar varieties now being imported to the United States from India, this dessert also borrows inspiration from the Southeast Asian dessert tradition. There, sticky or sweet rice is served warm with a drizzle of sweetened coconut milk and some chilled spears of the perfectly ripened fruit. Three temperatures work together on the plate here: coconut milk flavors the cooking liquid for the rice, which is then molded into rings and served warm, encircling a cold ginger pudding and a frozen mango *lassi*, inspired by the frothy sweet or slightly salted yogurt-based drinks popular in India. Gracefully curved over the dessert is a candied ginger and coquito-studded florentine, lending an airy, crisp contrast to the otherwise soft and yielding textures of the dessert.

The order of things:

1. If using fresh coconut, process as shown below to yield fresh coconut milk
2. Soak in water, rinse, and then cook sticky rice
3. Complete sticky rice and mold
4. Make steamed ginger puddings
5. Make frozen mango lassi
6. Make florentine batter
7. Bake and shape florentines
8. Make mango compote
9. Make ginger syrup plating sauce

Equipment list:

Twelve bottomless round rings measuring 4 inches in diameter by ¾ inch tall, for sticky rice

Round metal cookie cutter, measuring 2½ inches in diameter, to cut out the centers of the rounds of sticky rice

Silform mold with six *timbale* or thimble-shaped indentations, each measuring 2¾ inches in diameter at the top, 1¾ inches in diameter at the bottom, by 2 inches deep, for ginger puddings; after baking and cooling, each of the ginger puddings are cut vertically into two equal pieces, yielding 12 servings

Six cylindrical molds, each measuring approximately 2½ inches in diameter by 2 inches tall, for frozen mango lassi. (Each lassi is cut vertically into two equal parts, yielding 12 portions.)

Tuile template with right triangle-shaped cut-outs, each measuring 8 inches long by 2 inches at the base

Sticky rice cooked in coconut milk

YIELD: APPROXIMATELY
24 OUNCES, 12 SERVINGS
2 OUNCES EACH

Oz	Grams	Name of ingredient	Notes
6.4	12	Sweet glutinous rice	
As needed		Water	To rinse the rice before cooking
6	180	Canned or fresh coconut milk	See Tip
14	420	Water	
	1	Salt	
2	60	Granulated sugar	
2	60	Unsalted butter	

TIP: *For a fresher, more quintes-sentially coconut flavor, it pays to process fresh coconuts to yield the coconut milk. Crack the brown outer shell of a fresh coconut over a large bowl to conserve the thin but flavorful coconut water that will flow out of the cracked nut. Peel the inner brown skin from the coconut, cut the meat into rough ½ inch pieces, and then process the resulting coconut meat along with the coconut water in a food processor using the steel knife attachment. Press the resulting mixture through a sieve to yield the coconut milk, discarding the solids, or saving them for another use.*

→ Spray the inside of 12 bottomless round rings measuring 4 inches in diameter by ¾ inch tall, lightly with pan release spray.

→ Place them on a parchment-lined sheet pan and set aside.

→ Place the rice into a strainer and rinse with cold water until the water runs clear.

→ Place the washed rice, coconut milk, water, and salt in a medium-sized saucepan.

→ Bring to a simmer and cook until rice is tender, stirring occasionally. Add sugar and butter and stir to combine.

→ Press the rice into the prepared round rings, flattening the mixture so that it is well compacted and flush to the top of the mold.

→ Then using a round cookie cutter, measuring 2½ inches in diameter, dipped into hot water before and after each cut, cut out a 2½ inch round circle of the rice from each mold and remove it, reserving for another use.

→ Refrigerate the now doughnut-shaped rings of rice on the baking sheet, covered well, until ready to serve.

Mango compote garnish

YIELD: 12 SERVINGS

Oz	Grams	Each	Name of ingredient
16	480	2 to 3, depending on size	Alphonso, Kesar, Atualfo or other variety of nonfibrous **sweet mangoes** with deep color
1	30		**Fresh lime juice**, sieved

→ In a food processor, puree all of the ingredients and then fill six cylindrical molds, each measuring approximately 2½ inches in diameter by 2 inches tall, with the mango lassi mixture.

→ Then freeze, covered.

→ When frozen, remove from the molds, cut each mold in half vertically, and reserve the 12 halves, frozen, covered, until ready to assemble the dessert.

Candied ginger and coquito florentines

YIELD: 12 TRIANGULAR-SHAPED FLORENTINES, EACH MEASURING 8 INCHES LONG BY 2 INCHES WIDE AT THE BASE

Oz	Grams	Each	Name of ingredient
4	120		**Granulated sugar**
0.71	21.3	1 T.	**Corn syrup**
4	120		**Unsalted butter**
1	30		**Heavy cream**
3	90		**All purpose flour**
1.5 to 2	45 to 60		**Candied ginger**, cut into ¼ inch dice
1.5 to 2	45 to 60		**Coquitos**, toasted and then shaved into thin crescent shaped shards

Coquitos are small seeds harvested from the several varieties of palm trees, such as the Chilean wine palm or the Quito palm. Similar in size to a nutmeg nut, this small round seed has the appearance as well as taste of a coconut, and therefore they are commonly referred to as "baby coconuts." The outer covering is thin and crisp while the inner meat is dense and chewy, providing a flavor exactly like coconut meat. If unavailable, substitute sliced almonds or shards of dried coconut.

- → In a small saucepan, bring sugar, corn syrup, butter, and cream to the boil.
- → Remove from the heat and add the flour, stirring to combine.
- → Allow to cool slightly and then using a small metal spatula dipped in hot water and then dried, spread the batter in an even layer onto a Silpat-lined sheet pan, using a tuile template with right triangle-shaped cut outs, each measuring 8 inches long by 2 inches at the base.
- → Scatter a few pieces of candied ginger and toasted coquito shards over each cookie.
- → Then bake in a preheated 350°F oven for 6–7 minutes.
- → Remove from oven, allow to cool slightly or until the florentines are cool enough to be handled without stretching.
- → Curve over a rounded surface (a small smooth bowl or bottomless entremet ring, measuring 5 inches in diameter would work here), with the candied ginger- and coquito-encrusted side pressed against the surface of the form upon which the florentines are being shaped.
- → Allow to cool thoroughly, gently and carefully remove from the form, and then store in an airtight container, in a single layer, outfitted with a piece of limestone or packets of silica gel to preserve crispness, until ready to assemble the dessert.

It is best to bake only a few of these at a time since they must be formed quickly once they are removed from the oven. If they become too cool to shape, they will be brittle and break easily.

Ginger syrup
YIELD: ENOUGH TO SAUCE 12 SERVINGS

Oz	Grams	Name of ingredient
1.5	45	Fresh gingerroot
4	120	Simple syrup

- → Peel and slice the gingerroot into thin coins.
- → Place the ginger coins and the simple syrup into a small heavy saucepan.
- → Bring the mixture to the boil and then remove from the heat, covered, to infuse for approximately 15 minutes. The ginger flavor should come through clearly in the syrup.
- → If not, infuse longer and taste to confirm that the liquid tastes clearly of ginger.
- → Pass the mixture through a fine sieve, pressing hard on the solids, reserving the infused liquid to be used as the plating sauce.

Assembly and plating

Just before serving, briefly microwave the ring of sticky rice just to warm. Center the ring on the plate. Place a half piece of the frozen mango lassi into the hole of the rice, curved side facing the curve of the rice. Then place a half piece of the ginger pudding in front of the frozen mango lassi with its flat side facing the flat side of the lassi. Place a curved tuile behind and slightly under the back of the ring of sticky rice, with the curved side facing toward the front of the plate. Sauce the plate with ginger syrup, as desired, and serve immediately.

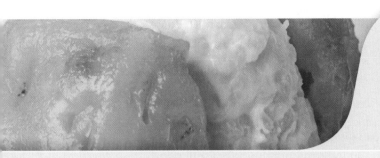

Tropical Getaway—Baby Pineapple with Coconut Rice Pudding

YIELD: 12 SERVINGS

Tropical getaway: Poached baby pineapple in white pepper syrup, enclosing jasmine-coconut rice pudding, with tuile garnish, caramel-rum sauce, and toasted coconut shards. This dessert all but evokes the hypnotic sound of swaying palms on a beach in some tropical paradise. Fragrant Thai jasmine rice, a long-grain variety, lends just enough starch to the cooking liquid in the pudding to thicken it lightly. White peppercorns, another tropical, particularly Southeast Asian ingredient, contribute a subtle hotness to the sweet poaching syrup, balanced by the mellowed notes in the vanilla. Baby pineapples grown in South Africa and Hawaii, and now becoming more readily available from specialty produce vendors nationwide, make for a neat presentation and due to their size, have an edible core, particularly when cooked. Creamy, crisp, chewy, and hot elements all mingle here for a satisfying year-round taste of the tropics.

The order of things:

1. Make white pepper syrup
2. Poach pineapples
3. Make jasmine-coconut rice pudding
4. Make the tuile batter
5. Make the caramel-rum sauce
6. Bake the tuiles
7. Toast the coconut shards for the plate garnish

Equipment list:

Twelve metal thimble-shaped molds, each measuring 1½ inches in diameter at the bottom (which will become the top when unmolded), 3 inches in diameter at the top (which will become the bottom when unmolded), by 2 inches tall, each holding about ¾ ounce, to mold the rice pudding

Acetate strips, 2 inches wide, to line the molds, for easy removal of the puddings

Apple corer to remove the cores from the pineapples, if desired

Tuile template, with a long strip–shaped cutout, measuring 8 inches long by 1 inch wide for each curved tuile garnish

White pepper syrup for poaching pineapple

Oz	Grams	Each	Name of ingredient
0.60	17		**Whole white peppercorns,** slightly crushed using a mallet or mortar and pestle
		2	**Bourbon-Madagascar vanilla beans,** split
64	960		**Granulated sugar**
64	960		**Water**

→ In a medium-sized heavy saucepan, place the peppercorns, vanilla beans, sugar, and water.

→ Bring to the boil and then reduce to a simmer, cooking for about 15 minutes, or until the flavor of the pepper and vanilla come through clearly.

→ Taste to confirm. If the flavors are weak, continue cooking and taste again.

→ When the liquid has a definite flavor of pepper and vanilla, pass through a fine sieve and then place the sieved liquid in a wide medium-sized heavy saucepan.

→ Reserve the vanilla beans, rinsed and dried, for another use, if desired.

TIP: *Madagascar vanilla has a particularly well-balanced, quintessentially "vanilla-y" flavor and aroma, not overly floral. Nonetheless, floral Tahitian and creamy, spicy Mexican vanilla beans, if fresh and highly aromatic, would work here, contributing their own distinctive flavor notes to the dessert.*

Preparing and poaching the pineapple

YIELD: 12 SERVINGS, EACH CONSISTING OF TWO HALF–BABY PINEAPPLES

Each	Name of ingredient
12, each weighing about 10–12 ounces, whole, before peeling	**Baby pineapples,** from Hawaii or South Africa, approximately 5–8 inches high, including the crown of leaves on top

→ Using a sharp knife, remove the crown of leaves from the top of each fruit.

→ Then remove the skin, without removing any of the flesh of the pineapple.

→ Make shallow cuts on the diagonal to remove the "eyes." (If desired, the pineapples may be cored.) However, due to their small size, the cores are tender, particularly after cooking, and therefore the fruits may be poached and served, uncored.

→ If you wish to core them, center an apple corer over the core of the pineapple and push down forcefully to remove the cores.

→ Cut each pineapple in half, from top to bottom, and place in the saucepan of poaching syrup, from above.

→ Bring the poaching syrup to a simmer.

→ Poach the fruits for about 20 minutes, carefully turning as necessary, to ensure that they are cooking evenly.

→ The pineapples should be fork tender but still hold their shape.

→ Once fully cooked, remove them from the poaching syrup, drain on a cooling rack, and set onto a half-sheet pan.

→ Reserve the poaching syrup to use as a plating sauce.

Oz	Grams	Each	Name of ingredient
3	90		Uncooked jasmine rice
10	300		Coconut milk
8	240		Whole milk
1	30		Granulated sugar
	1	Pinch	Salt
1	30		Unsalted butter
16 plus additional, as needed, used to soften the pudding just before assembling the dessert	480 plus additional, as needed, used to soften the pudding just before assembling the dessert		Heavy cream

→ Wash the rice in cold running water until the water runs clear.

→ Drain rice.

→ In a medium-sized heavy saucepan, place washed rice with coconut milk, whole milk, sugar, and salt.

→ Over medium heat, cook the rice for approximately 1 hour, stirring occasionally, until tender and most of the liquid has been absorbed.

→ When tender, cool slightly and then add the butter, stirring to blend.

→ Allow the mixture to cool further to room temperature.

→ In the bowl of an electric mixer outfitted with the whisk attachment, whip the cream to soft peaks.

→ Fold the cream into the rice base and set aside, covered, in the refrigerator, until ready to assemble the dessert.

→ After refrigerating, the rice pudding may become firm.

→ Loosen by stirring in a bit of heavy cream, as needed, just to soften the pudding slightly.

→ Spray lightly with pan spray and then line 12 thimble-shaped molds with acetate strips.

→ The molds should measure 1½ inches in diameter at the bottom (which will become the top when unmolded), 3 inches in diameter at the top (which will become the bottom when unmolded), by 2 inches tall, each holding about 3 to 4 ounces.

→ Lightly pack the rice pudding mixture into the molds.

→ Cover and refrigerate until ready to assemble and plate the dessert.

TIP: *For a fresher, more quintessentially coconut flavor, it pays to process fresh coconuts to yield the coconut milk. Crack the brown outer shell of two fresh coconuts over a large bowl to conserve the thin but flavorful coconut water that will flow out of the cracked nut. Peel the inner brown skin from the coconut, cut the meat into rough ½ inch pieces, and then process the resulting coconut meat along with the coconut water in a food processor using the steel knife attachment. Press the resulting mixture through a sieve to yield the coconut milk, discarding the solids or saving them for another use.*

Tuile sculptures

YIELD: 12 TUILES, EACH
WEIGHING SLIGHTLY LESS
THAN ¾ OUNCE, PLUS EXTRA,
ALLOWING FOR BREAKAGE,
OVERBAKING, OR TUILES
WITH LESS THAN OPTIMAL
SHAPE

Oz	Grams	Name of ingredient	Baker's percentages
2	60	**Unsalted butter,** room temperature	80
0.60	1.8	**Mild-flavored honey,** such as clover	25
1.4	42	**Granulated sugar**	56
2	60	**Egg whites**	80
2.5	75	**All purpose flour**	100

TIP: *It is best to bake only three of these at a time since they must be shaped while still warm and pliable. If they cool and harden, you may place the tuiles back into the oven briefly to soften. Then remove from the oven and shape, as desired.*

→ In the bowl of an electric mixer outfitted with the paddle attachment, cream the butter, honey, and sugar until light.

→ Add egg whites.

→ Add flour and mix just until flour disappears.

→ Place a Silpat on the back of a half-sheet pan.

→ Using a small metal spatula, spread a thin but not translucent strip of batter into the cutouts of a tuile template, each measuring 8 inches long by 1 inch wide for each curved tuile garnish.

→ Bake in a preheated 375°F oven for about 8 minutes, or until the batter looks set and just lightly golden brown.

→ Remove from the oven, allow to cool for a few seconds, and then using a thin spatula, release the tuile from the Silpat, curving it in a free-form spiral. (See photograph on page 362.)

→ Repeat the process of baking and shaping the tuiles until you have made 12 perfect tuiles.

→ There will be extra tuile batter left.

→ Reserve, refrigerated, for another use. It keeps well for at least a week.

→ Place the baked tuiles carefully in a single layer into a large plastic box, with a tight-fitting lid, outfitted with a piece of limestone or a package of silica gel, to help retain the tuiles' crispness.

→ Store at room temperature until ready to assemble the dessert.

→ Make the caramel rum sauce as follows.

Caramel rum sauce

YIELD: 12 SERVINGS
APPROXIMATELY
1 OUNCE EACH

Oz	Grams	Name of ingredient
8	240	**Granulated sugar**
4	120	**Water**
1	30	**Dark rum**
4	120	**Heavy cream**

→ In a small heavy saucepan, over medium-high heat, cook the sugar and water, without stirring, to golden amber stage, approximately 320°F.

→ Immediately remove from the heat and carefully add the dark rum.

→ Return to the stove, cooking again, over low heat, to burn off the alcohol in the rum. The liquid may flame so stand back from the stove during this process.

→ Over very low heat, keep the mixture warm.

→ In another saucepan, heat the heavy cream until boiling.

→ Once boiling, remove from the heat and add to the warm caramel sauce, stirring to combine.

→ Remove from the heat and store over a water bath, if using immediately, to keep the sauce flowing.

→ Otherwise, refrigerate, covered, and then reheat over warm water as needed, to reliquefy, when serving the dessert.

Oz	Grams	Name of ingredient
1 to 2, approximately	30 to 60, approximately	**Dried coconut shards**

If using *fresh* coconuts for the coconut milk, reserve some of the coconut meat and toast them lightly as directed below.

→ In a preheated 375°F oven, on a baking sheet, toast the coconut shards for approximately 5 minutes, stirring occasionally to ensure even browning.

→ Watch these carefully, as they burn easily.

→ Once they are golden brown, remove from the oven and set aside at room temperature until ready to assemble the dessert.

Assembly and plating

Unmold rice pudding onto the center of each serving plate. For each serving, use two halves of a pineapple. Place one half of the poached pineapple on the left side of the rice pudding and the other half on the right side of the pudding. Spoon approximately 1 ounce of caramel rum sauce in front of the pineapple. Dot the plate with tiny amounts of the reserved white pepper syrup. Balance one tuile on top of each pineapple/rice pudding construction, strew a few shards of toasted coconut on the caramel sauce, and serve immediately.

Carrot-Beet Cake with Sour Cream Sorbet and Carrot & Beet Chips Garnish

YIELD: 12 SERVINGS

Carrot and beet cakes with sour cream sorbet, carrot and beet plating sauces, and carrot and beet chips as garnish. With their inherent sweetness, root vegetables cross over from the savory side of the kitchen to the sweet pantry with ease. This dessert illustrates that when properly treated, vegetables have a place in the dessert maker's arsenal of ingredients. Unlike the standard quick-bread formula, which can often yield a cake that is dense and leaden, this variation on that theme is enriched with sour cream and uses butter instead of the usual liquid fat such as oil. The cakes are also lightened in texture thanks to the addition of beaten egg whites, gently folded in just before baking the cakes. Five spices lend the right aromatic warmth to the cake batter, which is divided into two uneven parts, the larger one used for the beet cake and the smaller one used for the carrot version. Walnuts in large pieces add textural counterpoint to otherwise fine-grained cakes, and instead of the usual cream cheese frosting that has come to be expected as a finish for vegetable-based cakes, sour cream here adds its tart dairy presence in a frozen accompaniment to the cakes. Geometry is strong here with vertical and horizontal elements tempered by the soft round of the sorbet and the gently curving edges of the vegetable chips and plating sauces.

The order of things:

1. **Make carrot chips and beet chips garnish**
2. **Make sour cream sorbet**
3. **Prepare pans** for baking cakes
4. **Make cake batters** and pour into prepared pans and bake
5. **Make carrot sauce** for plating
6. **Make beet sauce** for plating
7. **Cut the firm frozen ice cream** and freeze until ready to plate the dessert

Equipment list:

Two **half-sheet pans**

Cardboard strips to "wall off" the baking pans for the carrot cake (create a baking area of 3 inches by 10 inches) and beet cake (create a baking area of 3 inches by 14 inches)

Heavy aluminum foil to cover the cardboard strips

Electrical tape to secure the "dams" in the baking pans

Round metal cookie cutter, measuring 1¾ inches in diameter

Rectangular pan measuring approximately 5¼ inches by 7 inches, by 1 inch deep for sour cream sorbet

Squeeze bottles for saucing cakes

Cake base for carrot cake and beet cake

YIELD: APPROXIMATELY 52 OUNCES TOTAL FOR BASE CAKE BEFORE DIVIDING THE CAKE AND ADDING THE GRATED VEGETABLES FOR THE CARROT CAKE AND BEET CAKE; CARROT CAKE SERVINGS WEIGH APPROXIMATELY 1¾ OUNCES EACH; BEET CAKE SERVINGS WEIGH APPROXIMATELY 3⅓ OUNCES EACH

Oz	Grams	Each	Name of ingredient	Baker's percentages
7.5	225	4.5	**Large eggs,** separated	17
15	450		**All purpose flour**	100
	2.3	1 t.	**Cinnamon,** ground	.5
	1.5	½ t.	**Cloves,** ground	.3
	1.5	½ t.	**Cardamom,** ground	.3
	1	½ t.	**Ginger,** ground	.2
	Scant 1	½ t.	**Allspice,** ground	.2
0.43		1 T.	**Baking powder**	3
	6	1 t.	**Salt**	1
10	300		**Unsalted butter,** room temperature	66
7.5	225		**Brown sugar**	66
1.25	38		**Granulated sugar** into beaten egg whites	33
5	150		**Sour cream**	33
5	150		**Walnuts,** roughly chopped	33
				8

→ Prepare two baking pans. You will need one for the carrot cake and the other for the beet cake.

→ For the **carrot cake,** you will need a baking area of 3 inches by 10 inches, by 1 inch deep. For this cake, you may use a 10 inch rectangular pan and wall off the pan at the 3 inch wide mark, using a piece of cardboard, wrapped with foil and then sprayed well with pan release spray.

→ Secure the cardboard "dam" using heavy electrical tape so that the cake batter remains in the 3 inch by 10 inch area designated.

→ For the **beet cake,** you will need a pan with a baking area of 3 inches by 14 inches. For this cake, you may use a 14 inch long rectangular pan and wall off the pan at the 3 inch mark, again using a piece of cardboard, wrapped with foil and then sprayed well with pan release spray.

→ Secure the cardboard "dam" using heavy electrical tape so that the cake batter remains in the 3 inch by 14 inch area designed.

→ Set the pans aside until ready to fill them and bake the cakes.

→ Separate the eggs, placing the yolks in one small bowl and the whites into another.

→ Into a large bowl, sift the flour, spices, baking powder, and salt and set aside.

→ In the bowl of an electric mixer, outfitted with the paddle attachment, cream the butter until light.

→ Then add the brown sugar and mix again to incorporate, scraping the bottom and sides of the bowl to ensure that all ingredients are well blended.

→ Add the egg yolks, one at a time, mixing to incorporate before adding the next one.

→ Then blend in the sour cream and the walnuts, mixing until just incorporated.

→ In the bowl of an electric mixer, outfitted with the whisk attachment, beat the egg whites to a foam, adding the granulated sugar, and continue to beat until stiff peaks form.

→ Fold the dry sifted ingredients into the creamed mixture, alternating with the beaten egg whites.

→ Then divide the mixture roughly into one third and two thirds.

For carrot cake, add the following to one-third of the cake base mixture above

Oz	Grams	Name of ingredient
4	120	**Carrots,** peeled, grated

Oz	Grams	Name of ingredient
6	180	**Beets,** peeled, grated

For the beet cake, add the following to two-thirds of the cake base mixture above

- → To the smaller amount of the cake base batter, fold in the carrots.
- → To the remaining batter, fold in the beets.
- → Pour the carrot batter into the smaller of the two pans and the beet batter into the larger pan.
- → Bake the cakes in the prepared pans in a preheated 350°F oven for approximately 40 minutes.
- → The carrot cake may take a bit less time since it is smaller, so check frequently until it tests done.
- → When done, place the cakes on a cooling rack and allow to cool at room temperature.
- → Make the sour cream sorbet as follows.

Oz	Grams	Each	Name of ingredient
6.5	195		**Simple syrup**
1.4	42		**Corn syrup**
2	60	From 2 lemons	**Lemon zest** in strips
8.5	255		**Sour cream**

Sour cream sorbet

YIELDS 12 SERVINGS, APPROXIMATELY 1.25 OZ EACH

- → In a medium-sized heavy saucepan, bring the simple syrup, the corn syrup, and lemon zest to the boil.
- → Reduce the heat and simmer the mixture for 5 minutes.
- → Remove from the heat, and cover the saucepan, allowing the liquid to infuse for approximately 15 minutes.
- → When well infused, pass through a fine sieve and remove the solids, reserving the liquid.
- → When the liquid has cooled to lukewarm, stir in the sour cream.
- → Transfer the mixture to the bowl of an electric ice cream machine and freeze until semi-firm.
- → Remove from the machine and spread into a rectangular pan measuring approximately 5¼ inches by 7 inches, by 1 inch deep.
- → Place the pan, covered, into the freezer, allowing the mixture to freeze until firm.
- → When fully frozen, using a 1¾ inch round cookie cutter, cut out 12 circles of ice cream in rows of three along the short side and in rows of four along the longer side, yielding twelve circles of the sorbet.
- → Remove each circle as you cut the sorbet, placing them, flat side down, on a parchment-lined sheet pan.
- → Cover the pan with plastic wrap and freeze until ready to assemble and plate the dessert.
- → Make the plating sauces as follows.

Plating sauces

YIELD: APPROXIMATELY
19 OUNCES, 12 SERVINGS,
APPROXIMATELY
1½ OUNCES EACH

TIP: *Farmers markets offer a great variety of different kinds of beets and carrots, in a veritable rainbow of colors, from yellow to red to orange, and varying flavor profiles, from earthy to candy sweet. Taste widely to settle on the varieties that yield the most intense, earthy, sweet and complex flavor, because this dessert derives its overarching flavor from the vegetables, used in two forms, as particulates in the cake and as the main flavoring elements in the plating sauces.*

Beet sauce

Oz	Grams	Name of ingredient
0.33	10	Cornstarch
1	30	Water
9	270	Fresh peeled **beets**, grated
1	30	Granulated sugar
8	240	Water

In a small bowl, dissolve the cornstarch in the first quantity of water and set aside.

→ Bring the beets, sugar, and second quantity of water to the boil.

→ Cook until the flavor and color of the beets is well extracted, yielding a deep colored liquid.

→ Pass the liquid through a fine sieve into a bowl, discarding the solids and reserving the liquid.

→ Return the liquid to a clean medium-sized heavy saucepan and reheat to a simmer.

→ Add the cornstarch mixture and cook until the sauce thickens slightly and loses the raw taste of cornstarch.

→ Remove from the heat and allow to cool.

→ Pour each sauce into a squeeze bottle, covered.

→ Store at room temperature if serving immediately.

→ If not, transfer the liquid to a container, covered, and refrigerate until ready to serve the dessert.

→ You may need to warm the chilled sauces over a warm water bath to re-liquefy when ready to serve the dessert.

Carrot sauce

YIELD: APPROXIMATELY
12 OUNCES, EACH SERVING
APPROXIMATELY 1 OUNCE

Oz	Grams	Name of ingredient
10	300	Fresh carrot juice
1.5	45	Granulated sugar
0.33	10	Cornstarch
1	30	Water

→ In a small bowl, dissolve the cornstarch in the first quantity of water and set aside.

→ Place the carrot juice and granulated sugar into a medium-sized heavy saucepan. Bring to the boil to dissolve the sugar and then reduce the heat to a simmer.

→ Add the cornstarch mixture and cook, stirring, until the liquid thickens slightly and loses the raw taste of cornstarch.

→ Remove from the heat and allow to cool.

→ Store at room temperature if serving immediately.

→ If not, transfer the liquid to a container, covered, and refrigerate until ready to serve the dessert.

Each	Name of ingredient
As needed	**Simple syrup** (equal parts water and granulated sugar by weight, boiled until the sugar dissolves)
24 slices	**Carrots,** peeled, and thinly sliced, lengthwise
24 slices	**Beets,** peeled and thinly sliced into rounds

*Carrot chips
and beet chips*

YIELD: 12 SERVINGS,
ALLOWING FOR EXTRA
CARROT AND BEET CHIPS,
IF SOME ARE UNDERSIZED,
MISSHAPEN OR OTHERWISE
IMPERFECT

→ In a medium-sized heavy saucepan, heat the simple syrup until hot.

→ First dip the carrot slices briefly in to the syrup.

→ Then place onto a Silpat-lined sheet pan.

→ Then dip the beet slices briefly into the heated simple syrup.

→ Remove from the syrup and place onto a second Silpat-lined sheet pan.

→ Place both pans in a preheated 225°F oven and bake the vegetable slices for 45 minutes, or until dry to the touch but not browned.

→ Remove from the oven and place the pans onto a cooling rack.

→ Allow to cool, and then carefully remove the chips from the Silpats to a parchment-lined sheet pan.

→ If not using within the day, store in an airtight container, outfitted with a piece of limestone or a packet of silica gel, to help retain the crispness of the chips, until ready to use.

Assembly and plating

Cut the carrot cake into 12 squat rectangular bars, approximately 2½ inches long by 1 inch square. Cut the beet cake into 12 rectangular bars, each measuring approximately 3¼ inch long by 1 inch square.

Place beet cake vertically in the center of the plate. Place the carrot cake cube lying horizontally in front of the beet cake. Place the sour cream sorbet in front of the carrot cake. Using the squeeze bottles of sauce, deposit the carrot sauce in a curved shape beginning just behind the beet cake and curving forward in a semicircular shape. Then deposit a similar semicircle of beet sauce on the right side of the plate, starting behind the beet cake and moving forward to the front of the plate. Place a cylinder of sour cream sorbet standing upright in front of and to the right of, the carrot cake. Garnish the beet cake by placing a carrot chip and a beet chip on top. Serve immediately.

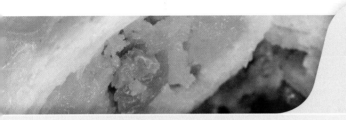

Carrot Halva

Carrot Halva in filo triangles, cardamom ice cream, ras malai sauce, with candied carrot curl garnish. Enclosing *gajar-ka-halva*, a classic Indian sweet, in layers of flaky crisp filo dough derived from the specifically Turkish, Greek, and broader Middle Eastern culinary traditions adds textural appeal to this dessert. The filling for the dough plays on the inherent sweetness of carrots, intensifying them with some added sugar, spice, and a small amount of lemon juice for contrast. An Indian-inspired plating sauce, simplified for commercial application, is made here using condensed milk instead of whole fresh milk, which is traditionally cooked and stirred over the heat in a shallow pan for hours to achieve its characteristic thick, rich consistency. Whole cardamom, commonly agreed to be the third most expensive flavoring, after saffron and vanilla, is used three times in this recipe. Indigenous to south India and Sri Lanka, and a member of the ginger family, the cardamom used here is green podded with a thin, papery shell containing small dark seeds. There is no need to remove the seeds from the pods for this dish since the refreshing eucalyptus aroma comes through loud and clear when the whole pods are infused in liquids such as milk or heated in the sautéed carrots as they are here. The pistachios, chopped and whole, used here echo the color of the green cardamom pods, and are mainstays of desserts in India and the Middle East, adding another welcome note of crunch to the dessert.

The order of things:

1. **Make carrot filling**

2. **Prepare filo triangles** by stacking layers of filo, brushing with butter, cutting and then folding to yield the triangles; bake triangles and store at room temperature if serving within the same day; if serving the next day, refrigerate, covered

3. **Make crème anglaise** for cardamom ice cream base, chill, elaborate, and then turn into ice cream mixture and then freeze

4. **Make candied carrot curl garnishes**

5. **Make ras malai sauce**

Equipment list:

Pastry brush to butter the leaves of filo and filled triangles of filo before baking

Ruler to act as a guide when cutting stacked and buttered filo into strips

Mandoline to cut carrots for garnish

Dowels to shape candied carrots into corkscrew garnishes

Oval-shaped ice cream scoop or two large soup spoons to form ice cream into quenelles

Carrot halva filling

Lbs	Oz	Grams	Each	Name of ingredient
1, approximately, weighed after peeling		480		**Carrots,** peeled
1		480		**Whole milk**
			10	**Cardamom pods,** whole
	0.5	15		**Fresh lemon juice,** sieved
	2.5	45		**Unsalted butter,** cubed
	Approximately 1, or to taste, depending on the sweetness of the carrots	30, approximately		**Granulated sugar**
	1	30		**Golden raisins,** soaked in hot water for 5 minutes and then drained
	1	30		**Almonds,** toasted in a preheated 350°F oven for approximately 12 minutes

→ Using the shredder blade of a food processor, shred the carrots and set aside, squeezing out any excess liquid.

→ In a heavy medium-sized saucepan, bring the milk and cardamom to the boil.

→ Reduce to a simmer and cook for 5 minutes.

→ Remove from the heat, cover, and allow the milk to infuse. The cardamom flavor should come through clearly.

→ If not, simmer again for a few more minutes and then remove from the heat, covered, to infuse further.

→ Taste to confirm and then pass through a fine sieve, discarding the cardamom and reserving the infused liquid.

→ Return the liquid to the saucepan and add the carrots and the sugar.

→ Cover, over medium heat, stirring frequently, until the carrots absorb the liquid.

→ Remove from the heat and add the lemon juice and butter, stirring until the butter melts.

→ Add the raisins and the almonds and set aside until ready to fill the filo and form into triangles.

Filling and forming the carrot halva filo triangles

Oz	Grams	Each	Name of Ingredient
16, approximately	480		**Unsalted butter,** clarified
16	480	30 sheets	**Filo dough,** measuring approximately 12 inches by 17 inches

→ In a small heavy saucepan, melt the butter, skimming the white foam that rises to the surface and discarding it.

→ Continue cooking until the butter has a nutty aroma and is light golden brown.

→ Spoon or pour off the clear liquid and reserve, keeping it warm and flowing.

→ During this process, be careful not to dislodge the browned residue (milk solids) at the bottom of the saucepan.

→ Discard this residue. Using six 12 × 17 inch sheets of filo, create a stack of six layers, layering each sheet on top of the next, brushing the melted clarified butter lightly between each layer.

- Using a small sharp knife and a ruler as a guide, cut the stack lengthwise to obtain five strips, each 3 inches wide by 12 inches long (a 2 inch strip will be left at the end; reserve for another use or discard).
- Place approximately 0.75 ounces of carrot filling at the end of each filo strip.
- Starting at the end where the filling has been placed, fold the strips into triangles, enclosing the filling, alternating the direction toward which the fold is made, first to the right, then to the left, and so on, until the filling is completely enclosed, brushing melted clarified butter on each exposed surface of the triangle as you go.
- Repeat the stacking, buttering, cutting, filling, and folding process four more times, using six sheets of filo each time, to yield 25 finished filled triangles. (If you are serving two triangles per portion, you will have one extra triangle. Try it fresh out of the oven!)
- Place half of the triangles approximately 2 inches apart on each of two parchment lined half size baking sheets.
- Bake in a preheated 375°F oven, approximately 15 minutes or until golden, rotating the sheet pans, if necessary, to ensure even browning.
- When done, remove from the oven, and place the pans on a cooling rack.
- When cool, remove from the sheet pans to allow air to circulate freely under and around the triangles to preserve crispness.
- Store at room temperature if using within the same day.
- If not, refrigerate and rewarm briefly just before serving to restore crispness.
- Make the cardamom ice cream as follows.

Crème anglaise base for ice cream

Cardamom ice cream
YIELD: APPROXIMATELY 1 QUART

Oz	Grams	Each	Name of ingredient
12	360		Whole milk
		10	Cardamom pods
6	180	9	Egg yolks from large eggs
4	120		Granulated sugar
10	300		Heavy cream

- Make crème anglaise base for ice cream as follows:
- Half fill a large stainless steel bowl with ice and water and set aside. This will be used as a water bath to cool the cooked mixture once it is removed from the stove.
- Place the milk and cardamom pods into a medium-sized heavy saucepan.
- Bring the mixture to the boil.
- Remove from heat, cover, and allow the cardamom to infuse for approximately 15 minutes.
- Taste to confirm that the liquid has taken on a definite cardamom flavor.
- If not, reheat and cook for a few minutes more, remove from the heat, cover, and then allow the mixture to infuse further.
- Taste it again before continuing.
- Pass through a sieve, discarding the cardamom pods.
- Return the liquid to the saucepan and keep it hot over low heat.
- In the bowl of an electric mixer, outfitted with the whisk attachment, whip the egg yolks and sugar until thick and light in color. The mixture should fall slowly off of the whisk in a thick ribbon.
- Gradually add one quarter of the hot milk to the egg-sugar mixture, whisking to combine.

- → Add this mixture to the remaining milk in the saucepan and cook over medium heat, stirring, without aerating until the mixture reaches 185°F.
- → Remove from the heat and immediately pour the liquid through a fine sieve into the stainless steel bowl set over the prepared ice water bath.
- → Stir to cool quickly. (This mixture may be made up to one day in advance, covered well, and refrigerated, until ready to complete the ice cream.)
- → When the mixture is cold, add heavy cream and stir to combine. Transfer the mixture to the bowl of an electric ice cream machine and freeze until semi-firm.
- → Remove from the machine, place in an airtight container and freeze until firm.
- → Now make the candied carrot curls garnish as follows.

Candied carrot curl garnish

YIELD: ENOUGH FOR TWELVE SERVINGS, ALLOWING FOR ADDITIONAL IF SOME ARE UNDERSIZED, MISSHAPEN OR OTHERWISE IMPERFECT

Oz	Grams	Each	Name of ingredient
6, approximately before peeling	180	3	**Carrots,** peeled and thinly sliced, lengthwise
2 to 3, as needed	60 to 90, as needed		**Simple syrup**

TIP: Note that traditional ras malai is made by boiling milk with sugar over low heat until it thickens, stirring constantly, over a period of several hours. This version closely approximates the flavor and texture of the original but cuts down preparation time considerably.

- → Using a mandoline, slice the peeled carrots lengthwise, slightly thicker than paper thin.
- → Dip into simple syrup.
- → Lay out onto a Silpat-lined baking sheet and bake in a preheated 225°F oven until dry but not browned, about 45 minutes.
- → Halfway through the baking process, turn the carrot slices over to allow them to bake and dry out evenly.
- → Remove from the oven and allow to cool slightly.
- → Then immediately wrap the carrots around wooden dowels measuring approximately ½ inch in diameter, to create a loose corkscrew shape.
- → When fully cool, remove from the dowels and set onto parchment paper or on a Silpat. Store in an airtight container, outfitted with a piece of limestone or a package of silica gel to retain crispness.
- → Next make the ras malai pistachio sauce as follows.

Ras malai pistachio sauce

YIELD: APPROXIMATELY 22 OUNCES, 12 SERVINGS, EACH WEIGHING APPROXIMATELY 1¾ OUNCES.

Oz	Grams	Name of ingredient
14	420	**Condensed milk**
4 to 5, approximately	120 to 150, approximately	**Heavy cream**
4	120	**Pistachios,** shelled, natural, peeled and roughly chopped

- → Heat the condensed milk and 4 ounces of heavy cream together over low heat, until the mixture flows easily, adding more heavy cream to thin, if needed. Do not overheat.
- → Add ground pistachios and set aside to cool.
- → Store, covered, in the refrigerator until ready to assemble the dessert.
- → Remove from refrigerator and place over a hot water bath to re-liquefy, stirring to smooth before using.

Oz	Name of ingredient
As needed to drizzle over the filo triangles, approximately 1 oz for each two triangle serving	**Mild-flavored honey,** such as clover honey

Oz	Grams	Name of Ingredient
2, approximately, enough for a few on each plate	60, approximately	*Whole* pistachios, shelled

Assembly and plating

Mask each plate with pistachio sauce. Cut each filo triangle across the middle, into two halves. Arrange the four halves on a serving plate. When the triangles are plated, drizzle honey evenly and lightly over the pastries. Garnish plate with a few whole pistachios, scattered over the sauce. Place quenelle of ice cream adjacent to the pastry. Set carrot curl garnish atop the pastry and serve immediately.

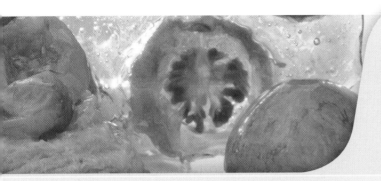

Tomato Tart with Lemon Clove Syrup, Basil Sorbet, and Pine Nut Ice Cream, with Tomato Glass Garnish

YIELD: 12 SERVINGS

Tomato tart with lemon clove syrup, basil sorbet, pine nut ice cream, and tomato glass garnish with confited lemon slice. Crossing easily from savory to sweet, ripe tomatoes reveal their true botanical identity as fruit in a sweet context. Inspired by the serendipitous mistake committed by the sisters Tatin in France who, having dropped their apple tart upon removing it from the oven, thought fast and served it pastry side down, this tart is intentionally baked with the buttery pastry placed on top, and then inverted so that the dough becomes the base for the tomatoes. Enhancing the flavor of the sweet though acidic tomatoes with spiced lemon syrup, the dessert ranges further into savory territory by accompanying the tart with a scoop of bright green, summery fresh basil sorbet, proving that tomatoes and basil are a felicitous marriage, regardless of context. A creamy and crunchy pine nut–flavored ice cream works well alongside the basil sorbet, echoing the crunch of the many-layered pastry beneath the tomatoes. Made to resemble a modern piece of stained glass art, the shatteringly crisp thin pane of sugar glass, encrusted with more of those sweet fruity tomatoes, completes the multitextural experience.

Making this recipe is a two-day process since the lemon slices for the confited lemon must be soaked overnight and the puff pastry yields best results after an overnight rest in the refrigerator before using. Therefore, bake and serve the dessert on the second day.

The order of things:

1. **On the day before serving the dessert, soak lemon slices** in a bowl of hot water overnight
2. **On the day before serving the dessert, make puff pastry** and chill
3. **Next day, make lemon clove syrup and cook the previously soaked and drained lemon slices in it,** reserving the cooking liquid to be used as a plating sauce
4. **Make basil sorbet** and freeze
5. **Make pine nut ice cream** and freeze
6. **Roll puff pastry and cut into desired shapes** and refrigerate
7. **Make oven-dried tomatoes**
8. **Make syrup for dried tomato "glass" garnish**

Equipment list:

Fine-meshed cooling rack set over a sheet pan to allow the confited lemon slices to drain

Silicone plaque with 12 round cavities, each measuring 3 inches in diameter, to form tomato glass garnish

Round metal cutter, measuring 4 inches in diameter to cut the puff pastry rounds for the tarts

Silform plaque with 12 cavities, each measuring 4 inches in diameter, in which the tarts are baked

Round ice cream scoop to portion out the basil sorbet and the pine nut ice cream

Quick puff pastry

YIELD: APPROXIMATELY
24 OUNCES, 12 ROUNDS
OF PASTRY, 3 INCHES IN
DIAMETER, EACH WEIGHING
APPROXIMATELY 2 OUNCES

Oz	Grams	Name of ingredient	Baker's percentages
9.6	288	All purpose flour	100
9.6	288	Unsalted butter, cool, waxy, not soft or greasy	100
	1	Salt	0.2
4.8	144	Ice water	50

This dough may be made either by hand or by machine, depending on the size of the batch.

Mixing by hand

→ Cut butter into 1½ inch chunks.

→ Place flour and salt into a large bowl. Mix to combine.

→ Add the butter and coat with the flour and salt mixture.

→ Add ice water all at once and lightly mix until the dough coheres into a rough mass. **Do not over-process.**

→ Turn the ragged mass of dough out onto a lightly floured surface and tap it firmly with a rolling pin to coax the dough into a roughly cohesive shape.

→ Check to be sure that the dough is not sticking to the surface.

Mixing by machine

→ Using the paddle attachment, mix the flour and salt at low speed to combine.

→ Then add the butter, cut into 1½ inch chunks.

→ On slow speed, mix just to coat the butter with the flour.

→ With the machine running, add ice water all at once, and briefly mix, turning the machine on and off rather than allowing it to run continuously, just until the dough becomes a rough mass. **It is better to underprocess rather than overprocess the dough.** The mixer should be turned on and off during this step rather than allowing it to run continuously.

Rolling the dough

→ Turn the ragged mass of dough out onto a floured surface and tap firmly with the rolling pin to coax the dough into a roughly cohesive shape.

→ Check to be sure that the dough is not sticking to the surface.

→ Use a plastic dough scraper frequently to free the dough from the work surface, as necessary, if it is sticking.

→ Flour the work surface *lightly* from time to time.

→ Once the dough has been rolled to a rough rectangular shape, mentally divide the dough in thirds and fold one third of the dough from the end closest to you toward the middle and the other third over the first third to create a package of dough made up of three thick layers.

→ Turn the packet of dough 90 degrees so that the short side is facing you.

→ Then roll the dough to lengthen it again to a rectangle measuring roughly 4 inches by 10 inches.

→ Fold in thirds again, turn it 90 degrees so that the short side is facing you again.

→ Now roll the dough again to a rectangle measuring roughly 4 inches by 10 inches.

→ Chill in between the rolling and folding steps if the dough shows signs of softening or sticking to the work surface. (The key to a flaky dough lies in keeping the layers of fat well chilled and separate from the layers of dough.)

→ Repeat the rolling and folding once more, chilling as needed if the dough shows signs of softening or is being resistant to rolling. (See process shots on page 143.)

- → Chill until firm.
- → The dough benefits from an overnight rest in the refrigerator ([reliably operating at 41°F] but for longer storage, freeze it and then thaw as needed in the refrigerator). Roll the chilled and rested dough to a rectangular sheet measuring approximately 12 inches by 16 inches by approximately ⅓ inch thick.
- → Then from the sheet of dough, using a round cookie cutter, measuring 4 inches in diameter, cut 12 rounds of dough, in rows of three along the 12 inch side and in rows of four along the 16 inch side.
- → Transfer the rounds of dough to a parchment-lined baking sheet, dock with a fork at ⅓ inch intervals all over the dough, and chill, covered, until ready to assemble and bake the tarts.

Oz	Grams	Each	Name of ingredient
		3	**Lemons**, medium sized
As needed			**Boiling water** to cover lemons for soaking
		16	**Whole cloves**
16	480		**Simple syrup**

Lemon clove syrup and confited lemon slices

YIELD: 16 OUNCES OF SYRUP AND APPROXIMATELY 24 UNIFORM SLICES OF CONFITED LEMON, EACH APPROXIMATELY 2 INCHES IN DIAMETER

- → Using a mandoline, slice the lemons into thin rounds.
- → Carefully remove the pits from each slice.
- → Place the lemons into a large stainless steel bowl and pour enough boiling water over them to cover.
- → Soak overnight.
- → The next day, drain the lemons, discarding the soaking water.
- → Now place the lemon slices, cloves, and simple syrup into a medium-sized heavy saucepan. Cook the lemons at the lowest simmer until tender but not disintegrating, approximately 45 minutes.
- → Drain the slices and set onto a fine-meshed cooling rack.
- → Reserve the slices to use as a garnish for the tarts, removing them gently from the syrup.
- → Reserve the syrup to use in the tarts below (approximately 12 ounces) and the remaining syrup (approximately 4 ounces) to use as a drizzle on the plate.

TIP: *Cooking the lemon slices slowly, with little turbulence of the cooking liquid, will help to keep the fruit intact and assure that it is tender.*

Assembling the tarts

- → Use a Silicone plaque with 12 round indentations, each measuring 4 inches in diameter.
- → Place the plaque onto a baking sheet and then pour about 1 ounce of the lemon clove syrup (from above) into each cavity. (Reserve the remaining syrup to use as a plating sauce).
- → Place the tomatoes into the syrup in a visually pleasing arrangement, alternating shapes and colors, as desired.
- → Then place a round of chilled puff pastry on top of the tomatoes.
- → Bake in a preheated 400°F oven, for approximately 40 minutes, or until the pastry is golden brown and well-puffed.
- → Remove from the oven, allow to cool for a few minutes, and then carefully invert the plaque onto a Silpat-lined full-size baking sheet.

- → Carefully remove the plaque, placing onto the tarts any tomatoes that may have stuck in the cavities.
- → Allow the tarts to cool at room temperature.
- → These should be served within a few hours of baking, which is when these are at their best.
- → If holding longer, refrigerate, covered, and then allow the tarts to return to room temperature before serving.

Oven-dried tomatoes for use in tomato "glass" décor

Each	Name of ingredient
96	**Small heirloom tomatoes,** each cut in half

- → Place tomato halves on a Silpat placed onto a sheet pan, and bake in a preheated 200°F oven for about 30 minutes.
- → They should be somewhat dry and a bit shriveled, but not browned.
- → Remove from the oven and allow to cool.
- → Arrange the tomatoes into the 12 indentations of a Silicone plaque, each measuring 3 inches in diameter.
- → Set aside and make the following syrup.

Syrup for dried tomato glass garnish

YIELD: APPROXIMATELY
16 OUNCES, ENOUGH FOR
12 ROUNDS OF TOMATO
GLASS, EACH MEASURING
APPROXIMATELY 3 INCHES
IN DIAMETER

Oz	Grams	Name of ingredient
12	360	**Granulated sugar**
3	90	**Corn syrup**
6	180	**Water**

- → In a medium-sized heavy saucepan, bring the sugar, corn syrup, and water to a boil.
- → Cook to a light amber.
- → While still hot, pour an equal amount of the syrup over the tomatoes in the molds, coating the tomatoes thinly but evenly.
- → Allow to cool completely.
- → When ready to assemble the dessert, remove the tomato glass rounds from the molds and use as a garnish on the plate.

Oz	Grams	Each	Name of ingredient
2	60		**Pine nuts,** toasted
12	360		**Whole milk**
		2	**Madagascar vanilla beans,** split
4	120		**Egg yolks**
3	90		**Granulated sugar**
6	180		**Heavy cream**
		3	**Salt**

→ In a preheated 350°F oven, toast the pine nuts on a baking sheet until golden brown, approximately 5 minutes, stirring occasionally to ensure even browning.

→ Watch carefully, as these burn quickly.

→ Remove from the oven and set aside.

→ In a medium-sized heavy saucepan, bring the milk, vanilla beans, and pine nuts to a simmer.

→ Cover the pan and allow to infuse for 30 minutes. The flavors of the vanilla and the toasted pine nuts should come through clearly

→ Remove the vanilla beans, rinse and dry, and reserve for another use.

→ In the bowl of an electric mixer outfitted with the whisk attachment, beat the egg yolks and sugar to thick ribbon stage.

→ When the whisk is lifted out of the bowl, the mixture should flow slowly in a thick ribbon from it.

→ Transfer the mixture to a stainless steel bowl.

→ Reheat the milk and temper half of it into the egg and sugar mixture in the bowl.

→ Add the remaining milk and then cook the mixture set over a hot water bath (the water should not touch the bottom of the bowl), stirring with a wooden spoon constantly, without aerating, until the mixture reaches 185°F.

→ When the mixture reaches temperature, immediately remove from the heat and pass through a fine sieve into a stainless steel bowl.

→ Stir in the salt and mix to dissolve.

→ Set the mixture over an ice water bath.

→ Cool quickly, stirring occasionally, and when cold, freeze the mixture in the bowl of an electric ice cream machine.

→ When almost firm, remove from the ice cream machine and transfer into a container.

→ Cover and place into the freezer until ready to plate the dessert.

Oz	Grams	Name of ingredient
12	360	**Fresh basil leaves,** stems removed
12	360	**Simple syrup**

→ Bring a medium saucepan of water to the boil.

→ Add the basil leaves and as they are wilted, immediately remove them to a bowl of ice water to set the color.

→ Remove the leaves from the ice water and squeeze out excess liquid.

→ Place on a double layer of absorbent paper and dry thoroughly.

→ In a food processor, puree the leaves with the simple syrup until finely chopped.

→ Pass the mixture through a fine sieve (you should have about 14 ounces of liquid).

→ Chill the liquid in the refrigerator until cold and then freeze it in an electric ice cream machine.

→ Remove to a container with a tight-fitting lid and keep frozen until ready to serve.

TIP: *Simply pureeing the fresh basil leaves without blanching will lead to a muddy brown–colored sorbet so it is important not to skip this step. Blanching and shocking the leaves stabilizes the green pigment of the leaves.*

Assembly and plating

Place a tomato tart to the left of the center of the plate. Place the tomato "glass" décor to the right and just behind the tart. Place a scoop each of the basil sorbet and the pine nut ice cream to the right, and in front, of the tart. Garnish the tart with a confited lemon slice and drizzle some of the reserved lemon clove syrup on the plate in front of the tart. Serve immediately.

Resources for Ingredients

For produce specialties:

Melissa's World Variety Produce

For imported specialty foods from France, Switzerland, Italy:

Swiss Chalet Fine Foods
9455 NW 40 Street Road
Miami, FL 33178
800-347-9477
www.scff.com

Made in France/Village Imports
6900 Beck Avenue
North Hollywood, CA 91605
818-985-9800
www. madeinfrance.net

For imported chocolates, specialty ingredients for pastry, and tools:

Qzina
16625 Saticoy Street
Van Nuys, CA 91406
www.qzina.com

Surfas Restaurant Supply and Gourmet Food
3975 Landmark Street
Culver City, CA 90232
310-559-4770
www.surfasonline.com

For chocolate molds and other equipment for confection making:

Chocolat Chocolat
8580 St-Hubert
Montréal (Quebec)
Canada H2P-1Z7
800-463-5837 or 514-381-6888
Fax: 514-381-7166
www.chocolat-chocolat.com

Design and Realisation Industries Inc.
Quebec, Canada
514-595-6336
info@dr.ca

Emkay Confectionery Machinery
3313 Mill Grove Terrace, Dacula, GA 30019
770-614-1302
Fax: 770-614-0515
www.emkaymachinery.com

Tomric
85 River Rock Drive #202
Buffalo, New York 14207
716-854-6050
www.tomric.com

For chocolate couvertures, single origin, blends, and all cocoa and chocolate products:

Belcolade Chocolate (Belgian chocolate)
8030 National Highway
Pennsauken, NJ 08110
800-717-4059
www.belcolade.com

Albert Uster—Des Alpes Chocolate (Swiss)
9211 Gaither Road
Gaithersburg, MD 20877
800-231-8154
www.auiswiss.com

Valrhona Inc.
1801 Avenue of the Stars, Suite 829
Los Angeles, CA 90067
310-277-0401
www.valrhona.com

Barry Callebaut
400 Industrial Park Road
St. Albans, Vermont 05478-1875
802-524-9711

Guittard Chocolate Company
10 Guittard Road
Burlingame, CA 94010
800-468-2462 or 650-697-4427
www.guittard.com

For nut pastes, marzipans, nut flours:

American Almond Products Company Inc.
103 Walworth Street
Brooklyn, NY
800-825-6663
www.americanalmond.com

For flavorings, compounds, spices, flavored oils, sauces, glazes, nut flours, extracts:

Amoretti
800-266-7388
www.amoretti.com

For molds, templates, cocoa butter colors, confectionery making equipment:

Chef Rubber
www.chefrubber.com

For natural flavorings, essences:

Mindy Aftel—Aftelier
1518 Walnut Street
Berkeley, CA
510-841-2111

For flavored oils, extracts:

Boyajian Inc.
144 Will Drive
Canton, Massachusetts 02021
800-965-0665
www.boyajianinc.com

For frozen fruit purees, sauces, compotes, glazes:

Frutta Prima
Available through Albert Uster Imports (see above)

Boiron
Available through distributors

RaviFruit
Available through distributors

Fruit purees, concentrates, and zest:

Perfect Puree of Napa Valley
2700 Napa Valley Corporate Dr., Suite L
Napa, CA 94558
800-556-3707
www.perfectpuree.com

For fresh dates:

Oasis Date Gardens
59-111 Hwy 111
Thermal, CA 92274
800-827-8017

For electric stand mixers, food processors, immersion blenders, specialized appliances, spatulas, mixing bowls, hand tools:

Kitchen Aid
www.kitchenaid.com

Cuisinart
150 Milford Road
East Windsor NJ 08520
800-726-0190
www.cuisinart.com

For silicone molds, silicon mats, metal frames for cakes and mousses:

Demarle
8A Corporate Center
8 Corporate Drive
Cranbury, NJ 08512
609-395-0219
www.DemarleUSA.com

For specialized professional equipment:

JB Prince
36 E. 31st Street
New York, NY
212-683-3553
www.jbprince.com

Martellato
www.martellato.com
Viala della Naviagazione
Interna, 97
35027 Noventa Padovana ITALY
39-049-7800155

For siphon bottles for foams, whipped cream dispensers:

Isi North America
175 Route 46 West
Fairfield, NJ 07004
973-227-2426
www.isiofnorthamerica.com

For sheet pans and other baking pans:

Author:
Vollrath 1236 N. 18th Street
Sheboygan,WI 53082-0611
800-558-7631

For rolling speed racks:

Channel Manufacturing
55 Channel Drive
Port Washington,
New York 11050
866-712-7283
Fax: 516-944-0625
www.channelmfg.com

For a wide variety of tuile templates:

Tuile Time
The Pastry Design Group Inc.
984 SW 1st Avenue
Pompano Beach, FL 33060
954-907-7292

For digital scales, thermometers:

Polder Online
PolderOnline.com
1141 Holland Drive
Suite #22
Boca Raton, FL 33487
www.polder.com

For precision refractometers to measure the density of sugar in syrups for sorbets, confits, and candied fruit:

Misco
3401 Virginia Road
Cleveland, OH 44122
866-831-1999
www.misco.com

For unique serving plates, platters, stemware:

Izabel Lam
204 Van Dyke Street
Brooklyn, NY 11231
718-797-3983
www.izabellam.com

Fortessa Inc.
22601 Davis Drive
Sterling, VA 20164
800-296-7508
www.fortessa.com

Steelite International
154 Keystone Drive
New Castle, PA 16105
724-856-4900
www.steelite.com

For premium whole leaf tea:

Upton Tea
Hopkinton, MA 01748
800-234-8327
www.uptontea.com

For fine teas sourced from the best tea growing regions of the world, specializing in white, green, oolong, and black teas produced in the best gardens of mainland China:

Peli Teas
8383 Wilshire Blvd.
Beverly Hills, CA
323-651-2282
www.peliteas.com

For freshly roasted limited-crop whole bean coffee:

LA Mill Coffee
1112 Westminster Avenue
Alhambra, CA 91803
626-202-0100
www.lamillcoffee.com

For disposable pastry bags:

One Way Plastics Ltd.
PO Box 399
Mt. Brydges
Ontario, Canada NOL 1 WO
519-264-9750
www.onewaypipingbags.com

For pastry bags, tips, pastry bag racks, sifting screens and other small wares for the professional baker:

Thermohauser of America, Inc.
44 Southbridge Road
Dudley, MA 01550
508-949-6843
www.thermo-us.com

APPENDIX B

Web Sites Useful to the Pastry Chef

Note that Web site addresses are always in a state of flux so it is possible that some of the sites listed below have either changed addresses or have simply disappeared. But there are new sites appearing on the Web all the time and it is worthwhile to keep visiting them periodically for updates of information about what's happening in the pastry world.

www.Michaellaiskonis.typepad.com

www.Eggbeater.typepad.com

www.ideasinfood.com

www.playingwithfireandwater.com

www.foodbeam.com

www.amabilia.com

www.christophemichalak.com

www.chadzilla.typepad.com

www.cannelle-vanille.blogspot.com

www.chocolateandzucchini.com

Organizations Offering Continuing Education Opportunities

Sources and Resources for further learning about a wide variety of subjects, including artisanal cheese, bread baking, produce, continuing education opportunities, pastry, confections, chocolate work, retail business, among other topics.

Artisanal Cheese Center   www.artisanalcheese.com

Bread Baker's Guild of America   www.bbga.org

The Chef's Garden   www.culinaryvegetableinstitute.com

Culinary Institute of America at Greystone's Worlds of Flavor conferences (Napa Valley, CA)   www.ciaprochef.com

French Culinary Institute   www.frenchculinary.com

King Arthur Flour's Baking Center   www.kingarthurflour.com

Notter School of Pastry Arts   www.notterschool.com

Retail Baker's Association   www.rbanet.com

San Francisco Baking Institute   www.sfbi.com

University of Massachusetts' Chefs Tastes of the World Conference
www.aux.umass.edu/chefculinaryconference

World Pastry Forum   www.worldpastryforum.com

Zing Train, retail training arm of Zingerman's specialty food store
www.zingtrain.com

Important Temperatures for the Pastry Chef

- Adding whole eggs to a pâte à choux base: 110°F

- Cooking sugar syrup for Italian meringue, to be used in Italian buttercream, mousses, or as a topping on pies and tarts: 246–250°F, soft ball stage

- Final temperature to which to cook crème anglaise, for use as a plating sauce, "soup," or ice cream base: 180°F

- Temperature at which sugar syrup is cooked to amber caramel stage: 320°F

- Temperature to cook sugar syrup for nut or seed brittles: 230°F before adding nuts or seeds, and then cook to 311°F final temperature

- Ideal temperatures of chocolate in three stages of tempering process (These temperatures may vary depending on which brand of chocolate is being used. Be sure to consult manufacturer's recommendations for specifics.)

	Dark	Milk	White
Melting	113–120°F	105°F	105°F
Crystallization by seeding or tabling	82°F	75–77°F	79–81°F
Holding	88–90°F	86°F	86°F

- Temperature to cook heavy cream for ganaches, before combining it with chopped or small pieces of couverture chocolate: 180°F, scalding

- Temperature to which liquids are heated to dissolve pre-bloomed gelatin: 86°F

- Setting temperature of mixtures containing gelatin: 68°F

- Temperature when butter begins to melt: 79°F

- Butter continues melting until it is fully liquid at a temperature between 90°F and 95°F

Bibliography

Alford, Jeffrey, and Naomi Duguid. (2003). *Seductions of Rice*. New York: Artisan.

Child, Julia. (1999). *From Julia Child's Kitchen*. New York: Gramercy.

Corriher, Shirley. (1997). *Cookwise: The Secrets of Cooking Revealed*. New York: William Morrow.

Davidson, Alan. (2006). *The Oxford Companion to Food*: New York: Oxford University Press.

DeGroot, Roy Andries. (1996). *Auberge of the Flowering Hearth*. New York: Ecco.

Figoni, Paula. (2007). *How Baking Works*. New York: Wiley.

Fortin, Jacques, Francois Fortin, and Serge D'Amico. (1996). *The Visual Food Encyclopedia*. New York: Wiley.

Jenkins, Steven. (1996). *Cheese Primer*. New York: Workman.

McGee, Harold. (2004). *On Food and Cooking: The Science and Lore of the Kitchen*. New York: Scribner.

Rinsky, Glenn, and Laura Halpin Rinsky. (2009). *The Pastry Chef's Companion*. New York: Wiley.

Saint-Ange, Madame Evelyn. (2005). *La Bonne Cuisine de Madame E. Saint-Ange*. Berkeley: Ten Speed Press.

Schneider, Elizabeth. (1998). *Uncommon Fruits and Vegetables*. New York: William Morrow.

Stevenson, Tom. (2005). *The Sotheby's Wine Encyclopedia*. New York: Penguin Group (USA).

Thomas, Cathy. (2006). *Melissa's Great Book of Produce*. New York: Wiley.

Thompson, David. (2002). *Thai Food*. Berkeley: Ten Speed Press.

Glossary

Bombe   A molded frozen dessert, usually made up of contrasting flavors of ice cream or frozen custard, the core layer of which is sometimes studded with candied fruits. When cut into wedges, the spherical or round bowl-shaped dessert reveals a pleasing pattern, and is frequently served with a sauce based on chocolate or fruit.

Butterfat   Also known as milkfat, this is the fatty portion of milk. Milk and cream are often sold according to the amount of butterfat they contain. In the United States, there are federal standards for butterfat content of dairy products.

Cajeta   A thick fudge-like mixture originating in south central Mexico, made from milk, traditionally from goat's milk although cow's milk may be used, which is cooked with sugar, in a heavy saucepan, stirring constantly until the water is evaporated from the liquid and the sugars are caramelized, yielding a fudgy thick, almost unpourable liquid. Used as a swirl in ice cream, as a filling in wafer cookies or spread onto crepes.

Chaudeau   Word from the French *chaud eau*, meaning literally "hot water" referring to a crème anglaise or liquid custard sauce–based dessert flavored with wines or spices and served warm.

Clarified butter   The semi-solid product of churned dairy cream, which has been melted and then heated beyond its melting point to separate the milk solids and water, each element of which has a different density. Some solids float to the surface and are skimmed off; the water and the remainder of the milk solids sink to the bottom and are left behind when the butterfat is poured off. The non-butter components are discarded. Without its milk solids, clarified butter has a much longer shelf life than fresh butter.

Cocoa butter   The liquid fat that results from the processing of the hard seed-like interior of the cocoa pod that gives chocolate its rich, melt-in-the-mouth character.

Cocoa solids   With cocoa butter, cocoa solids are one of the two major components of chocolate liquor, the product of the hard seed like interior of the cocoa pod, which is ground into a thick liquid. Approximately 42 to 50 percent of chocolate liquor is made up of cocoa solids, with the rest being cocoa butter.

Confited fruit   Partially candied fruit, this process involves cooking fruits such as citrus in order to preserve them over a short time (contrasted with fully preserved **candied fruits** [*fruits glacés*] which are shelf stable indefinitely). The fruits are cooked in a sugar syrup, brought to a boil, simmered, and then removed from the heat, repeating this process over a few days or a long period of time, increasing the concentration of sugar in the syrup gradually (from approximately 40 Brix to 75 Brix, meaning the percentage of sugar in the syrup) so that the water in the fruit is driven out of the fruit, allowing the sugar to penetrate the fruit fully.

Consommé   From the French for "finish" or "complete," this term usually refers to a meat bone or poultry bone–based stock that has been long cooked, then concentrated by further boiling, and finally clarified by adding beaten egg whites to attract any impurities, before passing the liquid through a cheesecloth-lined fine sieve to yield a perfectly clear liquid. For the pastry chef, fruits including berries and citrus and even some vegetables (such as fennel) form the basis for a highly flavored liquid in which other sweet elements may be floated.

Contrast   In the multicomponent desserts making arena, contrast refers to the way one element in a dessert is different from another, such as serving a crunchy or crisp element alongside a creamy one, or a frozen mousse or other frozen element served with a hot sauce such as hot fudge or ganache.

Couverture   High-quality chocolate usually with a higher percentage of cocoa butter than ordinary chocolate, which makes for glossier coatings and a richer flavor, used in baking and confectionery making, from the French word for "coating" or "covering."

Crème anglaise   From the French, meaning "English cream," a mixture of milk and/or cream with eggs, sugar, and flavoring, cooked gently over a water bath, without aerating, until it reaches a coating consistency (185°F), used as a plating sauce, the basis for light Bavarian creams (a combination of crème anglaise, gelatin, flavorings, Italian meringue, and whipped cream), and rich, dense ice cream.

Curds   The part of milk that coagulates, or sets, when the milk sours or is treated with enzymes. Heating milk and then adding a coagulating ingredient such as rennet or acid causes the milk to form into solid irregular pieces which when drained and pressed become cheese. See **paneer**.

Desiccated   This refers to products that have been dried, such as shredded or grated coconut, whose moisture is low and work well in baked goods such as macaroons.

Entremet ring   A heavy-gauge, thin, bottomless metal form, available in many different shapes, sizes, and heights (used to give form to chilled or frozen mixtures such as ice cream, sorbet, mousses, and Bavarian creams). Frequently a thin cake layer is placed in the bottom of the ring, and additionally as a lining for the sides of the mold before the creamy mixture is deposited into the form.

After freezing or chilling the contents to firm up, a torch is used to heat the outside of the ring to facilitate removal of the contents.

First crack stage of coffee roasting   This refers to the stage of the coffee roasting process when the flavorless green beans show signs of cracking when exposed to high heat, measured at approximately 356–435°F. This leads to flavor development. At this stage in the roasting process, the bean doubles in size, becomes a light brown color, and experiences a weight loss of approximately 5 percent.

Flavor   The totality of taste impressions perceived by the palate.

Florentines   Thin, crisp cookies made from a runny batter comprised of a mixture of sugar, honey, and butter or other fat that is heated to emulsify, elaborated often with nuts and candied or dried fruits, and then deposited on a nonstick baking surface and placed into a moderately hot oven where the batter will spread, bubble up, and caramelize. After removing from the oven to cool, the cookie will firm up and become crisp but is subject to softening due to humidity in the air and therefore should be used quickly after baking or stored in an airtight container outfitted with a humidity-absorbing ingredient such as silica gel or a piece of limestone.

Food costs   An important part of the business of baking and dessert making, food costs refer to the total sum of money spent on ingredients, exclusive of labor, overhead, or any other costs attached to the operation of a business. As part of managerial responsibilities, pastry chefs must be able to calculate food costs accurately as part of determining a selling price for that product in order to be sure that the product can be profitable.

Ganache   A combination of high-quality chocolate and heavy cream (sometimes with butter added) made by boiling the cream (from 50 percent to 100 percent the weight of chocolate) and pouring it over the chocolate, which has been chopped into small pieces and placed into a bowl or other heat-proof vessel; the mixture is then usually stirred without aerating until melted and smooth, resulting in a dense, rich, and creamy mixture. Used as a room temperature, warm, or hot sauce and the base for a mousse when additional aerated heavy cream is folded into it. Alternatively, it may be whipped until lightened in color and texture for a mousse-like filling for cakes or other layered desserts.

Gianduja (zhahn-DOO-yah)   A smooth paste of Swiss origin combining dark or milk chocolate, roasted hazelnuts (and sometimes almonds) and sugar, used often as the basis for confections and pastries.

Gluten   Flour itself has no gluten. The naturally occurring proteins in wheat flour, *glutenin* and *gliadin*, which make up about 80 percent of the proteins in the endosperm of the wheat kernel, combine to form gluten when the flour is combined with liquid. Controlling gluten development through the proper amount of mixing and the use of fat in the dough, which shortens strands of gluten formed, is important to the baker and pastry chef. Overmixing a dough, whether yeasted or not, can lead to a baked product that is tough and rubbery instead of tender. Undermixing a yeasted dough, for instance, can lead to a finished product with poor volume since the leavening process creates a web structure within the bread dough that is supported only when there is enough gluten developed through adequate mixing.

Hard crack stage of sugar cooking   Refers to the temperature of a sugar syrup cooked to 295–310°F (146–155°C), often used for clear sugar decorations as plating garnishes.

Hygroscopic   Describing the characteristic of a food, such as honey, that readily absorbs moisture, as from the atmosphere. When a hygroscopic ingredient such as honey is used in baking, the resulting baked products tend to remain softer or more moist over a longer period of time than if made with sweeteners such as granulated sugar.

Italian meringue   Beaten egg whites lightened with a hot sugar syrup cooked to soft ball stage, 240°F, used as a lightener for mousses, butter creams, in marshmallows (with gelatin added), and French macaroons, and on its own as a topping for cakes, poached fruits, or baked Alaska (ice cream covered with meringue and then torched to highlight the design of the piped-out meringue).

Limited lots   In the arena of cultivated food products, particularly specialty coffee and tea, this refers to beans or leaves available in small supply for a short time, exhibiting a special and prized flavor profile that may or not be replicated in the next available batch, normally commanding a higher-than-would-be-expected price at market. Typically these products are grown and cultivated at a coffee estate or tea garden within a sharply defined geographic area. These are of interest to the food and beverage expert who may wish to feature the beverages made from these products as accompaniments to desserts for special pairings.

Market forms   This term refers to ingredients used in baking, for instance vanilla, produced from the same basic component but available as a liquid extract, dried and powdered and as a paste, each of which has its own particular applications, strength, and flavor profile.

Marrons glacés   A specialty of the confectioner's art, these are chestnuts that have first been roasted, hard shells and skins removed, and then candied slowly in a sugar syrup, sometimes flavored with vanilla. A delicacy around winter holiday times throughout Europe, they are considered a luxury food, priced accordingly.

Mellow   Descriptor for foods that are soft, sweet, and juicy, such as ripe fruit.

Milk solids   The combined yield of fat and protein in milk.

Mouth feel   The totality of impressions about a food, either solid or liquid, as it is being eaten.

Mulled wine   The alcoholic fermented liquid made from grapes, usually red, which is served warm, flavored with spices, and sometimes sweetened with honey. Served throughout Europe, Scandinavia, Russia, and even South America as a holiday drink.

Noble rot   A naturally occurring and desirable fungus called *Botrytis cinerea* (*la pourriture noble* in French, *edelfaule* in German) found on grapes, which causes the fruit to lose much of its moisture and acidity, concentrating flavor in the process, leading to sweet wines of floral complexity; famous examples include the sweet Sauterne of Chateau d'Yquem, one of the preeminent dessert wines of the world, produced in the Bordeaux region of France. Sweet, complex-tasting wines, painstakingly produced from grapes affected by this fungal growth, are particularly good partners for fruit-based desserts.

Origin   The place where a food product is grown or produced, important to pastry chefs when evaluating the taste of that product as compared to similar products grown and produced in other regions of the world.

Over roasting   This refers to the stage in coffee roasting that obliterates or masks the underlying desirably complex flavors inherent in the coffee bean. Over-roasted coffee tastes burnt, losing all of its subtler floral, sweet notes of flavor.

Paneer   The basis for sweet and savory dishes in Indian, this is fresh, unripened cheese, made by heating milk to which a curdling agent such as lemon or lime juice is added. As the mixture is heated, the milk separates into curds (soft semi-solid) and whey, the watery liquid part and is then transferred to a cheesecloth-lined fine sieve, suspended over a bowl and weighted or tied tightly to press out excess moisture. It is then ready for use, eaten as is, or served in desserts in a spiced sweet syrup or with a thick spice-scented milk–based sauce, or in savory applications in curried dishes. Also spelled **panir.**

Particulates   This term refers to the solid additions to a cake or cookie batter or pastry dough, which lend texture and flavor to the dough but are not necessary to form the structure of the product. Examples of particulates include shredded vegetables, chocolate chips, nuts, and dried fruits.

Polenta   The ground and dried meal made from white or yellow corn, common to Italian cuisine, where it is used as a starchy side dish. Sweetened and elaborated with fruits and served with a sweet sauce, polenta serves as the basis for a homey, comforting, sweet pudding.

Puff pastry   A flaky, nonyeasted laminated dough in which a block of fat, preferably unsalted butter, is flattened in a packet of dough, folded and rolled repeatedly, chilling the dough in between roll-outs to firm the fat and rest the gluten, to create multiple thin layers of fat alternating with layers of dough. When baked, the water content of the butter in the dough, when heated, turns to steam, causing the layers to expand and separate, yielding a flaky dough with thin horizontal air pockets between layers.

Quick puff pastry   As used in this book, a handy shortcut version of puff pastry in which instead of rolling a packet of butter into a packet of dough, the cold fat, preferably unsalted butter, is cut into large pieces and lightly mixed with flour and water just until the mixture coheres into a ragged mass. This is then rolled and folded to create layers as above but requires less refrigerator resting time since the gluten in the dough is not fully developed when the dough portion is mixed, as it is in the classical puff pastry. Since neither dough has sugar in it, it is equally well suited for use in sweet or savory applications.

Quill   The curved, rolled piece of bark from the cinnamon or cassia tree, which is sold as cinnamon sticks.

Rancidity   The state of a food becoming rotten, stale, or inedible.

Resinous   Slightly aromatic with a piney flavor, referring commonly to Greek or other Mediterranean style wines or herbs such as rosemary.

Rhizome   A plant growing as a root, under the ground, such as ginger, turmeric, or galangal.

Rule of three   An artistic principle, which states that a well-balanced artistic composition such as a plated dessert should be composed of three main elements. It states further that three elements on a plate create dramatic tension among the elements. As a corollary to this informal rule, using more than three elements on the plate tends to confuse the eye (and the palate). Using fewer than three elements on a plate might be considered too predictable, static, and even boring to the eye and palate.

Seasonal produce   The fruits and vegetables that reach their peak of ripeness or maturity during a particular well-defined period or time during the year. These tend to be most flavorful and usually available for the best price.

Second crack stage of coffee roasting   The stage in coffee roasting where the bean structure itself begins to fracture, usually measured between 435°F and 474°F. The darkness of the roast correlated to this stage is important to the final taste of the coffee brewed from those beans. At this stage, the roast color is defined as medium-dark brown. The second pop is much quicker sounding than the first and the beans take on an oily sheen.

Semolina   The granular, high protein wheat flour from which the best pasta is made, with a slightly gritty texture that works well in steamed and baked puddings and cakes.

Single estate tea   A premium quality blend of teas from one particular estate or garden.

Single origin   Refers to a produce cultivated and produced in one particular place with its own special climatic and soil conditions, particularly applied to coffee, cocoa beans, and tea.

Soft ball stage of sugar cooking   Refers to the temperature of a sugar syrup commonly agreed to be 240°F (115°C), deriving its name from the description of how the syrup forms when placed into a vessel of ice water. The sugar when combined with water reaches this stage when much of the water content has been cooked away, leading to a thick syrup used while hot, poured over beaten egg whites for Italian meringue, folded into mousses to lighten them, and far use in French macaroons, marshmallows, and frozen confections such as nougat glacé.

Taste memory   A desirable skill of seasoned chefs acquired over a period of time, through repeated experiences of experiencing the flavor of an ingredient. Useful when comparing the flavor of numerous ingredients in a single category to decide which one would work best in a particular application, for instance, deciding which chocolate or vanilla would marry best with the other ingredients in a specific dessert.

Temperature   A measure of the relative hotness or coldness of something; as it is used in a dessert making context, this measure would impact on the how the dessert is perceived by the diner so the hotness or coldness would be measured at the time the dessert is served.

Tempering   Used for dipped and molded confectionary, garnishes, and decorative showpieces, this is a process involving successively melting, cooling, and rewarming couverture chocolate to cause cocoa butter crystals naturally occurring in the chocolate to align so that the chocolate crystallizes. The result of this process leads to chocolate that is shiny with a smooth mouth feel and sets firmly at room temperature with a good snap when broken into pieces.

Texture   How a food feels in the mouth.

Timbale or thimble   Refers to a flowerpot-shaped cylindrical mold with sides tapering from the open end down to the bottom, often used as a vessel in which to bake or steam puddings and cakes.

Torte   European style cake, usually flourless, often made with ground nuts replacing the flour.

Tuile   A thin, crisp cookie, similar to **stencil paste** or **hippenmasse,** generally made from equal parts butter, granulated or sifted confectioners' sugar, egg whites, and flour, spread through a template with cutouts in any shape desired, onto a nonstick silicone mat and baked until lightly browned. When warm, these are flexible and may be shaped around dowels, rolling pins, or bowls to create three-dimensional edible sculpture. Perfect as a container for ice cream, mousse, and sorbet or as a garnish for a plated dessert.

Verrine   From the French word for "glass," this refers to the clear glass or the dessert made in it, featuring layers of different ingredients, served in combination to yield a multicomponent, multitextured dessert. Savory versions are also made, using vegetables, fish, smoked fish, herbs, layers to please the eye as well as the palate. An ice cream sundae could be considered a simple version of a verrine. Fruits, sauces, whipped cream, crispy elements, puddings, or mousses, all might be appropriate elements in a verrine.

Whey   The watery part of milk that separates from the curds, as in the process of making cheese.